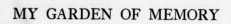

MY GARDEN OF MEMORY

Kate Douglas Wiggin

MY
GARDEN OF MEMORY

AN AUTOBIOGRAPHY

BY

KATE DOUGLAS WIGGIN

WITH ILLUSTRATIONS

" There's rosemary, that's for remembrance;
...and there is pansies, that's for thoughts."

BOSTON AND NEW YORK
HOUGHTON MIFFLIN COMPANY
The Riverside Press Cambridge
1923

The Riverside Press
CAMBRIDGE · MASSACHUSETTS
PRINTED IN THE U.S.A.

And if I have done well, and as is fitting the story, it is that which I desired, but if slenderly and meanly, it is that which I could attain unto.

For as it is hurtful to drink wine or water alone; and as wine mingled with water is pleasant, and delighteth the taste; even so speech finely framed delighteth the ears of them that read the story. And here shall be an end.

JJ Maccabees, v. 38, 39.

We should never write save of that which we love. Forget-fulness and silence are the penalties we should inflict upon all that we find ugly or commonplace in our journey through life.

ERNEST RENAN

CONTENTS

CONTENTS

ILLUSTRATIONS

FOREWORD

"I have considered the days of old, the years of ancient times."

"OUT of the eater came forth meat and out of the strong came forth sweetness." Such was the riddle that Samson put forth unto his thirty companions, and at the end of three days and nights they could not expound it. Such a riddle does heredity put forth unto us, and at the end of three hundred times three days and nights we are equally unable to give the correct answer.

For how much do Indian fighters count to their posterity? What do teachers, preachers, lawyers and doctors, pioneers, Revolutionary heroes, Pilgrim mothers and fathers, and many score of ordinary, commonplace progenitors bequeath to their great-grandchildren? Does the leaven quicken the lump, or the lump prove too much for the leaven? "Rich man, poor man, beggar man, thief, doctor, lawyer, merchant, chief," goes the old rhyme, and the order is followed, no doubt, in most genealogies. There is no mention of a thief among my kindred, although such a record would hardly be treasured with meticulous care; but on the other hand, no one of them ever painted a great picture, carved a great statue, or wrote a great poem; or if he did, no trace of his achievements has been preserved.

As I look back over the long roll of my mother's and father's people, I see that they are all, without exception, English and Welsh by blood, that they have been Americans about as long as any folk save the redskins, and that they must have been natural warriors, for they have been to the fore in every armed conflict in which our country has engaged, from the French and Indian Wars to the Revolution, and down to the present day.

My sister and I, on the contrary, can hardly kill a fly without a shudder, so I cannot think how, when, and by whom this splendid fighting stock was watered.

My father, Robert Noah Smith, was born in Providence, Rhode Island, was educated at Brown University, and took his legal degree at Harvard; but Noah Smith, Jr., my grandfather, removed his family in 1830 to Calais, Maine, with which town, with Machias and its neighboring hamlets, Englishman's River and Carleton Stream, my mother's people, Knights and Dyers, were closely associated.

My mother, Helen Elizabeth Dyer, born in Calais, was the daughter of Jones Dyer, 3d, and Lydia Knight, Jones Dyer, 2d, having been a native of Bristol, Rhode Island, and Jones Dyer, 1st, of "gallant little Wales." My grandfather, Jones Dyer, 3d, is referred to as Jones Dyer, Gentleman, in the old family deeds and papers, while his father is described as Jones Dyer, Yeoman. A man of great individuality and marked business ability was Jones Dyer, Gentleman, who conducted his fortunes so successfully that he was able to retire from business at forty years, and thereafter to wander from place to place, seeking rest for the sole of his foot, the which, apparently, he never found.

My mother, last but one of the fourteen buds on the family tree, and thus the child of her father's later years, recalled him only after his retirement, and described him as an unusually silent and reserved person, and as a furious and omnivorous reader, his "Websterian" head — for so it was always described — constantly bent over books and papers. In spite of his apparently adequate family, my grandfather took into his home and cared for two orphan relatives, and, as his aged father and mother were also

under his roof, it may well be imagined that my splendid
and heroic maternal grandmother was seldom at a loss for
occupation.

To his keen business sense, clear reasoning power, and
executive ability, Jones Dyer, Gentleman, added, what
must have been rare in a man brought up on the outermost
edge of things, a distinct sense of the artistic and unusual
and the instincts of a collector. Whatever he bought for
his family was valuable and beautiful, although his restless removals from place to place often scattered to the
winds his various treasures. While living in New Haven,
Connecticut, at one time, where my uncle was studying
law at Yale, grandfather bought from an old French *émigré*
a house and its contents which my mother described as the
most interesting and beautiful of all that the family had occupied up to that time. The French gentleman was going
back to Paris to end his days, and, when I contemplate the
few pieces remaining to me from this New Haven house,
the mirrors, brasses, mahogany, and silver, I can but applaud the *émigré's* taste and discrimination.

The grandparental *wanderlust* descended to his children in full measure, the members of my immediate family, mother, sister, brother, and I, being so possessed with
it as to be almost unable to endure life unless the furniture
of our rooms is changed in position often enough to make
us feel, at least, that we are in a strange place, though Fate
may, in fact, chain us at home.[1]

Packets of letters from my mother's sisters, written in
their exquisite Italian hands with a life and vigor that

[1] We have lived in seven cities or towns of the United States, rather by
force of circumstances than by "natural selection." But since my marriage to
Mr. George Christopher Riggs in 1895, we have spent such long seasons abroad
— in London, Edinburgh, Largo, Lochearnhead, Inverary, Dublin, Killarney
(having been householders in some of these places) — that it is difficult at times
to realize that we are New-Yorkers, although we undoubtedly are, in spirit
and in truth.

throb through the yellowed paper, invariably recount
journeys made or planned. "My trunk is packed and I am
waiting for father's sloop, the *Challenge*, to take me to Philadelphia," writes Emily. "When father's ship, the *Pilgrim*, comes back," says Joanna, "he promises that I may
go to New Haven to take further music lessons." "If
father is willing," writes a married daughter, Harriet, to
her mother, "I could go to Boston on one of his ships and
make you a little visit in Charlestown." And so on and so
on, gay, laughing letters from happy girls equally careless
and care-free, and well knowing that father's doubloons, if
not always his approval, would back their hopes and plans.

The family lived about the time of these letters in an
old-fashioned mansion on Town Hill (Calais, Maine), a
residence formerly owned by the Honorable Edward Everett, President of Harvard, and, as there were eight daughters growing up under its roof, each one, according to tradition, something of a belle and a beauty, it may well be imagined that, as a misanthropic young uncle once said, "the
Hill was black with beaux day and night!" One of my
mother's rare memory-pictures was of her elder sister,
Sophia, sitting (perhaps not accidentally!) under the parlor
chandelier, its full light shining on her wavy auburn hair,
while a bevy of gallants around her rivaled one another in
efforts to disentangle the "kinks" in a long, slender gold
chain she always wore about her neck. The impression of
this scene as given by my mother implied that the pranks
of the chain were not wholly a cause of regret to the lovely
Sophia.

The family chronicles of the Knights, my maternal
grandmother's people, are particularly picturesque and
splash with bright color the pages of the old records. One
of them was cast away on a lonely island and with an axe
saved from the wreck felled two trees and fashioned a canoe

in which he and his companions escaped to safety. Another, Captain Jonathan Knight, fired the first gun in that little naval engagement known as "The Lexington of the Sea," when the British armed cutter, *Margaretta*, was captured off Machias (June 12, 1776) by the *Unity*, under Captain Jeremiah O'Brien. As the identical musket, a queen's arm, was long treasured in the Knight family, there seems to be concrete evidence of the fact, as well as that set down in local chronicles.

This particular ancestor I cannot but hold in high esteem, for not only is he to be credited with the *Margaretta* exploit, but it is written of him that for many years his home was "a trysting place for the merry and a sure refuge for the poor, the weary, and the stranger." No better epitaph need man desire, nor could a more striking characterization be made of a good man and a good citizen. The Knights were also known as the "friends of the Indian," and my grandmother told many stories of the squaws and braves that came familiarly to her father's house at Englishman's River, Machias, and who were fed and lodged there, well-advised and comforted.

These Indian visitors were numerous even in my mother's day, and often brought to the old Knight farm, which fronted the river at Salmon Falls, huge pails of wild strawberries, blueberries, and cranberries, which my mother and her nosegay of blooming sisters were expected to look over and prepare for preserving. Knights and Dyers both were pioneers in the District of Maine, and so were backwoodsmen, salmon-fishers, lumber-dealers, land-surveyors, sailors, skippers, and ship-owners. The record of their deaths is in itself a chronicle of pioneer history; such an one killed in the Colonial Wars; such an one scalped by Indians; such an one drowned on a surveying-trip; such an one fell from the masthead; such an one gored by an ox; such an one died of fever in the West Indies, and so on and so on, unconscious martyrs to the cause of ever-advancing America.

Not less dauntless and adventurous were many of the women in my mother's family. There was the famous "Aunt Polly," who held the blockhouse for hours against a roving band of Indians, ordering, with such a ringing voice, the sick men and women who formed the garrison to load their muskets and take their stands for firing, and calling the roll in so confident a manner, that the savages, convinced that reinforcements must have arrived, held off until the men came home at sunset.

Then there was the great-great-great-Aunt Hannah who, set to guard an upper window in a blockhouse, and seeing an Indian climbing up toward her and clutching the window-ledge with his hands, closed her eyes and brought down her hatchet, full force, with a result which toppled the heroine over on the inside of the building as swiftly as the unfortunate savage on the outside. These details of pioneer history have been interesting to me mainly as material for family story-telling at the fireside, and with that end in view I have gathered together certain of the exploits of my forbears, both legendary and attested, and delighted, on winter evenings, to recount the sagas of the Marys, Mehitabels, and Susans, the Jonathans, Jeremiahs, and Davids, who dot my small page of American history.

My father's people seem to have been less adventurous than my mother's, although they have given good account of themselves in all our wars, but on the whole they would appear to have been of a more studious, professional, and stay-at-home habit. My father and his six-foot brothers were mighty hunters and anglers, however, and great friends of the Indians who guided and accompanied them. Peol-Tomah, the well-known chief of the Passamaquoddy tribe, to whom General Charles Hamlin erected a monument, was one of their valued friends, and "Mila," the name of his daughter, was given to one of my aunts and is still proudly borne by three of her descendants. At one time Peol captured two yearling moose on Anejon Stream and brought them down to Calais to one of my uncles, who had them trained to draw his sleigh in winter. The novel team attracted great attention and proved satisfactory at first. As the moose grew older, however, they showed a desire to jump fences, sleigh and all, when in high spirits, and they were finally presented to Fairmount Park in Philadelphia, where another uncle, the Reverend James Wheaton Smith, was then settled.

The family traditions seem to give conclusive evidence that the first of my father's ancestors to come to this country was a certain John Smith of the *Mayflower*, and that he was among its passengers appears the more likely, as no large party was ever gathered together, either in England or America, at any period of history, without the enlivening presence of at least one John Smith. There were always preachers and lawyers among the paternal kinsfolk, and my grandfather, Noah Smith, Jr., was a man of high standing in politics, being a member of the Maine State Legislature for several years before becoming, first, Speaker of the House (1854), and then Secretary of State (1858). He resigned the latter post at the earnest request of his intimate friend the Honorable Hannibal Hamlin, who, upon being elected to the Vice-Presidency, secured my grandfather's appointment as Secretary of the United States Senate in Washington and afterwards Legislative Clerk of the same body. It was while he was holding this office that he was taken ill and died at the home of his son, James Wheaton Smith, at Philadelphia. His gavel, used as Speaker of the Maine House, is an ornament of my desk, but no more precious to me than the battered copy of "The History of Cock Robin," a wonderful book with movable pictures which he ordered from London and presented to me on my fifth birthday.

His wife, Hannah Wheaton, my father's mother, was a woman of remarkable ability, so it is related in the family, and a descendant of the Robert Wheaton who was an early emigrant from Swansea, Wales, to this country, settling in Rehoboth, Massachusetts, about 1636. From this same stock descended Henry Wheaton, the distinguished diplomatist and authority on international law, and also Judge Laban Wheaton, founder of Wheaton College, and the name, a beloved and honored one, is still borne as a Christian name by members of my father's family. Some of the Wheaton gift of expression and literary facility undoubtedly descended to my father and his brothers, for they were famous story-tellers, noted for their fund of good anecdotes, their wit and spontaneity, and a certain laughter-compelling audacity that distinguished them as *raconteurs*. An old gentleman in Philadelphia, in describing Robert, my father, said that, if ever three of the brothers, Jim, Charles, and Bob, sat at the same table, the rivalry was such that no guest at the meal could ever forget the occasion. That such family characteristics are often handed down is a commonplace of tradition, though, alas! I cannot remember any three members of the present generation who could dominate and hypnotize a company at dinner.

A certain gift for story-telling may have descended to my sister [1] and to me from another branch of the family, for my great-grandfather, Captain Noah Smith, of South Reading, Massachusetts, is described in the Town Chronicles as having "in profusion, the qualities of hope, of

[1] Nora Archibald Smith.

friendship, of mirthfulness, of language, of conscientiousness, and memory." It is also said of him that he was "always social and cheerful, had a keen relish for 'Attic salt,' and possessed an unfailing supply of it himself. His memory contained an exhaustless fund of anecdote and story, and it was ever his delight to entertain his friends with a relation of them."

We are right, perhaps, in treasuring up and in recounting such few memorials of our ancestors as the vicissitudes of American pioneer life have allowed us to retain, for they throw a light upon bygone days and perhaps also upon inherited tastes, ambitions, and characteristics of our own. As to that, who can say how far these influences reach? Does the leaven, as I said in the beginning, really influence the lump, or the lump heavily, persistently, absorb and swallow the leaven? "Blood tells!" I remarked one day in a would-be experienced manner to the wise old San Francisco minister who honored me with his friendship. "Yes, my child," he replied, laconically, bending toward me his wonderful gray head — "blood tells, but remember that it sometimes tells lies!"

KATE DOUGLAS WIGGIN

MY GARDEN OF MEMORY

I

"I REMEMBER"

"How is one to write? Well, there is only one recipe I have ever heard of," said an old Frenchman; "take a quart or more of life-blood, mix it with a bottle of ink and a teaspoonful of tears, and ask God to forgive the blots." He said nothing specifically about smiles, but I am sure he meant that they had a part in the life-blood.

I ought — indeed, I should like — to begin at the very beginning, after the manner of the best and most logical autobiographies. But is it possible for one to decide what is the true beginning? Perhaps it does not come even at the hour of birth; for a great many facts have preceded that vital moment when we first broke into this world that we know best. It may be that we trailed Wordsworthian "clouds of glory" with us, and "Heaven lay about us in our infancy," in which case it was, indeed, a felicitous beginning, that shed its luster over many long months, even years of life. On the other hand, many a child trails nothing but gray clouds and shadows behind him and glory cannot live forever in this murky atmosphere.

Now that the more active years of the journey are over, I understand better than before the bearing upon my life of those events that seemed to have no special value at the time they occurred, but which might have been turning-points given me, not by decree, but for choice, perhaps; — and in one's choice lies all the difference!

Nothing that I shall inscribe on these pages is anything

but true; but the record as a whole will tell far less than the whole truth. A New England pen can hardly set down for an army of strange readers causes, circumstances, motives, judgments, and reasons — poor, indifferent, questionable, or good. One can hardly explain them to one's own soul, for they were not clear even at the time, and now, years afterward, they are lost in the mist. Character has been formed, somehow, somewhere, all along the way, when one least realized it, and now there is nothing to set down but incidents and events of the journey; the red-letter days, the higher levels, the view from the hills one may have climbed; for there is never much to say about the valleys where one worked, not always with joy, nor even with sense of service, though an autobiographer's "hard times" are thrilling to himself, and exciting to the reader. My memories, vague, uncertain, always undated, and never recorded in diary form save for three months during my whole life, are as clear as crystal as to my early childhood, and here then will be my beginning.

When I was a little girl!

I have said before, and very likely shall say again (since iteration, I have heard, is next to inspiration), that these six words are perhaps the most charming in the language. If you have any doubt of their eloquence, experiment with them upon any group of children, however unsusceptible or undisciplined, and observe their almost hypnotic effect. Breathed even to your own heart in some quiet moment, they have a like influence, sending your thought back to some fragrant memory-garden, some hidden corner of the "little past," where you re-live the care-free, eager, impetuous, poignant hours when self was first beginning to be conscious of self, and all you have since become was in the glowing bud.

My very earliest recollections seem to me to be all too few in number, too blurred and ill-defined to be put into words. They begin in something too fugitive to be called a memory, but I never cease to capture, lose again, and recapture, a moment at a children's party in Calais, Maine, when I could not have been more than two years old. This glimpse — it is nothing more — is of many children, and a man who was the idol of all, the center of attraction, the source of all merriment, the fount of all delight; and, with the picture, a sense of personal pride of possession; for this bewildering being, whom the children followed as they did the Pied Piper of Hamelin, was my very own father, and the feeling in my heart was certainly pride, if the psychologists are willing to admit that a child who has only lately learned to lisp can feel an emotion that ordinarily comes a little later.

There is a second picture of a great green space filled with trees; a space of winding paths and groups of children, that I now know to have been Independence Square in Philadelphia, and I must still have been at the toddling age, for we lived there only until I was three years old.

I can see groups of nurses, companies of children, and, threading his way through them and entering a wide-open, wrought-iron gate, a tall, handsome man whom I ran to meet gladly and who caught me in his arms and kissed me. I remember that I waved my hand to him when he left me a moment later, and that my face was wet, not with my own tears. It was my father again, my brilliant, gifted father, a young lawyer, who went on a business journey to a Western State and died there shortly after, so that my clearest and most fully conscious memory of him is also my last. There is an old proverb, "Thy mother is a vine in the blood"; and I, whose mother tarried on earth for more than ninety-one precious years, often feel her in my veins, in very truth. What is stranger, perhaps, is my conscious sense of close kinship with my father. It did not haunt me in childhood, but began when I myself began to "do things." I have often finished a book and thought: "My father would have liked that!" or, "My father would have done this, in something this way, only better."

I have known many persons who have no feeling of belonging to the man and woman who gave them life. Their personalities, instincts, tastes, tendencies, attractions, repulsions seem to have been inherited from some unknown source farther back in the line of ancestry; but I have a strange, almost uncanny, assurance of springing directly from my father and mother and bearing within me the traits of both. My father's peculiar gifts have the stronger influence upon my mind, but I am well aware that the mother-part of me has its own hold, and that what is "me" is the blend of these two individualities.

The vision of the child parting with her father in Independence Square has no companions for a long time, and meanwhile the scene has shifted from Philadelphia to a New England city.[1]

An early recollection in this epoch is my first spanking, and a timid and sentimental effort it was, as was just, perhaps, for my offense was merely against conventions. The kind rector of the Episcopal Church had come to bring me a present and my mother summoned me to the parlor to receive it. The gift, when taken from its wrappings and disclosed to my eager gaze, proved to be a prayer book, and as I took it, I remarked, indiscreetly and ungratefully: "Thank you ever so much, Mr. F., but I do wish you had given me almost anything else!" The rector departed in a few minutes, and thereupon I was practically (though feebly) introduced to the necessity of concealing

[1] Portland, Maine.

one's own feelings if, thereby, one can avoid hurting the feelings of somebody else. The spanking reduced my mother to tears, but, beyond some faint idea that I had annoyed her and been impolite to a clergyman, my sufferings, mental or physical, were infinitesimal.

Surrounding these two episodes in a general haze there is the memory of the house in which I lived; and there is the larger house across the street, with a magnificent horse-chestnut tree in the side yard, a tree that I could sketch to-day, so vividly can I see the shape of its trunk, the spread of its branches, and the glory of its blossoms. Above all, and more vividly than all, there is "Mary," who belonged to the tree as the tree belonged to her; — the first bosom friend of my infancy, I should think, was this same Mary.

There is also a very dim and evasive memory of a "dame school," where I see myself sitting on a low bench in the company of three or four other children with brief legs, white stockings, and ankle-ties. This is undoubtedly the first educational experiment to which I was subjected, and the dead-and-gone dame who conducted it would doubtless turn in her grave if she knew that I recall only the bench, and nothing of the knowledge, for the imbibing of which it was really sat upon.

Another gap occurs here. Many months must have passed, but real life, conscious, coherent, continuous, begins with me when I see myself driving from the New England city to the village of Hollis, sixteen miles distant, — a rough and dusty, rather hilly, road, two horses, and a huge, heavy, dignified "carryall" holding four people. My mother, after some years of widowhood, had married a distant cousin, Dr. Albion Bradbury, the beloved physician of a large countryside. My stepfather, already well known and liked as "Cousin Albion," sat with me on the front seat, my mother and the Small Sister behind, and existence, during every moment of the marvelous journey, grew more thrilling, more enthralling.

Were we not going to the country "for good and all," casting off the life of the great metropolis of Portland as the nautilus flings aside its outgrown shell? We were going to live in the country forever and ever, and the house was on the bank of a swift-flowing river! Oh! horses, gallop your fastest! (There was little Arabian stock in the State of Maine and a jog-trot was the customary gait!) Gallop your fastest, good horses, for the child is knowing the joys of anticipation for the first time, and happiness, without a shadow of doubt, is at the end of this epoch-making drive!

I was nearly seven, we will say, and the Small Sister on the back seat three, but I seem never to have observed her definitely before this red-letter day. As to her first appearance on this planet, her reception by a grateful family circle, her infant graces, or any wonder at having a sister at all, remembrance fails! I can atone for this unsentimental blindness and deafness in early days only by saying that after I once succeeded in taking note of her she looms very large in all later memory pictures.

The carryall arrived in due course of time, and, as it was late in a June afternoon, there must have been supper and bed-going, but these episodes passed unnoted by my capricious brain. It took cognizance only of the awakening next morning in an unfamiliar upper chamber. The features of no other room in all the universe are so well remembered, and the picture of no other single moment is so fresh, so deeply etched on my heart of hearts.

The room had slanting walls that cozily shut out all fear and wrapped a child about with soft content. It had yellow-painted furniture, a buff wallpaper, and a brown ingrain carpet. When I opened my eyes and ran to the

THE AUTHOR'S CHILDHOOD HOME IN HOLLIS, MAINE

single window, I looked out upon a Porter apple tree laden
with tiny, just-set fruit, some white Brahma cocks and hens
and chickens clustering near the door of a shed, a girl
scraping something messy and delicious from a tin pan and
feeding the greedy flock, and, above all, I met the impassioned, upward gaze of Brent, a black, wavy-haired
dog — a rather foolish, addle-headed, irresponsible, lovable
dog who became a fast friend within twenty-four hours.

The back wheels of the carryall, observed through the
open barn doors, assured me that all I saw was real —
although the universe had an air of having been made to
order especially for my delectation, and I realized gratefully that I was a human being, with joyous opportunities
of sharing the life around me. I felt that I was going to
sleep forever in the yellow-painted bedstead and look forever on the apple tree, probably also that I was destined to
join in the intoxicating occupation of scraping food from
the tin pan and feeding the white flock; for I was a born
"participator," and I fear that from the beginning of
time nothing ever occurred in my immediate vicinity in
which I did not long to take a hand.

I had been in this village once before, and I remembered
that I knew a little girl up the hill and across the fields.
Accordingly I dressed hurriedly, slipped downstairs, and
made my way through the grass "over to Annie's." The
attire of children in those Dark Ages was so simple that
any chit past babyhood could dress herself without aid.
Underclothing was looked upon merely as a covering for
the body, the shape of the child when covered being a matter of complete unimportance. In fact, the question of
shape did not concern our elders very much, I fancy.
The drawing on of white cotton stockings presented no
difficulties, though the lacing of copper-toed boots was an
art that had to be, and was, learned at a very early age,

long before it appeared as one of the features of the Montessori system. The one-piece frock of gingham or calico slipped over your head, and then, if you were moderately clever and self-helpful, you could squirm and wriggle about until you had pushed the half-dozen pearl buttons into the companion buttonholes that closed your waist in the back.

If your hair was long, you braided it in a pigtail, and if it was short, you brushed it back under a round comb and regarded your shiny Websterian brow without any compunctions. Moreover, nothing had to be done to your clothes when they were once made, save to take out tucks and let down hems of skirts according to the stretching and lengthening of your infant legs; and all this greatly simplified life, as you can well imagine. There was no variety in sleeves, nor any change in silhouette in those days; a frock was worn until it was definitely shabby.

The charm of that first walk in the early morning is still potent. I can still see the waving daisies and buttercups, feel the dew on my ankles, hear the birds singing in the leafy elms, sniff the fragrance of the pine woods near at hand. The world seemed so fresh, so new, so ready to be lived in, and, though so big and untried, so kind, so sympathetic, so helpful!

One can get used, I suppose, even to such divine things as early summer mornings, dew-drenched daisies smiling in the sun, blue skies and song of birds — though the lover of beauty would never tire of them; but to the child the newness of it all comes with a passionate intensity of joy; a "first, fine, careless rapture" that, indeed, can never be quite recaptured later in life.

The world is always a new plaything to children, while to the old it seems falling to pieces from sheer dryness. Everything loses its value with time, but it is not the fault of the fruit, but of the mouth and the tongue. "Ask the children and the birds how the cherries taste," says Palacio Valdes. "I do not know how they taste to the birds," he adds, "but as for myself they tasted so delicious to me sixty years ago that when I saw a basket of them I fell immediately into an ecstasy like Saint Theresa in the presence of the Sacrament."

II

CHILDHOOD PLAYS AND PLEASURES

My childish pleasures were many, though so simple that a little girl of to-day would certainly think them woefully dull. We played paper dolls, jackstraws and jackstones; we "tiltered"; we built houses from "stickings" and "cut-rounds"; and gave parties with dishes made of broken china. We pulled hairs from the horse's tail and put them in the brook to grow snakes, which, to our surprise and regret, they never did; we waded in the river and ran to and fro on the rafted logs; we fished for "shiners"; we made cakes of rose-leaves and brown sugar, folded them in paper and buried them in the earth for a week, when we dug them up with great ceremony and ate them with much lip-smacking.

In the spring we searched for mayflowers, and waded in the full brooks and gathered fluffy pussy willows. There were anemones and frail hepaticas in the woods and blue flags and wild violets in the marshy places. We watched the yellow dandelions come, one by one, in the short green grass, and we stood under the maple trees and saw the sap trickle from their trunks into the great wooden buckets placed underneath.

If spring seemed wonderful, summer was even more joyous, with strawberrying and blueberrying and hay-making; — long days of play and long twilights and moon-light nights.

One of our pleasures was a little out of the common. I asked my stepfather one day if he would give us a part of the garden brook for our froggery. The garden in question covered an acre or two of ground, with little up-hills and down-dales, while a dashing, tumultuous brook, with here and there a bit of quiet water, ran through it. There were many trees, with flower-beds bordering the road, and there was a green-and-white latticed summer-house on the brink of the hill at the foot of which flowed our beloved Saco River. In one of the deep, quiet pools of the brook, hidden by green alder bushes, my father put pieces of fine wire netting, and so arranged them that the frogs we caught and placed there lived a pleasant and secluded life free from the cares and dangers that we fancied existed in large ponds.

Here we used to wait for gay young polliwogs to grow into frogs, one leg at a time. Repeated and prolonged observations by the pond never once permitted us to see a leg actually coming out. Nature somehow decreed that it should happen in the night.

We found two wounded bullfrogs by the side of the water-lily pond, magnificent bass singers, stoned by cruel small boys. We bound up their broken legs and bruised backs and coaxed them into health again in one corner of the froggery that we called the hospital. In another corner was the nursery, kept only for the tiniest frogs; but with a dawning pedagogical instinct we let them out once a day so that they might not be cut off from the advantages of adult society. All our frogs had names of their own and we knew them all apart. They always had plenty of fat juicy flies and water-bugs for dinner, and sometimes we put little silver shiners and tiny minnows into the pool. "They will know now, you see, that there are other things in the world except frogs," I explained to the Small Sister, who did not favor the idea, principally because she could never lean over the fishy part of the brook to catch minnows without tumbling in head foremost.

We held a frog singing-school once a week. It was very

troublesome, but exciting. We used to put a nice little board across the pool and then catch the frogs and try to keep them in line with their heads all facing the same way during the brief lesson. They never really caught the idea, and were never in a singing mood until just before our own early bedtime, when the baby frogs were so sleepy that they kept falling from the board into the pool. They could never quite apprehend the difference between school and pool; but at the end of the summer's training we twice succeeded in getting them into line, quiet, docile, motionless, without a hint of the application of force; tact, moral suasion, and superhuman patience being the only means employed. It was a beautiful sight worth any amount of toil and trouble! Twenty-one frogs in line, for a minute and a half, all graded nicely as to size, all in fresh green suits with white shirt-fronts. What wonder that in various sojourns in Paris I have never been able to regard a frog's leg as an appetizing delicacy, or to hear its resemblance and superiority to chicken discussed without a shudder. As soon dine upon the breast of the family kitten!

It does not need the prophetic gift of an Amos or an Ezekiel to see in this sort of play a foreshadowing of my future absorbing interest in education; and it is strengthened in my mind by the fact that in playing paper dolls I went outside the usual routine of country child — city child — brides — mothers — boy and girl babies; and created orphan asylums of dolls dressed alike in pink or blue. Their pasteboard mother or matron was firm in discipline, and given to daily instruction in the three R's, but she allowed them to wear pink and blue gingham. She thought brown gingham cruel, and so, at that eager, beauty-loving age, did I, by a curious coincidence! I have on my desk a tiny Doll's Spelling Book, brown with age, an inch and a quarter square, with fifteen neatly printed pages of words set down for "Nellie," my favorite orphan paper doll. On the inside of the cover is the only evidence extant of any intuition on my part regarding the author's craft. In the proper place there appears in the clearest of print:

HOLLIS

ENTERED ACCORDING TO

ACT OF CONGRESS

1864

It seems like a simple statement of intention on the editor's part to preserve her work against all persons of piratical tendencies, yet, on the other hand, I was in complete ignorance of publishers, royalties, circulation, or anything regarding the profession of the author, nor had I the slightest interest in it.

Summer waned, but in the fall we went nutting and pressed red, yellow, and bronze autumn leaves between the pages of our great Webster's Dictionary. We gathered apples and watched the men working at the cider presses and the farmers as they threshed their wheat and husked their corn.

Then came winter, with snowballing and coasting down-hill, and long evenings before the open fire popping corn and roasting apples. We made snow ice-cream for Saturday afternoon parties: snow, milk, sugar, and vanilla stirred together and partaken of immediately after mixing, not realizing that later generations would pronounce the product crowded with poisonous microbes.

There was a sawmill on the brink of our river and groups of board-piles near the bridge. One board could always be taken from the top and laid across a block to form a see-saw; and overhanging boards, reaching out from the pile, left mysterious caves and shelters here and there, into which we could creep and pretend many things. Sometimes we were distressed princesses awaiting a romantic and chivalrous rescue; or, our husbands being away clearing the land, we were secreting ourselves from the wolves or the Indians that surrounded our log cabin.

The board-piles afforded the best possible place for playing "Hide and Coop," and also unparalleled opportunities for falling and scraping one's infant shins. "Annie" was the most adventurous of our number, her unspoken motto being "Excelsior," her skull apparently being made of unbreakable material and her arms and legs of India rubber. I was always panting at her heels, though never quite achieving her heights; one perennial obstacle in my path of progress being the all-too-frequent presence of the Small Sister.

The Small Sister was plump, but in no way elephantine; her feet, while neat and pretty, were sufficiently large to bear the weight of her body, yet she was hopelessly unsteady in her movements. Clad irreproachably in clean buff or blue calico, she lagged behind us on the country road, puffing, blowing, and shrieking: *"Wait for me! I can't keep up!"* If there were a puddle anywhere within reach, it exercised a magnetic attraction for her. She tried tremblingly to skirt it unscathed, but always hovered totteringly on its brink and then sat down in it.

As for a stile, or any elevation that had to be climbed, she was never able to decide which leg had to be put over first, where to put it when over, or what to do with the leg left behind. She would always clutch the nearest post desperately and call in clarion tones: "I won't be long!" She was everything that was most desirable, however, when it came to story-telling, and the management of large and ever-increasing families of paper and rag and china-headed dolls.

We both read without being taught. No power on earth could have kept us from ferreting out the momentous secrets that lay between the covers of books. We never heard that there was an alphabet that had to be learned before we could read. We played with our letter-blocks and picture-books quite by ourselves, and presently divined the relation between spoken and printed words. Thrilling two-line tales in large type with explanatory pictures proved the necessary missing link, and then with one intrepid leap of the mind we seemed to land in the heart of a book. There might be a few puzzles in it, a few questions to ask, but we could dig out the story quickly enough, you may be sure of that!

In this way books grew to be a vital part of our life. Books, books, books! There was always plenty of time (incredible statement!); therefore books before breakfast, after playtime, before bedtime, between-times.

This, then, is the record of the recreations of long ago. At the very recounting of them my heart softens and grows younger. I look from my library window upon the sky-scrapers of New York, but I cannot see them because the hills of the Maine village hide them and obscure the view. I know that the hum and noise and blare of city streets is just outside, but I am deaf to it all because the music of the swift-flowing river, to which I went to sleep in my childhood, is the sound I am hearing as I write.

Life was by no means all play with an old-fashioned New England child, but the idea never dawned upon us that there was anything wearisome or obnoxious about work. Our childish duties and cares were as many and as diverse (thank Heaven!) as our plays and pleasures. We "helped" in everything, and divided the responsibilities of the household as if we belonged to the working class instead of being the children of a well-to-do physician. There was one man, and one maid-of-all-work, but each of us had special responsibilities. That we took care of ourselves goes without saying, but we did much more than that, regularly, faithfully, and without question.

When I was nine or ten I had weekly music lessons for a year or two with a maiden lady who herself had been privileged to study in Boston for three solid months and who was looked upon in our little community as an artist of the first rank. She was more than that, she was a woman of the first rank and an admirable teacher. To hear her play "The Maiden's Prayer" or "Monastery Bells," both hands moving at once, and an occasional change of pedals, was a musical event of well-nigh national importance in our small society.

Miss Martha Rumery's cottage on a hillside country road near our own was one of my pleasure-palaces, and the old-fashioned Hallett & Cumston mahogany piano, with its tinkling keys, opened vistas of new delight to my rather sensitive ear. Practicing and studying, then, had to be added to our days' duties (we had lessons at home chiefly); but household tasks were many, and so vital a part of the great business of life, that we accepted them joyfully and without question.

I may as well say here as elsewhere that my memory is a capricious and treacherous one. It holds with tenacity what I should regard as wholly unimportant events, and completely buries others, well remembered by members of my family. I have never paid any attention to dates, from my childhood to the present moment. It seems an inexplicable and indefensible thing that an intelligent person can go through life writing thousands of undated letters, filing business documents with no record of the settlement of the issues involved; omitting to set down even in a dozen words occasions of surpassing interest, forgetting the exact year in which occurred serious family events such as births, marriages, deaths, and removals to new homes in far-away places; but it can be done, alas! Experience has taught me a little; not very much, and only at the expense of profound and exhausting effort. This fatal weakness, this entire absence of chronological faculty, prevents a properly made autobiography, and it accounts for mysterious lapses on my part. For instance, why should I so clearly remember the "froggery" and have so little memory of the Civil War? It was not because I lived among people unaffected by it, for the villages of Hollis and of Buxton, just across the river, were famous for sending out soldiers before the draft began. Yet I recall only three events as having registered themselves firmly in my mind.

First, the surrender of General Lee, when our village was illuminated with candles and kerosene lamps to a brilliancy entirely beyond the imagination of man to conceive. Broadway in 1923 seems murky and dim beside the effulgence of my memories.

Next, the return of one soldier after another, several from Libby Prison, and the outbreak of various contagious maladies which kept my stepfather continually in action day and night.

The third far surpasses the other two in its intensity; the death of Abraham Lincoln. Instead of being a vague picture, it comes back like a great, dark, overwhelming shape obscuring the sunlight; a dull blow; gloom blacker than ordinary gloom; a portentous cessation of activities. Families ate little, work in the fields stopped, men gathered in yards and by roadsides and talked in low voices. My mother sat with folded hands and my father paced to and fro on the grass in front of the house. I stole out, uncomprehending, but profoundly moved, and walked up to my grandmother's house to meet Uncle H., who was always very sensitive and emotional, with the tears running down his face, and I heard a man say: "Squire Bradbury feels it like the rest of us and he a Democrat and a Copperhead."

Finding that nobody paid any attention to me, I came down the street heavier-hearted than ever. The children now had come under the influence of their elders, and were crying, they scarcely knew why. When they met, one said to the other: "Isn't it dreadful that Abraham Lincoln is dead? Mother cried when she read the paper"; and another would answer: "So did mine, and Father says he won't go on planting till Lincoln is buried. He says he can't think what will become of us without Lincoln!"

And so the days wore on in sadness and there was a weight on the public heart that it took many weeks to lighten. I am grateful that I remember that episode so clearly and that I had the opportunity to sympathize and suffer in my childish way. It was my first conscious recognition of the greatness of individual character, the first conscious stirring of "admiration, hope, and love" in my heart for something bigger than I had ever known, or heretofore imagined. It leads directly to an influence that came into my life three years later; one that made a never-to-be-forgotten impression in a wholly different way; one that persists to this day and which I will recount in its proper place.

III

DIARY OF A "TRULY" LITTLE GIRL

I once kept a journal when I had attained the ripe age of ten summers. I set down in a mottled-covered blank-book daily, for a portion of one season, all the doings of my life in a small New England hamlet. There is not a trace of literary talent in this childish effort, I am ashamed to say. I was, in reality, a creature of dreams and fancies, of ardent enthusiasms and unflagging energies, but the idea of a journal, in my mind, seems to have been a rigid record of the day's activities. The getting up in the morning, the going up and down stairs, the preparation for breakfast, the everlasting "going for the milk" (in the temporary absence of a cow from our family possessions) — these completely crowd out any reflections or imaginings that may have flitted through my brain.

When I read the thrilling matters and speculations that occupied the infantile attention of Marie Bashkirtseff long ago, and Mrs. Asquith in our own time, I blush with embarrassment at the barrenness of my mind at the same age! I am not conscious that I concealed anything, so I must accept the obvious verdict that I was either extremely backward, or not mentally alert.

The journal lies before me as I write, and with the reading of every page "airs from the Eden of youth awake and stir in the soul." It is an innocent, humdrum, human little document, chiefly interesting as a chronicle of a child's life in a Maine village more than fifty years ago.

The fine old house of my stepfather's family, a short distance up the maple-shaded street, looms large in the chronicle, for Grandmother lived there, and there was much visiting to and fro. Every meal "at Grandma's" is described with much particularity in the journal, and my offices in the great old-fashioned kitchen, with Grandma at the helm, seem to have been matters of enormous pride, not to say self-glorification. Nothing was extenuated and I believe naught set down in malice, but the regularity with which I pounded beefsteak with a broken pie-plate before it was cooked seems to show that the meat of that period was not so tender as might have been desired, and Grandma herself would have blue-penciled some of my pages.

Here is one extract showing a busy day and apparently foreshadowing, not a future author, but a cook or, at any rate, a laborer in the realm of domestic science.

The book in which to keep the diary does not seem to have been given me at Christmas or New Year's, for my first records are set down in March and cease abruptly and altogether in mid-July of the same year.

The first entry reads as follows:

March 24th: I got up this morning at twenty minutes past seven; then I went downstairs and dusted the parlor, which took me until breakfast time. After breakfast we read the prayers for the day and two chapters in the Bible. Then Nora and I went out to feed the hens. We found one egg. After we got through I put on my things and went for the milk. After I got home we went up to Grandmother's to spend the day — Mother, Cousin E. and all three of us children.[1] I read a little while in the new "Harper." The story that I read first was "My Fathers-in-Law." It was real funny, but it didn't sound true. Then Grandma said she wanted me to help her. Cousin E. went out with me; she mashed turnips, and I pounded beefsteak with a broken plate to make it tender; then I fixed the sausages for dinner, helped set the table; then we sat down. We had a real nice dinner — sausages, beefsteak, pickles, turnips, potatoes, cheese, biscuits; for dessert — pumpkin and apple pies, coffee, apple sauce. After supper I

[1] There was a little half-brother, Philip, by that time.

dressed and went to the Bible class. I read once, and answered three or four questions.

March 25th: Upon looking out of my window this morning I found it was raining in torrents. I was very much disappointed as Father and I expected to go to Hollis Center to buy a lamb and two more hens. Ours seemed so cold and hungry that I took hay and stuffed it in all the little holes of the hen-house and then took a nice clean board and put it in a place where the wind didn't blow, and put their food and drink on it. I caught the tame hen too, and had a little fun with her. Then helped Mother make the beds, then studied for two hours. I had California for a lesson in Geography to-day. It was easy and real interesting; I had a long Latin lesson and I suppose it seemed the harder for me because I hate it so; did four or five sums, and then practiced till dinner time. After dinner I went to see if there were any eggs, but there were not, so I went indoors, went upstairs, brushed my hair, washed my face, and went downstairs, and worked on my night-gown case. By that time it was five o'clock, time for me to make the milk toast for supper. I put the milk in the frying-pan, and then mixed the thickening, and put that in with a large piece of butter. Nora came out then and toasted the bread for me, and I dropped it in the drawn butter and let it soak a good while till it was soft, and then laid it in the dish. Afterwards I poured the rest of the milk over the toast. I guess it was nice, but you can't save butter. If you do, the gravy tastes like paste. After supper Mother played for Father and me to dance by, and then I for Father and Mother.

March 26th: I did not wake up this morning till Cousin E. called me. I was sleepy, but I had to get up, so I did. The first thing I did was to run to the window to see if it was a pleasant day. It was, so dressed quick, for if it was pleasant we were going to get the lamb. (The lamb is not for use, but for fun.) There wasn't anything to do for breakfast, so I cleared up the parlor; then when Father and Mother came down we read the Bible. After breakfast I made the beds, and then with Father and Nora went up to Grandmother's to harness the horse. After I had been there a little while I saw Mr. F. riding up the road. I ran down to ask him if we could have the lamb if we came over for it. He said he should have to ask a dollar and a quarter for it instead of a dollar. I ran up and told Father, and he said the lamb wasn't worth it. I couldn't help crying, I wanted him so much. Mother said she was real sorry, and she didn't care anything about the extra quarter, but it was too much for a lamb. Father came down in a minute with the horse to go over to the Center for the hens, so I got a basket and we started. On our way over we called at Mrs. E.'s; she wanted to give me the quarter, so that I could have the lamb, but Father wouldn't let her. We stopped at the blacksmith's to get the horse shod; waited to get warm a minute, and started for the hens. We had such a time catching them! We had all but one, and Mr. K. said she was the "slipperiest critter he ever see." *Father stopped at Mr. F.'s after all and bought the lamb* (*!!*) Afterwards we had to study. Everything went wrong; had to get my lessons twice. People came in every three minutes. Fed the lamb, then ate my supper, and went to bed early.

The aforesaid "lamb" deserves this last extract as showing the point of view concerning the unwise expenditure of twenty-five cents in that era of economy and discretion. It also shows that parents had hearts of flesh in all ages, and that an extra quarter of a dollar for a pet lamb, though an unjust charge, must be paid now and then unless the ears of posterity are to ring with charges of undue severity or incredible parsimony:

April 1st: Rose early this morning and practiced a half-hour before breakfast. After breakfast I went for the milk, also for a dozen of eggs for one of our hens that wants to set (or sit). After I got home we read the prayers, and then I thought of some way to make an April Fool of Uncle H. I should have fried some cotton-wool doughnuts, but he was sick and couldn't have eaten them. I had to carry up some medicine to him. Father was down at the store then, but soon came and went into the house, but came out in a few minutes, and said, "Here is a little maple sugar that I bought for you; divide it among you." So I went out and sat down with Janie on the sled and opened the bundle and saw — an old hammer, a piece of bark and one of tin! I felt cheap then, I tell you! I took the bundle then and made April fools of all the people in the place with it, came home, read the Bible and practiced, before dinner. After dinner dressed Phil and myself, then went down to Miss R.'s to get her to show me about my music lesson and how to make a pair of garters for Aunt J.'s baby. After supper, as it was too rainy to carry the garters in to

Aunt J., I practiced a half-hour, then went upstairs, and Mother read out loud a beautiful war story about Benjamin F. Porter, a boy only sixteen years old and a Lieutenant.

April 2nd: Practiced half an hour before breakfast; after that went on some errands for Mother, then went to the pond and saw F. and W. take the ice out. I sat on the sluice with a bean-pole and poked the ice, which the boys sent down over the falls, but Nora got her feet wet as usual, and went into Grandma's to dry them. Then we had to rip my embroidered blue dress because Miss R. was going into Portland and was going to take it in to be colored. After dinner went into the kitchen to see Billy, the lamb, washed. He had a long piece of his tail frozen, and when he was washed it came right off, which was a horrible surprise.

April 3rd: Rose early and went downstairs, practiced a half-hour before breakfast. After breakfast we read the Bible, then went for the milk, and invited Miss T. and Mrs. C. over to tea, for we were going to have Grandma's family besides. Came home and went up with Cousin E. to Grandma's to borrow some milk, butterplates, and muffin rings. Miss T. taught me a polka in the forenoon; after dinner ironed a good while, all the handkerchiefs, towels, napkins. Then went into the parlor, and read till it was time to dress. After supper Miss Jennie Usher sang; I don't know the real name of it, but I call it "Jamie," then "Maggie's Secret," "The Brook," "Too Late," "The Bridge," — all beautiful songs. Then I played Mozart's Turkish March, and was clapped; then we had a game of "Muggins" till the company went.

Housework of all kinds seems to have been accepted in a cheerful spirit, as witnessed by the following excerpts chosen at random:

April 4th: This morning we commenced house cleaning, or at any rate we moved *down*stairs to clean *up*stairs. We carried great armfuls of clothes and threw them with feather beds and mattresses downstairs, and after we had thrown them all down we tumbled down on them, and carried them by armfuls into the bedrooms. After we got the beds made up, Mother swept and we went upstairs; while she was sweeping, we took tacks out of carpets, as many as we could, and then, when she came up, we had to clean up the playroom. Hannah was taking up her carpet, so Mother and I had to get dinner. I dressed myself and went to take my music lesson. It was a lovely thing called "Departed Days."

Before supper I went with Nora into the storeroom and got some apples for mincemeat. Mother peeled them, and Nora and I chopped to the tune of "Yankee Doodle." It makes it much easier.

Here is an item very interesting to me:

April 9th: After breakfast we read the prayers as usual, then I made the beds, and there was still time enough to have a play before studying, so we went over to Carll's to see them dig the cellar under the new ell.[1] Came home and studied, which with reciting and practicing took me till dinner. After dinner I went in to Aunt J.'s to see the baby, then came home and wrote my journal; then Nora and I went up in Dunn's woods to get some boxberries. Practiced till supper time when I fried the pancakes. Uncle H. came down, and I played for him till bedtime.

April 17th: Helped Hannah fry the cakes for breakfast. After breakfast I quilted a little and then studied. It never took me longer to get my lessons, for my head ached dreadfully. After dinner I quilted twenty-four squares, then Nora and I stripped up a lot of rags and sewed them together, and I braided a little on them to make a rag mat for our play house. Carried Mrs. C.'s book back to her, and afterwards took down a book to both Mrs. D. and Mrs. S., "Uncle Tom's Cabin" to the former, and "Yusef, or a Crusade in the East," to the latter, also borrowed two bound numbers of "Littell's." Oh, how splendid!

April 21st: After breakfast Uncle Henry came down and asked us up to dinner, so Mother said she would and bring something. Hannah and I went ahead, I with a lemon pie, and she with some parsnips. After we had given them to her we went out in the garden by the brook, and stayed there till dinner time. After dinner we all went up in the woods, and got Grandma a lot of things to make root beer of, "Linkum Piny," Liverwort, Motherwort, Ivory Leaves, etc.

April 28th: After dinner read a little out of a book of poems, "The Hidden Way," then went out in the kitchen and played

[1] The Carll house is now my own "Quillcote," and the child who saw the cellar dug little thought it was directly under the room which would one day be her study, where she would write *Susanna, Waitstill, Mother Carey, The Old Peabody Pew, Rose o' the River, New Chronicles of Rebecca*, etc.

jackstones for a while, after which we went to walk, came home quite early, *had perfectly splendid tarts for supper.*

May 12th: After breakfast we read the Bible, then I helped get Nora off for meeting. Then sat down and read awhile in my favorite book "Uncle Tom's Cabin," after which I wrote a letter, also my journal, then Mother read a very interesting account of the great Paris Exposition out of the " Tribune." I want to go aw-fully, but, of course, there is no possibility of it. Cousin E. came in just as she had finished and brought me some beautiful wild flowers, Hepaticas, Anemones, and May Flowers. Pretty soon Nora came and brought me a nice Sunday School book — "Pa-tience, or the Sunshine of the Heart." All the children in the Sunday School books are as good as pie.

May 19th: Rose at seven this morning. After breakfast we put on our new calico dresses. They fitted nicely and I think they are beautiful. Then after waiting some time Willie came up with the horse and we started for church, had a beautiful ride up, and got there just in time. We had our Sunday School lessons good and our Commandments also. We had some very nice books; my most interesting one was "Mary Lewis, a little Orphan but a Christian girl."

I have finished the "Minister's Wooing." After supper I watered the plants. I am to do it for a cent a week. (!!)

May 21st: I did not miss in school this morning and had good lessons in the afternoon. Got up two in spelling, *so I am now Number Six.* (!!)

May 24th: Father gave me a piece of land to make me a vege-table garden, so I went right to work. First I hauled manure in Phil's little cart, and hoed and mixed it in with the earth, then Nora and I went up to Grandma's and got some Beet seeds, Corn, Potatoes, Lettuce, Tomato, Peas; it took us a great while to plant them and make a fence round it and it wasn't a very big garden either.

June 2nd: Miss R. asked me if it was pleasant if I did not want to ride up to Moderation with her the next time when she goes to give a music lesson. I said I should be delighted to. I jumped rope till bedtime. Oh, I hope it will be pleasant! I have got to be down at Miss R.'s house by six, ready to start. It is eight miles. Even with her good horse we cannot make it in an hour.

June 7th: Hannah called me at five o'clock this morning. I dressed myself in a nice clean gingham dress, then ate a little breakfast and went down to Miss R.'s. It was a perfectly lovely day, and when we got on our way it was so early and everything was so fresh that we were having a beautiful ride. The birds were all singing and the apple trees all in bloom, and so many weeping elms and other splendid trees I never saw before.

June 8th: I cut up some rhubarb for pies and for sauce, then helped make cake and cream pie, after that I wrote my journal, and then practiced till dinner time. I had my pinball cut out, but could not make it because it had to be ironed. As I couldn't think of anything else to make I thought I would buy some calico at the store to make baby's bibs. Well, I got some pink calico, a quarter of a yard; it will make three and it was only four cents. I had time to bind one before supper; after it Nora and I went over the other side of the river and played hide and coop in the lumber yard.

June 11th: Nothing happened during the day, but when I got home from a drive they told me that Lambie had choked to death. Oh, how sad I did feel; it seemed as if I couldn't keep from crying, and I did when I got into my room alone. He cost a dollar and a quarter and only lived two and a half months! We are never going to have another. He wound himself up in his rope and then fell down a steep bank.

July 4th: It has been a very hot day and not much fun. I was unhappy quite a while remembering last Fourth of July when Mother was away and Aunt J. was taking care of us and she gave me five cents to spend and told me to divide it with Nora. I took three cents and gave her two because I was the oldest; and next day, and ever since, sometimes at night, I feel ashamed, for it was mean and I know I ought to have given her two and a half and been fair.

July 6th: Made Phil's cart into an ambulance and Nora and I are going to have a hospital for sick bugs and other things. I got four little willow branches and dropped them into the cart for a bed and then made a cover of white curtain lace. It is perfectly lovely and we soon hope to have it full of invalid insects, though Nora hates worms and crawling things.

July 13th: I have had some trouble with lessons this week, but none at all with behavior for a very long time. It seems quite natural to be good. (!!)

So ends the commonplace little chronicle! I could not have been a Pharisee at the age of ten, so I hope this allusion to the ease with which I attained perfection of conduct may be pardoned by the reader. The record was made on a Saturday night, and I was probably in a happy and serene state of mind, looking back upon several days of unusual virtue.

Armando Palacio Valdes says in his charming auto-biography: "Childhood is happiness. Every child is happy if no brutal hand is interposed between it and happiness. Air, light, liberty, a little sand and mud — in childhood we need nothing more for being happy. And God gives us these things."

Simple, busy, contented child of the long ago, peering at me out of the haze of the past, I wonder how much of her survives in me to-day! Monotonous as the diary is, it does give one a sense of home, of ancestral acres, the spot where childhood and youth were lived, the spot where memories cluster. Father, mother, brother, sister, grandmother, uncle, cousin, playmates, all rise in their accustomed places as I turn the leaves of the journal and read the faded childish handwriting, but I see them on a background of the hills and fields of New England, with its summer heats and its drift of winter snows. I see the fast-flowing river, the sawmill on its brink, the little red-brick district school, the white-painted meeting-house. All together they make the picture I love best, that of the dearest of all my many homes.

BEGINNING OF HERO-WORSHIP

OUR little Maine village had not only many people of more than ordinary intelligence, but several of quite unusual culture, so that the conversation we children overheard among our elders was good substantial stuff. That there was gossip in the post-office, the stores, and on the benches at either end of the bridge, is true enough, but I remember none at all in any social gathering under our own roof, although we were only allowed on the outer edges of such gayeties as whist parties or the like. Yet, our hamlet being somewhat isolated from the exciting issues that constitute the life of large cities, heroic figures like Senators, Governors, and millionaires were seldom entertained, and thus my instinct for hero-worship confined itself to personages in books, or to the authors of them.

I remember, however, the passion of interest aroused in me by the afternoon call of my mother's friend, a certain Miss Martha Ripley, newly arrived from France and Italy. This lady had boarded at the celebrated Carll house on our street, and it was a matter of general assent that she was an extraordinarily learned as well as an unusually gifted person. She had translated several well-known novels from the French and had traveled extensively. My father and uncle likened her to Madame de Staël and George Sand, giving us the idea that a society graced by her, and by another local favorite, a witty spinster named Louisa Titcomb, was probably equal in brilliancy to that of any salon in France.

I distinctly remember the day when Miss Ripley arrived in our sitting-room after a year of absence, absolutely direct from Paris. Her hat, dress, shawl, shoes, with her visible body inside of them, had unquestionably trod the streets of Paris, and there she stood, tolerably calm, in our sitting-room.

She was embraced by my mother, who said, "Is it really you, Mat Ripley?" — and I was astounded at the familiarity under the circumstances of abbreviating the Martha to "Mat." She greeted my sister and me as having grown enormously in two years, and seated herself by the open fire for a long account of her travels and adventures in foreign lands. She had a straight, slim, erect figure encased in a tight black cloth dress relieved by a pale blue belt that held our youthful eyes enchained. Oh! that intoxicating blue belt, when first we beheld it! It spelled Parisian fashions and "Godey's Lady's Book" to us, and, although it would seem to have been an uneventful and inexpensive adjunct to any frock, it had never been seen before in Hollis. It was easy to copy, and nearly every lady in the village wore a colored belt within a week, though they never dared to wear one while walking up the middle aisle of the Congregational Church. The belt seemed not exactly immoral, nor even irreligious, but too conspicuous for "meeting."

Miss Ripley had an olive skin, dark hair drawn back very tightly, irregular but piquant features, and a certain air of masculinity that attracted instead of repelling; — in fact, as I look back upon her now, I can see quite clearly that she was a type calculated to fit like a glove in Paris, and that she did not break up the serenity of matrimonial relations in Hollis is all to her credit. She was witty, ironic, and intrepid, being afraid neither of mice nor snakes.

Her adventures were thrilling! They could all have been told to our Sunday School without editing, but they held me breathless, as so very different from the daily life we led on our elm-shaded street. She opened unexplored worlds, and I palpitated to think how the people lived whom I read about in my geography, in such searching analyses as: "*The French are a gay and polite people fond of dancing and light wines.*"

When she rose to leave, I whispered to my mother, "Oh, Mother, *may* I give her my amethyst ring?" — that being a natural votive offering that one could lay on the altar of genius. The treasure reposed at the moment in my bureau drawer, as it was not *de rigueur* for children to wear jewelry at that epoch in history. I mention the episode chiefly because it is a sort of forerunner of my eager interest in people who "did" things, and how infrequently celebrities appeared on my humble horizon — just the right horizon, after all — wide enough for a child's eyes and growing wider day by day.

My sister and I had few playmates, but I cannot remember that we were ever dull, for dullness in a child, as in a grown person, means lack of dreams and visions, and those we had a-plenty. We were fortunate, too, in that our house was on the brink of one of the loveliest rivers in the world. When we clambered down the steep bank to the little cove that was just beneath our bedroom windows, we found ourselves facing a sheet of crystal water as quiet as a lake, a lake from the shores of which we could set any sort of adventure afloat; yet scarcely three hundred feet away was a roaring waterfall — a baby Niagara — which, after dashing over the dam in a magnificent tawny torrent, spent itself in a wild stream that made a path between rocky cliffs until it reached the sea, eight miles away. No child could be lonely who lived on the brink of such a river; and then we had, besides our studies and our country sports, our books, which were the dearest of all our friends.

Oh! the unconscious misery, the dullness, the loneliness of the child who does not care for reading! No one pretends that a book is the only open sesame to knowledge, for we learn a thousand things by other means: by first-hand observation, by the cares and responsibilities of existence, through skill in handicraft, through creative work of any sort; but the book, the dear, enlivening, enchanting, stimulating, informing, uplifting book, is the most faithful of all allies, and, after human friendship, the chief solace as well as the most inspiring influence in human life. For periodical literature we read "Harper's Magazine" and "Littell's Living Age," faithfully and passionately. No books were too old for us! We not only read "Robinson Crusoe," "The Lamplighter," "Typee," "Scottish Chiefs," "Thaddeus of Warsaw," "The Minister's Wooing," "Undine," "Uncle Tom's Cabin," and such old-fashioned treasures, but Thackeray, Dickens, Scott, Shakespeare, and the Bible.

There was, besides, my stepfather's good medical library in the many shelves surmounting a professional cupboard which, when opened, exhaled undesirable perfumes. (I can at any time still call up the repulsive odor of Podophyllin, although I have not sniffed it for more than half a century!)

There were huge brown-covered volumes on another wall, Blackstone and Coke, and other legal tomes inherited from some ancestor, but none of these were the stuff of which my dreams were made; — these centered in a certain set of black-walnut book-shelves, hanging on the wall of the family sitting-room. There were other cases here and there through the house, but I read and re-read the particular volumes in this one from year to year, and a strange, motley collection they were, to be sure, representing the tastes of father and mother, friends and relations.

Children were not supposed to have any separate enthusiasms — save for Rollo, Maria Edgeworth, and Letitia Barbauld.

On the two lower shelves were most of the novels of Charles Dickens, more eagerly devoured than all the rest, although no book in the case had escaped a second reading, save Bailey's "Festus," a little of which went a very long way with us. I can remember certain times when I used to scan the thrice-read volumes and mutter: "Nothing but Festus! Nothing but Festus! How *can* I bear Festus? I will read 'David Copperfield' over again; it was last week that I finished it for the fourth time!"

It seems to me that no child nowadays has time to love an author as the children and young people of that generation loved Dickens; nor do I think that any living author of to-day provokes love in exactly the same fashion. From our yellow dog, Pip, to the cat, the canary, the lamb, the cow, down to all the hens and cocks, almost every living thing was named, sooner or later, after one of Dickens's characters; while my favorite sled, painted in brown, with the title in brilliant red letters, was "The Artful Dodger." Why did we do it? We little creatures couldn't have suspected that "the democratic movement in literature had come to town," as Richard Whiteing says; nevertheless, we responded to it vigorously, ardently, and swelled the hero's public.

We never read newspapers save the weekly "Portland Transcript," so that there was a moment of thrilling excitement when my mother, looking up from the "Portland Press," told us that Mr. Dickens was coming to America, and that he was even then sailing from England.[1] I re-

[1] *A Child's Journey with Dickens* made its first appearance as a speech at the banquet at Delmonico's, February 7, 1912, celebrating the hundredth anniversary of Dickens's birth.

member distinctly that I prayed for him fervently several times during the next week, that the voyage might be a safe one, and that even the pangs of seasickness might be spared so precious a personage. In due time we heard that he had arrived in New York, and had begun the series of readings from his books; then he came to Boston, which was still nearer, and then — day of unspeakable excitement! — we learned that he had been prevailed upon to give one reading in Portland, which was only sixteen miles away from our village.

It chanced that my mother was taking me to Charlestown, Massachusetts, to pay a visit to an uncle on the very day after the one appointed for the great event in Portland. She, therefore, planned to take me into town the night before, and to invite the cousin, at whose house we were to sleep, to attend the reading with her. I cannot throw a more brilliant light on the discipline of that period than to say that the subject of my attending the reading was never once mentioned. The price of tickets was supposed to be almost prohibitory. I cannot remember the exact sum; I only know that it was mentioned with bated breath in the village of Hollis, and that there was a general feeling in the community that any one who paid it would have to live down a reputation for riotous extravagance forever afterward. I neither wailed nor wept, nor made any attempt to set aside the parental decrees (which were anything but severe in our family), but if any martyr in Fox's "Book" ever suffered more poignant anguish than I, I am heartily sorry for him; yet my common sense assured me that a child could hardly hope to be taken on a week's junketing to Charlestown and expect any other entertainment to be added to it for years to come. The definition of a "pleasure" in the State of Maine, county of York, village of Hollis, year of our Lord 1868, was something that could not reasonably occur too often without being cheapened.

The days, charged with suppressed excitement, flew by. I bade good-bye to my little sister, who was not to share my metropolitan experiences, and my mother and I embarked for Portland on the daily train that dashed hither and thither at the rate of about twelve miles an hour. When the august night and moment arrived, my mother and her cousin set out for the Place, and the moment they were out of sight I slipped out of the door and followed them, traversing quickly the three or four blocks that separated me from the old City Hall and the Preble House, where Dickens was stopping. I gazed at all the windows and all the entrances of both buildings without beholding any trace of my hero. I watched the throng of happy, excited, lucky people crowding the streets on their way to the hall, and went home in a chastened mood to bed — a bed which, as soon as I got into it, was crowded with Little Nell and the Marchioness, Florence Dombey, Bella Wilfer, Susan Nipper, and Little Em'ly. There were other dreams, too. Not only had my idol provided me with human friends, to love and laugh and weep over, but he had wrought his genius into *things;* so that, waking or sleeping, every bunch of holly or mistletoe, every plum pudding was alive; every crutch breathed of Tiny Tim; every cricket, and every singing, steaming kettle, had a soul.

V
A JOURNEY WITH DICKENS

THE next morning we started on our railroad journey,
which I remember as being full of excitement from the
beginning, for both men and women were discussing the
newspapers with extraordinary interest, the day before
having been the one on which the President of the United
States had been formally impeached. When the train
stopped for two or three minutes at North Berwick, the
people on the side of the car next the station suddenly
arose and looked eagerly out at some object of apparent
interest. I was not, at any age, a person to sit still in her
seat when others were looking out of windows, and my
small nose was quickly flattened against one of the panes.
There on the platform stood the Adored One! It was un-
believable, but there he was in the flesh; standing smiling,
breathing, like ordinary human beings. There was no
doubt, then, that "angels and ministers of grace," called
authors, had bodies and could not only write David Cop-
perfields, but could be seen with the naked eye. That
face, known to me from many pictures, must have looked
in some mysterious way into the face of Dora, of Agnes, of
Paul Dombey, of Little Dorrit! My spirit gave a leap and
entered a new, an unknown world.

Dickens's hands were plunged deep in his pockets (a
favorite gesture), but presently one was removed to wave
away laughingly a piece of famous Berwick sponge cake,
offered him by Mr. Osgood, of Boston, his traveling companion and friend. I knew him at once! — the smiling,
genial, mobile face, rather highly colored, the brilliant
eyes, the watch-chain, the red carnation in the buttonhole,

and the expressive hands, much given to gesture. It was only a momentary view, for the train started, and Dickens vanished, to resume his place in the car next to ours, where he had been, had I known it, ever since we left Portland.

When my mother was again occupied with her book, I slipped away, and, borne along by some resistless and hitherto unrecognized force, I entered the next car; which did not seem at all to me a vehicle carrying Tom, Dick, and Harry to Boston, but a sort of traveling shrine or altar. I took a humble, unoccupied seat near the end, close by the much patronized tank of (unsterilized) drinking-water and the train-boy's basket of popcorn balls and molasses candy, and gazed steadily at the famous man, who was chatting busily with Mr. Osgood. I remembered gratefully that my mother had taken the old ribbons off my gray velvet hat and tied me down with blue under the chin, and I thought, if Dickens should happen to rest his eye upon me, that he could hardly fail to be pleased with the effect of the blue ribbon that went under my collar and held a very small squirrel muff in place. Unfortunately, however, his eye did not meet mine, and my toilette made no sensation in any quarter, but some family friends espied me, and sent me back to ask my mother to come in and sit with them. I brought her back, and, fortunately, there was not room enough for me with the party, so I gladly resumed my modest seat by the popcorn boy, where I could watch Dickens, quite unnoticed.

There is an Indian myth which relates that when the gaze of the Siva rested for the first time on Tellatonea, the most beautiful of women, his desire to see her was so great that his body became all eyes. Such a transformation, I fear, was perilously near to being my fate! Half an hour passed, perhaps, and one gentleman after another came from here or there to exchange a word of greeting with the famous novelist, so that he was never for a moment alone, thereby inciting in my breast my first, and about my last, experience of the passion of jealousy. Suddenly, however, Mr. Osgood arose, and with an apology went into the smoking-car. I never knew how it happened; I had no plan, no preparation, no intention, certainly no provocation; but invisible ropes pulled me out of my seat, and, speeding up the aisle, I planted myself breathlessly and timorously down, an unbidden guest, in the seat of honor. I had a moment to recover my equanimity, for Dickens was looking out of the window, but he turned suddenly and said with justifiable surprise:

"God bless my soul, child, where did you come from?"

My heart was in my mouth, but there was still room to exercise my tongue, which was generally the case. I was frightened, but not so completely frightened as if I had been meeting a stranger. You see I knew him, even if he did not know me; so I became immediately autobiographical, although palpitating with nervousness. I had to tell him, I thought, where I came from, who I was, where I was going, or how could I account for myself and my presence beside him in Mr. Osgood's seat? So I began, stammeringly, to answer his question.

"I came from Hollis, Maine, and I'm going to Charlestown to visit my uncle. My mother and her cousin went to your reading last night, but of course three couldn't go from the same family, it was so expensive, so I stayed at home. Nora, that's my little sister, is left behind in Hollis. She's too small to go on a journey, but she wanted to go to the reading dreadfully. There was a lady there who had never heard of Betsey Trotwood, and had only read two of your books!"

"Well, upon my word!" he said; "you do not mean to say that *you* have read them!"

"Of course!" I replied; "every one of them but the two that we are going to buy in Boston, and some of them six times."

"Bless my soul!" he ejaculated again. "Those long thick books, and you such a slip of a thing."

"Of course," I explained conscientiously, "I do skip some of the very dull parts once in a while; not the short dull parts, but the long ones."

He laughed heartily. "Now, that is something that I hear very little about," he said. "I distinctly want to learn more about those very long dull parts."

And, whether to amuse himself, or to amuse me, I do not know, he took out a notebook and pencil from his pocket and proceeded to give me an exhausting and exhaustive examination on this subject; the books in which the dull parts predominated; and the characters and subjects which principally produced them. He chuckled so constantly during this operation that I could hardly help believing myself extraordinarily agreeable, so I continued dealing these infant blows, under the delusion that I was flinging him bouquets.

It was not long before one of my hands was in his, and his arm around my waist, while we talked of many things. They say, I believe, that his hands were "undistinguished" in shape, and that he wore too many rings. Well, those criticisms must come from persons who never felt the warmth of his handclasp! For my part, I am glad that Pullman chair cars had not come into fashion, else I should never have experienced the delicious joy of snuggling up to Genius, and of being distinctly encouraged in the attitude.

I wish I could recall still more of his conversation, but I was too happy, too exhilarated, and too inexperienced to take conscious notes of the interview. I remember feeling

THE CHILD OF THE JOURNEY
WITH DICKENS

that I had never known anybody so well and so intimately, and that I talked with him as one talks under cover of darkness or before the flickering light of a fire. It seems to me, as I look back now, and remember how the little soul of me came out and sat in the sunshine of his presence, that I must have had some premonition that the child, who would come to be one of the least of writers, was then talking with one of the greatest; — talking, too, as it were, of the author's profession and high calling, for were we not discussing books? All the little details of the meeting stand out as clearly as though it had happened yesterday. I can see every article of his clothing and of my own; the other passengers in the car; the landscape through the window; and above all the face of Dickens, deeply lined, with sparkling eyes and an amused, waggish smile that curled the corners of his mouth under his grizzled mustache. A part of our conversation was given to a Boston newspaper next day, by the author himself, or by Mr. Osgood, and was long preserved in our family archives, while a little more was added a few years after by an old lady who sat in the next seat to us. (The pronoun "us" seems ridiculously intimate, but I have no doubt I used it, quite unabashed, at that date.)

"What book of mine do you like best?" Dickens asked, I remember; and I answered with the definite assurance of childhood, "Oh, I like 'David Copperfield' much the best. That is the one I have read six times."

"Six times — good, good!" he replied; "I am glad that you like Davy, so do I; — I like it best, too!" clapping his hands; and that was the only remark he made which attracted the attention of the other passengers, who glanced in our direction now and then, I have been told, smiling at the interview, but preserving its privacy with the utmost friendliness. I had never looked behind to see how my mother was faring. There are great crises in life when even mothers must retire to the background. For the moment I had no mother, family, friends, or acquaintances, no home, no personality; I was a sort of atom floating in space, half conscious that I could not float forever, but must come to earth again.

"I almost said 'Great Expectations,'" I added presently, "because that comes next in our family. We named our little yellow dog 'Mr. Pip' out of your book. They told Father when they gave him to us that he was part rat terrier, and we were all pleased, because, if he was, he wasn't all mongrel. (That means mixed-up.) Then one day Father showed him a trap with a mouse in it. The mouse wiggled its tail just a little, and Pip was so frightened that he ran under the barn and stayed the rest of the day. That showed that there wasn't enough rat terrier in him to be right, and the neighbors made fun of him and used to call 'Rats!' when he went down the street. We loved him just the same and he had as hard a time as Pip in 'Great Expectations.'"

Here again my new friend's mirth was delightful to behold, so much so that my embarrassed mother, who had been watching me for half an hour, almost made up her mind to drag me away before the very eyes of our fellow passengers. I had never been thought an amusing child in the family circle; what, then, could I be saying to the most distinguished and popular author in the universe?

Dickens here told me little stories about English dogs, but I remember them too vaguely to repeat them or give them their inimitable mingling of fact and nonsense. "Have you only one dog?" he asked.

"We had another," I answered, "a big curly one called John Brent, out of a novel, but he died, and we take all our names from your books now. We know a dog who stays with us most of the time. He doesn't belong to anybody and he likes to visit Pip, so we named him Mr. Pocket after Mr. Pip's friend. The real Mr. Pip and Mr. Pocket met first in Miss Havisham's garden and they had such a funny fight it always makes Father laugh till he can't read properly! Then they became great friends. Perhaps you remember Mr. Pip and Mr. Pocket?" And Dickens thought he did, which, perhaps, is not strange, considering that he was the author of their respective beings.

Mr. Harry Furniss declares that "Great Expectations" was Dickens's favorite novel, but I can only say that to me he avowed his special fondness for "David Copperfield." I can never forget that and never be mistaken in my remembrance of it.

"Did you want to go to my reading very much, child?" was another question. Here was a subject that had never once been touched upon in all the past days — a topic that stirred the very depths of my disappointment and sorrow, fairly choking me, and making my lip tremble by its unexpectedness, as I faltered, "Yes, I did, more than tongue can tell! I know how I feel when I read one of the books, but I wanted to hear how it sounded."

I looked up a second later, when I was sure that the tears in my eyes were not going to fall, and to my astonishment saw that Dickens's eyes were in precisely the same state of moisture. That was a never-to-be-forgotten moment, although I was too young to appreciate the full significance of it.

"Do you cry when you read out loud, too?" I asked curiously. "We all do in our family. And we never read about Tiny Tim, or about Steerforth when his body is washed up on the beach, on Saturday nights, for fear our eyes will be too swollen to go to Sunday School."

"Yes, I cry when I read about Steerforth," he answered

quietly, and I felt no astonishment. "I cried when I wrote it, too! That is still more foolish!"

"Where do you cry the worst?" I asked. "Our time is when it says, '*All the men who carried him had known him and gone sailing with him and seen him merry and bold*' "; and here I grew tearful and reminiscent.

We were now fast approaching our destination — the station in Boston — and the passengers began to collect their wraps and bundles. Mr. Osgood had two or three times made his appearance, but had been waved away with a smile by Dickens — a smile that seemed to say, "You will excuse me, I know, but this child has the right of way."

"You are not traveling alone?" he asked, as he arose to put on his overcoat.

"Oh! my goodness!" I said, coming down to earth for the first time since I had taken my seat beside him — "certainly not; I had a mother, but I forgot all about her." Whereupon he said, "You are past-mistress of the art of flattery!"

But this remark was told me years afterwards by the old lady who was sitting in the next seat, and who overheard as much of the conversation as she possibly could, so she informed me. Her penciled notes, read to me when we met by chance in South Reading, Massachusetts, have helped me greatly in the minor details of the interview and my own phraseology, which amused her because of its chatterbox fluency and the amazing response it elicited from so great a man.

Dickens took me back to the forgotten mother, and introduced himself, and I, still clinging to his hand, left the car and walked with him down the platform until he disappeared in the carriage with Mr. Osgood, leaving me with the feeling that I must continue my existence somehow in a dull and dreary world.

That was my last glimpse of him, but pictures made in childhood are painted in bright hues, and this one has never faded. The child of to-day would hardly be able to establish so instantaneous a friendship. She would have heard of celebrity hunters and autograph collectors and be self-conscious, while I followed the dictates of my countrified little heart, and scraped acquaintance confidently with the magician who had glorified my childhood by his art.

He had his literary weaknesses, I suppose, Charles Dickens, though faithful love will always blind me to them, but they were all dear, big, attractive ones, virtues grown a bit wild and rank. Somehow when you put him, with his elemental humor, his inexhaustible vitality, his humanity, sympathy, and pity, beside the Impeccables, he always looms large! Just for a moment, when the heart overpowers the reason, he even makes the flawless ones look a little faded and colorless!

As I am writing, there comes into print an autograph letter of Robert Louis Stevenson's written at Bournemouth, England. It is undated, but covers several pages in diary form. It says, and my heart echoes every word:

I wonder if you ever read Dickens's Christmas Books? I have read only two of them yet, and I have cried my eyes out, and have a terrible time not to sob. But, O dear God, I feel so good after them, and would do anything to make the world a little better for people. I wish I could lose no time; I want to go out and comfort some one. I shall never listen to the nonsense they tell me about not giving money. I shall give money; not that I haven't done so always, but I shall do it with a high hand now. Oh, what a jolly thing it is for a man to have written books like these books, and just filled people's hearts with a desire to do good!

VI

SCHOOL DAYS AND HOME TEACHING

SCHOOL days play an extraordinarily small part in my life. I should probably pass for a fairly well-educated person, so long, at any rate, as I do not frequent the too-intimate society of scholars, or of those human horrors whose conversation resembles a questionnaire, or who presume so confidently on your acquaintance with the Neanderthal Man, Hammurabi, Tiberius Gracchus, or the Venerable Bede that no amount of ingenuity can extricate you from disgrace. If one has, like Rosamond in "Middlemarch," "a small mind in a very active state," life does not become wholly unbearable even to the ignorant. W. E. H. Lecky, the Irish historian, once told me about sitting beside a young, charmingly dressed American lady at a dinner where the guests were mostly celebrities in one field or another. She was a stranger and begged him to identify the principal personages for her delectation. Finally she asked: "And what do you do, sir?" "I am a writer," he replied; "I suppose I may say I am by way of being an historian; are you by any chance interested in history, Madam?" "Oh! no, not a bit," she answered blithely; "I always say let bygones be bygones!"

She was doubtless a pretty ignoramus, but Lecky, the brilliant talker and the man of wide knowledge, had contrived to remember her for a dozen years or so, notwithstanding!

In our early days my sister and I were taught at home under the capable, slightly impatient, somewhat sporadic direction of our busy stepfather, whose large practice distributed over a wide territory did not permit regularity of hours. He was a graduate of Bowdoin College, an excellent scholar, and a good teacher, if his pupil answered his questions instantly. My Latin Grammar was much damaged by his irritable pounding of it on the table; while the Small Sister's Greenleaf's Arithmetic was once flung into the orchard when she was particularly and distractingly dense about the multiplication table, which she detested. A flow of tears always followed this lesson, and she invariably dried them over a Hans Andersen fairy book.

I cannot say just how, when, where, or whether I ever acquired any substantial body of knowledge, or any adequate degree of mental training, for when one's years from seven to sixteen are passed in a small New England village, continuity in education, a rather valuable factor, is almost impossible. A hunger for companionship, and for learning in company with others, led finally to my going to the little district school in a small white building farther down our village street. This school I have somewhat veraciously described in "Rebecca of Sunnybrook Farm," which book, while wholly fictitious in story, is in background as true as my modest art could make it. The schoolroom had many windows, plenty of light and air in moderate weather, and there was an ugly stove in the open space in front of the desks and blackboard. The wooden desks had shelves for books underneath, useful also for apples, peppermints, cinnamon-sticks, slates, balls, and tops. The wooden benches were very uncomfortable, and were always made for two pupils in that time. Both desks and benches were battered, scarred, cut, and stained by ten or twelve years of use and abuse by badly bored children, who for the most part resisted the acquisition of learning as something wholly outside their idea of the universe.

The teacher's desk was on a platform in one corner near the door, and the personality in the chair of power changed nearly every term, as the salary was something in the nature of four dollars a week, and the dust of the village was shaken off the pedagogic feet whenever a larger school and salary loomed on the horizon. The phrase "pedagogic feet" calls to mind one teacher who had somehow strayed into a profession unmatchable for influence, and in my opinion unequaled for the most heavenly opportunity of service to growing humanity.

The instructress at this time was thin, sallow, censorious; the glance of her cold blue eye pierced one's very marrow; her lips were too thin for sweetness; but she knew her textbooks, I will say that for her. One of the minor punishments then in vogue for an idle, obstinate, or disobedient child was to put her in a corner under the teacher's desk for ten minutes. This secluded nook was generally occupied by young persons of the masculine gender, but alack! under the discipline of this particular educator I was sometimes there — why, I cannot remember.

The climate was close and stuffy, the space contracted, and the floor, though fairly clean, too dusty for my nice fresh gingham dresses, so I used to put my skirt over my head before I sat down. This could be done quickly and discreetly, unnoted by any one except the teacher, who was much irritated by my fastidious habit. Once ensconced in semi-darkness, I used to repeat to myself softly:

"On Linden, when the sun was low,"
and
"Not a drum was heard, not a funeral note,
As his corse to the ramparts we hurried."

At the same time Miss X, always seated with feet crossed, disclosed to my searching gaze a Congress boot, with the triangle of elastic on the side which characterized that creation of the late sixties. How I longed to put my fingers in the slightly stretched top and give it a sudden snap; not for revenge, just for experiment, and "*pour passer le temps*," which hung heavy!

I met Miss X many years later after some modest success or other which no doubt had surprised her. "Do you remember me, Kate, dear?" she asked with a honeyed inflection I had never hitherto observed in her voice. "I think I do," I answered, with sweetness equally fictitious, "though there were many teachers at the little white schoolhouse in my time; but there is one point on which I never can be mistaken, and that is your feet, and your Congress shoes! The pupil, rhetorically speaking, always sits at the teacher's feet, but I often sat there physically. I must have been a naughty child to have been put under your desk so frequently, Miss X."

"Not really naughty, dear, as I remember; but there was a certain extreme gayety, a desire to look out of the windows, a tendency to mirth on slight provocation that had to be checked."

"I dare say!" I answered; "but life has already gone on with the 'checking' process and it was sure to be done, sooner or later; I can't help feeling that you began it a trifle too soon, Miss X." And with that we parted.

It may have been under this administration — I am not sure — that the Small Sister made a sort of experimental advent into the school. I led her in proudly, her hair polished until it shone like mahogany, while her frock of blue gingham, adorned with white tape trimming, and starched until it stood out like a balloon, was so clearly *le dernier cri* that it almost provoked applause from the school. All went well at first, but on a later day she provoked the displeasure of the teacher who snapped the child's ear with her thimble-finger, one of her ways of registering disapproval. This was too much for me. I, at the age of nine, was a responsible human being. I could be put under the desk with impunity, but no other scion of our noble house should submit to indignity, and, rising from my seat on the other side of the room, I took the weeping infant by the hand, saying, "I will take my little sister home, please," and walked majestically from the school, not to come back that day. As viewed by the general public, it was an impressive and dramatic scene, and my courage (the neighbors called it "spunk") was secretly approved. My father arranged my return to the seat of learning, but the Small Sister went on with her studies at home, and Greenleaf's Arithmetic almost lived, though it never multiplied, in the orchard.

I remember nothing more of this school, and I loved only one of the many teachers, Miss Nancy Emery, who also loved me, and for that matter has kept on loving me till this moment, bless her heart! Such a clear red-and-white skin she had, such smooth bands of softly parted dark hair, such a nice waist for a child's arms to squeeze, such a kind voice, such a gentle manner!

A term at the little red-brick schoolhouse across the river in Buxton followed at some time or other, but I can recall nothing about it. The next memories are of being a boarding pupil during three terms, from November to June inclusive, at the Gorham Female Seminary eight miles away! This I concluded (somewhat hazardously) was to be life at its most significant and pregnant possibility, life altogether new, varied and incredibly adventurous. I have paid my respects to this institution in "Rebecca," never as to facts and real experiences (my invariable custom), but as to externals.

The Seminary had achieved much good work in its time, and enjoyed a later period of rejuvenation and power, but it was not at its best during the year of my attendance, when the classes were not of their accustomed numbers and the general teaching was not of its usual high grade. Still, to a youthful "female" of thirteen years or so it gave a feeling of belonging indirectly to the great educational institutions of the universe.

It was a co-educational school, boys being admitted to the Academy on the hill, and it is a startling, a well-nigh incredible fact that I do not remember the name, face, or personality of a single boy! I recall a blur of boys in recitation rooms, and in the Gorham streets, but I must have been both a highly unsusceptible and an extraordinarily unattractive "female of the species," or I should have, at any rate in the secret chambers of my memory, some recollection of the male element in that school. It is true I could have been only thirteen (no diaries and no dates of anything whatsoever have been preserved in my family), but even so, consider Marie Bashkirtseff at that age, and recall the Young Girl Diaries of to-day, not to be read by elderly married women save in private, where blushes cannot be perceived. I see now that I was unusually slow in development, and I should call myself wholly abnormal, sub-normal, or super-normal, save that, later on, say at sixteen, I was able to recognize the presence of a boy or man in the room, and "register" interest or indifference as the case might be; at any rate, I knew he was there, which shows progress!

I learned little or nothing at the Gorham Female Seminary for some reason or other, although I sometimes wonder just when we really do learn anything. At all events, I did grow in vision, instinct, and wisdom, because of an intimate friendship with my Latin teacher, Miss Mary Smith,[1] who lived in the village. Her house was a pleasant old Colonial mansion at the foot of the wooded hill behind the Seminary. There were open fires, plenty of books, a sunny

[1] Now Mrs. Waterman, widow of Judge Waterman, well known in Maine.

sitting-room, and Miss Mary herself, a very miracle of old-time grace, distinction, and charm. I already loved books, but she directed my reading, and formed my taste for the right things. I always read aloud to her the poems I was to recite at school exercises, and they were generally chosen by her.

Like steel to the magnet I darted down the hill through the grove of pine trees and appeared at her door in the late afternoons, at dusk, or sometimes, with permission, in the evening, always to find a warm welcome and a long talk during which I could almost feel myself grow. It was she who gave me the Latin prayer of Mary, Queen of Scots, with which I won an unimportant prize, probably because I could never speak it without tears, always imagining my head on the block and the knife descending!

POEM COMPOSED BY QUEEN MARY IN VIEW OF HER
APPROACHING DEATH
"O Domine Deus, speravi in te!
O care mi Jesu, nunc libera me!
In dura catena, in misera pœna,
Languendo, gemendo, et genuflectendo,
Adoro, imploro ut liberes me."

Another feat in which Miss Mary took great pride was my sudden call to take part in the competition for the Tower Gold Medal for Elocution. It was an awkward situation, for there was an Elocution Class, and I was not in it; but the illness of two competitors made the number to appear at the Town Hall altogether too few to be impressive, so Miss Mary suggested my being flung to the lions, and chose for my martyrdom Tennyson's "Saint Agnes' Eve."

It is a very beautiful poem and for a long time afterward I used to brush my hair off my face, cover it with a long white flowing scarf, and repeat the poem with the moonlight streaming in at the window; or, barring that marvelous dramatic aid to inspiration, have the lamps turned down and recite it by the light of an open fire.

It was far and away the best piece of literature in prose or verse on the programme, and I had simply one advantage over the other competitors, that, although I was compounded of the very essence of New England, I could always "let go" of myself in these things; indeed, the trouble was, not to "let go" too thoroughly. There was never any audience for me after the first line. I was Saint Agnes, looking through the convent window at the snow-covered, moonlit landscape, and awaiting her miraculous transfiguration. I could feel the "first snowdrop of the year" lying in my bosom, the touch of the "pale taper" in my hand; and in the long pause that my instinct told me should follow the two impassioned lines —

> "For me the Heavenly Bridegroom waits,
>   To make me pure of sin"

— I felt a sensation of billows submerging me, a complete absence of body, until I could say with a sort of rapt serenity:

> "The Sabbaths of Eternity,
>   One Sabbath deep and wide —
>   A light upon the shining sea —
>   The Bridegroom with his bride!"

I was given the Tower Gold Medal for Elocution, notwithstanding the fact that Elocution played no part in the proceedings; and the reason was that my beloved Miss Mary chose for me the poem that suited my voice, and one that was totally unlike any other *tour de force* selected by the teachers for their contestants. Of course, if I had not possessed a little talent hidden away somewhere, I should have proved unequal to the test, but it was never suspected nor called upon for many years afterward.

That was a lucky June for me, for I bore away two other

prizes, one for French, and another for general excellence in English, not because I was better than others in these studies, but because they were still worse. At the closing exercises in the church, when I went up the aisle several times to receive my trophies, very curled as to hair, very grand as to Roman sash, my father whispered to my mother: "If she is mentioned again, I shall drive home and let her come back in the railway train. She is abominably conspicuous."

It is necessary to remark here that the only glory I missed was the one for which I tried — the one for English Composition! My theme — "Cloud Pictures," copied in violet ink — was the feeblest effort sent in to the judges, one of whom remarked to a teacher that the girl who won the Tower Gold Medal had better confine herself to speaking and let writing alone.

The next winter was spent at South Reading, Massachusetts, with one of my mother's sisters, and I attended for a few months the senior class of the grammar, and the freshman class of the high school. Arriving after the term had begun, I was taken by an elderly cousin for a private examination in a lawyer's office. I made a positive sensation there by reading from Shakespeare's plays at sight, but fell down completely on an example in cube root and the capital of the United States. The first would always block my entrance into any institution of learning; but the second is difficult to explain.

Part of a winter at the Morison Academy in Baltimore, where an aunt and uncle lived, left me in the same disordered, unfinished, and unsymmetrical state of mental development, but my horizon was distinctly widened and my first deep spiritual awakening occurred under the influence of a certain Dr. Richard Fuller, a Baptist divine of extraordinary magnetism and eloquence. I did not have to be converted. I was born with a simple faith, not to be discussed nor argued about, but seemingly "built into" the foundations of my being.

It was a year or so later than this that the rest of my family left Maine for many a year, and embarked for Santa Barbara, where it was hoped that my father, who had a little weakness of the lungs, might grow stronger in the mild and beautiful climate of California. I, still "uneducated," strange to say, having sipped momentarily at five founts of learning, was left behind for six months at Abbot Academy, Andover, Massachusetts, one of the best boarding-schools for girls in New England. I was a sore trial to the Faculty, for I was, in a manner of speech, a senior in Literature, a junior in French and Latin, a sophomore in Grammar, a freshman in History, and a poor risk for the preparatory department in Mathematics!

It was a good atmosphere for a girl; simply and sincerely religious, refined and gracious in its social life. Punctuality, decorum, studious habits, good manners and speech, obedience to rules — these were all presupposed and they actually existed. I made a few dear friendships there that were faithfully maintained until a new life, far away from New England, claimed my time, my thoughts, my heart, indeed, the very soul of me — all this hidden behind what seemed to be only another mile of the long trail from childhood to womanhood. "Stepping westward" was, symbolically, only another mile of a life-journey, but "the long trail" carried me to heights and depths of experience never suspected in all my former wanderings in the land of dreams.

VII

"STEPPING WESTWARD"

THE journey to California was taken after waiting many weeks in Maine for a proper duenna. One was never found, and my parents, being anxious that I should join them, consented at length to the only available escort, a newly resigned Lieutenant of the Navy, going as far as Utah to the ranch he had recently bought. I knew him well, and so did all my elderly friends. He was an engaged man, which rendered him in their minds as safe as a man is ever likely to be, even under the most favorable circumstances, and he was to be joined in Albany by a younger brother who was to share his ranching experiences, so that we should be a party of three.

Never could a girl of seventeen be chaperoned more imprudently, safely, and delightfully than by two gentlemen aged respectively thirty-eight and twenty-two. Both were like big brothers; both were knights of chivalry; reminding me of Mark Twain's story of the wayfarer who showed him the right road to a hotel when he was lost in a strange country at midnight. He pays his debt of gratitude to the unknown friend laconically by remarking: "He had a harelip and a heart of gold; such men are all too few!" My two friends had the hearts of gold minus the facial deformities, and we were very sad when we parted at Ogden, for I had to make the rest of my journey alone, until I met my stepfather in San Francisco.

The Lieutenant carefully scanned the various travelers going beyond Ogden with a view to putting me in the special care of some one, but at length decided against it, as I was on bowing terms with two or three ladies in my Pullman car.

"There is one man you might consult if you get into any real trouble before you meet your father," he said — "that tall, large, elderly person we have noticed at all the eating stations. He looks reliable and interesting, and, if he looks after you as much as he looks at you, he might prove serviceable, though I have an instinct that he might enjoy being a chaperon a little too much."

The Lieutenant was partially right in his analysis of character. The man was interesting, although he could not be described as reliable, save in assiduity of attendance where he was not wanted. I was obliged much of the time to cover my face with a handkerchief and feign sleep to avoid his too frequent visits to my section. At the end of the second day he laid his heart, hand, and exceedingly uncertain fortunes at my feet, embarrassing me to such an extent that I sat most of the time with a feeble-minded old lady of eighty in the opposite end of the Pullman.

I have one recollection of him, however, which has never faded. He was an inveterate quoter of poetry, and on the whole he was less dangerous when invoking his memory than when he indulged in sentimental remarks which I was too young and inexperienced to elude. He said he had lately visited an old-time acquaintance in an institution for the insane, a man who had always been a great lover of poetry, especially that of Robert Burns. On his last visit to him, the deranged friend had said: "You remember the last verse of 'John Anderson, my jo, John'? It ends:

> "'We'll sleep thegither at the foot,
> John Anderson, my jo!'

"Now, Burns," my fellow-traveler continued, "never would have ended the poem there, for he believed in immortality. He would have written another verse, like this:

"'John Anderson, my jo, John,
We winna mind that sleep;
The grave so still and cauld, John,
The spirit canna keep.
But we will wake in Heaven, John,
Where young again we'll grow,
And ever live in blissful love,
John Anderson, my jo!'"

This comes perilously near to being as good as the original. I don't know whether the lunatic wrote it, or my fellow-traveler, and I have sometimes thought they were the same person. My modest charms, physical or intellectual, have always made a peculiar appeal to gentlemen just going into, or coming out of, institutions treating mental disturbances.

Santa Barbara was at this time (the late eighteen-seventies) a Paradise on earth. I do not know the precise date, for, as I have intimated before, I come of a family strangely uninterested, oblivious even, of genealogy, and of dates. We never kept diaries or preserved any memoranda. I, in my later years, have scribbled, on paper, notes of important occasions, but I can seldom find the notes afterwards. My friends suggest a filing cabinet, an article of furniture for which I feel a strange repugnance, but nowadays I have little to file, compared with the rich eventful years of youth and middle age.

Santa Barbara is still a Paradise of a different sort, they tell me; but in my day there were no great hotels, and no magnificent villas in the Montecito and the Mission Cañon. There were no motors, of course: one casual, dilatory, and informal street-car line; deep dust everywhere, save in the rainy season, and a multitudinous army of fleas, since vanished; but it was a heaven upon earth, nevertheless.

My first appearance there had one drawback. The Lieutenant, while joyfully greeting and feeding me in the railway station at Albany, introducing me to the unknown younger brother and gayly prophesying a wonderful journey, became a little confused and mixed the luggage checks, four or five in number. Accordingly he arrived on his ranch with a trunkful of pretty dresses and hats intended for a girl's triumphant début in society, and I found at the Santa Barbara wharf two battered trunks bursting with tin pots, pans, and cooking-utensils of every sort, uncouth masculine underwear, corduroys, leggings, riding-breeches, and high boots.

My father's remarks on the masterly executive ability of my chaperon cannot be printed. He was an emotional man and spoke hastily and fluently when occasion warranted; but which of us suffered the more from this exchange of luggage, the two ranchers or the girl, would be difficult to tell. At the end of three months of telegraphing and writing, together with the expenditure of liberal sums of money, we all regained our individual effects and the incident was closed, save that my father declined to meet the Lieutenant when his Nevada ranch failed and he came to California to buy another.

Now ensued what proved to be the most irresponsible, delightful, entirely healthful and enchanting year or two of my life. No words can describe the loveliness of Santa Barbara, with its semi-tropical atmosphere, its luxuriance of foliage and flowers, its lovely semi-circle of mountains, its blue, blue sea!

I had been used to the deep snows, and late reluctant springs of Maine. In California, when the rains had ceased, April was a revelation of beauty hitherto unimagined. We had a pleasant house, although there were no positively unpleasant ones to be found; for where fuchsias and geraniums climb up and hang over the fences, and rosebushes, staggering under their wealth of bloom, hide all defects of architecture, or lack of paint, the enchanted eye refuses to find a flaw.

On and near the foothills and in the cañons the wild hyacinths were out, lupins and poppies, too, and acres upon acres of baby blue-eyes in damp hollows and shady places. There was a breath of sweetness from budding fruit trees, fragrance of orange blossoms, and every poor man's garden was the equal of a millionaire's conservatory.

The sun was never shy, surly, indifferent, or capricious; he seemed to have an adequate idea of his duty in the world. So also had the myriads of stars (there seemed to be thousands more than in New England); and as for the moon — that orb is responsible for enough mischief in temperate climes, but the Southern California moon is in a class by itself. This assertion may not be strictly scientific, but its admirers, or those who have been affected by its rays, will swear that the moon is far brighter, bigger, yellower, and more dangerous than elsewhere, and that it is suspended in its clear blue canopy of sky in a way unlike other moons in other skies.

There was good society in Santa Barbara both for young and old. There were few dances save those under the famous grapevine in the Montecito Valley, because there was so much bathing and horseback riding, so many picnics in the Cathedral Oaks and along the many trails through the cañons, so many suppers on the beach — in short, such a habit of living out of doors morning, noon, and evening, that there was little time for indoor gayeties.

Our attending squires were charming companions, mostly Eastern college men of good family, sometimes looking (not too energetically) for bargains in fruit farms and sheep ranches; now and then needing a soft climate for some slight throat trouble; oftentimes merely resting

a season, after stupendous intellectual labors at Harvard
or Yale.

How stimulating were our horseback rides on the beach
at low tide; our country gallops along trails leading,
through towering groves of wild yellow mustard, to some
hospitable ranch for luncheon; our return, winding up in
a hilarious attempt to "lope" twelve abreast down Santa
Barbara's main street; a dangerous and reckless experiment that never ended in, though it often appeared to
presage, a universal slaughter of the inhabitants.

My little white bronco, Blanquita, was saddled and tied
to the horse block every morning, and I frequently rode
in the afternoon a *palomino* horse from the livery stable,
hard of mouth and heavy of foot, but strong and handsome.

That we never had any accidents worth mentioning
shows our horsemanship, for almost all broncos "buck"
when so disposed, and to keep one's seat while they are
clambering up some slippery mountain trail with loose sand
and rolling pebbles underfoot means something in the way
of pluck and ability. It was a free, eager, venturesome,
joyous life altogether, and if I had a dozen daughters
I should like those born in the East to have a breath of the
West, while I would send Californian girls to the East for a
year or two.

I sang in the choir of the Congregational Church, and
enjoyed the rare and inspiring friendship and tutelage of
Mr. John P. Morgan, a talented New York organist who
had come to Santa Barbara for his health, and who played
the very indifferent organ and trained the inexperienced
choir of the church, because music was the mainspring
of his life. I went often to his house, and learned to sing
and to love great songs, buoyed up by his enthusiasm and
his matchless accompaniments. Without any range of

voice, I somehow succeeded in interpreting such master-pieces as Beethoven's "Adelaïde," Schubert's "Hark! Hark! the Lark," "Thine is my Heart," and everything of Schumann's that was anywhere within my powers. Old Italian and French songs were in our repertory, too, but, although I sang in many concerts with other amateurs, I was always glad that Mr. Morgan never went out in the evening, so that he could not be in the audience.

VIII

GIRLHOOD GAYETIES

Two episodes in this gay, irresponsible girlhood stand out with peculiar clearness, both being visits from Santa Barbara to other parts of the State. The first was a month's stay in Los Angeles, whither old friends of the family, Mr. and Mrs. Hayden McClellan, from Baltimore, had migrated, and gathered about them all the best elements of the younger set. It was one of those haphazard youthful affairs in which a girl simply put into her trunk all her prettiest clothes and took a steamer down the coast for what she knew was destined to be a "good time."

There was a delightful "camping out" at Santa Monica, with many moonlight evenings on the sands, when members of the McClellan house party came from Los Angeles, with young bankers and professional men, and young Englishmen and Canadians from neighboring ranches. Then we went back to town life with many new friendships and perhaps a few budding affairs of the heart. These grew into the real thing in one case, I remember, but for the most part they were vague explorations into an unknown land where the "not impossible he" that might command her heart, might be.

The particular reason for going back to town was the first ball of the season, a ball with a "cotillion" which Mrs. McClellan was to lead with a young Harvard man whose mere appearance on any social occasion lifted it at once from mediocrity to ineffable distinction.

He was clever, good-looking, danced like an angel, talked like Demosthenes, and was a natural winner of hearts. All the unmarried girls envied Mrs. McClellan, but agreed that they suffered less at her good luck than if it had happened to one of their own group. I think, perhaps, if asked, we would all have married young Harvard, even had it involved the establishment of a harem in Los Angeles society, for it was generally felt that the possession of one tenth of his affections was worth more than a whole regiment of ordinary hearts.

Young Harvard, however, was the temporary captive of Juliet McClellan's bow and spear for this great occasion, and I had troubles of my own that prevented my dwelling too much on her triumph. There had been previous cotillions, and I had been mysteriously and reluctantly "annexed" by the least interesting man, the least coveted partner, in the dancing set. He was an Englishman, badly damaged in his own native hunting fields and in a highly adventurous life in most of Great Britain's various colonies. Some of his bones had been broken in Australia, others in New Zealand and South Africa, but he had thriftily retained all that were necessary for dancing, riding, and shooting. His dancing was a *tour de force*, beginning always with a flying leap and a prolonged slide down the entire length of the hall, followed by the gradual swinging of his breathless partner into a peculiar waltz, one that happily could never be imitated. Frequently his dancing mate slipped to the floor, or so disliked his temperamental darts and swoops, or his sudden and violent "reverses," that she never tried him again. We all called him privately Junius Brutus; Junius, because he had an aged father with the same Christian name, well known in social circles, and Brutus because of his rough treatment of ladies in the dance.

Floor-managers had difficulty in finding him partners, and his forlorn condition awoke pity in my youthful breast. Also, though not at all a conspicuously good dancer, I had somehow fathomed the secret of his method. At the very first attempt I did the flying leap without accident. We did not encounter other couples in our progress because everybody cleared the way for J. B. The crowd parted, and we proceeded unscathed like the Israelites through the Red Sea.

I soon found that a long stride, combined with complete surrender of my own person to his powerful leadership, kept me on my feet; but presently Junius Brutus, when he could find no intrepid stranger, claimed me for his perpetual victim, and, of course, I was his chosen partner for the coming cotillion.

Later on, when he discovered how wonderfully our "steps suited," he had an idea that we might swoop and slide through life together with the same success, but I thought differently. I was sympathetic, but fastidious, and disliked the prominent wen behind his ear; the bump on his forehead; the tendency of one eye to wander in its orbit; and his habit of showing me how his broken thumb could revolve on some hidden axis.

We were three girls and three bachelors staying with Mr. and Mrs. McClellan on the night of the ball. My bedroom was on the ground floor of the house with a door opening into the garden. California was still so new to my New England eyes that the tall fuchsias, the geranium hedges, and the wealth of roses kept me in a continual state of transport; but I had other reasons for special delight.

On one side of my room was a wide, shallow bay window, and the upper half of one section had never been closed summer or winter. An orange tree with thick, glossy foliage protected the room from even a drop of rain, and in this opening had grown a branch drooping with buds and with half-ripe balls of greeny-gold. The fragrance of the blossoms and the fruit drifted into the room, the last thing my senses took note of at night, and the first in the morning. My orange-tree bedroom symbolized to me all the charm and romance of Southern California.

The ball and the cotillion were great successes from every point of view, and my state of mind was peculiarly blissful because I had survived the evening without any private interview with J. B. and because my dress had been admired. In itself it was simple and white and fluffy, a thing to be scorned by the débutantes of the present time; but it was lifted to a higher level by garlands and garlands of artificial sweet peas brought me from abroad by a friend. Everybody noted them, for California was then farther from France, and Los Angeles from Paris, than is the case nowadays, and they were lovely enough to turn any girl's head — pink and darker pink, rose and white, delicate blue and pale purple — exquisite in color, and so real that one could almost inhale their perfume. Sprays of them dotted my cheap, airy little flounces, encircled my short sleeves, and made a wreath for my hair, — oh! happy girl, who went to a ball in 1876 at a cost of twenty-five dollars, including her white satin dancing slippers! Well, the sweet peas, hardly aided at all by me, worked wonders, and at two o'clock I went home from the ball with aching feet and head in the clouds, though practically uninjured by several athletic and daring waltzes with J. B.

We were three girls in my orange-tree bedroom that night; two in the broad bed and one on a cot in the corner. Our host and hostess, with their bachelor guests, were upstairs.

Sleep came quickly, and it hardly seemed an hour, although it really was six o'clock in the morning, when I was awakened by the feeling that the bed was moving under me. I lay for a little while with closed eyelids trying to account for my sensations, then, opening them, I leaned over the bedside and saw that the floor was several inches deep in water, with a sediment of sand at the bottom. I looked again and again, unable to believe my eyes; then, hearing a sound of rushing water in the street outside and the excited talk of men, I awoke the others and we sat bolt upright in bed, quite mystified at the situation. Then we screamed in unison, after the manner of eighteen.

The voice of our host through the closed door of our room answered us.

"The reservoir up the street has burst, girls," he cried, "and this place lies in the main path of the flood. The house is in a hollow, so we are catching it worse than anybody. Get up, dress yourselves, and go upstairs out of danger! I've made stepping-stones of boxes for you in the hall. Junius Brutus wants to carry you up!"

"Never while we live!" — "Don't let him come in!" — "How can we dress?" cried the girls. "We shall have to wade to the closet."

"Then we must!" I said. "I'll do the wading and bring back our dry clothes to the big bed. Then we'll all stand on it and dress, looking into the tall glass opposite; but before I begin I'll put two chairs between the bed and the door and we can leap from chair to chair and reach the hall and the box-bridges. Oh! how heavenly to be in a real flood! But how awkward if it rises, for J. B. is six feet two and the only possible means of transportation to shore!"

Laughing, panting, and shrieking with excitement, we carried out this programme; I, the wader of the party, waiting till the other two girls had made hurried though fetching toilettes, for I brought water and towels to and fro and held mirrors with the utmost unselfishness. Then my turn came, and, hanging my white dress and sweet-pea garlands so high that no water could reach them, I hurried to make myself as nice as possible to meet the excitements that were near at hand.

They were many, and the thrills were attended with few fears. We knew that the water must recede in course of time and that our host would certainly be reimbursed for any damages. It would be dull staying on the bedroom floor upstairs, we reflected, save for the view from the windows, and there would be lack of food; but I had no sooner made up my mind to this imprisonment and the comedy of being borne down the lightning rod to a place of safety in the arms of my partner of the night before than I heard loud laughter from the kitchen. We disdained safety; we wanted fun, so we skipped across our chain of chairs to the chain of boxes in the hall below, thence across the dining-room chairs and tables till we faced the kitchen door, where our hostess and the beaux of the party stood on pantry stools, wooden chairs, and inverted tubs.

J. B. gave me an enamoured glance from the vantage-ground of a nail keg which enabled him to build a roaring fire in the stove, the kindling and wood being passed from hand to hand like the buckets in a country fire-brigade. Our host was barefooted and had his trousers rolled to the knee, so that he could attend to all the more disagreeable and menial tasks, while Juliet, his wife, who had the prettiest feet and ankles west of the Rockies, had adopted a suitable and even necessary shortening of her skirt — rather audacious for 1876!

What a breakfast we had! — for a real breakfast it was! The Chinese cook did not sleep in the house and could not reach us in the flood. J. B. and I somehow found ourselves paired like all the others and sought uncooked food in the refrigerator just outside the kitchen.

"I must speak!" he murmured. "I never cared for —"

"You must care for the eggs, and the eggs only," I interrupted; "there seem to be only seven and we are eight!"

"Don't be cruel," he begged, "let me —"

"I'll let you shave the bacon while I hold it down. Food is the only consideration now; — besides, they're waiting for us. Do be sensible!"

"How can I?"

"I don't *know* how, I'm sure, but you can try."

We passed bread slices, with a fried egg on top and a bit of bacon, from hand to hand; while a loving-cup of coffee, in the shape of a two-quart tin dipper, sped (most unsanitarily) from lip to lip. In the middle of the repast, the pair seated on the rail of the sink, where they could ply the pump, suddenly flung their arms around each other and exclaimed:

"We can't keep it to ourselves another minute! It happened last night when we were coming home from the ball. We are engaged to be married!"

As they had parted at two in the morning and slept until six, we could hardly praise them for remarkable self-control and secrecy, but our congratulations and their ecstasy added to the general gayety, though it brought on a brief scene with J. B., after which I never danced with him again!

Alas! the flood steadily receded from this point, leaving a disagreeable ooze in its wake. My orange-tree room alone kept its two inches of water until nearly noon, when our guests had all departed save the accepted lover, who was invited to remain and work for his board the rest of the day.

Delicious, unique breakfast; the only one of its kind in the world, perhaps! Would that I could have a photograph of the merry party standing on tottering edifices of one sort and another, eating, drinking, joking, and making light love at six-thirty in the morning!

That was my first visit to Los Angeles! As for J. B., he really was unlike all other men! He berated my host for the embarrassing position in which I had placed him.

"Devilish awkward!" he said. "I sent the old Governor back to Australia a fortnight ago, so there'd be more room in the ranch-house when I was married."

"Had you asked the girl before you dispatched your father?"

"No; I supposed it would be all right. No girl would dance with me, I thought, unless she meant business!"

"Served you right, old man! Don't be so sure next time!" said my host; and that was the end of that story!

IX
AN OPERATIC FRIENDSHIP

THE second episode was far more important; indeed, it was of a semi-miraculous nature. Annie Louise Cary, our great American contralto, came from Maine, as all will remember. Arriving in California with the first grand opera company that had ever visited San Francisco, she asked a friend: "Where is that young girl — Kate Somebody — who used to write letters to the Usher family in Hollis? I have heard them read many a time. She is very fond of music, and I dare say has never seen an opera in her life. I'm going to have her up here. Find out where she lives and I will do the rest."

The astonishing invitation from a celebrated singer whom I had never met fell like a bomb into my family circle; a harmless, magical bomb that when it burst scattered surprise, confusion, and joy.

"She says four weeks and you haven't anything to wear!" said my mother.

"She has even sent steamer tickets!" exclaimed my father. "Most extraordinary! She must be eccentric, or a genius."

"What *did* you write about in your letters to the Ushers?" asked my sister, who was now sufficiently grown up to go to the root of things.

I sat quite still and dumb, staring at Miss Cary's incomprehensible invitation. "They were always just plain letters," I said after a pause. "I don't remember mentioning music. The only way I can find out *why* she invited me is to go and see. When I know her, I can guess the reason. Of course, I don't deserve such an honor, but, if we only got what we deserve, life would be awfully dull, so I'd better go at once; she might change her mind."

The family agreed that there were no obstacles whatever to partaking of manna that fell from heaven without the slightest provocation, and I left for San Francisco on the first steamer, to be welcomed by Miss Cary in her luxurious suite of seven rooms at the Baldwin Hotel.

"I can't think why you wanted me," I said, almost tearfully, as she gave me a friendly kiss and handed my coat and hat to her maid.

"Neither do I, but I did!" she answered, with a laugh that was one of her many charms. It was not a sweet, merry, light-hearted treble, but a full-throated, golden, contralto laugh, with a lot of heart in it, the note that always won her audiences.

We were friends in two minutes and a half, and almost at once a door into fairyland opened before my unsophisticated eyes. I had had glimpses of unknown worlds before, but I had never been invited to walk in and make myself at home, so to speak; yet in twenty-four hours I fell into line as a member of a grand opera company in good and regular standing.

Max Strakosch was the impresario, Clara Louise Kellogg the prima donna, Tom Karl one of the tenors, Mr. Behrens the leader of the orchestra, but I cannot recall the names of all the supporting artists; I know that the critics and public pronounced it an admirable *ensemble*, and the productions were thought of remarkable excellence, although I dare say the scenery of "The Masked Ball" was also used for "Aïda" and "Martha," since I am writing practically of the Dark Ages.

There were only four performances a week — three evenings and one matinée — and the repertory included "Faust," "Aïda," "Mignon," "Il Trovatore," "The Masked

Ball," "Martha," and "La Favorita." I attended all the rehearsals for orchestra, chorus, or principals. In fact I lived in the opera house except for meals and grudged even the time for these, save for the private company dinners which were at three in the afternoon on opera nights. Every successful dish was followed by a message from Mr. Strakosch to the chef, who appeared in person to be roundly applauded by the artists and to hear the welcome words:

"Bravo! Admirable! Perfection! Come to the opera to-night and bring your family!"

Miss Kellogg was beautiful in looks and in splendid voice, at the height of her career as an artist, charming everybody with her intelligent and spirited performances; but it was Miss Cary after all who had the ovations, the flowers, the crowds, the "standees," the frenzied applause; she who evoked laughter in comedy as well as thrills and tears in tragedy. She was especially fine as "Azucena" and "Amneris" in "Il Trovatore" and "Aïda"; a most mirth-compelling and bewitching "Nancy" in "Martha," and a sensation as the heroine in "La Favorita." What she did as "Siebel" in "Faust" and how she contrived her effects I cannot imagine, since she never "stole" the center of the stage, but "Siebel" seemed a star rôle in her hands, although it has only one aria.

I remember well a final rehearsal of "Faust," when she was in gorgeous voice and in such plenitude of spirits that the dimly lighted opera house seemed irradiated with her vitality. When she came to her aria in the garden, "*La parlata d'amor*," she sang it with her usual beautiful ease and the velvety quality that always entranced the ear; but on a repetition for some reason, a half-hour later, she amused and delighted the orchestra by prankishly singing parts of it an octave higher than it is written, simply skylarking up and down with it in a musicianly, but wholly nonsensical, way, until, at the end, the laughing musicians rose to their feet *en masse* with cries of "Brava! Brava!" while those standing in the wings, keenly appreciating the triumphant audacity of the feat, applauded to the echo.

And I, hidden away in the shadows at the back somewhere, would say to myself, "I am visiting her, sleeping in the room next to hers, and she likes me!" — and a glow of affection, gratitude, and girlish pride would warm me through and through! I did not know then that her voice was of such extraordinary range (three and a half octaves) that she could sing any rôle entrusted to her from soprano to baritone.

I do not forget that I am speaking through the mists of bygone years and that my opinions were those of a very young, enthusiastic, prejudiced, and ignorant person, but contemporary criticism bears me out in my admiration of Annie Louise Cary as an artist. Her voice was beautiful, her acting power far above the average, considering the standards of that day, when it was not "polite" to act too strenuously lest you should agitate your *bel canto!* Her personality was warm, magnetic, compelling, lovable, and she had won her spurs in a hard school. Her popularity abroad was amazing, and I can never forget some of the things she said when we were sitting quietly together sewing. I was probably darning stockings, but Miss Cary, when at leisure, hemmed dusters or innumerable pieces of fine muslin in which she packed toilet articles, private papers, photographs, and the like, when traveling.

"My dear child," she said once, "the very best thing that can happen to an artist is to be obliged to work with an undoubted superior. No time then for vanity or self-consciousness; no chance for idleness, for half-hearted performances, for self-satisfaction. Your 'job,' if your wagon is hitched to a star, is not to trail too far behind."

"Isn't it discouraging?" I asked.

"If you are a weakling, yes; but if you have any good stuff in you — no! I have sung with Patti, Gerster, Tietjens, Campanini, Brignoli, Capoul, Galassi — indeed, always with great artists. If I amount to anything it is because I sang with Christine Nilsson during the earlier, indeed, the larger part of my stage life. The contralto who appeared with her had to strain every nerve to be worthy, or to be noticed at all, for that matter! At every performance there stood that beautiful, distinguished-looking creature riveting all eyes, her lovely voice caressing every ear; her simplicity rebuking all theatricalism! What was a practically unknown contralto from the State of Maine to do in order to 'hold up her end'? In Russia, where I learned that they had never heard of Maine and thought I must be an Indian, I worked harder than ever; and when I took curtain-calls with Nilsson, and finally scene-calls by myself, I felt more proud of being her associate than I did of my own success. — Oh! yes, it is a poor thing to mistake yourself for a number one when you haven't learned yet to be a good number two!"

"Composers don't favor contraltos as much as I should like," I complained.

Miss Cary laughed. "No," she said, "we generally have to do the best we can with the little given us, while the sopranos and tenors live in the limelight; — not because they are eager for it, but because it is so decreed by fate. I enjoy singing 'Amneris' because, although 'Aïda,' the slave, has to be loved by the tenor, as usual, the scorned Princess has her dramatic chance! She is defeated, to be sure, and her love rebuffed, but that is nothing! Generally the contralto is 'back stage' listening to thrilling duets sung by the high-contracting parties! They cannot keep 'Amneris' in the background!"

Miss Cary's triumph in this rôle was complete. Her magnificent appearance, the beauty of her voice, and her powerful acting produced an unparalleled effect upon the operatic stage.

These talks with her made a deep impression upon me, as coming from a great artist, then the most popular singer in America. I had learned something of her experiences in Europe; — her début in Copenhagen, her successful appearances in Stockholm, Paris, Moscow, St. Petersburg, and London. I had heard of the really extraordinary furor she created in Russia, but her rather unique conviction that her steady growth had come from being pitted against superior artists at the outset and obliged from loyalty, as well as self-respect, to do her level best with such powers as had been entrusted to her, impressed me tremendously.

My long visit ended in a blaze of glory, for Mr. Strakosch, when the week's repertory was announced, allowed me to choose the opera for my birthday treat. I selected "The Masked Ball," because many friends of Miss Kellogg and Miss Cary were "going on" in the dancing scene, for the fun of the thing. We were all disguised in dominos and masks, but I could not convince myself that every eye in the opera house was not riveted on ME, and, after once circling the stage in a semi-comatose condition, I forsook the gay throng to hide myself in Miss Cary's dressing-room.

After the opera my beloved friend gave me a gay little birthday supper in her private sitting-room, asking two or three intimates, Mr. Strakosch and four or five members of the company. There was much singing of an informal sort, but all at once I was stricken with panic by Miss Cary's saying: "I want you to hear this child sing something; — no, you needn't play for her, Enrico; she likes to accompany herself, because she knows that she can hide her own weaknesses, and she will be afraid that you won't! Go to the piano, child, and sing some little thing! Don't be frightened! Mr. Strakosch isn't engaging any new artists! This isn't an 'audition,' my dear. Nothing hangs upon it! — The little creature hasn't a bit of voice, but good gracious! what common sense! If she had anything to sing with, she could actually sing. — Go on, child!"

I tottered, rather than walked, to the piano, consoled by this extraordinarily chastening introduction; hardly knowing how I could demonstrate my "common sense," though sure of my ability to live down to her description of my voice. An impertinent idea came to me, to sing a favorite encore of Miss Cary's, "The Cows are Coming Home," with as much of her well-known manner as I could muster on short notice.

It was a simple little thing that would cause present-day critics to leave the hall in scorn and fury. It had memories of early evenings in the country, of leaning over the pasture-bars, of tinkling bells in the distance, of watching the slow, tranquil line of cows coming along the grassy path, the recital of their familiar names, and a refrain with a tear in it — something about the singer's looking back to child-hood remembering certain twilight hours when the cows were coming home. I suppose — indeed, I know — that it was absolute balderdash, and I am certain that no artist could maintain her self-respect and use it as an encore nowadays, when cows are never mentioned on a concert programme — and yet!

Annie Louise Cary, from the village of Wayne in the State of Maine, gazing back at her country childhood, and the familiar scenes of life on the farm, could somehow reconstruct a picture that kindled every one's imagination.

One might dislike and despise cows, either going to pasture or coming home, but not when she was singing about them! How the men in the audience swallowed lumps in the throat — men who had never leaned over (pasture) bars or taken any interest in milking! How the handkerchiefs came out when the singer, her own eyes swimming, came to the lines:

"When jingle, jangle, jingle,
  'Way down the dusky dingle,
    The cows are coming home —
  Malvine and Pearl and Florimel,
  Red Rose and Sue and Bonnie Bell.
  Like shadows in the sunset light
  They tell the soft approach of night
    When hearts no longer roam.
  And bygone hopes and bygone fears,
  Seen dimly, through a mist of tears,
  Come trooping down the lane of years
    When the cows are coming home —"

After all, the contralto voice is the only one on a level with our hearts; sopranos may soar, however high, but the vibrations are too rapid to stir our pulses.

I transposed the song to as low a key as I dared, and my somewhat irreverent imitation of my dear prima donna, especially in the lines that always caused a flow of tears in the audience, was thought so creditable that all laughed heartily, and she, after kissing my cheek, gave me a sound shaking by way of reproof.

Miss Cary's career upon the stage was not a long one, and her star was still in the ascendant when she left it forever, for, after her marriage to Mr. Charles Monson Raymond, in 1882, she never sang again save for some favorite charity.

Although Mr. Raymond was a modern American stock-broker, he succumbed as quickly to the charm of the great contralto as did the early Italian Romeo to the spell of

Juliet, for, on the night he first saw her as "Siebel" in "Faust," his mind was made up to marry her, if marry her he might. He was not an habitual opera-goer, had been dragged by a friend against his will to this particular performance, and sat speechless and motionless until its close. As the curtain fell, he turned to his friend and said, with decision: "I'm going to marry that woman!"

"What woman?" gasped his bewildered companion.

"The one who has been singing 'Siebel,'" answered Mr. Raymond; and sure enough he did, although it was nearly two years before he even obtained the kind of introduction to the beloved which he desired.

This operatic experience with Annie Louise Cary gave me a view of the hitherto unknown side of the footlights and induced intense interest, but I was not intoxicated by it. I learned a little about ordinary stage routine by watching good and bad exits, stiff and graceful gestures, natural and theatrical poses, and a dozen other practical factors in an artist's profession. These I promptly put into effect in my first appearance in amateur theatricals after my return to Santa Barbara. Four weeks with Annie Louise Cary were supposed to be worth four years in a dramatic school, and there was some thought of trying "Camille" in order to give me an opportunity.

The play was a pretentious affair for charity in Lobero's adobe theater. The house was wonderfully decorated with slender spires of yucca blossoms five feet high, gathered from the slopes of the Santa Ynez foothills. The effect of these plants, each with its towering apex of creamy, wax-like flowers, was uniquely beautiful and created a sensation. The theater was crowded and the drama finally chosen was Byron's "Our Boys," I playing the *ingénue* part of "Mary" in the usual white muslin, blue sash, and two braids ending in curls.

There is no record that the theatrical world was shaken to its center by my performance; but the breathless joy with which I passed hours of rehearsal in the damp, stuffy, adobe theater; the light feet with which I trod the dusty floor of the dim, murky wings; the positive ecstasy that flooded my being when I slipped off my own personality and dress, and slipped on that of the somewhat attractive but wholly imbecile "Mary" — all these sensations meant something of which I was then unconscious. Here and there, now and then, first and last, I have stood on the brink of a totally different career from the one I finally followed. Dazzling glimpses of a life, for which in some ways I had a sort of rudimentary fitness, have appeared to me as I trod the long trail that winds into the land of dreams; but I always ended by voluntarily choosing the quieter, sometimes even the wearier path, as the one for which my feet were shod, the one that God meant me to tread. The "nightingale" has sung and the "white moon" has always gleamed for me, nevertheless, when the scene may have seemed very drab and very barren to the casual onlooker. It is not always in gold days, but in gray ones, that the soul grows and the purpose of life unfolds.

X

A TURN IN THE ROAD

"HARD trial. Great tribulation, bred'ren!"

The scene changes now, and it is quite time that it should; high time that something should happen. My life had been as simple, as free from adventures, as uneventful as a girl's life could be, up to this moment. If nothing had occurred to change it, I might have continued to be a rather lively and versatile young person of uncatalogued tendencies. As a matter of fact, I was still in the egg-stage, although quite unaware of it until circumstances broke the shell; but, when things began to happen, they happened hard and fast, as if to make up for lost time.

My family had arrived in Santa Barbara on the crest of a "land boom." They did not observe that it was the "crest," for very few persons were observing either ebb or high tides closely; they were too busily occupied in planning for the acquisition of somewhat sudden though legitimate fortunes, small or large according to the sums invested. There seemed nothing very speculative about the boom, and most certainly nothing that resembled gambling. The security appeared as solid as the earth itself. Mr. A would buy a few feet of ground on Monday for a hundred dollars and sell it on Wednesday for two hundred. Mr. B would purchase a thousand acres or so in April and, cutting them up into large and small ranches, make a fortune on the enterprise in a few months. The climate of Santa Barbara, its mountains, its sea-bathing, its soil — in which you stuck a rootless sprig of something and after the first rains found it clambering audaciously into your bedroom window — its college, its churches, its Mission, its inevitable displacement of all other health and pleasure resorts on the map — these subjects of conversation assailed the ear on every side. They were tolerably new then, and were at least approximately true, although when the excitement subsided there were perhaps as many land-poor as land-rich persons in local society.

The land-poor ones had not bought at the right moment, at the right price, or in the right quarter. My father and mother had joyously and hopefully put their entire substance into land, buying plots here and there, with and without buildings, and on the usual terms of a substantial sum in cash and the remainder on mortgage. When nearly all the choice land was in possession of this particular body of enthusiastic purchasers, my father, in despair at finding anything else to buy, purchased a drug-store on the main street for several thousand dollars, the universal opinion being that its speedy sale would place us in the millionaire set. He made up his mind to be firm, not to throw it away at five times what he paid for it, but to hold it. These timid, instantaneous "turn-overs" were foolish, many people thought, and my parents determined to resist temptation and make a self-respecting profit on their holdings.

I remember little of all this land-buying business, being interested in youth's own affairs and hearing nothing but optimism on every side. I must record now one fact that, judged by the confidences of my contemporaries, seems unusual. I had never once heard money matters mentioned in our household from childhood up to this moment; never any talk about income; never a word of debts, credits, hopes, fears, economies, or extravagances. We were never told to save, and never given presents that seemed to indicate riches; the whole subject of finance was left untouched. My mother in her first widowhood had a comfortable living income on which to support herself, my little sister, and me. This inheritance came from her father; and if he had not, with truly Rooseveltian fervor, furnished fourteen children as heirs-at-law, or if he had not retired from business at forty, his less acquisitive grandchildren might have been quite well-to-do in this year of our Lord 1923.

My stepfather's practice supplied the rest of the annual budget (if there ever was a budget, which I very much doubt), and, as I say, there was an extraordinary lack of discussion as to ways and means. This may have meant indifference, but it certainly did not imply debts or difficulties, for, when these occur, children can never be kept in ignorance, since the very atmosphere breathes a nameless misery and continual argument in and out of season.

So, into the hopeful, contented, wholly untrained, and, I fear, unbusinesslike family, there came the death of my stepfather after an illness of only a few months. It occurred when the ebb tide of that particular land speculation was only too obvious, the fortunate and far-seeing buyers having departed with their legitimate gains, while a couple of hundred disappointed ones were left behind to regret their too enthusiastic, ill-selected, and promiscuous purchases. Within a year the growth of the town had veered in an unexpected direction, and we were among those who had not prophesied discreetly.

To be left with many parcels of unsalable land, all mortgaged, as was the invariable custom, the mortgages to be paid out of the profits that never came; to be left with our own cottage, horses, carriages, harnesses, and household effects in peril because of the lack of income: all this is disagreeable enough; but to be encumbered with a drug-store and two clerks needing continual advice and skilled superintendence as well as salary, this was tragedy. A widow with two youthful daughters and a boy of twelve might well despair, and she did.

Even the drug-store cat ran away; — a handsome Maltese tabby who lazily reclined near the ornamental jar of roseate liquid in the window, attracting much notice, but, as I remember, no custom! She must have been intelligent, and having heard, no doubt, that rats desert a sinking ship, forsook our fated drug-store and went to one farther down the street, curling herself disloyally but effectively round a blue jar, fully as becoming as the pink one.

My mother was down-hearted, but we were not, and we managed to keep up her courage. Oh! blessed youth! Nothing matters very much when, if ill fortune seems to be transiently present, good fortune is sure to be just smiling round the corner! At sixteen, eighteen, twenty, life is all ahead, glowing with rosy possibilities. Sudden and unaccustomed poverty is easy to bear compared to the dull, dreary misfortune that clouds middle age.

The undeclared motto of some people is: "Expect nothing and you'll never be disappointed." Ours was: "Expect everything and some of it happens!" With us poverty had its humorous side! In the first place, when we discovered that there was less than two hundred dollars in the bank and that interest on mortgages was to be paid regularly (out of nothing), we were sure that something must happen shortly to end what seemed a highly colored melodrama.

We were three thousand miles from relations and there were no vulgarly rich ones to extricate us from our formidable difficulties. We did not suffer agonies over seeing our lands go one by one for the mortgages; we did not weep when horses and carriages were sold; we still had a mortgaged roof, food, and our feet; but, if these had been suddenly removed, I confess we might have been brought to reason. My sister, just out of Santa Barbara College, gave two French and two Spanish lessons a week at a rate per hour which I do not dare quote, because it will seem to

THE SISTERS

show that as a family we were high-grade imbeciles, but as a matter of fact we were considered above ordinary intelligence.

My first attempt at adding to the depleted treasury came when the young rector of the Episcopal Church called on a certain Monday night to see if I would play the church organ for fifteen dollars a month. I accepted the offer cheerfully, and thought it unwise to mention that I had never touched the keys of an organ, reflecting that the first Sunday was five days away and that I at least could always read simple music at sight and play piano accompaniments. I took the key of the church that same evening and issued from the front door of my house at nine next morning, a full-fledged organist.

The instrument was a large cabinet organ with two banks of keys and foot pedals. I confined myself to one bank and three stops on my début the following Sunday, and I did not use the foot pedals for some time, save when in my agony of nervousness I stepped on a wrong bass note by mistake, expecting, of course, to be discharged the next day. The hymns and anthems gave me little trouble, as there was an excellent and sympathetic unsalaried choir, but the preludes, postludes, and voluntaries were a source of great anxiety at first. I could not read difficult music quickly and attend to the two banks of keys, the stops, and the blowing of the instrument at the same time, so I improvised for the most part, and worked up old melodies as I had been accustomed to do on the piano from childhood. One Sunday, being quite bereft of ecclesiastical themes, I wandered half unconsciously into the old Scots ballad: "Charlie is my darling." I reverently disguised it, I thought, by changing the time, diverting its majors into minors, and *vice versa*, and weaving into it fragments of other themes until it became to my mind as sacred a composition as I ever heard. Nevertheless, the rector, after receiving and depositing the offering, gave me a passing glance that spoke volumes. I hid my blazing face behind the hymn-books and "played out" the congregation to an impassioned rendition of "Oh! for the wings of a dove." No one in the choir or in the pews had noted my lapse in piety, but the young rector was a singer and had recognized an old favorite. The next morning came a note saying: "My dear Miss Kate, I am very fond of Charlie, but think perhaps he had better be left at home on Sundays."

While we were eating up the horses and carriages and harnesses, I wrote a story partially based upon an experience occurring during the time that I was a boarding pupil at the Gorham Female Seminary. I don't know why I wrote it, save that a certain Mark Sibley Severance, passing a winter in Santa Barbara, had written a book on Harvard College life and used occasionally to chat about literary matters with me. I admired him extravagantly as the only author with whom I had daily acquaintance, and perhaps he suggested my trying my hand at composition.

The thing was called "Half-a-Dozen Housekeepers," and was sent as soon as finished to the "St. Nicholas Magazine" in New York. Weeks passed, running into months. I called daily at the post-office, but was not really surprised that I received no answer. I thought little of the story, and wondered I had had the impertinence to offer it in so high a quarter. One dreary day of the first autumn rains I made my usual call at the post-office, feeling a little more grown-up and practical than I had before, for I had heard that morning of an entirely new and unknown fatality called "taxes." I had been so carefully brought up that when a thing was due it never occurred to me that there was anything to do save pay it; the only question was — how?

The angelic being disguised momentarily as a postmaster handed me an envelope, not knowing that he was a fairy godfather. It had "St. Nicholas Magazine, 33 East 17th Street," printed on it and appeared like any ordinary letter, but on being opened by trembling fingers disclosed an acceptance of "Half-a-Dozen Housekeepers," which was to be printed in three installments, and a check fluttered to the ground beside me. I had never seen a check before, but I picked it up and departed eagerly to a secluded spot to find that it appeared to call for a payment of a dollar and fifty cents which I thought was fair value for a first effort, though inadequate for taxes. Concentrated scrutiny gave me the idea after a moment that it was perhaps for fifteen dollars, though that seemed a large amount for my services to art. I continued to study it, arithmetic being my weak point and ciphers particularly distracting, but I could read and understand written words, and my eyes finally slipped to the plain statement that one hundred and fifty dollars was to be paid me by the misguided, the extravagant, the romantic editor of the "St. Nicholas." (Dear Mary Mapes Dodge, of blessed memory!)

I ran home like a whirlwind and entered the sitting-room, saying breathlessly, but without a smile: "The 'St. Nicholas' has answered me."

"Of course they wouldn't take it —" sighed my sister.

"Ye-es," I allowed, "they took it!"

"Why, I call that glorious, to have it printed at all! Did they pay anything?" asked my mother.

"Ye-es, something!"

"Never mind if it isn't much, dear," said my mother; "it shows they liked it."

"Was it as much as five dollars?" my sister asked.

"More."

"More than ten?"

"More than fifty."

Gently, slowly, tirelessly they raised the sum, and I answered, until suddenly my strength left me, and shrieking, "One hundred and fifty," I flung myself sobbing on the sofa while my mother and sister wept in unison.

"We must frame the check and hang it on the wall!" suggested my sister, wiping her eyes. (She knew even less of checks than I did!)

"Then we don't get the money," I answered sagaciously.

"Well, it must never be spent on common things like food!" said my mother, who in turn wiped away her tears.

"Certainly not!" exclaimed my sister. "A monument in the back yard is the only picturesque and proper thing."

There never was any monument erected to that check, or to any succeeding one, but something strange happened about this sudden and successful breaking into authorship. It ought to have been either the beginning of a long line of similar successes or a "flash in the pan," a happy accident, followed by many failures. What really occurred was something in which I now take infinite pride, though at the time it seemed merely sensible. I thought quite soberly the rest of the week about the whole affair; the comparatively short time in which I had written the story, its speedy acceptance, its generous recompense. Manifestly the right and obvious thing was to sit down and write another, and then another, and maintain my responsibility as the head of the family, but I found to my surprise that I had nothing in particular to write about! No themes, no convictions, no powerful urge to express myself, no background of culture, no experience, no knowledge of human nature! What was there in me, I thought, out of which to make a successful author? Nothing! The right thing for me was to learn to do something well, to have a profession of some sort; not one requiring long study and apprenticeship, for that was impossible under the circumstances, but a modest vocation. What should it be? Teaching of some sort was one of the obvious channels of activity, but how could I teach when I possessed so little knowledge? The younger the children, the less book-learning I should need, but, on the other hand, the more wisdom. How should I gain this indispensable asset?

Well, there is no use in denying it! Happiness, good fortune, or at all events opportunity for service, is always just around the corner, perhaps only waiting for the signal that each human creature must give for himself. I was not conscious of giving any signal, but presently my vocation was calling, calling to me; at first in tones I could not understand, but that gradually grew intelligible. The call came unexpectedly, but the moment I really heard and comprehended it, I answered — all eagerness and gratitude and joy; — but the vocation did not seem to be authorship! My "call" was not to write books; but hidden in it, all unsuspected, was the experience of life, and sympathy with human nature, without which the most valued book is but waste paper.

XI

A FAIRY GODMOTHER

I HAD "been East," as we say in California, for several months following my stepfather's sudden death. There were a few technical business affairs to be settled; although, as a matter of fact, they never were — every attempt to disentangle them resulting in tying them into harder knots.

I had thought a position might miraculously open to my wistful search for something profitable to do — I being a nice girl who had never before had any financial responsibilities, but who now found herself with a young sister, a still younger brother, and an inexperienced mother to be kept in circumstances resembling our former modest affluence; but nobody wanted me for anything! What wonder! I could sing a little, play a little, act a little, write a little! I was well versed in ordinary household duties and sewing, but one casual glance at me would not have revealed a capable domestic assistant to an employer seeking that precious article. I had no well-digested, well-classified knowledge to impart to my juniors, although I was intelligent, eagerly interested in life, and possessed of an alert mind. No district or State superintendent would have considered me as an applicant for public school teaching. The first examination would have revealed the fact that I was not mistress of the particular subjects that had to be taught, nor of the latest method of teaching them.

I returned to my family in Santa Barbara, therefore, convinced that I might be an agreeable young person in general society, but of no possible value in making a living.

Why, when I had sold a brief three-part story [1] to the "St. Nicholas Magazine" for one hundred and fifty dollars, did I not sharpen my lead pencil and sit down and be an author? The answer breathes incredible conceit, but it is true. As I have hinted in my last chapter, I realized that I had no knowledge or experience of life; no well-formed opinions or convictions; no message to convey; that the little vein of passable metal that I had struck in writing my first youthful story was not deep enough to yield any adequate return for subsequent mining operations; that never out of literature alone could I support myself, nor the members of the family until they could stand on their own feet. I did not need to be *told* that I had too little to say at that period, to be a successful author — I knew it, without a shadow of doubt.

I suppose I was possibly the most sensible person in the State of California when I determined that I was unfit to attempt authorship as a means of livelihood; yet it was never once remarked, by any one, and never would be, even at this day, did I not myself declare it to an ignorant and undiscriminating world. Sensible I was, am, and ever shall be; sometimes worse, but always sensible, though entirely unappreciated in this regard.

At this crucial moment, in the early summer of 1877, came a remarkable woman to Santa Barbara, Mrs. Caroline M. Severance, of Boston, sometimes called the Mother of Women's Clubs. She had left mountains of accomplished work for women in Massachusetts, and at the age of sixty-eight or seventy, perhaps, was on her way with her husband and two sons to make a home and plant an orange grove in Los Angeles.

We soon became fast friends, just why I am not quite clear. She was modest, unassuming, sympathetic, broad-

[1] " Half-a-Dozen Housekeepers."

minded, and an obvious leader among women who were then called of the "advanced" type. She was a born reformer. She advocated dress reform, low heels, no corsets, new systems of diet, universal suffrage, feminism, single standard of morals, and the economic independence of women; but perhaps her dominant interest was in methods of education, then in the hopelessly muddled and inchoate state that has prevailed since the days of Confucius and Socrates, both of whom were convinced that they had settled the problem for all time.

She interested me greatly in the kindergarten method, which was then gaining ground in Massachusetts under the name of the "New Education," and through the efforts of Elizabeth Peabody, who, not long returned from the land of Froebel, was fully assured that she had solved the riddle of the universe. Her brother-in-law, Horace Mann, had introduced the system into his famous school, and Marie Kraus-Boelté, a pupil of Frau Froebel, had also made a beginning in New York.

If I had been made of tinder and a lighted match had been applied to me, I could not have taken fire more easily, when Mrs. Severance told me of this new educational enterprise with young children.

When she remarked one day that her first duty in Los Angeles was to find a suitable house and garden for a certain Miss Emma Marwedel, a trainer of kindergartners then established in Washington, who was to follow her to Southern California as soon as possible, I sighed to think that Santa Barbara was not to be the chosen field of this glorious experiment. The complete regeneration of humanity by any series of simple expedients had never been put before me seriously up to this time, either as a graceful occupation or a noble form of self-sacrifice, and I kindled to it warmly, though secretly.

When, a fortnight later, Mrs. Severance wrote from Los Angeles that Miss Marwedel had arrived and was certain that every unrealized dream of her adored Froebel could be brought to perfection in the heavenly climate of Southern California, I held my breath. She added:

The training-school will open at once, even if there is only one pupil, and, my dear Kate, I beseech you to be that one! You were born for this work and are peculiarly fitted to do pioneer service because you are musical, a good story-teller, and fond of children. I have studied you carefully without your knowledge, and at my age I am a fair judge of the necessary requirements. You have the play-spirit in you, but you also love work! If you can manage the hundred dollars for tuition and perhaps twenty-five extra for books and working materials, I beg you to enroll yourself at once and become our guest and a member of our family for the necessary nine months' course. I consider I am doing as much for Miss Marwedel and the cause as for you in this matter, so pray do not disappoint me.

Personally I felt as if Elijah had alighted from his chariot and asked me to accompany him to some unknown Paradise, but I felt that there would be a slight awkwardness about the hundred and twenty-five dollars. We were now entirely out of debt (we were out of everything, in fact!), but the sale of our various plots of land from time to time had only satisfied all mortgages thereon and sometimes left a few dollars in the home treasury.

I called a family council on the receipt of Mrs. Severance's letter. The Small Sister was no longer small, as I have said, but had graduated with high honors from the Santa Barbara College. She was an admirable French scholar and spoke Spanish as fluently as English, so she would soon be ready to fly from the home nest to some locality where these accomplishments would be appreciated, but meantime had come this invitation to try my own wings.

The family came gallantly to the rescue. We remem-

bered that we owned a small undesirable adobe house on
the outskirts of town. Why not mortgage that (being at
the moment all out of mortgages) and study kindergarten
on part of the amount received?

The motion was carried without a dissenting vote, and I
went to seek my fortune, promising to do honor to, and
"lead," whatever training-class there happened to be,
especially if it contained only myself!

Great-hearted, generous, wise Mrs. Severance! One of
the dearest and most helpful of all the friends that have
aided me in passing the many milestones of my journey!
How kind she was, how stimulating, how interested in
every step of my progress! And what a happy year it
was for me, a member of her delightful family!

There were only three of us in Miss Marwedel's first
training-class, for the idea was new and there had been no
advertising; but twenty-five children had been gathered by
Mrs. Severance by the day I arrived in Los Angeles, and
they were a lovely group from four to seven years old.

I shall never forget the hour when I first joined the circle
game in Miss Marwedel's beautiful California garden and,
with the hand of a new child-friend clasped in each of my
own, received my first glimpse of what "guided play"
might mean in early education.

There were established laws, I could see that, although
they were evidently unwritten. No child could break the
circle and rush off to follow his own personal activities, for
that would prevent collective pleasure and friendly coöperation. The games were to be chosen by the children themselves when they were familiar with them, but Miss Marwedel would have to be the arbiter at this early stage of development. Any game chosen would naturally be accepted
by the circle, even if not the favorite of the majority, for
that course was plainly to be viewed as common politeness.

I found later that, if any child did not desire to play, and was rude in the expression of his indifference, he could sit at ease on the piazza and watch the cheerful fellowship going on in the garden, and, when his abnormal egotism or selfishness had been modified a little by solitude, he would ordinarily rejoin the circle and play heartily. The individuals who cannot work with, or for, anybody had better be shown from the cradle that the universe is made on such a plan that "togetherness" is the only possible solution of happiness, peace, and prosperity.

The game Miss Marwedel announced was The Little Teacher. One child was to go into the center of the ring and give us motions of his own contriving while the circle of children sang the words (of greater economic than lyric value):

> "Look at little Harry
> Who shows us the game —
> Look at little Harry,
> Now we'll do the same."

Chorus of tra-la-las with soft clapping of hands and imitation of Harry's (or Lucy's) activities were to accompany the song.

Miss Marwedel gave the words, which were repeated twice, but thereafter we met our first obstacle; — she could not, alas! sing the tune, Nature having deprived her of that one talent.

"There will be a music teacher next week, children," she exclaimed, "and then we will have beautiful plays, yes? — Do any of the ladies — do you, Miss Kate — chance to know the German folk-song 'Ach! du lieber Augustin'? You do? Wunderbar! Is it not wonderful, children, the kind Miss Kate knows the air of The Little Teacher!"

I sang the exceedingly simple words to the equally simple tune, and the children learned it in two minutes. Then a volunteer was asked to go into the center of the ring. A certain "Edgar" bounded from his place in the circle with almost unparalleled haste and energy. One glance at him showed me that he would be in the center of the ring whenever he was not forestalled by a person still more agile and devoted to the limelight, and so it turned out.

Having arrived at the point of his ambition, the aforesaid Edgar had no idea what to do, and Miss Marwedel had to go to his side and whisper a suggestion. Boys of four or five years, by the way, never conceive of any movement other than jerking a leg up and down or swinging an arm to and fro; self-expression at this age is acrobatic rather than rhythmic or æsthetic. Miss Marwedel advised the arm, and suggested that it was the pendulum of a clock, and we all followed. Edgar then reluctantly chose some one from the circle to succeed himself, murmuring: "I could swing the other arm as well as not!"

The game progressed to the great delight of the children, and at length a miracle happened. Bertha was chosen. Bertha had a Brain. Bertha had a Sense of Drama. She took her little white skirt with both hands, stretched it to its full width, sank slowly to the first measure of the tune, and rose to the second, having made a perfect curtsy! The effect was enchanting, electric, almost reducing Miss Marwedel to tears. We in the circle imitated Bertha as nearly as possible, the boys sticking out a foot and struggling to extend their semi-masculine garments gracefully, while the little girls ducked in various ways, scraped each other's legs, and struck attitudes of acute stomach-ache. Some even fell to the earth, and none of us would have made a good appearance at the Court of St. James.

The grace of Bertha's performance, and the frightful clumsiness of our efforts to approach it, made repetition necessary, and before we finished the game we taught the youthful males of the company how to bow when the females of the species were curtsying.

Miss Marwedel said, with emotion, when the performance concluded: "Bertha has been with me only two days; my children are always so inventive; you will see how it goes, ladies. — You took note of little Edgar, ladies? I wish to cultivate your observation! Little Edgar will shortly need some abridgment. Is that the right word?"

I thought it an admirable, though unusual, word, and reflected that Edgar probably needed "abridging" as far back as his grandfather!

After the game came a miniature luncheon of a small cup of milk and a cracker, with some casual hints as to table manners and conversation, and then a half-hour of clay modeling in which the laurels placed on my brow during the musical exercises were quickly wrested from me by the youngest child in the group, who, when requested to make a nice carrot or turnip, modeled a pig that was a real pig, and so acknowledged by all. Edgar remarked that he could make splendid pigs and was accustomed to doing so daily if not hourly. On being asked to produce one for our pleasure, he said he'd rather go home, he had a loose tooth.

The period of handiwork brought me another vision. The child who had talent, who had tidiness in using his material, or swiftness in the attainment of his objective (the clay turnip, potato, or pig) was thereby released for the service of the community. He could help the four-year-old baby to get his lump of clay into some sort of shape; show some clumsy-fingered five-year-old that his clay was too wet, and that he could not model in mud. Oh! noble ideal to instill unconsciously without any sermonizing into a child's mind! — that greater talent was in itself a joyous responsibility; that it was an honor to help the weaker brethren; that it was better to aid his fellow-worker to put a handsome tail on *his* pig than to go on making two pigs of his own. When I found in a few days that work in the kindergarten was always a reward, never a penance; and that being deprived of it was a punishment, I divined the (to me) new, more orderly, more brotherly world that was a human possibility. Certain of these principles of Froebel can never be outgrown, or superseded by better ones, in the opinion of any woman who has studied them, taught them, or learned to live by them. They have been voiced by all great teachers in one form or another; they are eternally right, eternally sound, eternally uplifting; — if a creature made in the divine image wishes to be a neighbor, a citizen, or a builder of new worlds.

At twelve, hats were distributed and the line was formed, Edgar unostentatiously slipping to the head as if by accident. Miss Kate played a march, while Miss Marwedel's eyes moistened with astonishment and delight, and the children went to their homes.

I was in an incredible state of excitement, for I felt that for the first time in my life I was clearly doing something that I was able to do well, perhaps in course of time superlatively well. I felt in my right place, happy, with entirely new springs of action touched, new powers awakened. I had never known any group of young children before. I had never consciously gone through any previous phase of the development of maternal instinct; but the very knowledge that this exhilarating morning was to be followed by others gave me enormous pleasure in anticipation.

The Little Teacher is a dull bit of verse and the game makes no appeal to the imagination as do many, indeed, most of the kindergarten games. It is merely a useful vehicle for bringing together a group of children who are strangers to one another, of uniting them in a common activity, and beginning to develop in them a sense of rhythm and time. I think it is a dull game, but I'd rather play it than Auction Bridge this minute, if I could get twenty-five children to play it with me! And then there was the pleasure of discovering Edgar and Bertha! The psychological study of Edgar as a human being would while away three or four hours at any time! He was only one of twenty-five differing personalities, but as a complete compendium of self-advertising I never knew his equal. No occupation was offered of which he did not pronounce himself a master since his birth. He had always forgotten how to do it, but it was all familiar to him in retrospect. No animal was ever mentioned in a story but Edgar had it in his back yard, and had petted and tamed it. No country on the globe that he had not visited, although his age was six and his circumstances humble. He was always bored at coöperative tasks, but if placed in a position of authority he would sweep, dust, water plants, open the door to visitors, gather the children's envelopes of work, straighten the line of march, and could be safely called upon for all showy and ornamental services. I have kept track of the Christian names of all Presidents of the United States and all Justices of the Supreme Court, but have never known an Edgar among them, so I am at a loss as to what use he has made of his commanding talents.

When the children disappeared, we three students went to a shady porch, opened our luncheon baskets, and discussed the morning.

Miss H. was a very tired public school teacher of long standing whose whole life seemed to have been passed in the drudgery of education without any of its compensating joys. Miss S. was about my own age, exceedingly practical, literal, and not given to self-expression. We were an odd trio, and I somehow thought Miss Marwedel would have difficulty in adapting herself to our several needs.

Our first lecture came at two. Miss Marwedel had mislaid her notes and had to unpack three boxes of books to find them, so she was a little flustered and discursive, but she gave us an interesting and sympathetic sketch of Froebel's life and work for which I was already prepared by the reading of various books lent me by Mrs. Severance. Still, the personality, the enthusiasm, and the spoken word made all the difference.

I am very grateful that my first training came from Miss Marwedel. She was not adapted to all pupils, her English not being perfect and her method not systematic. Her feet never trod the solid earth; she was an idealist, a dreamer, and a visionary, but life is so apt to be crammed with Gradgrinds that I am thankful when I come into intimate contact with a dreamer. Dreamers and visionaries are not always comfortable members of families; that, I allow. They are unpractical, unpunctual, not given to toiling and spinning, prefer sunsets to sewing and poetry to cooking; but, for outside intercourse, give me a dreamer or two to stir the imagination and kindle the heart's desire for noble things. This has been and can be done at the cookstove and in the business office, but candor compels me to state that a sunset, a quiet hour on a hilltop, a "book of verses underneath the bough," all prove more serviceable in my experience.

When Miss Marwedel painted the possibilities of the children with whom we were working, when she recounted Froebel's vision of the future of the race if children from the earliest years could be self-governing and creative, instead of disciplined like soldiers and "standardized," I escaped temporarily from a world of rigid realities. I remembered the line: "Iliums like a mist rise into towers." Miss

S., for instance, was a little troubled by Miss Marwedel's "mists," but the dear lady always succeeded in making me see the "towers" through them. We all had to consult other authorities for details, for practical directions about this or that, translate her messages to mothers into less abrupt language, get into more intimate relation with the children than she could at her age; nevertheless, she had the vision and she gave it to us. A brightness "fell into the air" that never faded until the years brought the "inevitable yoke" of Wordsworth's immortal Ode, and custom began to lie upon me with a weight "heavy as frost, and deep almost as life." That "inevitable yoke" and "weight of custom" never falls early upon those who live with children.

XII

THE STUDY OF KINDERGARTEN

THE winter was one of steady application and study, including the making of many books of manual work, the execution of which was to prove the student's ability to conduct the kindergarten occupations with children. There was much study of psychology, history of education, Pestalozzi, Rousseau, Herbert Spencer, Froebel's Mother Play. There were classes in Games and Story-Telling, there was the daily work with the children, not only the four- and five-year-olds, but the highly advanced youngsters of six to seven who had some book instruction. There were themes to be written; there were metaphysical problems to be discussed and answered. The daylight hours were full to the brim, and the evenings required a couple of hours' preparation for the coming day; still, I was never tired, the work was so novel, so interesting, so fruitful.

The Christmas holidays brought one decided change in my daily life, and books were laid aside for a brief but very dramatic and exhilarating period.

The Severances were devout Unitarians, and had induced a Massachusetts minister, to whom climate was of temporary importance, to join our little colony in Los Angeles and preach in a hall in the city. Mrs. Severance's hope was for a small church building, and the weekly audience of a hundred persons seemed to make this possible in time. The service and the choir were inexpensively conducted! I played the cabinet organ, Seymour Severance sang tenor, Sibley bass, a niece was the soprano. Mr. Severance, Senior, took up the collection and Mrs. Severance superintended the Sunday School, which under her dispensation was an intellectual and spiritual treat.

An entertainment was projected for monthly expenses and future building, and Mrs. Jarley's Wax Work Show, then (1876) in great popularity in Eastern cities, was chosen as the vehicle. Turnverein Hall was engaged for one night, and longer if we achieved success, so we began rehearsals, I being the only "Mrs. Jarley" to be found. We took only a few of the "stock figures" and descriptions then in use, but we had nearly every notable man and woman in the town to assume the characters in the Historical Chamber and Chamber of Horrors, and in the Chamber of Beauty the belles of Los Angeles were assembled, drawing to the audience all the beaux within twenty miles. I wrote my speeches of introduction, prose and verse, by day and by night, and we made preparations for many original characters in order to give me a chance for allusions to local politics, town history, and harmless California gossip. I padded myself into an elderly figure, wore a wig and spectacles, and, as a final sacrifice to art, covered one of my teeth near the front with a piece of court plaster. I was hideous, but I was broad comedy, and I believe that I was "funny." I have taken part in many modern successes and not a few failures, but in no such dazzling achievement as this Wax Work Show became, most unexpectedly, to all concerned. The first-night audience returned *en masse* for the second, and the third and fourth brought no reduction in numbers. The introduction of several new figures daily, and the writing of material for chats with the audience, with the borrowing and making of costumes, taxed all our energies, but we were exhilarated beyond measure by the apparent glory of our performance.

I remember a dark, swarthy man sitting on the front

bench, who nightly gazed at me with a kind of sad but profound interest. He turned out to be Captain Jack Crawford, the poet scout of the Sierras, who was in Los Angeles waiting for a free night to engage Turnverein Hall for his own spectacular entertainment. On the fourth night we concluded that we had not sufficient strength to coruscate before another audience that season, and announced our farewell. My friends had all along disapproved of my comedy "make-up" and begged me to use some subterfuge to appear in my own person. I adopted the idea of going through the performance as usual until the intermission preceding the showing of the Chamber of Beauty. Then I appeared as the daughter of Mrs. Jarley, explaining that my mother had gone heroically through the three preceding nights of excitement, but had finally succumbed to fatigue, and I was obliged to take her place at a moment's notice. My neighbors had provided a pale blue taffeta dress with flounces, pink silk stockings and slippers, a lovely little poke bonnet of blue with rosebuds on the crown, and an enchanting flowered scarf to throw over my shoulders.

When I appeared as a proper blonde, minus my black wig, with my own teeth all in place and the padding removed from my figure, there was an amazed, glad roar from the strangers and a frenzy of delight among my friends. By abruptness of contrast I could have stood momentarily for a professional beauty. The wax figures all helped in the dramatic effect, some of them melting into apparently helpless heaps with admiration, and the two footmen (the Severance brothers) who had lifted the figures in and out, and wound them up for action, pretended to be so spellbound by my appearance that they forgot their duties, greatly amusing the audience and inducing roars of laughter.

The next morning Captain Jack Crawford wrote me a courteous letter, saying that if I did not object to appearing in the make-up of an Indian princess he would like to engage me as his leading lady! This was one more of the strange roads to notoriety, if not to fame and fortune, that I decided not to tread!

Studies and long days of practice with the children, an appointment as special musical assistant by Miss Marwedel, at a salary of ten dollars a month, lectures four times a week, filled the following months to repletion. I had no moment of leisure to remember the triumphs of Mrs. Jarley and her Wax Works, for I was living in a world of children. I knew, indeed, the Mayor of the city and the Governor of the State, but I knew much better the egotistic Edgar, the graceful Bertha, the stodgy Jane, and the willful Jimmy of our own little flock.

The date of the training-school graduation approached. The children were to be an integral part of it, as Miss Marwedel thought in no other way could we so clearly illustrate the theory we were so anxious to popularize. When the great day came, the house and piazzas and garden were filled with parents, teachers, and interested persons, but inside the two schoolrooms chaos secretly reigned. My fellow-student, Miss H., had tonsillitis, and Miss S. was paralyzed with fear at taking her place.

Miss Marwedel's white dimity dress had not come back from the laundry, so, while Mr. Severance went to seek the missing garment, would Mrs. Severance graciously explain Froebel's method of education to the waiting audience?

Edgar, true to type, gladly offered his services in all these directions, and, when we explained that they were a trifle out of his range, he hotly declined to beat the drum for the entrance march. It might be explained that we had found the drum to be the only efficient substitute for the otherwise unceasing flow of Edgar's suggestions and activities. When drumming, his physical and mental operations were confined to the instrument, though even then strangers might conceive that Edgar hired the house, paid the rent, gathered the children, employed Miss Marwedel, and very likely had introduced Froebel's educational method into Los Angeles.

I had suspected Edgar's agony if some one else should really supplant him at the head of the line, so with a magnificent gesture I hung his beautiful soldier's cap, with its enormous tissue tassel, on a bust of Pestalozzi in one corner, and took the drum from the shelf, saying, "I will lead you in myself, children," at the same time taking a few timid steps and tapping the instrument feebly.

It was enough! Edgar tore the leader's cap from Pestalozzi's head, dragged the drum from my willing grasp, and, with the air of a Wellington or a Napoleon, opened the door of the smaller schoolroom where we were gathered, and the long line of lovely children entered the audience-room, while Miss Marwedel in her chamber above was donning the white dimity and I was at my usual place at the piano.

The students in training were each to read a brief theme, but my individual part of the graduating exercises was the management of the songs and circle games, entirely unrehearsed, of course, and played according to the daily inspirational method. I was also to tell the story; but as the afternoon wore on, Miss H., now totally dumb, and Miss Marwedel, distraught by her stiffly starched dress, which engendered strange projections when standing, and upward swoops when sitting down, it seemed as if the graduation were composed entirely of Edgar and Me. To make matters worse, Miss Marwedel whispered a request that I should say her farewell words to the audience in her place, as the starched dimity was now not merely recalcitrant, but positively aggressive.

"Say to them," she murmured, "that I am fatigued and enfeebled by the heat. Say to them some of the things I have so faithfully taught you, and tell them that you are my assistant and are familiar with my method of your so-difficult English speech! Then play the march at once and let the so-serviceable Edgar lead the dear children to the piazza to rejoin their parents. (Such agreeable persons, the parents! Mr. Smith thanked me for Edgar's development.) Mrs. Severance will no doubt bring some of them to introduce to me. I will sit in this large chair, and, if you will put the heavy German-English dictionary in my lap, it would perhaps relieve me of some of my difficulties — yes? I do not like the Chinese method of laundry."

The graduation was over, and, if I had been a prima donna engineered by a publicity department, no one (save Edgar) could have been so eternally in the center of the stage; but I had my diploma; and if it did not describe me as the source of prodigious power and learning, it did mean that I had a profession; that my feet were set upon a most beautiful path, full of charm, of gayety, and of real service to the world if only I proved myself worthy.

For my first experiment I rented a most lovely old adobe house in Santa Barbara called "The Swallow's Nest," on a quiet street bordered with eucalyptus trees and blooming with rose-gardens. It had a charming space for playground and a long veranda, and when my twenty-five rush-bottomed red chairs, each with its movable table, were put in place, all my working materials tucked away in a great cupboard, and a few pictures hung, not even Alexander Selkirk himself could have exclaimed with greater joy and pride:

"I am monarch of all I survey,
　My right there is none to dispute."

Then I began to learn and to grow; then I began to use my psychology, study human nature, and learn the difference between one child and another; then my sister joined me for the hour of work between twelve and one o'clock. After the departure of the younger children, we taught reading and writing to those of six years, at the request of ambitious parents who believed these subjects the only key to knowledge.

I approach this theme with embarrassment, because, as a matter of fact, I never did, and am sure I never could, teach a child to read. We had a much-recommended book entitled "Reading Without Tears." It is true that there were no tears, but neither was there any reading. To this day I am haunted by the weary, pathetic, boring spectacle of a certain Alpheus Van Valkenberg, standing daily by my side, and, after several weeks of alphabetical instruction, use of building blocks, combined with the "word method," reading correctly:

"Up, up, my boy!
　Day is not the time for sleep."

My heart beat high with joy until I discovered that he was holding the book upside down! Some fond friend or parent must have given Alpheus private instruction. I am providing him with his right name, because I hope that he did not die young and may see this book and realize my penitence; though there is the tragic supposition that he made an infantile vow never to learn to read because I made the art so obnoxious.

We were a very happy family in "The Swallow's Nest" that summer, and we taught one another more than any of us realized. The only lack I ever felt was that I longed consciously for a larger group of children, and I had a vision of how wonderful it would be to plant a child-garden in some dreary, poverty-stricken place in a large city, a place swarming with unmothered, undefended, under-nourished child-life.

This was the vaguest of visions, for I had never had the smallest experience with crowded neighborhoods, or with any but carefully brought up, well-trained, silk-stockinged children, not even having attended a large public school myself, with its varied types of foreign birth or foreign parentage.

Had I known it, at this very time the way was opening for me to do the thing for which I was half-consciously groping.

Felix Adler, the noted preacher, teacher, lecturer, author, philanthropist, came to San Francisco from New York in the summer of 1878, and in a brief visit gathered a company of men and women interested in education, forming a board of directors, which raised sufficient money to rent a building and assume the task of opening the first free kindergarten west of the Rocky Mountains. There were but few trained kindergartners from whom to choose and I was called from Santa Barbara to organize the work.

How gladly I packed my belongings and set out alone and unattended to undertake that Herculean task! How little I knew of what was to be done and how best to do it! I was only a girl, but I felt that a kingdom awaited me in that unknown city. I cannot do better than include a small part of that life in these pages; for the youth, the heart, the soul of such an experience cannot be easily re-created after a long lapse of time. The first distinct emotions set down freely, soon after the events occurred, are fresher and have a certain element of revelation.

These marvelous experiments of ourselves with the world, or with such a fraction of it as we have chanced to meet, have a glow at the beginning that we fail wholly to recapture at the end, for they were bathed in the "light that never was, on sea or land." The past is irradiated by the imagination if it has been a happy past, while the present is shadowed by fuller knowledge, experience, and self-consciousness — perhaps, too, with a sense of the failure of our highest ideals. My "career" was rather like that of the famous White Knight in Lewis Carroll's "Through the Looking Glass." You remember that he fell off behind when the horse started, in front when it stopped, and now and then sideways for a change. My falls and my remountings are all pictured in the following pages.

The scene is a long, busy street in San Francisco. Innumerable small shops lined it from north to south; horsecars, always crowded with passengers, hurried to and fro; narrow streets intersected the broader one, these built up with small dwellings, most of them rather neglected by their owners. In the middle distance were other narrow streets and alleys where taller houses stood, and the windows, fire-escapes, and balconies of these added great variety to the landscape, as the families housed there kept most of their effects on the outside during the long dry season.

Still farther away were the roofs, chimneys, and smokestacks of mammoth buildings — railway sheds, freight depots, power-houses, and the like — with finally a glimpse of docks and wharves and shipping. This, or at least a considerable section of it, was the kingdom. To the ordinary beholder it might have looked ugly, crowded, sordid, undesirable, but it appeared to be none of these things to the lucky person who had been invested with some sort of modest authority in its affairs.

The throne from which the lucky person viewed the empire was humble enough. It was the highest of the tin-shop steps at the corner of Silver and Third Streets; odd place for a throne, but one commanding a fine view of the inhabitants, their dwellings, and their business pursuits. The activities in plain sight were somewhat limited in variety, but the signs sported the names of nearly every nation upon the earth.

The Shubeners, Levis, Ezekiels, and Appels were generally in tailoring or second-hand furniture and clothing, while the Raffertys, O'Flanagans, and McDougalls dispensed liquor. All the most desirable sites were occupied by saloons, for it was practically impossible to quench the thirst of the neighborhood.

There were also in evidence barbers, joiners, plumbers, grocers, fruit-sellers, bakers, and venders of small wares, and there was the largest and most splendidly recruited army of do-nothings that the sun ever shone upon. These forever-out-of-workers, leaning against every lamp-post, fence-picket, corner house, and barber-pole in the vicinity, were all male, but they were mostly mated to women fully worthy of them, their wives doing nothing with equal assiduity in the back streets hard by. — Stay, they did one thing, they added copiously to the world's population; and, indeed, it seemed as if the families in the community that ought to have had few children, or none at all (for the country's good), had the strongest prejudice against race suicide.

Well, there was the kingdom and there were the dwellers therein, and the lucky person on the steps was a girl. She did not know at first that it was a kingdom, and the kingdom never at any time would have recognized itself under that name, for it was anything but a sentimental neighborhood. The girl was somewhat too young for the work she was going to do, and considerably too inexperienced, but she had a kindergarten diploma in her pocket, and, being an ardent follower of Froebel, she thought a good many roses might blossom in the desert of Tar Flat, the rather uneuphonious name of the kingdom.

Here the discreet anonymity of the third person must be cast aside, for I was the girl, and the modest chronicle of my early educational and philanthropic adventures must be told after the manner of other chronicles.

The building in Silver Street, which I hoped was to be the scene of such beautiful and inspiring doings as had been seldom observed on this planet, was pleasant and commodious. It had been occupied by two classes of an overcrowded primary school, which had now been removed to a fine modern building. The two rooms rented for this pioneer free kindergarten of the Pacific Coast were in the second story, but were large and sunny. A broad flight of twenty wooden steps led from the street to the first floor and a long stairway connected that floor with the one above.

The first few days after my arrival in San Francisco were spent in the installing of stove, piano, tables, benches, and working materials, and then the beautifying began, the creation of a room so attractive and homelike, so friendly in its atmosphere, that its charm would be felt by every child who entered. Inspiration to cleanliness and courtesy, by furnishing an atmosphere of beauty and shining neatness everywhere, was my thought. A child may note for the first time that his hands are dirty when dainty, bright-colored working materials are given him. Will he be as likely to roar and shout if he is always spoken to in tones that are musical? Beauty of tone, of color, and of line appeal to him unfailingly. Children's souls are starved for the want of these things in crowded, untidy, noisy, ugly neighborhoods, with their squabbles and fights, their foul smells, their rudeness and vulgarity.

I was a stranger in a strange city, my only acquaintances

being the trustees of the newly formed Association. These naturally had no technical knowledge (I am speaking of the Dark Ages, when there were but two or three trained kindergartners west of the Rocky Mountains), and the practical organization of things — a kindergarten of fifty children in active operation — this was my department. When I had anything to show them, they were eager and willing to help; meantime they could and did furnish the sinews of war, standing sponsors to the community for the ideals of education we were endeavoring to represent. Here is where the tin-shop steps came in. I sat there very often in those sunny days of late July, 1878, dreaming dreams and seeing visions; plotting, planning, hoping, believing, forecasting the future. "Hills peeped o'er hills and Alps on Alps."

I take some credit to myself that when Settlements and Neighborhood Guilds were as yet almost unknown, I had an instinct that they furnished the right way to work.

"This school," I thought, "must not be an exotic, a parasite, an alien growth, a flower of beauty transplanted from a conservatory and shown under glass; it must have its roots deep in the neighborhood life, and there my roots must be also. No teacher, be she ever so gifted, ever so consecrated, can sufficiently influence the children under her care for these few hours a day, unless she can gradually persuade the parents to be her allies. I must find then the desired fifty children under school age (six years in California) and I must somehow keep in close relation with the homes from which they come."

How should I get in intimate touch with this strange, puzzling, foreign community, this big mass of poverty-stricken, intemperate, overworked, lazy, extravagant, ill-assorted humanity leavened here and there by a God-fearing, thrifty, respectable family?

Buying and borrowing were my first two aids to fellow-ship. I bought my luncheon at a different bakery every day and my glass of milk at a different dairy. At each visit I talked, always casually, of the new kindergarten, and gave its date of opening, but never solicited pupils. I bought pencils, crayons, and mucilage of the local stationers; brown paper and soap of the grocers; hammers and tacks of the hardware man. I borrowed many things, returned them soon, and thus gave my neighbors the satisfaction of being helpful.

To each craftsman in the vicinity I showed the particular branch of kindergarten handiwork that might appeal to him, whether laying of patterns in sticks and tablets, weaving, drawing, rudimentary efforts at designing, folding and cutting of paper, or clay modeling.

I had the great advantage of making all of my calls in shops, and thus I had not the unpleasant duty of visiting people's houses uninvited, nor the embarrassment of being treated as peddlers of patronage and good advice are apt to be treated. Besides, in many cases the shops and homes (Heaven save the mark!) were under one roof, and children scuttled in and out, behind and under the counters and over the thresholds into the street. They were all agog with curiosity and so were the women.

I know, by long experience with younger kindergartners and social workers in after years, that this kind of "visiting" presents many perplexities to persons of a certain temperament, but I never entered any house where I felt the least sensation of being out of place. I don't think this flexibility is a gift of especially high order, nor that it would be equally valuable in all walks of life, but it is of great service in this sort of work. Whether I sat in a stuffed chair or on a nail keg or an inverted washtub, it was always equally agreeable to me. The "getting into relation" perfectly, and without the loss of a moment, gave me a sense of mental and spiritual exhilaration. I never had to adapt myself elaborately to a strange situation in order to be in sympathy. My one idea was to keep the situation simple and free from embarrassment to any one; to be as completely a part of it as if I had been born there; to be helpful without being intrusive; to show no surprise whatever happened; above all, to be cheerful, strong, and bracing, not weakly sentimental.

As the day of opening approached, an unexpected and valuable aide-de-camp appeared on the scene. An American girl of twelve or thirteen slipped in at the front door one day when I was practicing children's songs, whereupon the following colloquy ensued:

"What's this place goin' to be?"

"A kindergarten."

"What's that?"

Explanations suited to the questioner followed.

"Can I come in afternoons, on my way home from school, and see what you do?"

"Certainly."

"Can I stay now and help around?"

"Yes, indeed, I should be delighted."

"What's the plants and flowers for?"

"What are all flowers for?" I demanded.

"But I thought 'twas a school."

"It is, but it's a new kind."

"Where's the books?"

"The children are going to be under six; we shan't have reading and writing."

We sat down to work together, marking out and cutting brown-paper envelopes for the children's sewing or weaving, binding colored prints with gold paper and putting them on the wall with thumb-tacks, and arranging all the kindergarten materials tidily on the shelves of the closets.

From that moment the Corporal, as I called her, was a stanch ally, and there was seldom a day in the coming years when she did not faithfully perform all sorts of unofficial duties, attaching herself passionately to my service with the devotion of a mother or an elder sister. She proved at the beginning a kind of traveling agent for the school, haranguing mothers on the street corners and addressing the groups of curious children who gathered at the foot of the school steps.

"You'd ought to go upstairs and see the *inside* of it!" she would exclaim. "There's a canary bird, there's fishes swimmin' in a glass bowl, there's plants bloomin' on the winder sills, there's a pianner, and more'n a million pictures! There's closets stuffed full o' things to play and work with, and there's a room with red rings painted on the floor and they're goin' to march and have games on 'em. She can play the pianner standin' up or settin' down, without lookin' at her hands to see where they're goin'. She's goin' to wear white, two a week. I tell her the children 'round here's awful dirty, and she says the cleaner she is the cleaner they'll be. . . . No, 'tain't goin' to be no Sunday School," said the voluble Corporal, "nor no Mission, nor no Lodge! It's a new kind of a school, that's all I know, and next Monday'll see it goin' full blast!"

XIII

LEARNING TO TEACH

It was somewhat in this fashion that I walked joyously into the heart of a San Francisco slum, and began experimenting with my newly learned panaceas.

These were early days. The kindergarten theory of education was on trial for its very life. I simply stepped into a cockleshell and put out into an unknown ocean, where all manner of derelicts needed help and succor. It was an experience of which I had heretofore known nothing; with lives miserable, sometimes entirely overburdened, and often criminal.

My cockleshell managed to escape shipwreck, and took its frail place among the other craft that sailed in its company. I hardly saw or felt the safety of the harbor or the shore for three years, the three years out of my whole life the most wearying, the most heart-searching, the most discouraging, the most inspiring; also, I dare say, the best worth living.

"Full blast," the Corporal's own expression, exactly described the setting out of the cockleshell; that is, the eventful Monday morning when the first free kindergarten west of the Rockies threw open its doors.

The neighborhood was enthusiastic in presenting its offspring at the altar of educational experiment, and we might have enrolled a hundred children had there been room. I was to have no assistant, and had provided seats only for forty-five, which prohibited a list of more than fifty at the outside. A convert to any inspiring idea being anxious to immolate herself on the first altar which comes in the path of duty, I carefully selected the children best calculated to show to the amazed public the regenerating effects of the kindergarten method, and as a whole they were unsurpassed specimens.

Of the forty who were accepted the first morning, thirty appeared to be either indifferent or willing victims, while ten were quite the reverse. These screamed if the maternal hand were withdrawn, bawled if their hats were taken away, and bellowed if they were asked to sit down. This rebellion led to their being removed to the hall by their mothers, who spanked them vigorously and returned them to me each time in a more unconquered state, with their lung power quite unimpaired, and their views of the New Education still vague and distorted. As the mothers were uniformly ladies with ruffled hair, snapping eyes, high color, and short temper, I could not understand the children's fear of me, a mild young thing "in white" — as the Corporal would say; but they evidently preferred the ills they knew.

When the last mother led in the last freshly spanked child and said as she prepared to leave: "Well, I suppose they might as well get used to you one time as another, so good-day, Miss, and God help you!" I felt that my woes were greater than I could bear, for, as the door closed, several infants who had been quite calm began to howl in sympathy with their suffering brethren. Then the door opened again and the Corporal's bright face appeared in the crack.

"Goodness!" she ejaculated, "this ain't the kind of school I thought 'twas goin' to be! — Miss Kate," she whispered, turning to me, "I've got the whole day off for my uncle's funeral, and as he ain't buried till three o'clock I thought I'd better run in and see how you was gettin' on!"

"You are an angel, Corporal!" I said. "Take all the

THE AUTHOR IN HER KINDERGARTENING DAYS

howlers down in the yard and let them play in the sand tables till I call you."

When the queue of weeping babes had been sternly led out by the Corporal, something like peace descended upon the room, but there could be no work for the moment because the hands were too dirty. Coöperation was strictly Froebelian, so I selected with an eagle eye several assistants from the group — the brightest-eyed, best-tempered, and the cleanest. With their help I arranged the seats, the older children at the back tables and the babies in the front. Classification was difficult, as many of them did not know their names, their ages, their sexes, nor their addresses, but I had succeeded in getting a little order out of chaos by the time the Corporal appeared again.

"They've all stopped cryin' but Hazel Golly, and she ran when I wa'n't lookin', but anyway she ain't no loss. I know, for I live next door to her. — What'll we do next?"

"Scrub!" I said firmly. "I want to give them some of the easiest work, but we can't touch the colored cards until all the hands are clean. — Shall we take soap and towels and all go down into the yard where the sink is, children, and turn up our sleeves and have a nice wash?" (Some of the infants had doubtless started from home in a tolerable state of cleanliness, but all signs had disappeared *en route*.)

The proposition was greeted amiably. "Anything rather than sit still!" is the mental attitude of a child under six!

"I told you just how dirty they'd be," murmured the Corporal. "But I never expected to get this chance to scrub any of 'em."

"It's only the first day; — wait till *next* Monday," I urged.

"I shan't be here to see it *next* Monday morning," my

young friend replied. "We can't bury Uncle *every* week!" (This with a sigh of profound regret!)

Many days were spent in learning the unpronounceable names of my flock and in keeping them from murdering one another until Froebel's justly celebrated "law of love" could be made a working proposition. It was some time before the babies could go downstairs in a line without precipitating one another head foremost by furtive kicks and punches. But better days were near at hand, and the children themselves brought them; they only needed to be shown how, but you may well guess that in the early days of what was afterwards to be known as "The Kindergarten Movement on the Pacific Coast," when the Girl and her Kingdom first came into active communication with each other, the question of discipline loomed rather large!

I had many Waterloos in my term of generalship, and many a time was I a feeble enough officer of "The Kids' Guards," as the kindergarten was translated in Tar Flat by those unfamiliar with the German word.

The flock was at the foot of the stairs one morning at eleven o'clock when there was a loud fire alarm in the immediate vicinity. No doubt existed in the mind of any child as to the advisability of remaining at the seat of learning. They started down the steps for the fire in a solid body, with such unanimity and rapidity that I could do nothing but save the lives of the younger ones and keep them from being trampled upon while I watched the flight of their elders. I was left with two lame boys, and four babies so fat and bow-legged that they probably never had reached, nor ever would reach, a fire while it was still burning.

Pat Higgins, aged five and a half, the leader of the line, had a sudden pang of conscience at the corner and ran back to ask me artlessly if he might "go to the fire."

"Certainly not," I answered firmly. "On the contrary, please stay here with the lame and the fat, while *I* go to the fire and bring back the other children."

I then pursued the errant flock, and, recovering most of them, marched them back to the schoolroom, meeting Judge Solomon Heydenfelt, President of the new Kindergarten Association, on the steps. He had been awaiting me for ten minutes, and it was his first visit! He had never seen a kindergarten before, either returning from a fire or otherwise, and there was a moment of embarrassment, but I had a sense of humor and fortunately he enjoyed the same blessing. Only very young teachers who await the visits of supervisors in shuddering expectancy can appreciate this episode.

The days grew brighter and more hopeful as winter approached. I gradually grew into closer relation with some homes than others, and I soon had half a dozen five-year-olds who came to the kindergarten clean, and, if not whole, well darned and patched. One of these could superintend a row of babies at their outline-sewing, thread their needles, untangle their everlasting knots, and correct the mistakes made in the design by the jabbing of wrong holes in the card. Another was very skillful at weaving and proved a good assistant in that occupation.

The improvement in these "little teachers" in capacity, as well as in manner, voice, speech, and behavior, was almost supernatural, and it was only less obvious in the rank and file. At the end of six weeks, when various members of the Board of Trustees began to drop in for their second visit, they were almost frightened by our attractive appearance.

"The subscribers will think the children come from Nob Hill," one of them exclaimed. "Are you *sure* you took the most needy in every way?"

"Quite sure. I have wished sometimes that I had selected humanity as it ran, good, bad, and indifferent, instead of choosing children from the most discouraging homes. I thought, of course, that they were going to be little villains. Some of them ought to be, if there is anything either in heredity or environment, but just look at them at this moment—forty pretty-near-angels, that's what they are!" (I remember reading a line somewhere: "He saw all his enterprises milk-white, rose-bright!" So, always, did I!)

California children are apt to be fine specimens; still, I refuse to believe that any other company of children in the universe was ever so piquantly interesting as those of the Silver Street Kindergarten, particularly the never-to-be-forgotten "first forty."

Many years have passed, but if I were a portrait painter I could reproduce on canvas every nose, eye, smile, hand, curl of hair, in that first group. I often close my eyes to call up the picture, and almost every child falls into his old seat and answers to his right name. Here are a few sketches of those in the front row:

Willy Beer, dubbed "Wriggly" Beer by the older boys in his street, because of a slight nervous affection that kept him in a state of perpetual motion. He was not uncomely; indeed, when I was telling a story it was a pleasure to watch his face all twitching with interest; first nose, then eyes, then mouth, till the delight spread to his fat hands, which clasped and unclasped as the tale proceeded. His mother sent me this unique letter when he had been with me a month:

Yung Lady:
  Willy seems to be onto his foot most of the time. These is all the butes Willy will half to Krissmus. Can you learn him settin' down? Respeckfully,

                                                    MRS. BEER

Hansanella Dorflinger now claims attention.

Hansanella sounds like one word, but they were twins, and thus introduced to me by a large, incoherent boy who brought them to the kindergarten. He was in a hurry and left them at my door with scant ceremony, save the frequent repetition of the watchword "Hansanella."

After some difficulty I succeeded in deciding which was Hans and which was Ella, though there was practically no difference between them excepting that the ash-blond hair of Hans was cropped still more closely than that of Ella.

They had light blue glassy eyes, too far apart, thin lips, chalky skins, and perennial colds in the head. They breathed together, smiled and wept together, rose and sat down together, and wiped their noses together — none too frequently. Never were such "twinneous" twins as Hansanella, and it was ridiculous to waste two names on them, for there was not between them personality enough for one child.

When I requested Ella to be a pony, it immediately became a span, for she never moved without Hans. If the children chose Hans for the father-bird, Ella intrusively and suffragistically fluttered into the nest, too, sadly complicating the family arrangements. They seldom spoke, but sat stolidly beside each other, laying the same patterns with dogged pertinacity.

One morning a new little boy joined our company. As was often the case, he was shy about sitting down. It would seem as if the spectacle of forty children working tranquilly together would convince new applicants that the benches contained no dynamite, but they always parted with their dilapidated hats as if they never, in the nature of things, could hope to see them again, and the very contact of their persons with the benches evoked an uncontrollable wail, which seemed to say: "It is all up with us now! Let the portcullis fall!"

The new boy's eye fell on Hansanella and he suddenly smiled broadly.

"Sit mit Owgoost!" he said.

"We haven't any 'August,'" I responded; "that is Hans Dorflinger."

"Sit mit Owgoost," he repeated thickly and firmly.

"Is this boy a friend of yours, Hans?" I inquired, and the twins nodded blandly.

"Is your other name August, Hans?"

This apparently was too complicated a question for the combined mental activities of the pair, and they lapsed comfortably into their ordinary state of coma.

The Corporal finally found the boy who originally foisted upon our Paradise these two dullest human beings that ever drew breath. He explained that I had entirely misunderstood his remarks. He said that he heard I had accepted Hans an' Ella Dorflinger, but they had moved with their parents to Oakland; and, as they could not come, he thought it well to give the coveted places to August and Anna Olsen, whose mother worked in a box-factory and would be glad to have the children looked after.

"What's de matter mit 'em?" he asked anxiously. "Ain't dey goot?"

"Oh, yes, they are good," I replied; adding mysteriously, "If two children named August and Anna allow you to call them Hansanella for five weeks without comment, it isn't likely that they would be very fertile in evil-doing!"

How can I describe Jacob Lavrowsky? There chanced to be a row of little Biblical characters, mostly prophets, sitting beside one another about halfway back in the room — Moses, Jeremiah, Ezekiel, Elijah, and Elisha, but the greatest of these was Jacob. He was one of ten children, the offspring of a couple who kept a second-hand clothing establishment in the vicinity. Mr. and Mrs. Lavrowsky collected, mended, patched, sold, and exchanged cast-off wearing apparel, and the little Lavrowskys played about in the rags, slept under the counters, and ate Heaven knows where, during the term of my acquaintance with them. Jacob differed from all the others of my flock by possessing a premature, thoroughly unchildlike sense of humor. He regarded me as one of the most unaccountable human beings he had ever met, but he had such respect for what he believed to be my good basic qualities that he constantly tried to conceal from me his feeling that I was probably a little insane.

He had large, expressive eyes, a flat nose, wide mouth, thin hair, long neck, and sallow skin, while his body was so thin and scrawny that his clothes always hung upon him in shapeless folds. His age was five and his point of view that of fifty. As to his toilettes, there must have been a large clothes-bin in the room back of the shop and Jacob must have daily dressed himself from this, leaning over the side and plucking from the varied assortment such articles as pleased his errant fancy. He had no prejudices against bits of feminine attire, often sporting a dark green cashmere basque trimmed with black velvet ribbon and gilt buttons. It was double-breasted and, when it surmounted a pair of trousers cut to the right length, but not altered in width, the effect would have startled any more exacting community than ours.

Jacob was always tired and went through his tasks rather languidly, greatly preferring work to play. All diversions, such as marching and circle games, struck him as pleasant enough, but childish, and, if participated in at all, to be gone through with in an absent-minded and supercilious manner. There were moments when his exotic little personality, standing out from all the rest like an infant Artful Dodger or a caricature of Beau Brummel, seemed to make him wholly alien to the group, yet he was docile and obedient, his only fault being a tendency to strong and highly colored language.

To make the marching more effective and develop a better sense of time, I instituted a very simple and rudimentary form of orchestra with a triangle, a tambourine, and finally a drum. When the latter instrument made its first appearance, Jacob sought a secluded spot by the piano and gave himself up to a fit of fairly courteous but excessive mirth. "A drum!" he exclaimed, between his fits of laughter. "What'll yer have next? This is a h——l of a school."

Now comes the darling of the group, the heart's-ease, the none-such, the Rose of Erin, the lovely, the indescribable Rosaleen Clancy.

We were all working busily and happily one morning when a young woman tapped at the door and led in that flower and pearl of babyhood, the aforesaid Rosaleen.

The young woman said she knew that the kindergarten was full, and, indeed, had a long waiting list, but the Clancy family had just arrived from Ireland; that there were two little boys; a new baby twenty-four hours old; Mr. Clancy had not yet found work, and could we take care of Rosaleen even for a week or two?

As I looked at the child the remark that we had not a single vacant seat perished, unborn, on my lips. She was about three and a half years old, and was clad in a straight, loose slip of dark blue wool that showed her neck and arms. A little flat sort of "pork-pie" hat of blue velveteen sat on the back of her adorable head, showing the satiny rings of yellow hair that curled round her ears and clung close to her neck. (No wonder!) She had gray-blue eyes with long upper and under lashes and a perfect mouth that disclosed the pearly teeth usually confined to the heroines of novels. As to her skin, you would say that Jersey cream was the principal ingredient in its composition.

The children had stopped their weaving needles and were gazing open-mouthed at this vision of beauty, though Rosaleen had by no means unmasked all her batteries. She came nearer my chair, and, without being invited, slipped her hand in mine in a blarneyish and delutherin' way not unknown in her native isle. There were dimples in the knuckles, and baby hand though it was, its satin touch had a thrill in it, and responded instantly to my pressure.

"Do you think we can make room for her, children?" I asked.

Every small boy cried rapturously: "Look, Miss Kate! Here's room! I kin scrooge up!" — and hoped the Lord would send Rosaleen his way!

"We can't have two children in one seat," I explained to Rosaleen's sponsor, "because they can't work to good advantage when they're crowded."

"I kin set on the pianner stool!" gallantly offered Billy Prendergast.

"Perhaps I can borrow a little chair somewhere," I said. "Would you like to stay with us, Rosaleen?"

Her only answer (she was richer in beautiful looks than in speech) was to remove her blue velveteen hat and tranquilly place it on my table. If she was lovely with her hair covered, she was still lovelier now; so that no one in the room would have been parted from the newcomer save by fire and the sword.

Two years that miracle of beauty and sweetness, Rosaleen Clancy, stayed with us, just as potent an influence as the birds or the flowers, the stories I told, or the music I coaxed from the little upright piano. Her face was not her only fortune, for she had a heart of gold. Ireland did, indeed, have a grievance when Rosaleen left it for America!

This is just a corner of my portrait gallery, which has dozens of other types hanging on the walls clamoring to be described. Some were lovely and some interestingly ugly; some were like lilies growing out of the mud; others had not been quite so able to energize themselves out of their environment and bore the sad traces of it ever with them; — still, they were all absorbingly interesting beyond my power to paint. Month after month they sat together, working, playing, helping, growing — in a word, learning how to live, and there in the midst of the group was I, learning my life lesson with them. They were naughty and willful sometimes, but, oh! I can remember moments in that room at Silver Street when one might almost hear the beat of angels' wings.

The study and practice of the kindergarten theory of education and of life gave me, while I was still very young, a certain ideal by which to live and work, and it has never faded. We kindergartners built our faith on Wordsworth's immortal Ode, and so, whether richer or poorer, whether for better or worse, in sickness or in health, in prosperity or adversity, we learned never wholly to lose our glimpse of that "celestial light" that in childhood "apparelled meadow, grove and stream, the earth and every common sight": and to hold that attitude of mind and heart which gives to life, even when it is difficult, something of "the glory and the freshness of a dream."

XIV
TEACHING *VERSUS* ACTING

As I look back across the lapse of time, I cannot understand how any creature, however young, strong, or ardent, could have supported the fatigue and strain of that first year! No one was to blame, for the experiment met with appreciation almost immediately, but I was attempting the impossible, and trying to perform the labor of three women.

I soon learned to work more skillfully, but I habitually squandered my powers and lavished on trivial details strength that should have been spent more thriftily. The difficulties of each day could be surmounted only by quick wit, ingenuity, versatility, by the sternest exercise of self-control and by a continual outpour of magnetism. My enthusiasm made me reckless, but I do not grudge a single hour of exhaustion or discouragement. All my pains were just so many birth-pangs, leaving behind them a little more knowledge of human nature, a little wider vision, a little clearer insight, a little deeper sympathy.

There were more than a thousand visitors during the first eighteen months, a circumstance that greatly increased the strain of teaching: for I had to train myself, as well as the children, to as absolute a state of unconsciousness as possible.

Among the earliest and most appreciative friends in the late autumn of 1878 were Professor John Swett and Mrs. Mary W. Kincaid, of the San Francisco Normal School, who thereafter sent down their students two at a time for observation and practical aid. The next important visitor in the spring of 1879 was Mrs. Sarah B. Cooper. She possessed the "understanding heart" and also great executive ability, so that with the help of her large Bible class she was able to open a second free kindergarten on Jackson Street in October, 1879, and until the day of her death worked devotedly and generously toward the development of the second organization, the Golden Gate Kindergarten Association. Her name not only recalls a long and intimate friendship and a talent to which I always paid tribute with every passing day, but it brings back a dramatic incident, a famous heresy trial in the spring of 1880 where I appeared as a witness.

Mrs. Cooper had a Bible class in a Congregational Church in San Francisco. It was held after the morning service, and sometimes called together as many as two or three hundred men and women, old and young. Many of them were strict in creed, but as a whole they were of all shades of belief and their questions were occasionally "radical," but Mrs. Cooper always controlled the situation and answered simply, sincerely, eloquently; also to my mind with true reverence. Such occurrences as the swallowing of Jonah by the whale did not bulk so heavily in the foreground of her theology as more spiritual or practical topics, but they loomed large in the thought of a certain deacon in the church who dropped in to the Bible class frequently and finally made up his mind that it was a dangerous institution.

He was a good man, true to every line of his orthodox creed, constant in attendance at church, and honestly convinced that every word in the Bible must be construed exactly as set down, but he never provided for symbolism nor for individual differences in vocabulary.

Mrs. Cooper's enthusiastic conversion to the kindergarten as a builder of character appeared to increase his dis-

belief in her orthodoxy, and he appeared at my kindergarten on three successive mornings promptly at nine and sat
through the opening exercises. If he expected to find
sixty or eighty infants on their knees in prayer, he was, of
course, disappointed. In the first place, the children were
less than six years old, four and a half being the average
age. The cosmopolitan population of San Francisco furnished us with many nationalities and the parents were of
many religious beliefs, as well, I fear, as of none at all. Our
ultimate ideal was to graft the kindergarten on the public
school system, when after a few years the State law might
be modified as to the proper age for admission to school
privileges. We wanted to surround the children with
ennobling influences, but we did not intend to give specific
instruction on topics unsuited to their age, only confusing
their impressions and blurring their perceptions.

I read pages of Froebel to the unhappy deacon, but in
vain he heard the words: "My plan of education is founded
on religion and must lead to religion." He was bewildered
by Froebel's metaphysics and could not comprehend the
spiritual basis of his educational method.

One of our many morning hymns was:

> "Father, we thank Thee for the night,
> And for the pleasant morning light,
> For food and rest and loving care,
> And all that makes the day so fair.
> Help us to do the things we should,
> To be to others kind and good;
> In all we do, in all we say,
> To grow more loving every day."

The deacon did not care for this, or for any other morning aspiration he heard in any of the kindergartens, so he
finally informed the church officers, and instituted an
inquiry into the orthodoxy of Mrs. Cooper, who had a
thousand ardent friends ready to stand by her, although

she was quite willing to carry on her teaching in another church if it seemed advisable.

I followed the trial in the newspapers with intense interest. It had occupied only two or three evenings, when I was astounded by being called to a meeting and asked to bring several kindergartners with me. We huddled ourselves together in a side pew, knowing that the only questions we should have to answer concerned the stand taken by the kindergarten in the matter of religious education, and we were eager to give testimony. Three of the younger kindergartners went to the space beside the pulpit when called, and repeated or sang the daily morning hymns they were accustomed to use.

How clearly I can see the well-filled church, the crowd of eager faces, the cheeks red with disapproval, the eyes filled with tears of sympathy! And my own were wet as I looked at the young, lovely teachers on the platform — simple, serene, womanly, motherly; all trembling a little at the expected attack on something they held sacred, and, in theory at least, above reproach.

Then I was called to the stand and questioned by the deacon himself. After my citing at his request various quotations from Froebel, all showing a decided spiritual basis of thought, he proceeded to say:

"You and your pupils have given us the forms of verse used in your morning exercises . . . Are you a Christian?"

"I hope I may say that I am, sir."

"Then of what value do you consider a prayer which does not mention the name of Christ?"

I could have answered this in many ways, but the Father of all mercies must have inspired me to reply:

"*What do you think of the Lord's Prayer, sir? Shall I repeat it?*"

The effect on the audience after a few seconds' thought

was electric. I hope I shall never be on the witness stand again, but I glowed with gratitude that my wits did not desert me on that occasion.

There were no more heresy trials. Mrs. Cooper's Bible class naturally doubled in size and the kindergarten spirit spread in every direction so that the desert began to blossom as the rose. I went to the Eastern cities for the three months of my summer vacation and learned by observation and instruction all that I could from my older and wiser contemporaries, Miss Susan Blow, of St. Louis; Dr. Hailmann, of La Porte, Indiana; Mrs. Putnam, of Chicago; the veteran Elizabeth Peabody, of Concord, Massachusetts; General John Eaton (then United States Commissioner of Education), and Miss Garland, of Boston.

The work in the St. Louis kindergartens was especially valuable to me, as it was organized in a way similar to that of my more modest one in San Francisco and had the same ambitions and ideals, although the leadership in St. Louis was unique. Dr. William T. Harris and Miss Susan Blow together made that city the best exposition of large public school kindergartens that the United States has ever seen. Boston was doing an interesting and beautiful work, financially supported for some years by Mrs. Quincy Shaw, and Chicago was a fine example of free and public kindergartens under the leadership of Mrs. Putnam and Elizabeth Harrison, but when Dr. Harris was the Superintendent of Schools and Miss Blow's genius was wholly devoted to the training and supervision of kindergartners, St. Louis was for a considerable period an electric fountain of influence. The metaphysical side of Froebel's philosophy was more developed there than elsewhere because of the extraordinary gifts in that direction of Dr. Harris and Miss Blow; but there was something more than metaphysics: there was complete devotion to the work and an infectious enthusiasm that was unequaled anywhere till we later handed on the torch in San Francisco, and from there up and down the Pacific Coast.

Miss Susan Blow was an imperishable ideal for me, from the time I first met her until she died in 1916. She was a vital force, at once intellectual and spiritual. Enthusiasm and magnetism issued from her in a veritable flood, if those who heard her had trained intelligence and an understanding heart.

I was very grateful and very proud when in later years I received the following note from her after a talk to all the kindergartners of the New York Association and all those from the public schools:

My dear and Gifted Fellow-Worker:

It should make you happy to know that you touched the deepest things in the kindergarten on Monday. Forty years have changed the kindergarten from a consecrated vocation to a profession. It was the spirit of the pioneer work which was sacred and exalted. They were glorious days when we never knew whether the kindergarten would last overnight, and never doubted that it would last forever. How to renew and perpetuate that spirit is the one problem of the Kindergarten Movement. You fired it anew on Monday.

Affectionately yours
Susan E. Blow

My visit to Miss Elizabeth Peabody happily coincided with the first summer of the then famous and much reported Concord School of Philosophy. I was too young and too unprepared for the soaring metaphysics of that body, and had some difficulty in absorbing the evening course on Pre-Existence, into which I was at once ushered; but I had such unequaled opportunities for meetings with remarkable men and women, that I shall give my special reminiscences of the great New Englander in the next chapter.

Returning in the late autumn with the commendation and approval of the leaders of the movement East and West, I opened in 1880 my own California Kindergarten Training-School. I took but four pupils the first season, my sister, Nora Archibald Smith, being one of them. She had just returned from a two years' pioneering excursion on her own account, among the Spanish-speaking children of Mexico and Arizona, and was prepared to be one of the torch-bearers of the new training-school.

The writing and delivery of lectures on kindergarten theory and practice, together with constant study and brief talks at educational conventions here and there, made this a very busy but not at all a monotonous year. Any one who has gone as a bidden guest to small teachers' meetings in country places knows the humors of the roads thither and back. Sometimes my fare was paid one way only, under the conception that I would prefer to end my days in the Paradise where the meeting was in session. Sometimes railway expenses were never mentioned at all, as though beneath the notice of educational idealists. I was sometimes met by a youthful, unmarried deputy superintendent, who, surprised that a person of my age should be talking to my superiors on pedagogical laws, "all but" asked me to be his, and help the cause. One particularly sentimental person introduced me to an audience as a lady "notorious to you all!" I well remember this town, as it had a local newspaper and its editor was absent for the night. The reporter in charge attended our meeting in a slightly bibulous condition. His article next morning was adulatory, but a trifle incoherent. It began (rather informally): "Say, boys! Oh! that kindergarten! Did you see her when she tripped up the aisle with that cute little unhitched topsy-sprig of a bonnet?"

My head was always clothed with dignity, but it was a

long time before any hat of mine failed to be identified by the above quotation.

There were two unexpected intervals of play during this period. In the girlhood days at Santa Barbara before my study of kindergarten I had often taken part in private theatricals. The community took a lively interest in W. D. Howells's brief dramatic sketches suitable for amateurs, and I had been cast for the verbose, light-hearted (and lighter-headed!) heroines of "The Register," "The Parlor Car," and "The Sleeping Car."

In San Francisco I had already played for kindergarten benefits the leading parts in Robertson's "Caste," "Our Boys" and "Our Girls"; also "The Morning Call" and "The Scrap of Paper."

Then came a Charity Carnival in San Francisco; a week-long affair it was, the forerunner of the mammoth bazaars of the present day. I was among those chosen for the little Stratford-on-Avon theater arranged in one corner of the enormous building, and great was my pride when I found that, in the scenes from "The Comedy of Errors," "Hamlet," and "Twelfth Night," I was chosen for the parts of Adriana, Ophelia, and Viola. I look back with some mental agitation on those probably crude and humorous efforts, and can console myself only by hoping that the Dromios, Hamlet, and Petruchio were as painful as my Adriana, Ophelia, and Katherine.

I played Katherine in "The Taming of the Shrew" only as a substitute for an experienced amateur and I had to learn the two scenes chosen for the programme in twenty-four hours. As far as I can remember, I think nobody bothered about rehearsals. The general idea was that Petruchio should stand where he liked and Katherine in whatever space was left for her. "Business" was not out-

THEATRICALS: "A COMEDY OF ERRORS"

lined, save a few suggestions about the value of facial expression, and the necessity of doing something with one's arms, so that they should not hang by one's sides like pump-handles.

I remember pacing up and down the big, bare waiting-room from which the players made their entrance on the stage, and of being arrested in my perpetual walk by a dear old lady who turned out to be the famous Mrs. Judah, one of the grand old women of the California stage who in "Romeo and Juliet" was the greatest "Nurse" of her time. My state of panic would have moved a heart of stone. She took my book and heard me through, commending my voice and reading.

"Where did you get your clothes?" she asked.

"The Committee sent them from the costumer's," I replied. "They were made for Mrs. B., you know. The dress doesn't fit behind, but the stage is small, and I thought I could keep my face to the audience."

"That's all very well, my dear," she remarked ruthlessly, "but your face is as much out of the way as your clothes!"

"You don't think I look like the shrew?" I faltered. "I was afraid I didn't. You see I had to wear my blonde Adriana wig."

"You look like Eva in 'Uncle Tom's Cabin,'" she answered. "Take off the hideous wig, for Heaven's sake! Who ever saw a flaxen Katherine?"

"I have only twenty minutes, dear Mrs. Judah."

"Never mind! You couldn't look worse!" was her comforting assurance.

A fair reproduction of the Indian scalping scene in the first entertainment of my childhood ensued. Help was called in, and every one flew to carry out the great Mrs. Judah's commands.

"That's better, though you are still more like a nice mouse than a shrew," she criticized as she viewed the metamorphosis. "But, after all, you have a fair share of brains, so they probably won't hiss you! There's your cue! Hold your head up! Forget how you look; just be what you're supposed to be, as nearly as you can. Go along, and the Lord help you."

Never while I live shall I forget the trembling voice of our mild and blameless Petruchio saying as his cue on my entrance: "Good morrow, Kate; for that's your name, I hear!"

We were well matched, for if I was a mouse, he was a bleating lamb.

I strode on the stage animated, not, I fear, by the spirit of Katherine, but by the spirit of Mrs. Judah, and, whenever I weakened, I was braced by a glance at her, standing in the wings, with a gesture that meant: "Hold your chin up, and if you can't be fiery, be as fiery as you can!"

I remember my exit, now a raging mouse, so flaming with passion that she felt like a combination of the great Rachel and Charlotte Cushman. I wrenched my hand from Petruchio's flabby grasp as he said: "And kiss me, Kate! We will be married o' Sunday!" and left the stage amid wild applause. I thought it might be an unexpected tribute to genius, but the stage manager said the fact that I swept the piano stool out on my train had its part in the general effect.

I fell into Mrs. Judah's outstretched arms and wept, while she said: "Cheer up! You might have been worse. There were times when you positively acted! Your mouse had its moments of being a tigress. You won't be so bad in Ophelia, and I'll help you through it!"

She did, and the Authors' Carnival ended my Shakespearean performances at once and forever, although I did have just one more chance, much later in life, a chance timidly rejected.

Not long after this, my dear friend Annie Louise Cary, of whom I have written in a previous chapter, made a second visit to San Francisco with an opera company headed by a charming soprano, Marie Roze, and herself.

I was chained to my daily tasks most of the time and too weary for much opera or theater-going in the evenings, but coincident with Miss Cary's visit came a most sensational triumph of Dion Boucicault in his first Irish plays at the Baldwin Theater.

I used often to take three o'clock dinner at the hotel with Miss Cary when there was to be an opera in the evening, and Boucicault was always present, witty — indeed, bewilderingly witty and alert — charming, and full of anecdote. He was even then a distinctly elderly man, but young and debonair in face and figure and spirit. He began to take a special interest in me from a certain day when he boasted facetiously that he could write more good Limericks about the people at the table in fifteen minutes than anybody present.

"Don't be too sure!" laughed Miss Cary. "You don't know what my young friend Kate can do in that line!"

"I said *good* Limericks," he remarked, with a merry Irish wink.

"I *meant* good ones; that's the only kind she writes," retorted Miss Cary.

"Test!" "Tournament!" "Pitched battle!" cried the dozen people at the table, pushing back the dessert plates, clapping their hands, and calling to the waiters for pencils and paper.

I knew that Mr. Boucicault couldn't do anything badly, and, as for myself, various celebrated protagonists of the Limerick were not then even born — Oliver Herford,

Carolyn Wells, Gelett Burgess, and others — against whom I should be sorry to be pitted in the present era.

We began scribbling, exhorting the guests to smoke, or be silent, or to leave us alone until the verses should be handed to the jury.

I may interject the remark that, if I can do anything at all, I can do it quickly.

The umpire called time when the fifteen minutes had passed and Mr. Boucicault and I were each struggling with a last line. With a sigh of despondency he handed in six sheets and groaned with despair when the umpire cried: "Six from the gentleman, eight from the lady! The question of quality will now receive a little consideration from the jury, though quantity was the point mentioned in this memorable contest."

Somebody read the Limericks aloud, amid bursts of laughter from the persons whose charms or foibles had been the subjects chosen. The jury was mostly composed of gentlemen, who were all chivalrous, and they declared, after consultation in a corner, that I had six first-class ones out of eight and Dion Boucicault four out of his six; so the gracious Irishman plucked flowers from the dinner-table, planted a few very unbecomingly in my hair, and sank on one knee beside my chair, laying the bouquet in my lap.

The month in which the opera company and that of Dion Boucicault's players were in San Francisco was a very hectic time for me, for two or three of the principal singers and actors formed a habit of dropping in on my kindergarten, generally during the hour for the story or the singing-games.

The voice-production of infants from four to six years old would not be interesting to an opera singer, and the dramatic features of a child's game might well strike an accomplished actor as a trifle weak; nevertheless, they were fascinated with the little people and with the novelty of the work itself. There was now an assistant teacher, and the children numbered nearly a hundred, of seven or eight different nationalities.

Mr. Boucicault came but twice, and I soon discovered that he called upon Miss Cary at her hotel immediately afterward and, pacing the floor, used strong and abusive language concerning my choice of a vocation. He called the work too fatiguing even for a blacksmith, and said it was brutal to allow a girl to immolate herself on a fantastic and imaginary altar. He was certain that I was overtaxed, physically and nervously, and that my natural gifts, such as they were, were being wasted on the exacting labor that I was doing for seventy-five dollars a month. Accordingly, he and Miss Cary put their heads together, and, much to my astonishment, he offered me the part of Moya in "The Colleen Bawn" and of Kate in "Kerry," at a salary three times larger than the one I was earning, with the inclusion of my mother's traveling expenses.

I think, perhaps, if there had been another trained kindergartner in California to carry on the work I had begun, and which was by this time flourishing like the proverbial green bay tree, this might have been an offer too tempting to refuse. I considered it nominally for twenty-four hours, although I never for a moment had any real doubt as to my decision; then I said to my kind and solicitous friend: "Thank you very much, but there are ever so many people to do Moya and Kate, but for the moment none to play my part here. If I hold to my task, there will soon be other kindergartens and many more hundreds of children in them. I belong where I am, Mr. Boucicault, and, anyway, how could I ever play against such an actor as you? It would be ridiculous!"

"I expected you to play with me, not against me!" he said, with a twinkling eye.

"But what about training, Mr. Boucicault?" I asked wonderingly.

(How well I can see the large marble-topped table in Miss Cary's sitting-room; Mr. Boucicault sometimes leaning over it persuasively, sometimes walking up and down puffing a cigarette, while I sat in a small chair trying to believe that the scene was real.)

"You've made good in amateur theatricals, haven't you?" he questioned.

"Ye-es, I suppose so."

"How many times?"

"Oh, two or three dozen, I should say."

"Well" (disdainfully), "that's certainly a disadvantage, but you're young enough to outgrow it. You see you'd have nearly six weeks on tour in small cities and large towns, before you faced a critical audience. Of course, if I had to 'make' you from the beginning — voice, speech, temperament, feeling, dramatic instinct — I couldn't do it in six weeks, or six years, for that matter, and I shouldn't try."

"I haven't the courage, Mr. Boucicault. I've never even seen a critic, much less acted before one."

"Did your audiences like you? That's the point. Tell the truth now!"

"Yes," I answered, with a good deal of embarrassment. "They always liked me better than I deserved."

"There you are! That's the sort of leading lady I need for simple, natural parts like Kate in 'Kerry,' the sort that the audience always thinks is better than she is — I dare say I think you're better than you really are!"

"I am sure of it," I said, laughing, but wishing desperately to cry at the same moment, "or you'd never have risked asking me to try. Do you remember what Tacitus said about a man of his time?"

"Great Heavens! the girl is making classical allusions! — No — what did he say?"

"That he was esteemed a great man whilst he remained in privacy, and would have been deemed worthy of governing — had he never governed! — No, Mr. Boucicault, I'm sorry, but I cannot, must not take this tremendous leap in the dark. Remember, I not only have a mother and a younger sister, but a brother of fifteen to look after."

And so he kissed my hand gently and kindly and went out to tell Miss Cary the result of our interview.

She came in wiping her eyes and sank into an armchair.

"You're a perfect idiot," she said, "but I'm not so sure but that you've decided wisely. I've been worried all along for fear your features are too small to 'make up' well."

I am much more dazzled by Mr. Boucicault's extraordinary proposition now, when I reflect upon it, than I was then. Any nice girl with good voice and a grain of talent could play Kate in "Kerry," a little gem of a play in which the great comedian was an unforgettable old Irish butler; but I fear I could never have given Moya her delicious Irish accent. At any rate, I said the instinctive "no" and never regretted it.

Dion Boucicault was more than an accomplished and ingratiating actor, more than a good adapter and playwright. He was one of the greatest *raconteurs* and one of the most inimitable conversationalists I ever met. He had known all the great figures of the stage and literature from Rachel down to Wilkie Collins and Charles Reade, with whom he collaborated on a well-known novel, "Foul Play."

He gave a most amusing account of the difference of opinion between Charles Reade and himself in writing this book. The hero and heroine of the novel, you may remember, were wrecked on a desert island and the hero had been very much in love with her before and after the wrecking episode. Now, the hero was a clergyman and, after several boring weeks or months on the island, proposed to marry himself to the heroine, using the church service and alternately asking the questions and reading the answers, putting in the "I wills" wherever needed, and finally blessing the heroine and himself, and pronouncing them man and wife. At least this was Boucicault's idea, foreshadowed in an installment sent to Reade by post. He thought it highly original. Charles Reade agreed with him when they met for discussion, but regarded it as a theory that would be decidedly objectionable and induce an acrimonious argument.

"Of course!" said Boucicault. "That's what we want, don't we? What's the use of writing a novel that nobody talks about?"

"But it's so foolish, so futile," argued Reade. "Who ever heard of a clergyman marrying himself to a woman?"

"Nobody," Boucicault answered, "and that's the delightful part of the idea."

"Probably he couldn't do it," Reade went on; "probably he would be defying both the church and the law. Probably 'Helen,' as we have drawn her, wouldn't lend herself to such an outlandish, melodramatic ceremony."

"All the better!" retorted Boucicault. "Either a clergyman *can* perform the marriage ceremony over himself — in which case we shall be benefactors of the human race, for he won't have to pay the 'other fellow'; or, we shall find that it can't be done, and our hero will have innocently committed a crime. It will be vastly exciting whichever way it turns out."

Nevertheless, the collaborators quarreled, and Charles

Reade finished the novel according to his own ideas, although he allowed the hero to *consider* performing his own marriage ceremony, but deny himself the privilege, for the good of his soul.

As an actor Boucicault was the idol of the San Francisco public at that time. Every seat in the theater was filled and there were always lines of laughing and applauding "standees." His method, if indeed he had any — it seemed sheer magnetism — was one that reached the best seats in the orchestra and the last row in the gallery. Nobody could resist him, for he was as touching in pathos, as tender in love-scenes, as he was in provoking laughter with his inimitable Irish wit. Yes, he was a great actor, and I should have inevitably learned much from him; but I cannot help thinking that I learned more at the tin-shop steps on the corner of Silver and Third Streets in San Francisco, where the children crossed in eddying throngs to a place where they were certain of a welcome. There is a Moorish proverb, you know, which says, "Work for the children is better than pilgrimage or holy war," and I believe it with all my heart.

I append here two brief and characteristic notes of Dion Boucicault's, one to Miss Cary, from Ogden, Utah, and a later one to me, from New York. We had accompanied him to the railway station to say good-bye when he and his company were starting on a long tour eastward, a road tour that would take them through the cities and larger towns between San Francisco and New York. The notes are undated, the first being penciled on the train, but posted at Ogden.

MY DEAR ANNIE LOUISE CARY:

Salt Lake City is before me, and I cannot help reflecting that if I were a Mormon I should invite two at least of my Baldwin Hotel friends to consider the question of plural marriages!

It was good of you to come down to see the poor exile on his road to prison. Solomon, son of David, what a fate!

If I dared to send a message to the charmingest of K's you would not deliver, nor would she listen to it, so I will breathe it to my pillow and whisper it in the night to the alkali dust. Oh, Lord! I wish I were six and twenty and had life to live over again and start afresh. By the way, I feel fresh enough, but the devil of it is I get cut out by the first young fool who has a narrow parting down the middle. (As if hair had anything to do with it!) Such is your sex!

Tell Miss K. that I never felt more flattered than when she set her back up and left the room at that nonsense of mine, when I pretended that her refusal to join my company arose from the fear that she might fall in love with me on better acquaintance. Instead of laughing in my face, she bridled and took it in earnest. That "fetched" me! Since that moment I have been hers to command.

For God's sake tell her to leave off making much of kids and teaching dirty-nosed young hoodlums. Let her shake the dust of San Francisco from her bottines and "go east, young woman!" Good-bye! Keep a little corner in your memory for a "vagabond," who will keep one warm in his heart for you. Manage it so that I may have an early opportunity after your arrival in New York to tell you how sincerely

I am Yours

DION BOUCICAULT

NEW YORK, 6 EAST 15TH STREET
June 16th, 1879 (?)

MY DEAR YOUNG FRIEND:

I must say it again at the risk of boring you — anything seems to me better than the life you are condemning yourself to lead — overworked and miserably paid, if it can be called pay at all.

If you want more advice, and from a woman, why not call in Ada Gilman and obtain from her the true and *inner* statement of what the stage-life is? She is clever, and what is better she is open and truthful. (She has one fault; she aspires to *be*, to *do*, and *suffer*, too much!)

She will tell you more than I can, having passed through all the early stages of the theatrical life. Then write and tell me if she has changed your point of view. I wish she might do so!

The difficulty is with women that they make up their minds in such loose parcels, and tie them with such weak resolutions, that they come undone very easily.

It is, I allow, a very serious and important step for you to take, and if you had a choice between a charming fellow that you liked — who had either fortune, or, better still, brains to make half a dozen — I might say "go for him!" But if there is no such fellow, then the stage is your foreordained world!

I am working fourteen or fifteen hours a day having to produce a play on September 1st, when Booth's Theater opens; and another on October 1st, the first night of the season at Wallack's. Then I appear in November at Wallack's in a new Irish piece and I must have another play ready in case of failure at Booth's! Do you pity me? Not as I pity you, my dear child!

Mind you write me a long letter about yourself, and don't forget to put me in a reserved corner of your heart, labeled

Your very sincere friend
Dion Boucicault

XV

THE CONCORD SCHOOL OF PHILOSOPHY

I SPOKE in the last chapter of my visit to the East for study, observation, and examination, if possible, before the opening of my own Training-School for kindergartners in San Francisco, the establishment of which had everything to do with the progress of the Pacific Coast movement. After St. Louis, Chicago, and Boston, Concord, Massachusetts, was the goal of my ambition, for there were gathered many persons distinguished in educational affairs, and Miss Elizabeth Peabody had invited me to be her guest. She had written:

You must not go back to San Francisco without seeing Concord. You are a hero-worshiper, and we have heroes of all sizes here just now at our great School of Philosophy. Come! we will study psychology, and make up our minds about pre-existence. You say you don't know very much about true Buddhism, metempsychosis, and man's fourfold being; but never mind! You shall slip into a little front seat by my side in the lecture room, you shall drink tea with dear Mr. and Mrs. Emerson, lunch at the Old Manse, and walk with good Bronson Alcott through all the beautiful haunts sacred to the memory of Thoreau. You shall sit at the feet of the Minute-Man with his famous young sculptor, Daniel Chester French, and he will doubtless make your heart beat with patriotism as he conducts you over the historic battle-fields. I am sure that in my life, as our favorite Mr. Emerson says, "the one event which never loses its romance is the encounter with superior persons on terms allowing the happiest intercourse." We are all old fogies in the house, and we want a fresh, young mind to help us with its happy intuitions. Come!

Yours

E. P. P.

P.S. You shall sleep in Charlotte Cushman's nightgown. She left it to me in her will.

The Concord School of Philosophy opened its first session in that summer of 1879. The dust of late July lay deep on all the highways; or, stirred by the passing wheel, rose in clouds, somewhat like the transcendental haze which filled the mental atmosphere.

Of those who had made Concord one of the homes of the soul, Hawthorne and Thoreau had been dead many years — I saw their graves in Sleepy Hollow; and Margaret Fuller had perished long ago by shipwreck on Fire Island Beach. But Bronson Alcott was still alive, though Louisa, his still more famous daughter, was in Boston and did not appear at the School. Dr. William Ellery Channing — Thoreau's biographer — was there, and F. B. Sanborn; above all, the "Sage of Concord," "the friend and aider of those who would live in the spirit," still walked his ancient haunts; his mind in many ways yet unimpaired, though sadly troubled by the failure of verbal memory. It was an instance of pathetic irony that, in his lecture on "Memory" delivered in the Town Hall, he was prompted constantly by his daughter Ellen.

Mr. F. B. Sanborn, Secretary of the School, was well known through his contributions to Concord history and biography. He was for years one of the literary staff of "The Springfield Republican" and active in many reform movements. Almost from his house John Brown started on his Harper's Ferry raid, and people in Concord still dwelt upon the exciting incident of Mr. Sanborn's arrest in 1860, as an accessory before the fact.

The School assembled in the Orchard House, formerly the residence of Mr. Alcott, on the Lexington Road. Next door was the Wayside, Hawthorne's home for a number of years, a cottage overshadowed by the hillside that rose behind it, thick with hemlocks and larches. On the ridge of this hill was Hawthorne's "outdoor study," a footpath worn by his own feet, as he paced back and forth and thought out the plots of his romances. In 1879, when I was in Concord, the Wayside was tenanted by George Parsons Lathrop, who married Hawthorne's daughter Rose. He had already published his "Study of Hawthorne" and a volume of poems, "Rose and Rooftree." His first novel, "An Echo of Passion," was yet to come.

After my brief journey from Boston, as I neared the celebrated village of Concord, I roused myself from my preparatory metaphysical studies to look at my traveling companions. Some of them were evidently to be my fellow-students, for once in a while I caught gentle murmurs of egos and non-egos, participations and self-determination. A fat, loquacious man walked up to me as I stood on the platform and offered to take me up into town for fifteen cents.

I told him where I desired to be driven, and, after treating me to a searching stare for a second, he asked, with sincere curiosity:

"Be you one of them Phy-loss-er-fers? The woods is chuck full of 'em now. I went in the hall the other day just a-purpose to hear 'em charnt with their eyes shet. I'd jest like to see one of 'em grubbin' stumps out of an old timber patch."

Nothing daunted, I reached Miss Peabody's house at seven o'clock, and received a warm greeting.

"Now, my child, you shall go to your room and have a good sleep, so that you may be fresh for to-morrow," said my friend.

"I shall not sleep at all while I am here," I said disdainfully. "Please let me tuck your hand under my arm, and we will walk slowly together toward the chapel to hear about the 'Psychic and the Material Body of Man.'"

Next morning we were early in our places. On one side

of the lecture room was the platform occupied by the Faculty. Behind it were four windows, and on this lovely August morning they were wide open, and the willow and elm branches hung into the room. Without, there was a concert of bees and birds and crickets, united in chirps and hum and song. On that day there sat upon the platform the venerable Mr. Alcott, Dean of the Faculty; Dr. William T. Harris, celebrated both in education and speculative philosophy; the Chinese Professor of Harvard College; Mr. Sanborn, the energetic Secretary; and Mrs. Julia Ward Howe, who was to lecture on Modern Society — for this was Woman's Day at Concord. By the east window sat a lovely creature with a matchless crown of red-gold hair. I knew her at a glance, for Mrs. Rose Hawthorne Lathrop had the beautiful Hawthorne hair, and a face, too, as perfect as sculptured marble.[1]

Emerson frequently came to the School and listened closely to the lectures, with a pensive, quiet expression, and eyes cast down. His face, so well known to all in its kindly simplicity, was full of sweetness, strength, and common sense.

He looked a thorough New Englander, and his bearing was full of dignity and reserve. Indeed, he was absolutely a law unto himself, and yet his personality was always kept in the background, so far as self-assertion or egotism was concerned. Yes, I thought, he is just what Mr. Alcott calls him, "a student of the landscape, of mankind, of rugged strength, wherever found. He likes plain people, plain ways, plain clothes, prefers earnest persons, shuns

---

[1] The beautiful young woman is now Mother Alphonsa Lathrop, and for many years has devoted her life to work among poor and incurable cancer patients, both in New York City and in Hawthorne, New York, where she has established a country home for unfortunates who will never leave it alive. Healer of pain, comforter in terrible distress, this saint among women carries on nobly a noble American name.

publicity, loves solitude and knows its uses"; and when I came to have the honor of knowing him, though ever so slightly, he was the identical man of his books, the essence of refinement in thought, full of serenity and cheerful faith, united with a simple plainness of speech.

As the days passed, I began to grow into Concord. The atmosphere was contagious. Before one knew exactly what transcendentalism was, one "caught" it — and for that matter it was impossible to resist the prevailing dreaminess. One began to believe thoroughly and honestly in plain living and high thinking.

Every morning I went to the nine o'clock lecture, which lasted until eleven or a little after, when the conversation began and went on until twelve.

After the lecture was ended, the subject was thrown open to discussion and there was an opportunity to ask questions. Usually there would be a silence of several minutes, and then Mr. Alcott would announce in his solemn, musical tones, "I have a thought," and, after a weighty pause, proceed to some Orphic utterance. Alcott, indeed, was what might be called the leader on the floor. He was ably seconded by Miss Elizabeth Peabody, whose sister, Sophia Peabody, was the wife of Nathaniel Hawthorne. Miss Peabody was well known as one of the very first persons who had brought the German kindergarten ideal to America, and for her lifelong zeal in behalf of all kinds of philanthropies and educational reforms. Henry James was accused of having caricatured her in his novel "The Bostonians," in the figure of the dear, visionary, benevolent old lady who is perpetually engaged in promoting "causes," attending conventions, carrying on correspondence, forming committees, drawing up resolutions, and the like, but, as a matter of fact, Mr. James never met her and denied the "soft impeachment."

After the morning sessions I usually walked along the homeward path with Mr. Alcott, and with Dr. Harris, of St. Louis, whom I had known previously in educational matters, and their kindly and helpful conversation always served as a sort of textbook to the often profound and metaphysical lectures. I visited Mr. Emerson's house on many different occasions; a plain, square wooden one, standing behind a grove of pine trees, concealing it from the passer-by. At the rear was a large garden, which had been famous for years for its roses and rare collection of hollyhocks — the flowers that Wordsworth loved.

There are spacious rooms on both sides of the house, divided by a long hall. On the right was the study, lined on one side with plain shelves of books. A large writing-table occupied the center of the room, which had on one side a huge fireplace over which hung a fine copy of Michelangelo's Fates. Here were many little curiosities in letters and books — reminiscences of Landor, Coleridge, Wordsworth, Carlyle, Thoreau, and the patriot John Brown; a photograph, too, of chatty little Frederika Bremer, who came there from Sweden in 1849, and whose dress-buttons, it is recorded, never were on terms of intimacy with their buttonholes.

I remember well a most beautiful portrait of his wife. Mrs. Emerson (always called "Queenie" by her husband) was as dainty and spirituelle a woman as one could imagine. Her complexion was as delicate as a rose-leaf, her eyes a vivid dark blue, and her snow-white hair was ornamented with an indescribable little tulle cap, tied under her soft chin with pale blue ribbons. It was such a lovely adjunct to a lovely personality that more than one "sonnet" or "ode" to "Mrs. Emerson's cap" was written during my visit to Concord. Her gown used always to be of plain black silk, and her exquisite appearance, in conjunction with her sweet, quiet manner, made her the center of admiration in that little circle. The eldest daughter, Miss Ellen Emerson, the last member of the home trio, was, indeed, "the angel of the house." Her daughterly devotion was unparalleled; she was her father's strength and comfort, and, when his memory began to fail, his best interpreter.

The house was rich in reminiscences, for almost every person of note who visited this country partook of its genial hospitality.

On one occasion, a voluble lady who was passing the Sabbath in Concord, went up to Mr. Emerson, saying, in rather a loud voice: "Don't you remember me, Mr. Emerson? I met you ten years ago at Dr. B.'s house."

I can see now the painful struggle of memory in the eyes, the patient look about the mouth, and hear the intensely pathetic ring in the voice as he answered brokenly, "I am a very old man, madam; I cannot remember many things."

He was still erect in his carriage, however, and seemed generally to be in good health, his only distressing symptom being his failing memory. He seemed to be always a glad and attentive listener, and, if he sometimes kept aloof from general conversation where there were many people present, he was always studiously thoughtful of the comfort and pleasure of his guests.

On the summer afternoons I often strolled through Sleepy Hollow burying-ground in company with Mr. Emerson, Mr. Alcott, Mr. Channing, and Miss Elizabeth Peabody. I can recall it as if it were yesterday: the walk in quiet mood from the hillside chapel, through fragrant orchards, to the ridge overlooking historic fields. The air was vocal with perpetual melody of birds and bees, the sun shone warm and bright, the air was sweet and balmy, and the whole landscape as tenderly serene as if death had never entered the world. — Now, to that little coterie of dear, old friends neither summer nor winter, bird nor blossom nor bee, can ever be the same again; for they have all drifted into the Great Silence.

We wandered slowly among the graves of the illustrious dead, while each of the honored living related happy anecdotes of the comrades passed over and yonder.

We lingered a moment by the resting-place of a certain Miss Abigail Dudley, for they have epitaphs in Concord burying-ground; and even quaint hollyhocks, dandelions, hardhack, whiteweed, goldenrod, and other flowers of Puritan stock, are allowed to grow peacefully about the fences and in the sunny places between the trees.

I was tired, I remember, for had I not just been precipitated into the full doctrine of Platonic philosophy and psychology, cosmologic and theologic outlines, and the Dæmon of Socrates, that morning? I sank on the grassy turf beside the marble stone designed

By its durability
To perpetuate the memory,
And by its color
to signify the moral character
of
Abigail Dudley.

I looked up. The day was warm, and they had all bared their heads to the breeze. Mr. Channing had helped Miss Peabody to a seat, while Mr. Emerson and Mr. Alcott rested at the foot of a great, leafy oak tree.

I never shall forget it: the sight of the four aged, benignant heads (three of them white with the snows of almost eighty winters) on which the mellow August sunshine poured its flood of light. There was no thought of time in the minds of these geniuses. They paused in their leisurely gait, sat down on a flat gravestone to discuss high themes, moved to another, always forgetting their hats or sticks or portfolios, which I gathered up in safety and retained until the proper moment when they might remember their next engagement. I shall never forget "Abigail Dudley's" stone, for there it was that Miss Peabody passed her hand over my ruffled curly front locks and said, on the last of these homeward journeys through the graveyard:

"Our young guest has developed much during this week! Another year she must be a real student, and I hope that her hair will be drawn back smoothly from her fine forehead."

My one task in life was to conceal the height of my Websterian brow, but my head was bowed with shame over this criticism by my dear old friend, when to my amazement Mr. Emerson said absent-mindedly from an adjacent tombstone:

"I have seen smoother heads with less in them."

Needless to say, I think I had never spoken in his hearing, save perhaps to ask a question of Mr. Alcott, who only remembered my presence when he needed his hat or cane or wished to be guided to the gate nearest his house. (None of them knew where they lived if a metaphysical point were under discussion.)

I sank under the glory of this unexpected tribute and silently concluded that the great man was thinking of some one or somebody else, but in any case he had said it in the presence of witnesses!

Every night that I spent in Concord was enriched by the conversation of that noble and venerable woman Elizabeth Peabody, the revered and eminent champion of childhood, who had been instrumental in inspiring a greater number of mothers and educators than any woman of her day. Her mind was a complete storehouse of fascinating and varied knowledge, and her memory endless.

After she had unbound her silvery hair for the night (there were always three soft, white curls drooping on each side of her face), she customarily settled herself for a season of reminiscence which often lasted till midnight, and was frequently interrupted by her brother, who came every half-hour to the foot of the stairs and called impatiently — "Elizabeth, Elizabeth! pray go to bed!"

"Ah, not quite yet, dear Mr. Peabody," I used to whisper pleadingly from the upper landing. "We are just remembering Mazzini and Browning, and Harriet Martineau is coming next. I shall go home in two days, and we must do Margaret Fuller and Dr. Channing to-morrow night, and finish Froebel and kindergarten on the next."

She told me of the home life of her two famous brothers-in-law, Nathaniel Hawthorne and Horace Mann, and talked by the hour of Thoreau, Dr. Channing, Edward Everett, and especially of Mr. Emerson with whom she had walked in friendship for over forty years.

Her first acquaintance with him was through the medium of Greek lessons. He was an extremely shy young man, and she a very bashful girl, terribly afraid of him and his superior attainments. For fear of shocking her teacher by ignorance, she prepared a third part of the Greek grammar for an opening lesson, and I cannot say how much of the Iliad and Xenophon for a rather supposable surprise. On arriving at the house, he seated her without a word at one end of a long extension table, while he took the other.

There was no conversation; she said her lesson; he heard it; and as she went out she asked timidly, "How much shall I study for next time?" "Finish the book," said he, and shut the door.

They had a strong bond of union in their mutual admiration of Edward Everett, who was his instructor in Greek.

Mr. Emerson one day chanced to look through Miss Peabody's portfolio of manuscripts, and, finding a paraphrase of the first chapter of St. John, thought it most remarkable, and sent for her, after which they became better acquainted. She told me, among other things, that during Emerson's first lectures in Boston, which had such a wonderful effect upon young people, Margaret Fuller, with whom she was most intimate, desired greatly to know the eloquent lecturer and philosopher, but no suitable opportunity offered, for he did not care to meet her. Miss Peabody tried to arrange an interview, but with no success. "I hear she has 'intense times,' and works them off in sonnets," said Emerson. "I'm rather afraid of her. What is there in her, anyway?"

Miss Peabody answered: "Why, Mr. Emerson, when first I called upon Margaret Fuller I felt, on leaving her, as if I had seen the universe!"

He then turned to his wife in despair, saying: "Queenie, we must have the young woman here if she can show us the universe!"

And so Miss Peabody brought them together, or, as she expressed it, fitted the hook into the eye, for there was no lack of appreciation afterwards.

My friendship with Elizabeth Peabody lasted until her death. I remember acting as her escort from Boston to a remarkable kindergarten convention in Detroit where we were the guests of Governor and Mrs. Bagley. Her memory was still wonderful. How well I recall her taking my hand as we sat beside each other in the Pullman car, and moved out of Boston, and asking me if I had ever read Stallo's Philosophy of History (or History of Philosophy, whichever it was). On my answering no, she said, "It is a remarkable book, but out of print. I will tell you what is in it."

I am sure that she did, and that the book was in four volumes, for her recollections of its contents consumed the better part of two days.

To show her complete ignorance of practical matters, she remarked during the journey, "My dear Kate, you must go abroad. The experience will be at once an education and an inspiration."

"I am afraid I shall be very old before I can afford it," I answered.

"But it is not so expensive a journey. I am not good at figures, but I think I did not spend more than two hundred dollars and I stayed in Europe two years."

I afterwards learned that she was escorted by a group of a hundred Boston admirers to the steamer in New York and sent directly to the American Embassy in London, where she made a long visit to her friend James Russell Lowell. In due time our Ambassador had her conveyed with all dignity to the Robert Brownings in Italy, who in their turn saw that she reached the house of the patriot Mazzini in safety. I cannot recall the great personages who managed her return journeys, but they were conducted with great care for her comfort. I imagine she thought herself the guest of the various railways and steamships honored by her company. I know that whenever she had a ticket given her she mislaid or lost it, but no conductor ever disbelieved her or demanded that she leave the train. I found her Pullman check for the Detroit journey in her copy of the Baroness von Marenholz's "Reminiscences of Froebel," and to my horror it was for an upper berth! It mattered not if I slept in the aisle, for aught any one cared, but every man in the car offered his section to this gentle, aged, white-haired child of seventy-eight. (A child in practical matters, but incredibly old in wisdom and spiritual vision.)

I myself had one example of her complete unselfishness and inexperience in human affairs. Before her eightieth birthday I raised among kindergartners a thank offering of a thousand dollars for a birthday present, sending it to Jamaica Plain where she passed the last years of her life in very simple fashion. It chanced that Sarah Winnemucca, a benevolent and highly cultured Indian Princess, had been lecturing in New York and Boston in an attempt to raise funds to give to the tribe to which she belonged farming utensils of all kinds with which to educate and support themselves by intelligent labor.

In due course dear Miss Peabody wrote thanking me and all her beloved young teacher-friends for the birthday gift.

"It came at such a welcome time," she said, "for I was able to send the good Princess Winnemucca eight hundred dollars out of your generous thousand, to carry on her noble and self-sacrificing work."(!!!)

I nearly fainted when I read the letter, but I loved her none the less. She herself was living without a single luxury. There are a few people (not so very many) who ought to be adopted by the world at large, and freed from every care.

I never went back to Concord again. It seems to have happened in my life that I seldom renewed and reviewed past experiences, but the first time a thing happens is perhaps the most precious. I shall never forget those meadows, and hills, and streams on which genius looked and made them its own. I was young, but as some one has said of another famous group: "The morning light had touched their foreheads: the youthfulness was in *them*, not in me."

> "No ray is dimmed, no atom worn:
> My oldest force is good as new;
> And the fresh rose on yonder thorn
> Gives back the bending heavens in dew."

XVI

MARRIAGE AND AUTHORSHIP

THE philosophic atmosphere of Concord gradually receded, touching me with a recovered glory now and then. I returned to California better fitted for my task. The months went on. There were no more operatic and dramatic experiences to disturb the six twelve-hour days' work in every week. Everything went happily, and our educational experiment was overwhelmingly successful from the point of view of public interest and the opening of new kindergartens in the more crowded quarters of the city; "Tar Flat" had been joined by "Barbary Coast," and many other picturesque localities were being covered. The demands for training-students became too many for me to deal with easily, as the applicants were naturally not all qualified for this particular work. I was so much interested in making converts, however, that I gladly accepted several persons peculiarly gifted and calculated to advance the cause even if they had not the requisite means for paying tuition.

My sister by this time had shown extraordinary talent and skill and had become associate principal at Silver Street. She had many of my special qualifications for teaching young children and a considerable number and variety of her own in addition! Visitors grew more and more frequent. I did not dare close the doors against them, for we were pioneers, you must remember, and we all felt that no sacrifice we could make for the work could be too great. We were constantly heartened by the wonderful approbation and sympathy of these daily guests.

One day, for instance, Joaquin Miller, the California

poet, wrote in the visitor's book, "*See the Yosemite Valley first and then the Silver Street Kindergarten*"! And though this was viewing things with a poet's eye and voicing them with a poet's tongue, it almost seemed to express the popular feeling.

The consequence of all this enthusiasm was that I carried on my circle-games, story-telling, dictations, and the children's occupations in the midst of fifty or sixty watchful eyes, sometimes critical, but mostly sympathetic.

I developed also a little bodyguard which was efficient in making a more harmonious atmosphere. It is neither wise nor kind to burden a child with responsibilities too irksome for his years, but it is never too early to allow him to be helpful to his fellows and considerate of his elders. The more I depended on them, the greater was their dependableness, and the little girls grew more tender, the boys more chivalrous.

No, I was seldom left without succor when I was in need of it! But I remember one afternoon when the world had gone very wrong! There had been a disagreeable argument with Mrs. Gump, who had sent Goldine to mingle with the children when she knew that she had chicken-pox; Stanislas Strazinski had fallen downstairs and bruised his knee; Mercedes Pulaski had upset a vase of flowers on the piano keys; and finally, Petronius Nelson had stolen a red woolen ball. I had seen it in his hand and taken it from him quietly as he was going down the stairs. I suggested a few minutes for repentance in the play-room and when he came out he sat at my knee and sobbed out his grief in pitiful fashion. "Only four years old," I thought, "and no playthings at home, so I must be very gentle with him." I put my arm around him to draw him to me and the gesture brought me in contact with his curiously knobby little chest. What were my feelings when I extracted from his sailor blouse three balls! I pointed the moral as quickly as possible so that I might be alone, and then, realizing the hopelessness of some of the tasks that confronted me, I gave way to such a flood of tears as I had not shed since I was a child. It was then and there that the Corporal found me, on her way home from school. She flung her books on the floor and took my head on her scrawny, young shoulder

"What have they been doin' to you?" she stormed. "Your hair's all mussed up and you look sick abed!"

She led me to the sofa where we put tired babies to sleep, and covered me with my coat. Then she stole out and came back with a pitcher of hot tea, after which she tidied the room and made everything right for next day. Dear Old Corporal!

She was at that time competing for a prize offered to all students in the public schools by a certain Dr. McDonald, of San Francisco, the subject being "Twin Evils: Tobacco and Intemperance." She had been told by certain advisers that great value lay in a good beginning to an essay, prejudicing the reader favorably in advance. I had some slight doubt as to her ability to treat the subject, but was quite willing to hear her beginning when she brought it to me for criticism. Alas! my apprehension was more than fulfilled, for her opening sentence ran:

"Twin Evils is a very bad Habit."

The local reporters exhausted themselves about this time in flowery and exaggerated encomiums on the school and its mistress. My courage in dealing with infants of four years must have been considered phenomenal when an impassioned scribe reported one day: "She goes among the wild little Spanish children in the free kindergarten and takes their knives from them, subduing them by her beauty and gentle manner." (!)

There was real gratitude and admiration, too, among the

mothers of the neighborhood. A certain Mrs. S. entrusted to us a pair of astonishing children who were wont to secrete themselves on the dark staircase whenever possible, playing with and testing the flavor of some well-worn lamp tops and wicks. Mrs. S. was so pleased with the gradual disappearing of these objects as articles of diet that she vowed her Jane should stay with me forever, if I wanted her, for I was bringing out powers in her that might have lain "dormount" for years!

Helpers arose almost every week, among them Miss Harriet Crocker, of San Francisco, now Mrs. Charles B. Alexander, of New York. Her generosity was such that we opened, furnished, and filled with children another room at Silver Street.

To take in more of the babies waiting wistfully in the back streets, I tried to replenish our treasury by writing "The Story of Patsy" (1882), dedicating it to Miss Crocker, thus:

To H. V. C.

In memory of gladness given
to sorrowful little lives.

I was far too close to the life I was picturing to make this book wholly worthy of its subject. I am well aware that it lacks perspective, and that it has more heart than art, but oh! how many kindergartens it brought to places that had never known one; how many girls read it and flew to the nearest training-school, unconscious, perhaps, that they were not only being fitted for teaching, but for motherhood and for life in general! It was not published, only privately printed, bound in a paper cover, and sold here and there for twenty-five cents for the benefit of the cause.

For the same reason, with no special literary impulse or ambition, I later wrote "The Birds' Christmas Carol" (1886), and I remember that the kindly printer remarked

casually that, if I gave the profits to the Kindergarten Association, I ought at least to keep the copyright myself. I
had no time to look in the dictionary and see exactly what
the terms of a copyright might be, but the printer acted in
my behalf and went through the necessary legal steps. (I
am grateful to him for the suggestion and so, I am sure, are
my publishers!) [1]

My volume of children's songs and games ("Kindergarten Chimes"), the fruit of my daily teaching, had now also
appeared under the imprint of Oliver Ditson and Company,
Boston, and was soon in steady demand among kindergartners and primary teachers. The writing of these
books, and of dozens and dozens of educational articles
and annual reports and appeals, I never considered as the
work of an author, but simply as useful propaganda and as
forming a record of interesting events.

The busy days went on and on, but at length the inevitable, although the unexpected, occurred. In order to entertain any notion of matrimony, it is necessary for a woman
to have a little leisure, say five minutes a day, at least.
I was wedded to a theory, an ideal, a vocation, a cause!
Such a state of mind makes one in a measure a little deaf,
blind, unsusceptible. Life was so crowded for a few years
by ceaseless activities of mind and body that my own
personal affairs remained in the background; but certain
subjects to which young women ordinarily devote much
thought were finally forced upon my attention, and in December, 1881, I married an old friend of my early girlhood,
Samuel Bradley Wiggin, a young lawyer of Boston and a
graduate of Dartmouth College, who had followed me to
San Francisco, hopeful that a legal career might open to
him in the West. In natural gifts and wide culture, in qual-

---

[1] *The Birds' Christmas Carol* was regularly published by Houghton, Mifflin
& Company in 1888; *The Story of Patsy*, by the same firm, in 1889.

ities of mind and heart, he was equal to any good fortune that might await him. Money, or prospects of money, neither of us had at the moment, nor could either of us assure the other of any probable future wealth. Even of health there was no superabundance to give on either side, for I was somewhat nervously exhausted by my three years of exacting labor, and the young partner in our perhaps perilous adventure was not of strong constitution, so that serious illness often disturbed the otherwise even tenor of our few years together; years never marred by difference of aims, ambitions, and ideals, many of them, alas! never to be realized by him!

On my marriage I left the kindergartens in the hands of my gifted sister Nora, who was already more than my equal, but I felt that I must persevere in the supervision and conduct of the Training-School to the extent of three lectures a week, or the development of the work would be temporarily arrested. Later on, I was not so necessary, but at the moment I was really a vital part of the movement.

About 1884–85 I removed to New York with my husband, but I returned to San Francisco each spring for the final lectures to the training-class, the examinations, graduating exercises, and signing of diplomas.

Each year I took the opportunity to visit the more notable Free Kindergartens and Manual Training-Schools in Chicago, Detroit, St. Louis, Washington, Philadelphia, New York, and Boston, consulting with all the best leaders of the movement and taking back the fruits of my observations and study to the West.

In September, 1889, while I was in California for a necessary stay of several months giving lectures to the Training-School, the end came suddenly to my husband in New York. His death came in a moment, softly, quietly, and without warning, and the whole current of my life was

NORA ARCHIBALD SMITH

changed. It seemed, after it had happened, as if I had always known that it must be so, and had always been preparing for it, in mind and heart. Existence was as full of financial responsibilities as it had always been, and my courage and strength were not equal to the pressing demands and excitements of the situation confronting me. My Training-School pupils, ardent young neophytes, were already at work in cities, towns, and villages from New Mexico in the south to Washington Territory (not then a State) in the north. Advice, encouragement, suggestions, and warnings had to be sent somewhere every day by post. The old woman who lived in the shoe, who had so many children she didn't know what to do, had a leisurely and care-free existence compared with mine, and, much as I loved my work, I saw I must soon leave it for a time to my sister and to the various associates who had grown into fitness for leadership.

I needed rest, recreation, change of climate, change of work, and all of these came to me in the course of a few years, but I returned to San Francisco for several seasons for visits to my dearly loved Training-School during the closing weeks before graduation. There came, alas! a time when it was no longer possible to go back to the dear old spot, for some years later, after my mother and sister had joined me in the East, the San Francisco fire and earthquake destroyed almost the entire quarter surrounding Silver Street, and the place of blessed memories was dynamited to stay the progress of the flames. A poet-friend felt the inner meaning of this sacrifice when he wrote in comment: "How strange and how beautiful that the building that had lived for so many years to help others should have died for the same reason!" [1]

Not a trace was left of the dear roof that at the height of

[1] Henry Johnstone, of Edinburgh.

my activities had sheltered three hundred children. The much-loved building, with all its treasured associations, its books, portraits, reports, and day-by-day records, perished in an hour, and nothing remained to tell the story that had been enacted there! But the four hundred young pioneers who first and last had gone out from the Training-School with spirits aflame for service have preserved its unwritten history in their hearts and lives, and when we meet one another now and then, at all-too-rare intervals, it is with something more than a mere handclasp, for we know that what we learned together in that well-remembered spot made life more fruitful and precious to all of us.

Sydney Smith will be recalled as saying that it is a very wise rule in the conduct of the understanding to acquire early a correct notion of your own peculiar constitution of mind, and to become well acquainted, as a physician would say, with your idiosyncrasies. . . . It is a prodigious point gained if any man can find out where his powers lie, and what are his deficiencies — if he can contrive to ascertain what Nature intended for him.

I am not at all sure even now about the precise quality of such powers as I possess, although I am well aware of my deficiencies as an author. When I recall those marvelous days in California, first with children, their mothers, fathers, and homes, and then with large classes of young women (though many of my pupils were twice my age), and also with many audiences in villages and towns in the vicinity of San Francisco, I half believe that Nature intended me, not for a writer, but for a teacher. I could always teach a thing whether I knew it or not, and I think I might always have remained a teacher had not my nerves been worn threadbare by "pioneering." At all events, I thank God for every enriching day spent with children.

XVII

FRIENDSHIPS THAT COUNTED

THERE had been another influence at work upon me in California added to the blessed one of daily life with children who needed me, and who fashioned the raw material and made me into a mother in all but the terms of the flesh. That other influence was the sustaining friendship and guidance of Dr. Horatio Stebbins, the successor of the well-known preacher, Starr King, of Civil War fame, minister of the First Unitarian Church of San Francisco. I might well include the whole family, for Mrs. Stebbins was like a dear elder sister; Roderick, the only son of an earlier marriage, then at Harvard, was a friend whose loyalty and affection have continued to the present moment; and the two younger children, Horatio and Lucy, who grew up under my very eye, were the delight of my heart.

I have always thought of myself as rather susceptible to influence of an inspiring sort; at least, I kindle quickly. I know that in childhood and early girlhood I was a hero-worshiper, though never a sentimental one; but when I look back and examine the facts, I find, to my amazement, that I have been on the whole singularly unmoved by the example of eminent or superior persons in any walk of life, though I have never failed to respect and admire them.

Preachers have preached, and I have listened; teachers have taught, and I have learned, a little, at least; but how many invigorating, stimulating figures, moulders of character, stand out in my life? Strange to say, only four! One of these was Miss Mary Smith, teacher of English literature and of Latin, at that seat of learning in Maine, the Gorham Female Seminary. Under her tutelage my

eyes saw new beauty on every side; she developed my
natural love for books and taught me discrimination,
gave me a fresh sense of harmony in words and opened my
ears to poetry. I can tell very surely when I am being
"lifted up" and shown a new and lasting vision, because
I always feel a distinct sense of expansion. I believe
that I grew under the influence of this dear friendship,
although it lasted less than a year.

While still a child, I met, traveled with, and talked
familiarly for two hours with the great Charles Dickens.
I have related the details of the journey in a former chapter
and can only say that I was never the same creature
afterward.

It was not in the least the contact of a little country girl
with a famous author. I had no so-called literary tendencies nor intentions. I knew Dickens's books and had loved
them unspeakably for at least three years, but never for an
instant did the seat beside him, the touch of his hand, the
sound of his voice, the warmth of his smile, the wonder of
his talk, stir any latent longing in me to follow in his foot-
steps and be myself a writer. I did not view him as an
author at all, but merely as somebody quite different from
all other beings who had crossed my path. I placed him
and his books, even then, in separate compartments, but
he was equally glorious, equally adored in both. He enthralled me! At parting I could not imagine how I was to
live without him, and I had a strange sense of exaltation;
of an ever-so-slight difference in my own stature; of being
just a little set apart by the experience of this day of days.
It was no turning of the head, neither vanity nor conceit,
only the buoyant, ecstatic feeling of having been in the presence of authentic genius. Dickens has always remained a
continuous influence in my life. I do not re-read him any
oftener than Jane Austen or George Meredith, but they

are merely favorite authors, and he is something more, an ever-fresh exhibition of human nature, magnetic, fully alive, unforgettable.

A good deal of water ran under the bridge before I encountered my next influence. Mrs. Caroline Severance, first of Boston, but in all her later life a resident of Los Angeles, begged me to study the kindergarten system in the new training-school established by Miss Emma Marwedel in that city. This experience I have told elsewhere and explained that it was "in the bond" that I should be her guest and a member of her family during the nine months' course of study. The intellectual life of the household, the table-talk of the mother, the father, and their two sons, was slightly different from any I had encountered before. It was occupied with current events, local, national, and international politics; "movements" of all kinds, discussions of every topic under the sun from physical culture and hygiene to equal suffrage, Buddhism, and theosophy. Mrs. Severance was interested in everything, and, although she was then called "advanced," she was womanly and, in my opinion, conservative; safe, sane, sound, and sensible in all things. She made my mind more alert, made me think, form opinions and convictions of my own, widened my horizon. I was "more of a person" when I left her roof; and, although the kindergarten training of that period was the more powerful agent in the forming of character, Mrs. Severance was, as a personality, a most valuable intellectual stimulus. Here, then, are three very different influences touching my life from the age of eleven to twenty-one.

How shall I find words to paint the portrait of Horatio Stebbins, who came next and who has never had a successor?

There are many people of my own age, as well as those

younger and older, who will read my tribute, and I long to have them say that I have captured some of the vanished glory of his personality and thereby illuminated these pages.

He was tall, strongly built, magnificent in mien, and his face might have been carved from a rock, with its broad forehead and regular features. It had a wonderful dignity that approached severity, until the flashing eye, the smile, and the humorous curl of the lip gave confidence. I was a little in awe of him at first, and later on, as he began to give me his friendship, I used to say to myself: "*Don't sink!* Pull yourself together and rise to him! Forget his 'bigness' and remember only his humanity. There is more sympathy, apprehension, and comprehension in him than in half a dozen smaller men, so just stand on tiptoe and be proud that he takes any notice of you at all!"

I used to breakfast with the family now and then on my way to the kindergarten, and I see him oftenest coming into the dining-room with dark-haired baby Lucy on his shoulder, her gypsy face leaning against his cheek.

"Shall we say grace, Jewel?" he would ask, to keep her from leaping too soon toward her high chair. Horatio, aged six, would bend his head, and Mrs. Stebbins and I would incline ours, until the few brief sentences were spoken. It was more than grace before meat, and the words were never the same, but how they blessed the food, the day, the task, and the gift of life itself! His briefest prayers made a hush in the heart. It was as if a cool finger were laid on one's pulse and a voice said: "Peace, be still!"

He simply "towered" in the pulpit, where, when he was especially eloquent, he looked seven feet in height and every inch of it in majesty. His lightest word took on gravity and meaning because of the forces inherent in him.

"I always try to be simple," I once heard him say, "but

it's a mistake to adapt your sermon to the dullest member of your congregation! About once a month I try to pitch my fodder so high in the rack that not a man can catch a straw without stretching his neck."

There is a story of Dr. Stebbins preaching to a new audience one Sunday, and a visiting minister, profoundly impressed, walking along the road with one of his deacons who had accompanied him to the service.

"Does Dr. Stebbins always preach like this?" asked the stranger.

"No," said the deacon, wiping a furtive tear from his eye. "Not always quite like this! Once in a while he lets us down a little mite, or we couldn't stand it!"

He grew to be my chief adviser in the work I was doing among the children and families of "Tar Flat." I have said that Mrs. Severance made my mind alert. Dr. Stebbins fortified my spirit, gave me strength, courage, philosophy, endurance. He was the first person to make me understand life, its meaning and purpose, and to help me live it. He was a lonely figure when immersed in deep thought or grave events, but at all other times a dear comrade.

One afternoon, the very last of an especially weary term when there was to be a vacation in the country beginning next day, I stumbled on the steep hill leading from the California Street trolley to my home on Pine Street, and sprained my ankle. A kind person picked me up, called a cab and took me home, at the same time sending for Dr. Ben F., our old family friend and physician. It was a case of a plaster cast and no vacation!

In a few hours came a messenger with a comfortable lounge, something we did not possess, as these were days of strict economy. Dr. Stebbins's card was pinned to it, and before night he followed his gift with a personal visit. I was on the lounge and my face was tear-stained with disappointment and pain. He stood over me, all comprehension and sympathy.

"My dear Kate," he said, with a twinkling eye, "we consider at our house that you are quite good enough for 'human nature's daily food,' but I don't think you're particularly strong on the passive virtues. Perhaps this is a good time for you to cultivate them."

That has not been my only opportunity, by far, but I find at a ripe age that the passive virtues, even yet, do not seem to be my strong point! I hope that where he is he can see me still "cultivating," when surely I should be gathering my harvest into barns!

My mother, my sister, and I took Sunday supper regularly with Dr. and Mrs. Stebbins during the winters of 1879 and 1880 and spent the evening with Mrs. Stebbins and the children while the Doctor went to evening service. He was preoccupied with his sermon on these occasions, but never too much so to be gentle and friendly and hospitable, with now and then a flash of his quaint humor, and more often still a single speech so full of wisdom, or spiritual significance, that it made the whole meal worth while. I cannot remember a single hour of the many I spent in that great man's company when I was not the better for it. An absolutely feather-headed woman or dull, mediocre man could never get far with Dr. Stebbins. He had a climate all his own, and, if one couldn't stand "altitude," one would simply have to pant and puff and blow on the level where one belonged. Triviality, meanness, hypocrisy, littleness of mind and temper, shriveled in his presence, and left the persons who conspicuously possessed these traits a trifle bare and uncomfortable. They sometimes called him "cold," laying the blame on him, not on themselves.

Yet he drew all sorts of men and women to him! His

Sunday evening service was attended by hundreds of people of no denomination and of all denominations, with men in the majority. He visited the sick whenever and wherever they needed him, whether they belonged to his parish or not. He married and buried all the uncatalogued, lately arrived, not-in-the-directory persons in San Francisco, so it seemed to his friends, and the poetic phrase applied to him by one of them was: "Priest of the wider parish of the heart."

As an extraordinary instance of his simplicity and his ability to search the deeps of a man and find something not visible to the many, I record an acquaintance formed in a Turkish bath to which he made several visits in order to rid himself of an obstinate cold.

I remember his saying to his wife at supper: "My dear, I met a most extraordinary man to-day. A man of wide experience, a student of human nature, and of most winning personality. I greatly enjoyed his company."

"What was his name?" asked Mrs. Stebbins.

"I did not ask him, my dear, nor did he ask mine. It was not a social occasion, you see, and the bath-attendant made no introductions!"

Three days later, another meeting of the same sort occurred in the steam room at the bath, and Dr. Stebbins again recounted his impressions of the interview. "A rare man," he said; "very ill in body, I fear, but magnificent in courage, and quite ready to face the inevitable. I think I must find out who he is."

By this time Mrs. Stebbins and I had become interested in the unknown being who had managed to impress the Doctor under such unusual circumstances. We did not have to wait long, for the friend of the bath, who possessed more worldly wisdom than his reverend friend, had learned his name and address, and had sent for him in an acute attack which ended in speedy death. We then discovered that he was the most audacious, most successful, most notorious gambler in California, a position not to be easily held in that State in olden times!

Mrs. Stebbins and I quoted to each other secretly her husband's unconsciously happy description of the man's "winning personality." The dear Doctor officiated at the funeral, of course, although there was naturally no eulogy, and the company in the church was somewhat mixed, but at supper the Doctor said thoughtfully, as he sipped his cup of tea: "A noble creature, my dear! Believe me, a noble creature at bottom! God knows why he was a gambler and only God is able to settle the matter with him. Meantime I am amazed that in two long interviews I discerned nothing but good in him. Our friend G. maintains that he did not deserve even the prayers I said over his coffin, though to my mind even a gambler (especially a delightful, genial, high-minded gambler) ought to have a farewell when he starts on his last long journey; but then G. knows as little about the spirit of God as a red heifer bellowing 'round the pasture."

I must give a little space to the Sunday evenings with the children who are now occupying places of pomp and power: Horatio, Assistant Professor of Mechanical Engineering at Leland Stanford, Jr., University in California, and Lucy as Dean of Women and Professor of Social Economics at the University of California — one of the most brilliant and executive deans of women in the country.

They were not precocious children, but very wise for their years, being much in the company of a remarkable father and mother. Horatio at four said: "God doesn't make flies one by one, Lucy! He says, 'Let there *be* flies, and there *is* flies.'" Also, after a very slight earthquake, he made an innocently heretical remark: "It seems to me if I held the earth in the hollow of my hand like God, I could hold it *still!*"

Lucy was less philosophic and didactic, but she once uttered a speech that has persisted in our family history. Dr. and Mrs. Stebbins were to dine with a particularly wealthy and critical widow whose dinners were banquets, but not always pleasant occasions. The Doctor and his wife sat on the edges of their chairs in the drawing-room, waiting for the carriage to be announced, while my sister and I were about to dine with the children. There was a heavy, brooding silence, broken by six-year-old Lucy, who said: "If you wore your pearl-gray dress, mother, mightn't it mitigate the gloom?"

Among the memories laid away in lavender to make fragrant all the years to come, none is more sacred to me than my association with the Stebbins family. Only two of that precious circle are gone; my own beloved mother and the Doctor himself, the unapproachable, the man among a million! He died in Cambridge in 1902, at eighty-one years, but my gallant little mother stayed with us until 1921, just after she had passed her ninety-first birthday. Roderick, the old friend of my girlhood, is now minister of the First Unitarian Church at Milton, Massachusetts. He officiated at my second marriage as his father had at my first, and he sustained us at the death of our mother and preached her funeral sermon in the winter of 1921 at Buxton, Maine.

On any night when I am wakeful I can hear Dr. Stebbins saying: "As we rise in the scale of being, the anxieties and sorrows of life pass into discipline, and discipline into virtue.... So, my soul, stand erect, and glory in thyself and in thy God!"

Here is a note to me in answer to a telegram on his eightieth birthday:

MILTON, MASS.
August 8th, 1901

MY DEAR KATE:

I cannot say anything equal to or worthy of your great salutation that comes like a voice out of heaven. I could pour out my heart like water, and my gratitude and love would burst forth in song, but believe everything that admiration and affection can bestow, and let my heart and voice be still.

HORATIO STEBBINS

And here is another that I value inexpressibly. It was in answer to one of mine to him in his last illness, trying to tell him of the part he had played in my life and the inspiration he had always been to me:

CAMBRIDGE, 20 ELMWOOD AVE.
March 31st, 1902

DEAR KATE:

What you say transcends all my powers of expression, and if I should "let go" I don't know where I should begin or end!

You have always been among my great admirations and my intellectual and moral delights; that I have had any influence or standing with you has increased my self-respect tempered by gratitude and humility.

I am sorry for your physical sufferings, Kate, and yet a creature like you, so keenly sensitive and so on the top of the world as you are, cannot escape the penalties of so expansive a being!

What can I say but repeat what you know already — my great affection for you all — your husband, your mother and Nora, the ever beloved and honored, whom to know is pride enough for a lifetime.

I am yours, indeed, always and ever more

HORATIO STEBBINS

HORATIO STEBBINS

Honored by humble men, he walks these streets,
Priest of the wider parish of the heart;
A tower of strength to the impetuous State,
Where steadfast and serene he fills his part;

Still offering wisdom — though the hour grows late;
Still lending courage — in the face of Fate.
Unterrified and kind, large as the light of day,
He passes on —
We lift our eyes, sodden with petty ills,
And lo! — visions of forests, of the silent hills,
And the deep tides of the obedient sea!

BRUCE PORTER
1898, San Francisco

XVIII

A FIRST JOURNEY TO EUROPE

ONE rather dreary day in the last years of my work in San Francisco, when I was thinking of my future, I read in a novel these lines: "There comes a time in most of our lives when in order to make any real progress it seems necessary slightly to change our direction." I wondered what "direction" along the life-trail I was best fitted to take, for I felt that it must be changed. I wondered if "Patsy" and the "Carol" had really any literary significance or whether they had been bought simply to aid a good cause.

I had done no writing for several years save on educational subjects and I had not the slightest sense of being an author. I had an ample supply of stories for use in kindergartens,[1] stories that my sister and I had constantly told to the children, also various essays of ours to be collected under one cover and to be called "Children's Rights," but these two possible volumes existed only in manuscript and were a natural part of my educational work.

Nobody had ever suggested that I could write; nobody had ever thought of any easier road for me than the one I had traveled; nobody had fancied that I could earn more than twelve hundred dollars or so in any year by any method. It was with no burning ambition, no special belief in myself, no idea of the ultimate outcome, but rather from languid curiosity that I sent the paper-covered "Carol" to Houghton, Mifflin & Company, of Boston.

That it had been printed and sold privately I felt must be, of course, a handicap, and so, indeed, it would generally have been considered. In spite of this drawback, Mr.

[1] *The Story Hour.*

Henry O. Houghton, the senior member of the firm, took
the book home in his pocket and read it aloud to his family
on the piazza of their country home. It was, as you will
see, a perfectly delightful family! The next morning Mr.
Houghton walked into the office of his firm at 4 Park
Street, Boston, and said: "If you folks don't happen to
like this book, I do, and I'll publish it on my own account
if necessary."

The interview was reported to me three thousand miles
away, the book was published, and I was an author. This
is a brief and simple account of the beginning of my new
vocation, for the edification of all those persons who
wonder how authors "happen," though, of course, there
had been a long and arduous, though quite unconscious,
preparation for the event.

The great and unexpected success of this unpretentious
Christmas story showed me clearly the new "direction"
in which I was bound to travel; indeed, it left me no choice,
for the book cleared the way for me from the first day of
publication, "easing my shoulders from the burden" and
"delivering my hand from making the pots."

"The Story of Patsy," much enlarged from its original
form, was published by Houghton, Mifflin & Company a
year later and received almost the same warm welcome as its
predecessor, but, in spite of these encouraging successes,
the early spring of 1890 found me still weary, depressed,
and much in need of entire change.

A gift of love and understanding found its way to me
just then, from a friend who appreciated my mental and
physical exhaustion. The gift was coupled with the stipu-
lation that it could be used only to add to my income
during a time of rest abroad, "strange countries for to
see."

I was not wont to accept favors from any quarter, but I

accepted this as manna falling from heaven! Never before in all the busy years had such a glorious thing happened to me. Somebody wanted me to be young and glad and relax my arduous labors for a little. Somebody wouldn't allow this particular sum to be put in the bank or be devoted to base practical uses. It was as much a miracle as the success of "The Birds' Christmas Carol," and these two delightful surprises taken together re-created me and gave me new joy and courage. They were "jam," indeed, and "jam to-day," in spite of the White Queen's declaration to Alice that the rule was invariably jam to-morrow and jam yesterday, but *never* jam to-day, an observation that sometimes seems singularly true in the course of a working life.

I soon found a dear Boston friend, Miss L., older than I, delighted to be my traveling companion, and Molly Blank, a charming young lady from Oakland, California, with plenty of money to spend and eager for new experiences, begged to join us and make a third in our coöperative excursion.

We sailed from New York on the Ems, of the North-German Lloyd Line, May 24, 1890. It was our first journey abroad, so we went where everybody else went, we saw what everybody else saw, and wrote back the same sort of enthusiastic letters to home friends. The only records of events that I ever kept regularly were those in a black notebook, the result of the months in 1890 from May to November inclusive, from the moment we docked at Southampton, June 2d, and went to Winchester the same day, and from there to Salisbury in true American fashion, within thirty-six hours.

Miss L. and I visited most of the English cathedrals during the summer, but Molly's tastes were neither architectural nor ecclesiastical, so we left her behind in London on these occasions. A couple of years afterward, I paid my debt to these beautiful and awe-inspiring buildings in the shape of my book called "A Cathedral Courtship," in which a pretty, lovable, and not very learned heroine sees a young Boston architect sketching a doorway in the cathedral at Winchester and meets him thereafter at Salisbury, Ely, Lincoln, Durham, and York, till their love-affair buds, grows, and at length bursts into bloom at Canterbury. I don't know whether the title of this story is misleading, but I am always dragging the volume from the piles of hymn and prayer books in large bookshops, the word "Cathedral" naturally taking precedence of the "Courtship."

The entries in the book when London is reached are mostly of social engagements and bewildered, excited accounts of meeting famous people. But there is space to show that we did our duty as Americans, for the pages bristle with Hampton Court, the various villages on the Thames, Crystal Palace, Grosvenor and National Galleries, Richmond, the Tower, Westminster Abbey and St. Paul's, Charter House, the Temple, Oliver Goldsmith's tomb, St. Mary-le-Bow, Henley Regatta, the Derby, Eton and Harrow games at Lord's, Ranelagh, House of Commons, House of Lords, Hyde Park, and many other famous haunts.

I am glad that I saw all these things with religious fervor, and had my one serious taste of London and its historic past; for in twenty or more subsequent visits in after years I never once went sight-seeing, but settled down into London life as if it were home, as, indeed, it always seems to me the moment my feet touch the beloved streets.

So the notebook proceeds, with records of Edinburgh, the Trossachs, Oban, Callender, Carlisle, Keswick, Ambleside, Chester, Warwick, Stratford; — but here I must pause a moment, for we went to Stratford, first as tourists, but I unexpectedly remained! A book, "Timothy's Quest," had already been begun in America and I had received, a week or two before, a request from my publishers saying that, if I were sufficiently recovered, they would like me to complete it at once.

The story of its writing will be found in a later chapter, and after I had penned its last words, "And this is the eternal magic of love," I went to London for a gay visit to Mr. and Mrs. Percy Spalding, Mr. Spalding being the senior partner of the fine old firm of Chatto and Windus, publishers of Swinburne and our own Mark Twain.

The first three days were spent in carefully re-copying the chapters of "Timothy" written and re-written in Stratford. If there were typists in 1890, I seem to have had no knowledge of them, and delighted in having my publisher's copy in clear, tidy pages of manuscript without a single correction. I was still rather young and inexperienced, but a certain neatness, tidiness, and exactness about detail have seriously interfered with my career as an artist. It is only necessary for me to glance at the horrible examples of true genius formerly sent to printers, to decipher as best they might, to realize how lacking I am in the divine afflatus!

When the thick package was safely on board an American-bound ship, I was happy beyond words. I knew "Timothy" was a "nice book," as good a one, at any rate, as I was capable of writing, and angels can do no more. A great deal of its success in Great Britain was due to the enthusiasm felt for it by Mr. Walter Gay, of the young publishing firm of Gay and Bird. He was his own "commercial traveler" at the beginning, and he never left any city in England without convincing the booksellers that they must read, must buy, must sell "Timothy's Quest."

WITH TIMOTHY AND LADY GAY
The children who played in the film production

Oh! how enchanting it would be for authors if publishers had shorter lists, and if they liked, admired, or loved (in varying degrees, of course) every book they published!

Of course, it is impossible. In the first place, the long list marks the successful publisher; in the second, every reader alive knows that no man could help being bored to tears by many volumes on the best of lists. There is one exception — the imaginative enthusiast whose duty it is to fall in love with every fresh book and sound its praises on the "jacket." He, indeed, is the author's friend, or, at any rate, if — or when — he goes too far, he is at least her dearest foe! She cannot help thinking that he exaggerates, and she blushes when she reads his encomiums, but occasionally — no, only semi-occasionally — she wonders if anybody else will ever agree with him!

Our party of three met again on August 4th after my solitary and delicious experiences in Stratford-on-Avon, and we left London — dear, beloved, unequaled London — and embarked from Harwich to Antwerp, Brussels, Cologne, the Rhine country, and last of all Munich.

We were on our way to the Oberammergau Passion Play of 1890, and, arriving at the village, a yellow-haired boy, who played "Ein Engel" in the great performance we had come to see, piloted us to Georg Lang's Hotel where we had engaged accommodations. We had rooms next an upper stable of sweet-smelling straw where the servants slept when the inn was crowded. I could have chosen no better quarters, and it seemed to me that Mary and the Holy Child were wondrously near, for we had breathed in the whole unforgettable story during our few hours' drive through the little village. Our eyes were constantly attracted by the beautiful faces of the children, and it has often been said that no mother in Oberammergau but hopes her child will grow into something fit for the Passion-spiel; if not for the Christus, then for John or Peter or Mary.

We rose at five on Sunday and reached the great theater at eight, remaining during the first part, which ended just before the brief interval for luncheon, the second half beginning at one and closing at five-thirty. After a lapse of thirty-two years I cannot write of the experience without emotion. I went into my own room alone, for the tears had been flowing throughout the afternoon and it was vain to try to stop them. Even when I was, as I thought, per-fectly calm and eating my breakfast in bed the next morn-ing, the pathetic voice crying, "*Eli, Eli, lama sabach-thani!*" came back to me and I pushed the food away.

We left Oberammergau next morning for Munich, and on August 12th at three o'clock we started for Innsbruck. Having settled ourselves in the railway carriage, Miss L. discovered that she had left a valuable pair of eyeglasses and her scarlet umbrella at the Munich hotel, and she hastily decided to return, recover her losses, and follow us in an express train next morning. Molly and I quickly made up our minds to proceed without her, for we had two good Tauchnitz novels and a great deal to learn about Innsbruck from the guide-book.

Arriving at our destination at eleven o'clock at night, we gesticulated until we secured a porter to carry our bags and hold-alls to the Hotel Goldene Sonne where we had telegraphed for rooms. The porter who spoke English had retired to his bed. The others waved us away, and we gathered after a while that they had not a single room vacant. Back to the station we went and found a German gentleman on the platform who spoke English, and who told us that he would get the railway porter to direct us to a lodging, but before we could understand his directions he disappeared, intent on getting a bed for himself, and not disposed to be over-chivalrous at that late hour.

Then ensued a walk of two miles at eleven-thirty o'clock with a porter who could not understand a word of our language, nor we a word of his. He passed different houses, and, tapping on the shutters, would call up some woman and apparently ask admittance for us, but we were always refused. We were becoming pretty well frightened when he led us into a kind of public-house, or beer-room, with long wooden tables and two men drinking. A man with a green Tyrolean hat came forward and our porter made a long explanation, finally laying down our baggage and disappearing. We tipped him liberally and wished that we might keep him as a sort of protector.

The man with the green hat called a chambermaid out of bed under the pretense that she spoke English. We divined nothing from her mysterious announcements except that we would have beds in a "little moment." We disliked to stay in such a place, but there seemed nothing else to do, so when the Green Hat picked up our luggage we followed him, as we thought, to our rooms. What was our surprise to have him take us through a long hall and out into the street again! There was not a possibility of explaining anything, so we followed him through dark alleys and deserted streets, the thunder and lightning of a coming storm adding to the growing terror of the scene. The man knocked on various shutters, and even wedged himself inside the door of two houses where women with very few clothes on came from their beds and shook their heads firmly in the negative.

Finally, in despair, at one o'clock he turned around a corner and, tapping at a shutter, cried "Madre!" — Then ensued a long conversation and we were admitted by a half-dressed lad. The Italian with the green hat bowed profoundly and left us. I offered him two gulden (a dollar), which he refused, so we shall never know what manner of man he was. The lad opened the door of a huge room and pushed us in, giving us a key at least a foot long. Then, presenting us with a match, he disappeared.

We lighted the one candle, locked the double oak doors, and, looking about us, saw one very narrow bed — without linen or pillows — no water or any toilet conveniences; but we had to endure it, as we were afraid of being turned into the streets again. Molly took the sofa and I the un-sheeted bed, as I was the elder and completely worn out and ill.

Before creeping into the unattractive cot, I arranged a candle on a table near and lighted it to see if it would be all right in case of burglary or murder. Leaning against the tall brass candlestick, what should I see but a small picture of myself! It *was* I, and I remembered a rather successful dress and hat of two years before. From where, from whom, and how, could it have arrived in that room?

"Molly," I whispered, "there is a picture of Me on this table!"

"Don't be silly; you are tired and probably can't see straight," she said sleepily, and, as was her wont, rather informally.

"I am not; it *is* a picture of me — I will show it to you!"

"Don't, till morning," she said testily. "I believe you. Perhaps there's a picture of you in every room in Austria. If you look on another table you may find a copy of 'The Birds' Christmas Carol.' Your head is turned by success!" — and then I heard her slow, gentle breathing and knew she had gone to sleep, but I lay awake for an hour wondering how that picture came to that lodging-house, as I had not, so far as I knew, a single acquaintance or correspondent in that part of the country.

At seven-thirty o'clock the next morning a nice voluble woman rapped at the door, but to all her conversation I was obliged to say, "*Ich spreche nicht Deutsch*," and let it go at that. I managed also to murmur, "*Brod und Butter und Kaffee*"; so we broke our fast. I wished ardently that the study and practice of kindergarten had left me any time to learn modern languages, but all my paper-covered Complete Guides to Travelers — giving advice in three tongues as to how the unhappy alien might extricate himself from difficulties — all these were of no avail. The situation was not covered, that is all there was to say. Soon after breakfast Molly started out "afoot and alone," armed with a bit of paper on which I had written three sentences from my phrase-book: "*Wo ist der Bahnhof?*" "*Wo ist der Hotel Sonne?*" "*Wo kann ich einen Wagen finden?*"

With these three questions answered, she came triumphantly back in an hour and removed me to the Hotel Goldene Sonne, where we found rooms, but were totally unfit for sight-seeing for twenty-four hours. That is the end of that particular story, but it unexpectedly turned out to be a serial and is continued elsewhere.

After several days in Innsbruck, Miss L. and Molly decided to join another lady who was going on a wearisome and expensive trip to the Engadine and over the famous Stelvio Pass. I did not feel equal to eight hours a day in a *diligence*, beautiful as the journey would have been, and, just as I was making up my mind how to use the two or three days of separation from my fellow-travelers, I received a letter from Dr. Ben F., forwarded by Brown, Shipley and Company from London. It began, "Dear Boofer Lady," as he had always called me, though I certainly had little in common with Miss Bella Wilfer in "Our Mutual Friend."

I had first met Dr. Ben years before in Los Angeles while I was studying kindergarten, for he was a friend of my hostess, Mrs. Severance. Then later on he came to live in San Francisco, and became our family physician, so far as we could be said to have one at that time.

His had been a sad life, spoiled almost at the outset by a cruelly unhappy and tragic marriage which could not be dissolved without much publicity and many mortifying consequences. (In 1875 or thereabouts people minded publicity and consequences more than they do nowadays!)

Mrs. Severance had known his story, and had always sympathized with him even when he was fractious or irritable. He was oversensitive, very loyal in friendship, had a sense of humor, but was subject to moods of great depression, always restless, and as much given to wandering as his slender means permitted. Different places in Germany had been his choice for a few years, and he had been most contented in the town of Graz, in Styria.

His letter, forwarded from London, would have melted a heart of stone. Not an acquaintance, a friend, a familiar face, not even an American, had ever come to Graz, which certainly was not on the tourist line of travel and eight or nine hours' journey from Innsbruck. Consulting the hotel porter, I found it rather an expensive journey for him to take, and I knew well that he could not afford it, so I telegraphed him that, if he could meet me halfway, I would come to Bruck-am-Mur, have a two hours' talk with him, and return to Innsbruck on a night train.

He accepted the plan with unspeakable delight and gratitude, and I started on what I believed to be an errand of mercy, but the journey also took me through a most beautiful country, going through the Austrian Tyrol and several well-known watering-places.

Providence helped me as usual, for I had not been

traveling an hour before a charming elderly lady made acquaintance with me and presented me with an enormous visiting card with wide mourning edge.

La baronne d'Egger
née du Fresne
Bischofplatz No. 7. 1 Etage. Graz.

She spoke only German, and how we got on I hardly know, but we did, and famously. She told me of an educational convention to be held the two following days in Graz, and begged me not only to take a peep at her beautiful town, but to see the educational exhibit. Her house she said was next the inn and she would take pleasure in entertaining me. I asked her if she knew my doctor friend. She replied in fragments of two languages that she had met the "*très malheureux*," the so-sad Herr Doktor, but my command of German was not sufficient to explain him and his background to her; indeed, I could scarcely have done it in English.

He met us when we alighted at Bruck-am-Mur and was overjoyed that I would go for a day to Graz, kissing the hand of La baronne d'Egger fervently in recognition of her kindness, and then lapsing into a state of considerable gloom because he had allowed me to meet him halfway instead of coming to see me at Innsbruck, as he should have done. In all our previous acquaintance we had both been as poor as church mice, but I told him that my financial condition was incredibly, almost miraculously, easy at the moment, and he was happier after that, so we journeyed the few miles to Graz, the capital of Styria, where I was deposited at the Goldene Birn, next door to the house of the kind Baroness d'Egger — "only for bed and *Frühstück*," she insisted, as she invited Dr. Ben to real breakfast next day at noon at a certain restaurant by the lake.

My intended visit of one day extended well into the

next, for Graz was too beautiful to be slighted, and my poor Dr. Ben too unhappy to leave until I had done my best to cheer him. By a strange coincidence, Innsbruck had been one of his favorite haunts, and the very lodging into which Molly and I tumbled after midnight had many times been his resting-place for days. That accounted for my photograph on the table, a loss that in his solitary life he had mourned continually. Scarcely more than forty-five years old, he looked sixty; pale, broken, and spiritless at first, but after various hours of friendly chat at table or in the lovely gardens he was, temporarily at least, more like himself.

Nothing on the Continent pleased me quite as much as this quaint, serene city of Graz. People lived out of doors and seemed to eat nothing in their own homes save their morning *Frühstücken*. The Stadt Park was a connected series of wide horse-chestnut avenues with benches on either side, and here and there a small open-air café. The band played every afternoon in a central enclosure where there was a beautiful fountain and tables where well-dressed people were seated. A great many of them were officers, for there were then one hundred and fifty military pensioners in Graz who sat serenely in the sun, reading newspapers, sipping coffee, and feeding the birds.

One eating-place by a little lake was filled with carp, which belong to the city and are taken out once a year. The tables are placed under the beautiful trees all along the edge of the water and "everybody" goes to breakfast there at eleven or twelve o'clock.

You break a crusty roll in two and fling it in the water. Presently one carp sees it and the rest follow till they flock around it by dozens, pushing, sucking, driving it about until the last crumb is eaten. A lady or gentleman given to practical jokes throws in an unbroken roll with a hard glossy crust that provides comedy for the spectators, for the hundreds of carp pursuing it make a sucking sound that can be heard a long distance. As *ein Brod* cost a kreutzer, the custom is valuable to the restaurant and an innocent amusement for onlookers.

Such delicious coffee as one gets in this part of Austria, and such charming manners as one sees on every hand! If one person or more comes to the table next yours, they salute you on coming and leaving. If they wish a seat at your table, they first ask, with infinite respect, if the *gnädige Frau* permits their presence. At one meal where I was the sole lady at one end of an outdoor café, seven strange men doffed their hats in passing and made a profound obeisance. Another, who asked politely for a seat at our table, inquired of Dr. Ben, when we rose, what language the "gracious lady" was speaking.

"English," said the doctor, "she is an American."

"So?" answered the gentleman (of course, in German). "And yet I have heard that the Americans speak a harsh language! My surprise is great! Convey my compliments to the gracious lady."

At the Goldene Birn all the servants say "*Gute Nacht!*" and "*Guten Morgen!*" and, as one passes them on the stairs or in hall or gives them a tip, they bow and say: "*Ich küsse die Hand.*" If one of our free-born or naturalized American waiters should murmur something like an imaginary kiss of the patron's hand on receiving a fee, the donor, unused to thanks of any sort, might perish with surprise.

Virtually no Americans and few English come to this quaint city, but it is well worth visiting. On my second and last afternoon in Graz, Dr. Ben and I took a droshky to the Schlossberg, dismissed it, and walked down the mountain, from the top of which one sees cities, towns, and villages for hundreds of miles. We walked along the beautiful winding path under forests of grand trees, with here and there a rustic bench, and, within short distances of one another, little bird-houses mounted on poles a few feet from the ground. Seeds and crumbs are scattered on the platforms that surround the houses, and often there is a contribution-box which asks the public to give a kreutzer that the birds may be fed in winter.

We were to meet our friendly Baroness for coffee at four o'clock, and, as it was only three, we paused to rest on a wayside bench. I shall never forget the scene nor the hour, for my poor Dr. Ben, in all the bygone years rigidly silent, though never wholly able to conceal his sorrows, told me the story of his life for the first time, not pretending that there was, or ever would be, any happy ending to it, in which I fully, although sadly, concurred. I could hardly bear to hear it, and, as if Nature itself were in a tragic mood, while we sat in utter silence for many minutes as he finished the somber chronicle, the sky grew dark, there was a rumble of distant thunder, and we rose and walked hurriedly to the Stadt-Theater Café where we were to meet our friend.

The café has a beautiful garden with tables under the trees, and three broad verandas enclosing the indoor restaurant. We had hardly reached the veranda when a sudden darkness fell upon the air, and immediately there began to fall hailstones, or balls of ice, some as big as one's thumb and others the size of a hen's egg. These fell in a cannonade on the veranda roof, and we had to move away from the end where we were sitting, for the ice-balls were scattering glass in every direction.

Soon the lamp-posts in the garden and the colored glass globes began to crash, while leaves and whole branches of trees fell on all sides, the noise being so great that one could hardly hear the voices of the servants hurrying frantically about the place. This continued for ten minutes, until the ground was thickly strewn with hailstones and ice. Then rain began to fall, and gradually the sky brightened, but before it cleared entirely the stones began to fall again more heavily than before. Between the storms the waiters picked up scores of little brown birds, bringing to my lap a dozen to be warmed and resuscitated, but, though many were only stunned, many more were killed or crippled, and on our way to the railway station we passed hundreds of broken-legged, broken-winged, and one-eyed little song-sters hopping about dejectedly, coming so close to you and with such confidence you felt how accustomed they were to kindness and protection on all sides. (Oh! what are those bird-loving, gracious, courteous old pensioners in Graz doing now, I wonder!)

At the hotel, just as I left, I received a telegram from my two traveling companions begging me to sleep that night at the Goldene Sonne in Innsbruck, where I was known, and meet them in Zurich next day, owing to a newly planned *diligence* trip.

Dr. Ben accompanied me a few miles to a little station along the line, and, when I had said good-bye and watched him walk away slowly like a man in a dream, a man without hope, my eyes filled with tears, for I felt I should never see him again.

But I did, in a way that neither of us could have expected, for, as I said, this is a serial story.

XIX

A HUNGARIAN COUNTESS

I SAT in my seat quietly, thinking of Graz and Dr. Ben, and wishing that some of the travelers in the corridor train would drop a word of English speech so that I might not feel so entirely alone. I looked forward eagerly to meeting the porter and the head waiter of the Goldene Sonne in Innsbruck, for the former spoke four languages fluently and the head waiter was seemingly master of all tongues. I had been feeling unspeakably ignorant in these last weeks, constantly at a disadvantage, constantly handicapped by the impossibility of truly expressing myself. The scant time for study that a tourist can muster is of little use, and I was timid at using the phrases I had learned, because I had an ear for accent, cadence, and inflection, and was therefore unhappy when I spoke badly, my discomfort being added to by a capricious memory. Heaven will be, indeed, heavenly to me if spirits converse in Esperanto or in any common tongue (as seems probable) without any thought of gender or irregular verbs.

An hour passed when a station approached at which I was told, as I thought, by the guard who looked at my ticket, that I was to change carriages. As a matter of fact, he could not have said this at all, but it was what I frantically understood him to say, and I buckled on my armor, though confident that I should never be able to perform the change successfully, surrounded by strange faces and made nervous by a Babel of strange voices.

The train stopped, and the usual hurly-burly ensued, dozens of persons alighting to smoke and to dart to and fro confusedly, while the only words I understood in the chatter and clatter were "*Zwei bier, bitte,*" which deafened me on every side. I was leaning out of the wide-open door steadying myself with my right hand, my eye searching for the guard to shift my small luggage, when a man in a linen duster crowded in behind me, apparently for the same purpose. He complained to the guard vehemently about some discomfort, pushing me aside the while. The guard answered unpleasantly, blew his whistle, and the Linen Duster, forgetting my existence, banged the door suddenly and irritably — banged it with my thumb in it, just as the train started.

I screamed with pain and terror; the man exclaimed, "*Ach Gott!*" several passengers flew along the corridor to my rescue, but could not open the door, which had a spring lock. It was probably only a half-minute before the general alarm brought the guard, and I was released more dead than alive and borne into a first-class compartment with only a single passenger, the one I had occupied having four ladies, all in hysterics, although their thumbs were quite uninjured.

Kind persons, murmuring incomprehensible words, stormed at the alarmed and incoherent Linen Duster, took off my glove and bandaged my hand. I sobbed for an hour, undeterred by the presence of the smart and handsome Austrian officer who shared my compartment, but who paced the corridor wiping his forehead and wringing his hands. He had asked me in German if I spoke French, and I had faintly replied in that tongue between sobs, "Yes, a little — but — not — when — I am wounded."

An hour wore on. The guard found ice at the stations and put my hand in a rubber sponge-bag and suspended it to the side of the window, as the bleeding was continuous. What would become of me in this extremity, I wondered!

Never would I travel alone again in a foreign country, I thought, even for six hours in a first-class compartment without change.

We stopped at another larger station, and my officer, who by this time was completely distraught by my suffering and his inability to help me, looked from the window and suddenly disappeared. In ten minutes he returned beaming with delight, and with him a beautiful girl, who said in quite perfect English: "What can I do to help you? Will you not come into my compartment where we can be quite alone?"

It seems that the officer saw from the window certain servants whose livery he recognized and also the young lady whom they were attending and whom he had once met in Court circles in Hungary.

I followed my lovely rescuer thankfully, sobbing more than ever at the sound of my beloved native tongue. She had an elderly companion with her who spoke French and German, and she summoned from a second-class compartment a maid and a man servant whose livery and the cockade on whose hat bespoke the fact that he was in the service of a noble family. My good Samaritan was a Hungarian, and her card bore the name: "Comtesse Andréa Csekonics." She was dressed in a pretty traveling gown of black and white shepherd's plaid, a long mantle, and a simple black straw sailor hat, and when she removed the gloves from her lovely hands she displayed wonderful pearls. But she did not mind blood or the sight of my truly horrible thumb. She did not let the companion touch me, but bathed me with her own hands, even to washing my disreputable, tear-stained face, removing my hat, and smoothing my sadly disarranged hair. How she even guessed I was a lady, under the circumstances, I hardly know, but she did; also she liked the lady in a few minutes, and the lady certainly liked, and subsequently loved, her, in return.

After the first attempt at rehabilitation she had her portmanteau opened and began to strip up exquisite linen napkins with crests and coats of arms on them. I could see a crown with twelve points, which to me seemed awe-inspiring.

She bound up my hand in ice as carefully as possible, and then composedly ripped off the broad black ribbons from her wrap and made a sling, adjusting it as cleverly as a surgeon.

From the fragments of the German conversation between the servants and the officer I concluded that it was the general opinion that I should lose my thumb, but I tried to be quiet and conceal my pain and natural anxiety.

Finally my charming nurse gave me hot milk and wine, and, drawing my head down on her shoulder, implored me to telegraph for friends.

"You are too 'yunk' to travel alone, my little dearest" (I was nearly fifteen years her senior). Whereupon I suddenly recalled, what I had been too ill to remember before, that Miss L. and Molly were on a *diligence* between Pontresina and Zurich and I could not be sure of reaching them by telegram for thirty-six hours.

I explained my hapless condition, and the details of my journey, which seemed all at once to be very heedlessly planned, because this accident had completely disarranged what had been most carefully thought out.

By this time my thumb was black and my arm scarlet to the elbow, with ever-increasing pain. Countess Andréa was to leave the train at Lend to visit her "grandmamma's" castle at Ischl, and after that I should have three hours alone. She announced a different plan every fifteen minutes, the first being that I should take her companion and send her back from Innsbruck to Ischl next day. She, herself, would be quite safe, she said, as her grandmamma's maid would meet her at Lend and drive with her to Bade-Schloss. This courtesy I declined with many thanks, for the companion spoke no English, and I hastily calculated that it would be a highly expensive expedient and place me under unbearable obligation.

Her next proposition was that I should accompany her to her grandmamma's castle, but it was a three hours' drive up the mountain, with no surgeon at the top, and rain was beginning to fall, so this enticing plan was dropped.

At length I said: "There is but one thing to do. I have a friend, an American doctor in Graz. It is the last thing I would wish to do, but I *can* telegraph him to follow me to Innsbruck immediately and perhaps he can save my finger."

This idea greatly relieved the young countess, and she sent a long telegram to Dr. Ben at the next station. The time was drawing near for our parting, and I paid a large sum extra to take on her compartment alone from Lend to Innsbruck. She dressed my finger for the last time, and laid me on the sofa with everything needful near at hand. She impressed the guard with all manner of orders — that he was to get ice constantly, bring me my dinner, and feed me with his own hands; also that no one was to come near me and that he was to take me off the train and deliver me to the Hotel Sonne porter, who had been telegraphed to meet me at the station. Finally the lovely creature left me with tears in her eyes, kissing me again and again while she said, "Good-bye, my little dearest. Gott bless you! The Herr Doktor must write me daily and you yourself when you are recovered."

I reached Innsbruck very ill, the only incident of my hours alone being a clandestine visit from the Linen Dusterman who had done the foul deed. He dropped on his knees and kissed my left hand, weeping at such a rate that I was obliged to reassure, and rid myself of him by murmuring: *"Das thut nichts! Gehen sie aus, bitte!"*

The hotel porter searched and found a German doctor, who came to the hotel and gave me a painful treatment and a sleeping draught, receiving the information that I was to have an American doctor next day with surprise and indignation.

And how about Dr. Ben? He had to wait at Loeben for an hour, and two hours at Bruck-am-Mur, before he could get a train back to Graz. Arriving there he walked a long time through the lonely streets, as he told me afterward, and at length entered his lodgings at eleven o'clock in the evening.

As he approached the center table in his sitting-room, his eye caught sight of a telegram propped up against the lighted lamp. He tore it open and read in English:

The Countess Andréa Csekonics begs to inform Dr. Ben F. that his American friend, Mrs. Wiggin, has met with a railway accident which, though it may not be serious, involves much pain. She has had every attention and care that could be given her, but she is in sad condition and her American traveling companions cannot be reached for twenty-four hours. Can you go to Innsbruck at once? Please telegraph answer to:
Wildbad-Gastein,
Bade-Schloss,
Lend.

Poor Dr. Ben! He had never failed to help the "boofer lady." He packed a few necessary things and, without taking off his overcoat, hurried to the station to find he was too late for the night express. That being the case, he took the first freight train and traveled fourteen hours before reaching Innsbruck, all this with no sleep and little food. Miss L. and Molly arrived a few hours later and helped him to get what he needed for my comfort, but it was his care, devotion, and truly exquisite surgical skill that saved my thumb without a scar.

My hand was crippled for six weeks, but I was able to travel in four days, during which time of convalescence we had a daily correspondence with Countess Andréa, of whom we learned much in Innsbruck. Her father, a Hungarian nobleman of great wealth, was in high favor with the Emperor and entertained him at his castle at Ischl every season for shooting. Letters and telegrams flew between us for some time, and a most enticing invitation came for me to spend a month with her in Budapest. ("You will like it, my little dearest! I have six magnificent brothers!" so she wrote.) It was some years before we finally lost touch with each other in the bewildering excitements of life that overtook us both, but she was an adorable creature, well worth love at first sight.

When Dr. Ben left us, he promised to return to America and his many friends within a year, and to give up his desolate life of wandering and exile, but I had no feeling that this would come to pass, and this time my premonition was right.

He died within a few months among strangers, far away from kith and kin, from acquaintances and friends, with no one near to keep up his courage or to say good-bye to him. This word of sympathy and of understanding is the only flower I can lay on the grave of a true friend, a grave I shall never see, and a friend I shall never forget.

I shall pass over Zurich, Lucerne, Interlaken, Bern, Geneva, Yverdun, since this is not a tourist's diary. Great mountains and lakes, great buildings, great pictures, great marbles, crowd and enchain the eye and fill the heart with remembered loveliness, but, though they influence one's taste, develop one's sense of beauty, and have a distinct value in widening one's horizon in a general way as to peoples, politics, national idiosyncrasies, customs, and manners, I am one of those who learn more from human beings. Passing a day or two in a town or city has always meant little to me. I want to live there long enough to participate, to be a neighbor, a sharer in some modest sort of way in the life about me. In such circumstances, without study, elaborate gathering of material, conscious observation, I become saturated with the spirit of the place, if by chance I belong to it and it belongs to me rightfully, the captive of my own modest bow and spear. That is the reason, I suppose, that I have used in my books so little of the background of Continental cities, save in Italy, where, three months in Venice and much time in Florence and Rome, seeing and sharing to some extent the social and family life of each city, I acquired sufficient familiarity with it all to furnish some chapters in "Penelope's Postscripts."

Even in Paris, where I spent three months on my way from Geneva, I do not remember the Tomb of Napoleon, Notre Dame, the Luxembourg, the Panthéon, Fontainebleau, Versailles, save as pictures floating in mist. My heart recalls only my French home with Madame la Marquise Le Mulier, her two daughters, Olga and Marie de la Vaissière, who taught French, and *petite* Bichette, a little convent-bred granddaughter who came to spend week-ends with the family.

I recall my bedroom with fresh green and white bed and window curtains, the crucifix and Mater Dolorosa over my head, the corner curtained off for a dressing-room, the family portraits and aquarelles, the *café au lait* at eight, the lessons from ten to twelve, *déjeuner* at noon; and the (to me) frightfully embarrassing dinners at seven, where the family (who spoke no English) sparkled, scintillated, coruscated, and gesticulated in a bewildering torrent of French, while Molly and I sat dumb, clumsy, lifeless, stupid, and unresponsive! It is good for one's vanity to be utterly submerged in this fashion, trying to stiffen one's self-respect by remembering the times one has been called in the past the "life of the party," though now one is conscious of being the probable death of it!

Madame la Marquise, though then in reduced circumstances, was a great lady, a tiny creature, seventy-four years old, with most exquisite manners and speech. Her father was a former Minister of Finance, her dead husband a Colonel and Commander of the Légion d'Honneur, her son a Chevalier of the Légion and bristling with many other distinctions.

The little drawing-room was filled with royal presents made to Madame's grandmother by Marie Antoinette, with one beautiful box presented to her father by Pauline Bonaparte — "*La Belle Pauline.*"

Madame had been a pupil of the great Malibran, and frequently favored us with an operatic aria in the evening. It was oftenest "*Robert, toi que j'aime,*" and she sat at the little piano playing her own accompaniments and singing like a tiny elderly canary, quite mistress still of her trills and roulades.

After the concert, which was delightful because Molly and I could applaud and smile in English, though we could make no exquisite compliments in French, there always followed a terrifying *divertissement*, valuable for the acquisition of French, in which we played juvenile games. They were more than juvenile, they were infantile; nevertheless they intensified brain-action to such a degree that I felt positively ill during and after them. Shame and degradation enveloped me like a garment during the decreed amusement!

Light feathery objects were flung daintily across the little salon into one's reluctant American lap by Madame la Marquise or by Vicomtesse Marie or Olga, always accompanied by gentle laughter and a tinkling volley of words, uttered with frightful velocity and ending in an interrogation point. We had ears and could discern the fact that we had been asked a question, but how reply when one had caught only an uneventful word or two of the torrent? It only remained to clutch the feathery object and remark stupidly, "*Je ne comprends pas, Madame la Marquise; je suis bien fâché!*" wondering, meantime, if I were obliged to write "*fâché*," whether, being a female, I should add another "e" to "*fâché*," for my mind sleeping and waking was filled with questions of gender — not the Freudian sex-complex of to-day, but an intellectual scramble for "*le mot juste.*"

Explanations voluble beyond belief followed the tossing of the missile, explanations half understood, and then the detested weapon would be tossed by us without words into any lap toward which our aim was certain. At this point Molly on the first occasion left the room with a plea, incorrect in form and containing many wrong tenses of the necessary verbs, her sublime finish being, "*Je suis mal à la tête,*" for which she was gracefully corrected *en route* by Mademoiselle Olga, I being left to bear the burden alone.

I learned to love the members of this family very much, and to win also the friendship of Mariette the cook, and gray-haired Albert, the *garçon, valet-de-chambre,* butler, and all else. My stay was almost over when my birthday came to pass, September 28th, and there was an affectionate and delightful celebration of the event. I remember the flowers, the delicious repast, and especially one course devised by Albert. He had apparently secured, perhaps from the Paris Exposition of several years before, a single

ear of corn, a veritable antique. Before the salad Albert
entered, bearing with infinite elegance a sizable platter, and,
placing it before Madame la Marquise and removing the
cover, he remarked, with infinite pride: "*Voilà!* Behold
the national dish of the charming American lady!" He
thereupon handed Madame a small carving-knife and fork
and retired, blushing and happy, to a corner to await the
service.

The single ear of corn looked very lonely on its platter
and displayed a very strange, brown color, whether acquired by extreme age or by Mariette's cooking, I could
not say. Madame took the carving-knife and fork in her
dainty little ringed fingers and, with a bow, said to me,
"*Permettez-moi, Madame?*" I bent my head and "permitted" her, but alas! my permission was futile. She first
attempted to carve and then to "saw" the unfamiliar object on the platter with her usual grace and distinction,
but nothing happened.

"Has it perhaps a bone that should have been removed
in the kitchen, Albert?" was her question, as well as I
could translate it.

"I think not," replied Albert, "but pray allow me to
carve it on the side table."

He disappeared behind a screen and struggled with my
"national dish," which finally, as nearly as we could judge
by sound, parted under extreme pressure and flew in two
directions. We were all embarrassed, I particularly so. I
murmured the word "ear" as related to corn, but it seemed
to them extraordinary that a part of the human body could
be used as the foundation of this rebellious article of food.
"Corn on the cob" was a difficult phrase, the word "cob"
was not in my slender French repertory and I doubted if it
were in the dictionary, so the incident was suffered to pass
with light laughter and persiflage.

That morning I had taken Bichette and a little convent friend to assist me in shopping at the Bon Marché. Both children were enchanted at the carriage drive, at being allowed to interpret and advise, at the little gifts with which I presented them, and the *déjeuner* at a quiet place near by. On the way home they embraced me fervently many times, and at dinner I found a bit of handiwork from Bichette, with a note which I have always kept as so characteristic of the grace and charm of a French child of twelve years.

MADAME!

J'espère que vous voudrez accepter ce petit travail comme le souvenir d'une petite fille qui vous aime de tout son cœur, et qui est bien triste que vous vous en alliez si tôt.

Permettez-moi, je vous prie, Madame, de vous souhaiter une bonne fête et tout ce qui peut vous rendre heureuse...heureuse...!

BICHETTE DE LA VAISSIÈRE

Le 28 Septembre 1890
PARIS

There is, in the last line of its tender little assembling of dots and exclamation point, a certain charm that is purely French, and to me it still seems miraculous that a child of twelve could master the intricacies of the verb "to go" and write correctly "*que vous vous en alliez*" — the present indicative, first person singular, being the only movement of which I was ever sure.

On one of the last afternoons of my stay in Paris, I went alone on an omnibus to the cemetery at Passy to see the tomb of Marie Bashkirtseff. I had read her diary when it appeared, and smiled a little at its vanity, its egotism, its restless ambition to be known, admired, and recognized; but I was always touched by the childlike confession of her inmost feelings, sure though she must have been that they would provoke criticism. One thing disarmed me, even when my taste rejected her not-quite-normal frankness, and that was her dogged pertinacity and devotion to her work — reading, writing, or painting. She scorned fatigue, though she was often, perhaps always, ill; yet no day, no night was long enough for this intrepid young creature to labor, in order that she should achieve fame and be remembered after death.

I approached the tomb, the finest one in the cemetery. Over the main entrance is this verse, cut in gold letters on stone:

> "O Marie, O lys blanc, radieuse beauté,
> Ton être entier n'a pas sombre dans la nuit noire.
> Ton esprit est vivant, vibrante est ta mémoire
> Et l'immortel parfum de la fleur est resté!"
>
> André Theuriet

On another side was the inscription:

À Marie Bashkirtseff

1860–1884

with a swarm of butterflies hovering over a star.

The third side had an openwork iron door and showed a long narrow chamber with an altar at one end where there stood two large candelabra with dozens of unlighted candles. A marble bust of Marie herself, some family portraits, and copies of her favorite books were in sight. Around the chamber were placed what must have been her old chairs, in use since childhood, her stools, sofa-pillows and *prie-dieu*. There were growing palms and fuchsias in pots, and quantities of the funeral wreaths common to France, beaded arrangements of purple, white, or black. A strip of Turkish carpet was placed on the marble floor leading to the altar, and over this entrance was an inscription from another well-known French poet.

Poor, pitiful, gifted child of twenty-four, she had achieved her cherished ambition more than most of us have done! She had been dead for six years then, but she was singularly alive for me, although I was not of her worshipers. I was struck with the fact that her commanding personality had, so to speak, outwitted, defied, and vanquished death! Some remnant of her feverish frail body was still there beneath the sod according to the inexorable law of Nature, but she, herself, her spirit, her personality, radiant, courageous, proud, indomitable, she, Marie Bashkirtseff, had somehow persisted, and I felt myself in her presence.

XX

AN ENGLISH COUNTRY HOUSE

A FEW days later I went back for a flying visit to my London friends, Mr. and Mrs. Percy Spalding. As soon as I arrived, I found an unexpected invitation awaiting me from Mr. and Mrs. Charles Nevill, of Bramall Hall, in Cheshire. I had met them at a London dinner earlier in the season, and there had been a decided friendliness between us from the first. I knew that Mr. Nevill was a wealthy business man in Manchester, but he was something entirely different in manner, in temperament, in tastes and proclivities from any other man of business I had ever met in England. That his father had built up the great manufactory and bequeathed it to his only son may have accounted for the fact that the son traveled about the world incessantly, collecting rare things from every country he visited and living a life of leisure, devoted to books and art.

Mr. Nevill the elder had purchased Bramall Hall from an old county family (the Davenports), who in the last hundred years had lost the money necessary to keep up so magnificent a property, and had given it to his son shortly after his marriage.

I had heard of it as one of the most wonderful old black-and-white half-timber houses in the whole county of Cheshire, and Mrs. Spalding insisted that I must not return to America without one visit in an English country house, even if it were to be necessarily brief, as my sailing date was near at hand.

The invitations were renewed every day by brief letter or by telegraph, and accordingly Mrs. Spalding and I left

BRAMALL HALL FROM THE COURTYARD

London for a five days' stay. I little thought, when I first beheld Bramall in all its picturesque beauty and grandeur, that it would become a sort of English home to me, revisited every year for more than twenty years, until first the lovely mistress, and then the clever and brilliant master, died and left a great blank in my list of English friendships. This first visit was in the autumn of 1890, but, after my marriage to Mr. Riggs, in 1895, he, as well as my sister, were welcomed into the heart of the family circle and passed many happy weeks in this marvelous old house every season, my husband becoming a much-loved friend of both Mr. and Mrs. Nevill.

My sister has preserved an enthusiastic letter written to her on the night of my arrival at the Nevills'. It is youthful, ecstatic, brimming over with surprise, admiration, and delight in the new environment.

BRAMALL HALL
NR STOCKPORT CHESHIRE.
October 30th, 1890

MY DEAR NORA:

Behold me in the lap of luxury! Behold me, the daughter of a youthful nation, disporting myself on an Elizabethan-and-Norman background! You didn't know that I was to be here, and have this experience, — even the angels didn't know, — yet here I am in a "baronial castle" at the end of the shooting season. (If I had arrived at the beginning, it would have done me no good, for the only weapon I have with me is my guitar and I find it much more useful, in my hands, than a gun!)

I have written you of the Nevills of Bramall Hall, but I can hardly bear to describe my surroundings when I remember that you and mother are living in a San Francisco "flat," and who am I, pray, that I should be dwelling in a house the newest portion of which dates from Queen Elizabeth's time? The Virgin Queen herself passed the night here on one of her royal progresses and sent her workmen afterward to model in plaster a marvelous ceiling in the drawing-room, leaving her royal coat of arms over the great fireplace as a memento of the visit. With its jeweled windows, its green terraces where peacocks flaunt their tails, its hedges of yew and holly and its own trout stream; with its armor, its tapestries, its silver and carved oak, it is a perfect example of the ideal English country house.

Part of it is several hundred years old (I can't stop to look up Queen Elizabeth or the earlier Norman architecture), but my host reminds me daily that other parts of Bramall were built when America was being discovered! He has been restoring the place steadily during the seven years of his ownership and the workmen are still on the premises, for he is doing everything with rare taste and devoting hours of study every day that the result may approach perfection. They are restoring the private chapel now (under the same roof, you know, on the ground floor) and I steal in for a moment now and then to sit in one of the ancient pews and lift one of the precious old prayer books chained to the oaken rail. I asked Mr. Nevill the reason of this ancient custom, and he replied exasperatingly that American tourists sometimes visit the chapel, but I am confident that there is a pleasanter explanation than this.

There is everything here we ever read about in a Disraeli novel. The great hall, its walls covered with arms and armor and its stained-glass windows emblazoned with colored coats of arms, has a fireplace large enough for two beautiful carved stone benches in the chimney, where we sit after dinner or at tea-time. The furnishing is of course entirely of antique pieces and altogether superb, while the bronzes and lacquers and ivories and porcelains reflect the firelight and intoxicate me with their beauty. Oh! my dears, if you could only see that hall lighted by candles at five o'clock, the men in their shooting clothes, Mrs. Nevill with her train brocaded with red Venetian flowers (all her dresses match the house), the beautiful tea equipage, crumpets, hot muffins, marmalade and pâté-de-foie-gras sandwiches, servants in livery, *and* a great gray boar-hound on the rug in front of the fire — I cannot go on, my hand trembles with excitement!

Later

Upstairs each guest's name is written on a card enclosed in a frame on the door (I am going to put mine on my hotel sitting-room door in New York! It is the only inexpensive feature of the establishment that I can find to imitate!) My room is at least thirty feet square. A mullioned window twelve feet long and four feet high, all leaded panes of glass, looks on the park, the terraces, and the little river that flows through the park. The walls and ceilings are paneled oak and my bed is seven feet wide. When I go to bed at night there is a procession of room-maids, ladies' maids, housekeepers and others, with warming pans, jugs of hot water, candles, eider-down quilts, and hot gin and water! In the morning a procession arrives with different articles, and oh! how I like it!

I had not a tea gown in my wardrobe and Mrs. Spalding said, after mature reflection, that she thought I had better buy one or stay at home. Accordingly I secured a much smaller stateroom than I intended for my return trip, and had a tea gown quickly made in Bond Street. It is soft white nun's veiling and white chiffon, long thin flowing sleeves, and a little silver ribbon and narrow white fox fur. It drapes gracefully, trails its expensive lengths across the priceless antique rugs, sweeps attractively over the boar-hound's tail, and surrounds the wearer with a sort of ethereal, heavenly atmosphere not entirely appropriate. I come down to tea as early, and stay as late, as possible, because my next costume is of the earth earthy — a somewhat shabby black lace rag, as of course I am not wearing colors. It is at tea-time that I sing with the guitar, and my still small voice in old English love songs and plantation melodies (greatly aided by the white tea gown and the dim candlelight) win me at least much temporary popularity.

This afternoon Mr. Nevill took me through the entire house (sixty rooms), explaining the nature of all his wonderful treasures, which are so arranged that, notwithstanding their value and rarity, and their extraordinary number, the effect is somehow kept from being that of a museum. One room has cabinets of exquisite Tanagra figurines, another hundreds of carved Chinese ivories, with Cloisonné and Satsuma. Another is filled with priceless specimens of old Spode china; while bronzes, from tiny bits to temple-pieces five feet high, adorn the broad window-sills and fill the niches up and down the oak stairways. There are many stairways, added, no doubt, at various periods, and the very afternoon of my arrival when I left the Davenport Room (my bedroom) for the great hall at tea-time — wandering along what I believed to be the right path, but a good deal occupied with the effect of my new white tea gown — I opened and threw back a heavy oak doorway and confronted, somewhat theatrically, the housekeeper's sitting-room where six maids, a valet, and a coachman were having their tea.

"I'm awfully sorry!" I said. "I have lost my way. Will you kindly show me the hall?"

They did so, thinking little of my mentality or sense of direction, I fancy, but the lady's-maid told me that the housemaid said that the valet told her that the coachman remarked that "first 'e thought it was a h'angel standing in the dark doorway."

England and Scotland are all I care to come back to, with now and then a sight of Wales and the Bavarian Tyrol. I don't care what becomes of the rest. Forever now I shall be chanting:

> "Far wave, far heaven, far hill,
> I dream of England still."

Your loving prodigal sister
KATE

Later on I wrote to my mother a letter about the cooking at Bramall Hall, "extra well" composed, as it was to be sent the rounds of the family. My mother, when she had to be, was a most delicious cook and much interested in bills-of-fare and in toothsome and unusual dishes.

DEAR MOTHER:

You ask me about the difference between French and English cookery, which lies largely in seasoning and ability to deal with "left-overs."

The English can make bread sauce suitable for a king, while ours is fit only for poultices. They can manage a wonderful onion relish for mutton, and excel us in a creamy horseradish sauce for roast beef. And how the best of their cooks can deal with parsley sauce! There are tender boiled fowls, borne into the dining-room on a silver platter, while you marvel at their beauty. They are stripped of skin and glazed with a sauce, pale green in color, and liquid velvet to the taste. At the head and foot of the fowl lie pieces of such boiled bacon as we never get on the American side of the Atlantic. Its tints of rose and white are vastly becoming to the green against which they lean, and when the host gives you a slice of the breast and another of the bacon, and the waitress says, "Please, 'm', will you have a little more parsley sauce?" you can hardly avoid smacking your lips after the manner of the Cratchit children when they smelled the celebrated Christmas goose.

I suppose, of course, that climate conditions all national cookery, and that each country eats what is best suited to its mode of life. At any rate, I cannot eat an English breakfast in America, but in England it fitly begins the day. Much choice is given you, not only between tea and coffee — and you usually choose tea, not because you like it more, but because you like the coffee less — but of a trio of good things to eat. There will be, perhaps, buttered eggs and bacon, a fried lemon sole, and a dish of broiled mushrooms and kidneys. Here again, mother, we Americans must retire modestly to the background. I know that kidneys are cooked better in Great Britain than in America, but the tragedy is blacker than that, for the kidneys themselves are better, and pray how can that be accounted for? Is it, perhaps, that the lamb and mutton are better, to begin with? Can a lamb or a sheep influence for good or ill its own kidneys? Do you ever find a roast or a boiled leg of mutton served at an American table without an apology that you have chanced upon a plain family dinner? And does the American mutton ever blush? No, but perhaps it has never been abroad and seen the little black-faced Welsh sheep, and what it can do in the way of a leg! No plain family dinner there, but a dish fit for princes of the realm.

However, having criticized the mutton of our own country and rebuked it for not paying more attention to the cultivation of its own kidneys, I return to the question of English cooking and find that the breakfasts and luncheons, as well as the teas and dinners of Bramall Hall in Cheshire, furnish an imperishable ideal of English excellence.

I sometimes steal a half-hour at tea-time, or just before luncheon, to collogue with the Scotch artist who presides over the Bramall kitchens, just to watch her combine the articles that her docile assistant has gathered on the table to await her skillful hand. From the wonderful old leaded glass windows of the kitchen I can see the velvety green terraces, the shining trout-stream, and the avenues bordered with blooming rhododendrons, while within all is peace. In the range burns a bright fire, the copper cooking-utensils gleam on the wall, the table and the floor are white as snow, and there are yellow bowls and old British luster saucers, with here and there on the great table dabs of green butter colored with spinach, hillocks of whipped cream, slices of red tomato and hard-boiled egg, snippets of scarlet pepper and minced olives, and little heaps of silvery anchovies, all waiting to be made into savories.

"Bring the croûtons!" says the genius of the place, and the kitchen-maid flies to her own lair where smoke and smell of frying and broiling may enter. When she returns the sculptor, painter, high priestess, with the more unassuming title of cook-housekeeper, stretches forth her untrembling hand and designs some little, blooming, fairy-like things that are to follow the sweet at dinner and produce thirst for the old port. Sometimes she permits me to try and make one "bloom" and the result is like a lump of quartz sitting among jewels!

KATE

Soon after this first visit to an English country house, I set sail for America, November, 1890, on the Red Star Line from Antwerp. On arriving in New York, I went at once to the Hotel Albert, University Place and Eleventh Street, and secured a tiny sitting-room and bed-room at a reasonable price, although my income did not promise much food when my rent was paid. I chose that hotel because it was filled with my literary friends — the Howellses, Frank Stocktons, Janviers; also Mr. Franklin Sargent, of the American Academy of Dramatic Arts, and his mother, who was all that any stranger-mother could be to me, and Heaven knows I needed one, with my own dear one in San Francisco!

Luncheons, dinners, and readings for Free Kindergar-tens followed in stimulating succession, for the rewards of even semi-successful authorship come quickly when one is young and full of the joy of life.

I had for intimate friends beside the hotel group, Carl Schurz and his daughters, Colonel and Mrs. Robert Ingersoll, Mr. Edmund C. Stedman, William Winter, Mary Mapes Dodge, Mary Wilkins, Mr. and Mrs. Lau-rence Hutton, Clyde Fitch, and many others.

Life was so delightful and so simple! A group of us used often to dine at the Hotel Griffou, in Ninth Street, a fifty-cent *table d'hôte* with pint of wine included, and such talk, such delightful interchange of views on books, pictures, and current events, such wit, and such merriment. The dinners were uniformly good, or seemed so to me, as my meals *à la carte* at the hotel were brief and uneventful. A new author with no income save her own earnings cannot indulge in luxuries, and I know that corned tongue and spinach at forty-five cents was my chief diet, being the cheapest article of the bill-of-fare! I mention this because, if there is one thing more delightful than another, it is the recalling and broadcasting of hard-time stories and the intrepid climbing of life's difficult ladder. An autobiographer's "hard times" have an indescribable interest for the reader as well as the writer. The struggles of a "self-made man" or woman, especially when they end inevitably in some degree of triumph, are as exciting as romance, and they encourage and thrill the poverty-stricken reader who bends over a kerosene lamp and wonders if his luck will ever turn.

XXI

A NEW CAREER

I THINK an entirely new path was gradually opening at this time, and persistently attracting me ever so little from the main road of a literary career, although I was quite unconscious of it. At Mrs. Sargent's notable Sunday evenings, many of the guests contributed a reading, recitation, or music, and I was now and then cajoled by Mrs. Sargent, her son, or by Clyde Fitch to add my bit to the entertainment.

A year before this I had done something really more important when I was living with Mrs. Alice Wellington Rollins at 150 West Fifty-Ninth Street. A group of us, all more or less "out of suits with fortune," had attended the performances of the Niebelungen Ring at the Metropolitan Opera House. We sat in the front row of the gallery and were the wildest of Wagner enthusiasts. In the spring, in honor of Mrs. Rollins's birthday, I wrote a nonsensical burlesque of a Wagner lecture-recital after the manner of Mr. Walter Damrosch, at whose very popular lectures I was always a faithful and admiring attendant. I took the melodramatic story of "Bluebeard" for the libretto of my opera, alluding to it as an unpublished work of Richard Wagner. Then, seated at the piano, I unveiled and interpreted one by one the various "motifs" and sang the entire opera, manufactured from various sources, much of it being my own composition, as was the libretto.

This was a laughter-provoking novelty, and I was asked for several years to do it for musical friends; indeed, I believe I might have "gone on the road with it" had I been so minded.

I read a chapter from one of my few published books now and then in Mrs. Sargent's or Mr. Stockton's hotel sitting-room, and once gave my "Bluebeard" recital when some distinguished musicians were present, but applause meant little to me save the transient pleasure one naturally feels in appreciation. I knew how wholly amateurish were all these trifles, but in later days I understood that they had formed a sort of basis for more exacting efforts, and were in a sense a self-training for wider experiences.

This "Bluebeard lecture-recital" was published years after with many revisions, and all the musical "motifs," by Harper and Brothers, and I gave it at my own house in its new form before Geraldine Farrar, David Bispham, Walter Damrosch, Emma Juch, Marcia Van Dresser, Gervase Elwes, Carlos Salzedo, Albert Morris Bagby, Arthur Foote, Albert Spalding, Frank Pollock, and other musicians. It was a performance calculated to reduce an amateur to nervous prostration as I sang, played the piano, and gave the lecture, thereby using the resources of three arts in which I had received no training. The bewildering fact was, that the more celebrated and learned were the musicians, the better they liked my nonsensical "Bluebeard"! Laymen thought it "clever" or "amusing," but Walter Damrosch, to whom I dedicated the book, confessed that he never afterward gave a lecture-recital on a Wagner opera without recalling my wicked burlesque.

Whether I went abroad that summer, as usual, where I stayed, and what was my manner of life can only be determined by a Court of Investigation, for my sister who was in San Francisco has not preserved letters and I have no records save a scrap of penciled paper saying that I sent "A Cathedral Courtship" for serial publication to the "Atlantic Monthly," December, 1891.

From that time on accounts of these readings or addresses are frequent, though briefly stated in my notes, generally without comment. They were all semi-private talks in behalf of New York Free Kindergartens, or readings at friendly dinners, among artist friends of one sort or another.

The first three in 1892 were January 7th, at the Women's Unitarian League, and January 11th and 13th, at the house of Mr. Carl Schurz. Then there was a more than unusually grand and fashionable occasion, on January 14th, at the beautiful studio of Mr. William Chase, the artist. Richard Watson Gilder, the President of the New York Kindergarten Association, introduced me as a sort of Joan of Arc for this cause, so that I felt overwhelmed with embarrassment and responsibility. Then Mr. Howells, in a few brief words, said that he always wished when he was introduced by a "personage" that the remarks could be preserved and printed on his gravestone. He said, too, amid applause and laughter, that an introduction was generally what a speaker would like to say of himself, but didn't dare!

I remember also that in the middle of one of my selections on that charming evening an antique tall clock in the corner behind me began striking, and not only began, but continued in defiance of all rules. Mr. Chase, the host, was too far in the rear to make his way through the crowd and interfere with the clock's eccentricities, and the audience was highly amused. I retained enough self-command to remark on the twenty-first stroke that I had no idea it was so late — a *mot* that served to enliven the interruption, and on the thirtieth stroke, when it deigned at last to stop, Mr. Gilder rose and remarked, "Your reading is, indeed, a striking occasion! Pray go on, Mrs. Wiggin!"

Then there was a delightful visit at my old school, Abbot Academy, on January 18th, in Andover, Massachusetts, where I had read the year before and was delighted to be welcomed again by a crowd of enthusiastic young people, as one of the "old girls of Abbot."

About this time I went to New England to help the Eastern Kindergarten Association in founding some new schools, notably one in Fall River for the children of factory workers, and this journey recalls an amusing incident.

I was a guest of the well-known Mr. and Mrs. Spencer Borden, who gave me a delightful dinner at seven o'clock, and their friends, to the number perhaps of one hundred and fifty, came at eight-thirty to hear my plea for the new enterprise. I went to my delightful guest-room very tired, at a little before eleven, and as I opened the door a small, expensive, but blatant cathedral clock on the mantel boomed forth the hour. I am a wretched sleeper and dislike vociferous clocks, and this one gave a loud stroke on the half-hour as well as the hour. I promptly put it carefully in a bureau drawer, but the wood acted as a sounding-board, and the noise that the clock made at midnight would have awakened the original Seven Sleepers. I rose and with considerable heat opened the closet door and set the offender on the floor. The closet had remarkable acoustic properties, and the twelve-thirty boom gave me a start that provoked further hostilities. I left my bed again, and, perceiving in the commodious closet several large drawers, found that they were filled with extra heavy blankets. I lifted one cautiously and respectfully laid the bawling and intrusive time-keeper on its back in the very middle of the pile, knowing that I could restore it to its unmerited and honorable place on the mantel at daybreak. Then I slept, as the righteous should, but seldom do.

At eight next morning my kind hostess rapped at the bedroom door and said: "Mrs. Wiggin, you were going on the ten-thirty train, but if you feel like being ready at

nine, Mr. Borden has to go to New York and will take care
of you all the way."

I liked Mr. Borden, was glad of his escort, made a
hurried toilette, breakfasted, and departed with him at
nine, and neither on the journey nor for long, long afterward did my brain revert to the sin I had committed in the
House of Borden.

On a certain night in Germany, many months after,
when the hotels were overcrowded, I was given a comfortable sofa in the proprietor's own sitting-room. At
eleven a small but vigorous and loud-mouthed gold clock
on the mantel gave the requisite number of undesired and
unrequested booms. Instantly my mind began to work!
Fall River! Borden House! Cathedral Clock! Bureau
Drawer! Closet Floor! Blankets! Then the secret scene
of suffocation and strangling of the hated object! Then
disappearance from the spot without confession!

It was now July. The blankets had been new and heavy.
Had the drawer been opened? What was my present
standing in the Borden family and in Fall River society?

I ran to a desk and poured out my soul in penitence to
Mrs. Borden. I would have cabled, but it seemed so
bizarre to say, after an interval of many months:

*Clock buried in guest-room closet between blankets and lower
drawer. Impossible to sleep with it! Forgive!*

No, I could only write the full history of my crime to
Mrs. Spencer Borden in Fall River, and in due course she
replied most indulgently that her new chambermaid had
searched for and recovered the clock immediately on the
receipt of my letter from Munich. (The phrase "*new
chambermaid*" struck me as inferentially tragic. Had the
old chambermaid been discharged for theft?)

Mrs. Borden said affectionately that the whole family

had more or less fallen in love with me and felt that I
was honest and virtuous. It was a trifle disturbing, of
course, to find that the "old" chambermaid (again that
worrying thought!) had wound the clock and set it just
before my arrival and reported its disappearance on the
next morning at ten. Mr. Borden said that he had carried
my dress-suitcase through the New York station, and that
it certainly was not suspiciously heavy.

All who discussed the mystery held the belief that I was
incapable of feloniously removing a small but weighty
cathedral clock from a house where I had been kindly
treated. Nevertheless, it was gone — a wedding gift, its
face surrounded with crystals, its body studded with
malachite and jade.

At twilight Mr. Borden would sometimes say, so his
wife facetiously reported: "I wonder where our dear Mrs.
Wiggin is!" "Yes," she would respond, "and I wonder
where our dear clock is!" I am glad that I wrote to her,
for had it not been for the experience in Munich I might
have been under slight suspicion until this very day,
although even millionaires must take out their fresh
blankets every few years!

In quick succession in the early winter of 1892 came two
invitations to read at Miss Masters's School at Dobbs
Ferry and Miss Aiken's at Stamford. The coaxing notes
from the girls' English and Composition classes were irresistible, and I read at both schools. It was in this way,
even before "Polly Oliver" and "Rebecca" were written,
that my life began continuously "to intersect the orbit of
youth." May it be so always till I die! Meeting young
people has always given me what Wordsworth calls
"vital feelings of delight," and I welcome it on every
possible occasion to this day.

There are records of readings at receptions given by the

Aldine Club, by Mr. Carl Schurz, by Clyde Fitch, and two talks on Kindergarten and Social Reform at Orange, New Jersey, and Wilmington, Delaware. There was one at Earl Hall, Columbia College, in a series of authors' readings begun by Mark Twain and George W. Cable, the latter a most beautiful reader. I have never heard anything lovelier than his voice in the French-Creole folksongs which he gave here and there in his stories of life in New Orleans and Louisiana.

Soon after this event came one day, very unexpectedly, a letter from a large town in a near-by State that set me thinking. The writer was the head of a certain Community Evening College. It was a pleasant, informal letter, saying that my name was a household word in his town, and that my picture, cut from newspapers and magazines, was pasted under the clock in dozens of kitchens and dining-rooms. (This touch was distinctly pleasant and unusual!)

The Community College wished to give a grand entertainment to celebrate its fifth anniversary, and the writer's married daughter had heard me read somewhere in New Jersey and thought that, if I would come for a hundred dollars and expenses, they could fill the church, which held six hundred persons, the tickets to be fifty cents, so that they could count on both pleasure and profit.

The town in question was a long, safe distance from New York. Why should I not steal away silently and read to a small but appreciative army of unworldly strangers, as I continually did in circles considered more select — fashionable and literary groups, where my pictures certainly were never pasted under the kitchen clocks — and come back with one hundred badly needed dollars?

On the success of this trial I could accept invitations to read in certain places where I was sure that a good cause

would be benefited over and above my fee. I had already
been asked by Mr. J. B. Pond to accept his management
and he had offered me first-class engagements in his
Lyceum Bureau, as many as I liked. I had declined this
appreciative offer, telling him that my physical strength
would never permit my keeping certain fixed dates nor the
weariness of many journeys. What I did not disclose was
the fact that I did not altogether like the idea of being a
"box-office attraction." Keeping myself free from "management" meant, of course, the burden of continuous
letters, plans, and arrangements on my own part, but it
would ensure my reading for the benefit of children's
charities, while I could accept compensation when I chose.

Letters from my interested public in the unknown place
came in quick succession, and, on being told that there was
no proper hotel for a "personage" like myself, I accepted
the hospitality of the head of the Community College and
his cheery, delightful wife. Every day proved that the
affair was to be of an epoch-making nature, for when my
tickets arrived there was an accompanying note from the
manager of the —— Railway assuring me that the express
train would be stopped at ——, though it had seldom been
done within the memory of man.

I alighted at four o'clock and was met by a committee of
cordial townsmen and women, and driven to the house of
my host. My hostess led me to a guest-chamber heated by
an airtight stove and begged me to rest, as twenty friends
were coming to supper at six. My heart sank, for I was
accustomed to quiet and solitude before a reading at eight,
but I graciously concealed my feelings.

I shall never forget the supper — delicious and bountiful
food, hospitably served by the ladies themselves, who
went to and from the kitchen, attending to every one
easily and well. The gentleman on my left, who was the

Chairman of the Entertainment Committee, was terribly nervous and shy, consequently somewhat embarrassed and clumsy, upsetting his glass, dropping his knife, fork, and spoon continually, and knocking my head against his when I stooped sympathetically to help him recover his tools. His face was crimson and bedewed with crystal drops of perspiration, for we were on the warm side of the dining-room, and my various remarks were received only with monosyllables. At last we reached the ice cream, and he gradually grew more at ease.

Suddenly he asked: "Did you notice the station you came into this afternoon, ma'am?"

"I noticed that it was new and very neat and attractive," I answered.

"Well I'm glad you liked it, ma'am, for it was finished off especially for you."

My teaspoon paused on the way to my mouth, as I said: "I don't quite understand — how do you mean?"

"Well," he answered, now voluble and friendly, "you see we've been building that station for three months and the work ain't gone smooth. Troubles with delivery, labor, bad weather, and one thing 'n' 'nother. I'm one of the Building Committee, and at the last meeting, when I found out you was coming here from New York to read, I says: 'Look a-here! Do we intend to have that lady come into an unfinished deepo when there ain't a week's labor to do on it? I, for one, would be ashamed of the town!' Well, sir, they all took fire and finished up the job inside and out in seven days."

"How simply magnificent!" I exclaimed.

"Not so bad, was it? Did you notice the waiting-room as you came through?"

"I saw that it was very comfortable, and somehow a little unlike other stations."

"Well, you see we couldn't get the stove and the right settees and tables and ice-water tank delivered for to-night, so the Entertainment Committee turned out and furnished the room themselves. Five or six of the ladies at this supper lent two sofas, five leather and two stuffed chairs, two black walnut, marble-topped tables, and some vases of chrysanthemums. They won't take 'em back till after you leave on the noon express to-morrow, neither — that's in the contract. 'We'll set where we can, till she goes,' that's what they said, and they meant it!"

I was certainly never more astonished, more grateful, nor more amused, than at this unprecedented tribute, and I was careful to let everybody know how thoroughly I appreciated it. At an authors' dinner in New York a few years later some one suggested over the coffee that each guest should relate the greatest triumph of his life. After Rudyard Kipling, Mark Twain, Mr. Howells, Mr. Stockton, Ruth McEnery Stuart, and others had told their tales, serious or humorous, as the case might be, I related my experiences in that reading in an unnamed town. The entire company at dinner decided that first honors should go to me, and that the table-decorations should be sent home with me in my cab, for never in their several lives had a railway station been finished and furnished in order that they might enter a town with propriety and dignity.

As a matter of fact, the entertainment went on from glory to glory. There were eight young men ushers, each wearing a huge American Beauty rose clipped from its stem and glued or nailed in some way to the lapel of his coat, and they insisted on preceding me solemnly up the church aisle in pairs to the pulpit platform, while the cabinet organ played melodious strains. I could only expect to find a father, bridegroom, and best man awaiting me at the end of the spectacular journey, and felt rather

lonely when I discovered myself alone with my book, surrounded with tall banquet lamps, and a floral display in
the background that must have greatly decreased the
profits of the College.

Never mind! I gave everything that was in me on that
memorable occasion! I changed my selections to suit the
audience, extemporized, talked to them familiarly whenever possible, told them a story now and then, never leaving any pauses for fear that they might march up the aisle,
salute the flag, and sing "The Star-Spangled Banner"
under the impression that I was the U.S.A. disguised in
one personality.

Dear people! Dear town! I dreamed for a time of living
there, but decided it would not be good for me. I needed
competition and drastic criticism, not railway stations
finished in my honor. New York is the place above all
others to keep one's head steadily poised in the precise
manner that the Lord intended, and above all to preserve
its accustomed size quite unenlarged under all circumstances.

XXII

SEMI–PROFESSIONAL READINGS

My life at this time was too exciting, too breathless, too crowded with events for the strongest woman to endure easily. I neither endured altogether, nor did I quite succumb. I drifted with a swift tide that carried me on without my having force to resist it. I never seemed to have strength to say "No" to three fourths of the requests that reached me; the appeals were so persuasive, the needs they represented so clamorous.

I had nothing practical, apparently, to do, so far as readings were concerned, but write half a dozen letters with regard to date, hour, and arrangement of light on a platform suitable in a large house, a church, or a hall. All these things attended to and dozens of hospitable invitations declined, there was nothing left but a short or long journey, the meeting of hundreds of strangers, the shaking of hundreds of hands, and the three readings each evening of twenty to twenty-five minutes in length, interspersed with the music which made up my afternoon or evening programme. How this could make such inroads on my vitality I cannot imagine! I read and read and read, sometimes under circumstances so delightful that I reacted to them with unspeakable joy; occasionally where matters were not well arranged and I had to mount a box between two large rooms, a glaring chandelier over my head, and the halls and stairways filled with people who could not be adequately reached. Sometimes there was a piano out of tune, sometimes a truly dreadful musician who, when I had succeeded in making "a composite mind" of the audience, tore everything asunder and left me to establish harmony again! At all events, I never met a single unsympathetic audience. Sometimes it responded in two minutes, sometimes in fifteen, but we always understood one another very soon. My few advisers said: "Reading is your vocation! Don't try to do anything else! If, as you say, you do not know how to read anything but your own stories, of course you will have to write enough of them to vary your readings, but, anyway, *read!*" And, indeed, it was perfect happiness — the part of it that was only reading and nothing more. I think two letters to my mother and sister in California, which have somehow escaped the flames, will give an idea of this semi-amateur, semi-professional, un-managed life I was leading.

HOTEL ALBERT, NEW YORK CITY
DEAR MOTHER AND NORA, FAR AWAY IN SAN FRANCISCO:
You will know how busy I must be when I have to dictate a home letter; but it seems as if I should never have leisure to write you in any other way. On Saturday last I was so unutterably weary, and found my letters accumulating to such an extent, that I sent for Miss B. and her typewriting machine, and we have been working together throughout the week, during which time I must have dictated a hundred letters.

I note what you say about these readings of mine. There is no doubt that they are overtaxing and overexciting, and if I continued them in rapid succession, they would be just as questionable spiritually and artistically. But I have read only ten or twelve times in four months, and the little money, together with the extended clientèle, is, of course, something to be thought of. My fee of one hundred dollars, though small, is a help, and I am enabling different organizations to earn thousands upon thousands for children's charities. I refuse half a dozen requests for each one that I grant. I read only when a good cause is to be benefited and never on any account for the entertainment of guests in a private house. I have declined no less than nine hundred dollars for nine different readings of this sort during the winter, solely because I did not wish to put myself on that footing, or to be paid money by my host or hostess. It would be perfectly dignified did I not wish to be a professional writer, but in

READING ALOUD FROM A MANUSCRIPT

brief, I will *not* be an Entertainer! (Unpleasant word!) I shall certainly read less next year and therefore shall ask a hundred and fifty dollars and expenses. I know well that the wear and tear is tremendous, but I am, as you know, very desirous of adding to our mutual savings in every way possible this season, in order that the risk of your leaving California and of our being together in the East next year may not be so great. Still, do not think I minimize the risks. The spotlight is dangerous for a woman who wishes to be a real literary artist. Too much attention and glorification are demoralizing to any talent.

The Benefit being planned for our Kindergartens is in Sherry's white and gold ballroom. Reception four to seven o'clock. Reading five to five-thirty. Music by Miss Leonora Von Stosch (now Lady Speyer) with her Stradivarius. She is a genius, a beauty, and a great friend of the Gilders. Mrs. Grover Cleveland is to receive the guests with five débutante assistants.

You will remember my friendship with Mrs. Cleveland, when in the first years of her married life she passed the summer in a cottage beside the Saranac Inn where I was staying? We had many evening games, amateur theatricals, and tableaux, and you will recall my foolish feat of writing once a week a poetical bill-of-fare for all the guests. Mrs. Cleveland is very good at verses herself, and as I have just come across some of hers to me, I send them to mother, as they are likely to be the only ones addressed to me by a President's wife.

> A certain young Mrs. Wigg*in*,
> Came once to the Saranac Inn.
>   She could act like a star,
>   Or play the guitar.
> She's remembered wherever she's been!
>
> She could act, she could play, she could sing —
> In fact, she could do any thing
>   From making a rhyme,
>   At 'most any time,
> To shooting a bird on the wing.
>
> We have lost her, our Mrs. Wigg*in!*
> She has gone from the Saranac Inn!
>   She drove over to Paul's,
>   And now memory's all's
> That is left us to show where she's been!

F. F. C.

I read in B. Monday evening, leaving there on the midnight train for Chicago. I have had a dozen invitations to visit people during my stay and finally have accepted that of Mrs. Blatchford, the soul of kindness and understanding. It seems in my present state of mind as if I could not endure the mental strain of visiting and being agreeable three times a day. Not that it would rest me to be disagreeable. Far from it!

I have engagements in March and April to read in Baltimore, Wilmington, and Boston, with provisional ones at Stamford and Northampton, but these can be omitted if advisable. The last is in Boston, April the twelfth; I think, however, that I shall leave New York the first of May and go somewhere in Maine, perhaps to Hollis or Gorham, and settle down to absolute quiet until the next thing happens. Things do happen to me in extraordinary profusion and unexpectedness.

"Polly Oliver" will be published in a few months; it has, of course, a California background, and I hope that girls will like it.

With all my love

KATE

HOTEL ALBERT, NEW YORK CITY

DEAR MOTHER AND SISTER:

The following is a detailed account of my "western tour of one-night stands." It was as enjoyable on the whole as such a thing can possibly be, although not altogether pleasant by any means. If I should catalogue the places alphabetically, although not in proper continuity, they would run, A — delightful, B — adorable, C — slightly stupid, D — dull, E — heavenly, and so on, but I confess that each affair was highly successful, only sometimes I am very tired and at other times tolerably well, and I am far too dependent on the place in which I read — the stage or platform settings, the kind of introduction I receive, etc., etc. This is ungrateful, for I am always presented by the most distinguished citizen, the most popular author, the Mayor of the City, or the Governor of the State. Sometimes they speak perfunctorily, but far oftener they submerge me in compliments. The Committee of Arrangements everywhere is without exception a group of charming literary and philanthropic women.

The last affair was under the auspices of a club of young ladies and was miserably managed, although a triumph in point of numbers, as far as the audience was concerned. The surroundings, however, put me all out of key with myself. The low platform was in a large chapel with Sunday School rooms opening out from it; these also crowded with people who could not see me and were constantly moving and buzzing. The platform was covered with a threadbare grass-green carpet and nothing on it but a marble-topped table and a hideous pulpit-chair too heavy to move. There was a large china water-pitcher and tumbler which I courteously banished. (If people cannot read without stopping every now and then to drink, they should stay at home!) A villainous, yes, a violent, terra-cotta background completed the awful picture! I wore my turquoise blue brocade and was tempted to ask the audience if I could go back to the hotel and change it. I hope the person who dressed the stage suffered half as much as I, at the tableau confronting the audience. It is foolish to be so sensitive to color, but I cannot help it. The programmes had not arrived at eight o'clock, but a few were brought me in the waiting-room a little later while the local violinist was opening the entertainment. The young ladies were evidently not proof-readers, for my selections appeared as:

1. The Story of Popsy.
2. Timothy's Guess.
3. The Bride's Christian Coral.

Popsy for Patsy, Guess for Quest, might have been excused, but the changing of The Birds' Christmas Carol to The Bride's Christian Coral made me hysterical! I trust the charitable young ladies will marry and have lovely children, but I never wish to meet them again!

My reading for the Chicago Children's Hospital was, I think, a great financial success, though I have come decidedly to the conclusion that I do not like such enormous affairs. I suppose there were about eighteen hundred people present. My voice filled Music Hall without difficulty, but I felt myself too far from the people to enjoy the evening thoroughly. If you ask why I have to enjoy it myself, it is because I must, or the audience fails to give full and warm response.

It was an unusually appreciative audience, and all the kindergartners of Chicago gave me a reception on Saturday afternoon, where I read five or ten minutes from the "Story of Patsy." It was a very pleasant affair and gave two hundred out of four hundred people an opportunity to call me "Wiggins." I have little time at any of these occasions to say more than that my name is Wiggin and that adding an "s" only makes it worse to the ear.

A Scottish poet-friend who received my plaint concerning those who "burdened my name with superfluous sibilants," as he phrased it, sent me the following verses:

To
KATE DOUGLAS WIGGIN

. . . .

Superfluous S's must denote
The feeble-minded bird,

Whose hissing voice and waddling gait
Among the fowls of air,
Mark it as one that has no great
Amount of brains to spare.

And he or she who spells your name
Kate DouglasS WigginS should
Be held to have advanced a claim
To goose- or gander-hood!

H. J.

Mrs. Coonley, who has a palatial house on the Lake Shore Drive, gave me a charming evening reception. Eugene Field offered me a luncheon "for men only" which I could not accept. He wants me to name a specific date in the summer, when the foreign luminaries are present in Chicago for the Exposition, saying if I give him due notice he will make the reception a "corker." He is a most amusing personage and was very anxious that I should make a short tour of the West with him and Bill Nye. I told him that I was an amateur and never read save where a good cause was to be helped and where the tickets were sold by patrons or patronesses. (This sounded "snobbish" after I said it.) Moreover, that I did not feel that I was suited to "one-night stands," and that I wished to save my strength chiefly for writing.

I was well and happy that evening and wearing a lovely pink satin dress with crystal trimming. Perhaps you will remember that neither Eugene Field nor Bill Nye was rich in personal beauty? I laughed until the tears came, and so did the little group in which we stood, when Mr. Field said coaxingly: "I wish you *would* go along with us! We need you! You see [in a whisper] we are so d——d homely! We simply can't dress the stage."

He pressed something in my hand at parting and asked me to

remember him by it. It turned out to be a stick of chewing gum. Five minutes later he returned with his hat and coat and said with the utmost solemnity (I really do not know to this day whether it was in earnest or not): "I am not generally an Indian giver, but will you please let me have half of that gum back; I haven't any to go home on." I wonder what Swinburne or Austin Dobson would think of our Western poets with their informality and American humor. One would have to know Eugene Field to understand him thoroughly. He was so lovable, so unique, so spontaneous in his humor, and so tender in his thought of children. He made even the gum-chewing episode quaint, not offensive.

People are radiantly kind everywhere! I try with all my strength to return these affectionate greetings in every possible way and lie down every night filled with gratitude, aches, and pains. There is no danger that all this friendly appreciation will ever turn my head, for it goes straight to my heart! Nor will the money I receive ever make me mercenary, nor swerve me from my chosen path, for you will remember in one of Grimm's Fairy Tales the Dwarf answered: "No, something human is dearer to me than the wealth of the whole world."

Yours with love

KATE

XXIII

LONDON EXPERIENCES

At the close of this somewhat tumultuous winter I went to San Francisco late in February to visit my mother and sister and to give for the last time the usual course of lectures four or five times a week to the Training-School and sign the diplomas.

Leaving there very weary, I arrived in New York early in April and am not surprised to read the following succinct record:

"Went to Dr. W.'s private hospital April 11th and left there May 26th for additional period of complete rest at my hotel."

I was young and had great recuperative power, so it is not remarkable that I sailed for London on the Etruria a month later. Before and after that time I was as frequently in a rest-cure as my income would permit, though commonly for brief periods. If any reader of statistical tendencies finds sensational gaps in the records of my activities, he will know that I was probably sojourning in a sanatorium. Quite a number of my more cheerful books have been written in hospitals or health resorts, particularly "Rebecca of Sunnybrook Farm," all of which was conceived in severe illness and most of the work done at Dansville, New York. My superiors, Robert Louis Stevenson and Mark Twain, wrote many novels in bed. Of course, they constantly smoked cigars or cigarettes, which seem to be a great help in stimulating constructive imagination, but my humble Muse would never lift an eyebrow or condescend to give me an idea in the atmosphere of tobacco smoke.

The only places where I can write are, first, in an empty room, with a large wooden table; second, in a hospital in moderate pain and with very little sleep; third, in a Pullman car filled with travelers whom I never perceive; then, fourth, in bed, with the rest of the house shut off and in as reasonable quiet as one can expect nowadays in a noisy, bustling, unreflecting world.

One cannot see callers, answer the telephone, go to luncheons or dinners, visit the dentist or shoemaker, address charitable organizations in or from a bed; therefore a bed, in my experience, is simply bristling with ideas. I don't know whether any robust person sitting up, in good health and spirits, ever reads my books, but, if any doubting Thomas wishes to find out if I am a favorite among invalids, he can write to thousands of nurses who will say that when they unpack a patient's belongings they invariably find, among the lingerie, photographs of the best beloved, dressing-jackets, and hot-water bottles, a book of mine for emergencies! The pallid sufferer sits on the edge of her cot while the nurse distributes her effects, and says feebly: "I thought if I happened to live, I might like to read *that*."

I arrived in London June 26th of that year, and began my annual frivolities. London for a few years was my only playground, my best source of intellectual stimulation, my chief place for meeting distinguished people representing all the arts.

Mrs. Louise Chandler Moulton, of Boston, had weekly afternoon receptions, where I met Thomas Hardy, Willard the actor, Henry Harland ("Sidney Luska"), Jerome K. Jerome, W. W. Jacobs, Mr. and Mrs. Kendal; also dozens of "knockers at the gate" — young journalists, novelists, and poets many of whom made a name for themselves in later years.

At Clyde Fitch's luncheons and teas, where I assisted in receiving, I first met George Alexander, Elizabeth Robins, Beerbohm Tree, John Hare, Irene and Violet Vanbrugh, Mrs. Patrick Campbell and her daughter Stella, James Barrie, Gerald du Maurier, Johnston Forbes-Robertson,[1] Madame Lillian Nordica, and many others.

On August 5, 1892, Mr. and Mrs. Laurence Hutton arrived from New York and I joined them at their lodgings in 19 Dover Street, Mayfair. They knew every one worth knowing in London, and not only received many social honors, but dispensed much hospitality. At that time I renewed my friendship with Mr. and Mrs. Henry Lucy ("Toby, M.P.") as well as with Henry Irving, Ellen and Marion Terry, and began others that existed until death came to interrupt the delightful association. Among them were Henry James, Mrs. Brookfield (famous as Thackeray's friend), Hamilton Aidé, Mrs. Alexander and Mrs. L. B. Walford, the favorite novelists, two young poets — Stephen Phillips and John Davidson — Justin McCarthy, and, greatest of all, George Meredith.

August 8th marked an interesting occasion, the informal celebration of Laurence Hutton's birthday at 19 Dover Street where the Huttons and I were stopping. I sent him the following little note in time for his breakfast:

> Dear Mr. Hutton, so glad you were born, —
> Wish you'd been *triplets*, for then, do you see,
> There'd be one for the world, that were else all forlorn,
> There'd be one for your wife, and a third one
> For Me!
>
> K. D. W.

That night there was a friendly supper with toasts and speeches and I recited some verses written for the affair:

---

[1] Alexander, Hare, Tree, Barrie, Forbes-Robertson, Irving, and Lucy all received knighthood in succeeding years.

AUGUST EIGHTH

WHEN HUTTON WAS BORN

Perch, Muse! on my shoulder, and Pen, run thou free!
The form of the verse makes no dif'rence to me,
So long as you just give me something to say
Concerning the great, unapproachable day
      When Hutton was born.

It must not be commonplace, must not be flat;
Quotations, allusions, must all be quite "pat,"
Since Hutton, whose birth is the theme of my rhyme,
Has fed upon praise for a very long time —
      Ever since he was born.

Indite, then, my Muse, in thy happiest manner,
A strictly appropriate Hutton Hosanna,
Extolling his virtue, exploiting his wit,
And hinting that Nature and Art "made a hit,"
      When Hutton was born!

That day I'm not sure that the morning stars sung,
But I am quite certain that bells must have rung,
That Authors and Actors and Angels were gay,
That wise men at once began gathering bay,
      When Hutton was born.

His friendship is genius; and this, by the way,
Is chiefly bestowed on the men, so they say.
The women, who saw that they'd get no assistance,
Just met and agreed to adore from a distance,
      When Hutton was born!

Yet woman it is who inscribes this poor verse,
(Which, poor as it is, might be very much worse,)
And woman it was who, perceiving the need
Of just such a hero, performed the good deed,
      And Hutton was born!

So, shout the glad chorus, triumphantly sing!
Your wreaths and your garlands of laurel then bring,
Tho' it's just a bit rosy to say to his face,
The world has become a much pleasanter place
      Since Hutton was born!

                    K. D. W.

LONDON, *August* 8

All this was town life, but how delicious were the excursions on the river and into the English country! If I had to choose between the darling little Thames and our vast Mississippi, what should I say? I might, of course, assert that the Thames stands for peace and quiet and beauty, and the Mississippi for its magnificent resources for trade and traffic, but the remark would not disarm the wrath of either country, so I can only hope that I shall not be examined on the subject.

The excursions, to an American woman, however friendly, even sentimental, her attitude, were always rendered amusing and exhilarating by the presence of one or two family dogs. I knew already that an Englishwoman would never allow bad weather to interfere with the dog's daily walk. She might have a sprained ankle herself and have two maids in bed with influenza, but willy-nilly, the faithful dog must be walked. It was not specifically set down in the Ten Commandments, but the duty was just as binding.

I went on an outing with a friend one sunny afternoon in London. He had not time to call for me, but we were to meet on Waterloo Station platform at three. He was prompt to the minute, but a maid had preceded him an hour beforehand with a family jewel, a very plain and uninteresting dog, by the name of "Bustle." He had been tagged and left with a guard, and we found him without trouble in the station *crêche*, safe-deposit, parcel room, or whatever the exclusive retreat for dogs may be called.

Bustle enjoyed the railway journey, the drive, the sail, and the tea, bread and butter and cakes, to the top of his bent. Never was such happiness displayed by any dog, particularly one minus beauty or brains. I was just as happy as Bustle, although I knew very well that had my attending squire been obliged to choose between my com-

pany and that of his canine friend, Bustle would have been
the winner.

On a steam launch going to the Henley regatta one day,
each man took his own dog. It was a small boat, and the
dogs were always "underfoot," and howled and barked
with joy so continually that conversation was almost impossible. Still, as one of our party (the owner of two dogs)
remarked: "A city is no place for a dog. Mine simply pine
for the river, and they enjoy boat-races beyond anything."
A lady of the party, whose little dog was approaching her
first confinement, left it at a farmer's house at Streatleigh
on the river because she thought that country air would be
beneficial both to mother and children. All this reads as if
I detested dogs, which is very far from the truth, though I
confess I should never exercise them in wet weather.

But there came a day when I had to renounce the City-
Of-All-Delights, for my conscience was growing more and
more uneasy and I knew that I must get away by myself
and write. I chose West Malvern in Worcestershire for my
retreat, but beautiful town as it is, I found it too crowded
and fashionable, and without unpacking my boxes went
to North Malvern, a mile away and not so popular for
tourists.

I believe I developed "Penelope's English Experiences"
for serial publication there and wrote a short story, "Fleur-
de-Lys," for the "Century," given years afterward to
Princess Mary for her War Fund Book.

After another gay visit to London I sailed for New York,
arriving October 25th, and the old life of traveling and
writing between-times was resumed.

A certain very interesting man with many literary
affiliations, Mr. Luther J. B. Lincoln, had an unusual
and successful series of evenings in several cities that
season in which various writers read chapters from their

still unpublished stories or books. He called these affairs "Uncut Leaves," and many prominent authors of the day read for him, either in large private houses or in club rooms.

I distinctly remember one occasion in a theater when I was to appear with Mark Twain. Feeling that no one could be so deliciously funny as he, I wrote a pathetic tale, with glances of humor now and then in the dialogue. He chose a story I had never heard before, however, one simply heart-breaking in its pathos, so that the audience, though interested, was somewhat sad, dejected, and tearful.

The mood was not quite right, for the preliminary offering on that evening was the reading in very monotonous style of a lengthy poem in perhaps a hundred or a thousand stanzas of ten lines each, semi-historical, with a tropical background of the South Sea Islands. I was extremely bored myself, but very curious as to its unexpected effect upon Mark Twain in the opposite box to mine. He leaned out farther and farther, fixing his eyes intently upon the speaker.

"The poem must be better than I think," I kept saying to myself, for Mark Twain's eyes never left the poet's face.

When the affair was over, Mr. Clemens joined Mr. and Mrs. Laurence Hutton and me for supper at the Huttons' house. I had never spoken with him before. Just after we had settled ourselves in the carriage, he asked with his inimitable drawl:

"Who — was — that man — that read — that — so-called — poem about Methuselah's life in the Indian Ocean?'

"That was Mr. So and So," answered Mr. Hutton. "He is not only a poet, but a literary agent."

"Well — he ought — to — go to — h——l!" drawled

Mark Twain venomously, and, leaving the painful subject, began a general discussion. He explained afterwards, less profanely, that he kept his eye fixed on the poet for fear that he should go to sleep and tumble over the railing of the box on to the stage. "'Livy" (his lovely wife Olivia) "always hates to have me do that!" he said. "She is so conventional."

After that there was a wonderful visit to Boston, a reading for a charitable institution and then dinners with Mrs. Deland, Mrs. Whitman, Mrs. Helen Choate Bell, Mrs. Homans, Arlo Bates, Judge Robert Grant, Thomas Bailey Aldrich, Mrs. James T. Fields, the Horace Scudders and Barrett Wendells. My visit was one round of memorable delight, for the guests at each table were the most witty, charming and clever people in Boston and it was an honor for any young author to be entertained by them.

I sailed to London on May 13, 1893, for a coaching trip in Wales with some New York friends. It was a most delightful experience and is fully recorded in "Penelope's Postscripts" (1915) — rather a nice book and far too little read! It is possible that people in general do not like women's postscripts; certainly men do not, always referring to them as proofs of a disordered mind.

There was a ten days' stay at Bramall Hall, Cheshire, according to custom; and a visit to my American friend, Lady Waterlow, whose husband, Sir Sydney Waterlow, was then Lord Mayor of London. From their town house in Chesham Place, one of the loveliest in London, we went to their country place, Trosley Towers, in Kent. Many long and inspiring friendships I owe to Lady Waterlow, the first in the series with the Bishop of Derry, afterward Primate of all Ireland, Mrs. Alexander his wife, and their daughter Eleanor. (You will remember, perhaps, that Mrs. Alexander wrote "There is a Green Hill Far Away," and "The Burial of Moses," which Lord Tennyson declared he would be proud to have written; also many other very beautiful religious poems and verses.) Lady Maud Stanley and Monsignor Stanley, of the Pope's household in Rome, I met at Lady Waterlow's; also Laurence, the gifted daughter of Sir Laurence Alma-Tadema.

"Toby, M.P." (now Sir Henry Lucy) was often there, and my friendship with him and with his wife grew with every season. Never were such luncheons as those they gave in their modest Victoria apartments. "Toby" brought home Prime Ministers, Under-Secretaries, Chancellors, and "Whips," as well as Lords and Ladies, and as London is fonder of authors, painters, and actors than it is of titles, Nancy Lucy's list of guests was one to envy, but never quite to equal.

The luncheon itself was absolutely simple and unostentatious, but everybody wanted to talk, not eat, though the cooking was perfect. There was one light wine, a single meat dish, a salad, a sweet and black coffee. I have seen beefsteak pudding there, meat pie and ragout of lamb as the principal course.

I remember once, before the first dish had been passed, I was beginning to tell my neighbors at table that I had come by omnibus instead of in a hansom, and had left a twenty-five-dollar Tiffany umbrella in the vehicle, this being my customary habit of economy. Everybody assured me that Scotland Yard would return the article within a day, but as a matter of fact nothing so fortunate occurred. I said I enjoyed the ride on the top of the 'bus and learned a good deal about London prices. I instanced the fact that at a restaurant near by a sign announced that one could get "sausage and mashed" for tuppence ha'penny. There was nothing wrong in the remark, but it was unfortunately timed, for at that precise moment the maid brought in to Lady Lucy three silver dishes of mashed potatoes and two platters of sausages bursting from their skins! The laughter was hearty and general, but Sir Toby determined that I should go without the dish to pay for my indiscretion. I was quite willing to be punished, but Baron Ferdinand de Rothschild, who had taken me in to luncheon, offered to "put up" the twopence halfpenny, and I was fed and forgiven.

I sailed for home from Liverpool, July 12, 1893, and my mother and sister came from San Francisco and met me in Chicago July 20th. They were on their way to Hollis, Maine, the home of my childhood, which finally became our country place, and at the instigation of Mr. Hopkinson Smith and Mr. Thomas Nelson Page I accepted an invitation to read at three Chautauqua assemblies, the meetings to be held in out-of-door pavilions. Monona Lake, Wisconsin, was the first place to be visited; Bay View, Michigan, and Chautauqua, New York, came later.

At the last place I read one morning to three thousand people and on the next afternoon to forty-five hundred. I can only say that I was heard as well as Mr. Smith or Mr. Page, though in one of the places there was a roof and at the others only a sort of sounding-board behind the speaker's platform under the trees. William Jennings Bryan, with a megaphone, would have better suited the scenery. I cannot think why we were ever desired under the circumstances, or ever paid, as we were, most generously. I had the advantage of my masculine comrades during these readings in having two offers of marriage from strangers, one of whom said he knew that he could make *me* happy and the other was sure that I would suit *him!* I could only remark that if I should ever marry again I should wish *both* conditions to be fulfilled, though I confessed it was asking a good deal.

At Monona Lake a newly-born baby accompanied by a new perambulator was offered me. The mother did not care for her offspring particularly, finding it very burdensome, nor could she support it, and as for "him," "he" wouldn't, but she thought probably that I could! Mr. Page and Mr. Smith both declined any share in the enterprise, saying that our partnership was for reading and had nothing to do with the adoption of babies.

Babies change very much (for the better or worse) between the ages of six months and three years, but this one seemed to have no pleasant potentialities in its face and no one could have yearned for the nursling of such an indifferent mother. Of course, all this is twenty-eight or thirty years ago and the baby may have grown up and become the wife of a prosperous pirate, but all the same, now and then, perhaps at Christmas-time, I remember that handicapped, unwanted little child and wonder if I turned my back on a duty, perhaps even on a blessing.

I cannot help remembering that that miserable, callous, immoral mother had looked over a large audience of eighteen hundred or two thousand persons and chosen me as the most suitable person on whom to unload her unwelcome responsibilities. She may have thought me an angel, slightly disguised, but Mr. Page and Mr. Smith both were fertile in suggestions as to many other things she may have thought me, and none of them, I must confess, were in the least flattering!

XXIV

A REUNITED FAMILY

THE Germans of Goethe's and Schiller's generation were probably in the right: a few years of wandering are good for the soul; in fact, we may almost consider them essential.

If I should tabulate the number of states, cities, towns, and villages in America and the various parts of Europe in which I have lived from six months to several years, it would seem that I must be at least a century old.

This tendency to wander was partly encouraged by circumstances and partly inherited, possibly from my maternal grandfather, who retired from business at forty years and never afterward lived long in any one place. This was perhaps a noble reaction from the tyranny of trade, though had he wrestled with financial problems a few years longer he might, with his talents, have been able to endow his less successful descendants with abundant fortunes.

A few of these descendants with purses less well filled were at this moment passing through a long-wished-for and almost miraculous attainment of desire.

Time, July, 1893; Place, Chicago. Everywhere excitement and jubilation! Crowds in the streets. Colored electric lights burning in profusion. Bursts of music now and then, alternating between dawn and dusk with roaring of lions in Hagenbeck's Menagerie.

If any one were sleeping, it was not easy to see how, or in what sequestered spot, and people seemed to think, to say, to proclaim (they being reinforced by newspapers declaring it in print twice daily) that all this excitement and agitation meant The World's Fair!

Nothing was farther from the truth, but the blind and deaf dwellers in the metropolis had a right to their more or less legitimate surmises, having lived on them for weeks and apparently traced them to their proper source. They were wrong, however; the fact that my Mother and Sister had arrived from San Francisco and that we were a united family once more, was, of course, the underlying reason for all this flag-waving and patriotic demonstration.

We did not argue the matter with the populace, knowing it would be a subject difficult of proof. We simply sat entranced and looked at one another, finding new virtues and graces quite forgotten.

We had met several times in the few years of separation, during which time my brother had married and settled in Southern California, but now we three were again a real family, in good standing.

It was true that I had to undergo a brief tour of readings in the West before we could begin our new life, but it would only be a question of a few weeks and a union of atoms would emerge from our present chaos.

> "O fortunate, O happy day,
> When a new household finds its place
> Among the myriad homes of earth,
> Like a new star just sprung to birth,
> And rolled on its harmonious way
> Into the boundless realms of space!"

Exactly where our roof-tree would be raised we knew not, nor did it seem a matter of much moment, though we perhaps held in our hearts one particular place, unknown almost to the map, that might be our final destination.

Archimedes said if he only had a spot of firm ground on which to rest his lever he could move the world. We had no special desire to embark upon so large a project, but we longed unspeakably for a home, and a definite place to work.

I recalled my delight some years before in a visit to that admirable woman and writer, Amelia Barr, at Cornwall-on-Hudson (author of "The Bow of Orange Ribbon," "Jan Vedder's Wife," "Friend Olivia," and dozens of other novels). Her library and sanctum almost made me envious. A great table seven feet by three was in the center of the room, crowded with manuscripts, and, by its side, another table with a Remington machine and a pile of neatly typed sheets, her morning's copying. Bookcases, low ones, for stacks of note and reference books, and three or four windows looking on the mountains — oh! what a place to work, I thought, and how I longed for a home and a study, instead of a lap and a blank book. It is but honest to say that I have had several "studies" since that time, but the *sanctum sanctorum* has never been my lot. My desk in New York has always commanded a view of unanswered letters and household accounts, while the sound of the vacuum cleaner or telephone in the distance, and the ringing of the front doorbell continually break the desired silence. There is generally a glimpse of a lampshade which the housemaid has arranged unsymmetrically, a picture hanging askew on the wall, or a Wedgwood teacup which has had its handle broken off and glued on since I last noted it. In the midst of a fairly good sentence, it is impossible for me to avoid the reflection that the window-cleaner must be ordered for the next day. All this goes to prove my fatal lack of concentration and that the part of me which is a writer is very much entangled with more mundane matters.

I knew one woman of very great talent who could write a sonnet in the library of her apartment, while her ten-year-old son, with four high-spirited and athletic schoolmates, played at Indian massacres in the adjoining rooms, with no other means of separation save portières.

Many a time have I chastened myself with the recital of Harriet Beecher Stowe's achievement of writing "Uncle Tom's Cabin" while rocking her baby in the cradle and peeling the vegetables for dinner. Granted that the baby was a quiet sleeper, I can conjure up the picture, although the continual alternation of knife and pencil or pen must have been difficult.

The moment during our brief Chicago visit that a quiet consultation could be held, we discovered that the only spot where we united in wishing to spend the summer was in Hollis, Maine, where our early childhood had been passed. Such a project may seem simple to the casual reader, but in reality it bristled with difficulties at the time and has always done so. The little village of Salmon Falls on the Hollis side of the river is a very small hamlet, and its inhabitants, though agreeing that many estimable people live in other parts of the township, contend that there is one stretch of street half a mile or so along the river-bank which is unequaled for beauty. It is to the dweller in Salmon Falls what Princes' Street is to Edinburgh or Unter den Linden to Berliners. The matchless Saco River has its famous Falls there, with a rather ugly iron bridge, which nobody minds because when he is standing on it he is always looking at the glorious rapids and the high-walled rocky banks gleaming with verdure and topped by lofty pines. This brief description shows how difficult it would be to find shelter in such a Paradise; rooms in Arcadia never are to be had on short notice! It is better to be born there if possible, but I know of no subject of such supreme importance as a birthplace, where the person most interested can never in the nature of things be consulted as to his preference.

Not having been born in Hollis, and a house in that favorable locality never being on the market, one's friends

would perhaps ask, "Why not build?" The trouble is that
for over a hundred years no house has been built in this
particular spot and such an unusual proceeding would be
very much criticized. There is no manner of house on
which the neighbors would agree with any heartiness,
either as to its site, its architecture, or the color of its
paint.

That brings up, of course, the question of boarding.
There was long, long ago a delightful boarding-house,
exclusive, distinguished, inexpensive, and willing to be
called by that name. My mother, my sister and I, during
our babyhood, had boarded there for two summers before
she married our stepfather, but for several years the dwelling had passed from one tenant to another or had remained
vacant. In 1893, however, boarders were not considered
particularly desirable. They were "confining," and one
could never depend upon their being agreeable for any
length of time. They might like the "table" in June and
be tired of it in December. (The "table," by the way, is
not an article of furniture in Maine, but the daily bill-of-
fare.) There was a certain grim New England spinster in
Hollis, who once told me that if her house should catch
fire in the night there was only one boarder out of nine
whom she wouldn't enjoy seeing burn up!

However, we knew one house on the top of Deacon
Akers's hill — the very one to which I flew through the
dew-drenched grass to see "Annie" on the morning of my
arrival as a child in Hollis — where persons of unblemished
character and angelic disposition could occasionally be
accommodated if strictly necessary. Not that they were
eagerly desired, but, if they insisted on coming and knew
all the attendant circumstances and rules of conduct, they
could be boarded. There was to be no humoring or cod-
dling. (Fortunately the question of special diet had never

entered the human mind at that time!) It was understood that a boarder was a boarder and nothing more; a human being, to be sure, but a human being much more admirable when he stayed in his own house.

We had known Mrs. Jane Akers from childhood; vigorous, plain-spoken, straightforward, full of good stories, a great reader, a little hard to please, but loyal to the bone. We knew, too, her fine square house with the twin elms in front, the pine forest almost opposite, and the unequaled stretch of western sky for sunsets.

There my mother and sister preceded me and there I followed them in a sort of bewildered and intoxicated joy at the enterprise. No more crowds, no more big audiences, no more compliments, for they never compliment anybody in Hollis; it is considered weakening to the character of the recipient.

The society in Hollis was unequaled at that time save that it lacked the masculine element. Almost all the men had died in the Civil War, gone West, or left the little village for towns where there was more lucrative work to be found. I always think one or two men make a party of twenty women a little livelier, even if they have no special talents to give to the entertainment and never open their lips until the refreshments are passed! In the old days (alas! they are no more!) I needed nothing more stimulating than an hour after supper spent with one of the village "Aunts." They are all gone and we shall never see their like again; witty, sharp in retort, keenly interested in life, thrifty, energetic, each dwelling in her little cottage alone, and on a very small income.

I remember leaning out of my bedroom window one morning on hearing the sound of a heavy truck, and saw that it was filled with split pine boards — "cut-rounds" and "stickin's."

"I think you have mistaken the house," I said, "for we have ordered no wood."

"Ain't there a widder in this house? — They told me to bring this wood down to a widder in Salmon Falls."

"Oh, yes," I replied. "The widders are all right, it's only the wood that's wrong. I am the Widder Wiggin, my mother is the Widder Bradbury, the lady who owns the house is the Widder Akers, but we don't need wood."

"Would it be for the house down the road a piece?"

"Very likely. The Widder Pennell lives there; and the Widder MacLeese at the end of the bridge; or, if you go up the street, the Widder Sweat lives in the white house and the Widder Dunn across the way in the brick one. Shall I make a list and throw it out the window?"

"Land, no," he grunted, "I don't want no list o' widders. I'll take the wood back to Clark's Mills, get the right name, and have somebody else haul it over. A man ain't safe in such a mess o' widders."

We had three plain, old-fashioned sleeping-rooms, mine with a large kitchen table between the windows; but my chief writing place in bright weather was under an apple tree in the field opposite the Akers house, a field that is now back of and a part of my own "Quillcote." Under its broad branches I wrote most, if not all, the stories in "The Village Watch-Tower," and to that apple tree I dedicated the book.

There was much other writing of reviews and short articles for the magazines, but I wrote, for the "Atlantic Monthly" "Tom o' the Blueberry Plains" (Christmas number, 1894), "The Nooning Tree" (June "Atlantic," 1894), and "The Fore-Room Rug" (March "Atlantic," 1894). This story is an especial favorite of mine because it "reads aloud" so beautifully. Hardly anything I ever wrote brought such quick response of smiles and tears.

Being an amateur, I never have had any "platform manner," sometimes standing, sometimes perched for a few minutes on the piano stool, moving a little now and then to be nearer different parts of the audience; and when I was to give "The Fore-Room Rug" I had always a little flag-bottomed rocker that I pulled forward informally and sat in it to read the scene where Diadema is holding Lovice's baby and rocking it to sleep as she sings an old-fashioned "Pennyrial" hymn. There was never a dry eye in the house during my little singing moments. Perhaps I could not do it now, and no elocutionist could ever read it. It had to be done with the utmost simplicity as if it were a true story; told, too, as to one person, with no one to hear but Lovice in her bed in the next room.

After that I wrote half or more of "A Village Stradivarius" and made notes for other stories, all printed in "The Village Watch-Tower."

It was a simple life we were leading, early bed and early rising combined with simple though remarkably well-cooked food. I never had the New England pie-habit at breakfast, but I did yield to one of Mrs. Akers's wonderful doughnuts with my morning coffee. I wrote her this irreverent hymn and gave it to her one morning:

PRAYER OF THE CITY BOARDER

Oh, Lord! whose law saith unto me
    My body should a temple be,
Protect me while I eat to Thee
    My daily doughnut!

Suffer it not to go astray,
    Nor tarry in one spot all day;
Let it, at least, be light, I pray,
    My daily doughnut!

But if it be both tough and hard,
    And soaked throughout in boiling lard,

Then may good angels haste to guard
    Me from that doughnut!

At night in dreams my lips repeat,
    Mouth-watering tales of butcher's meat.
Alas! I do but wake to eat
    My daily doughnut!

So, if some morn I am not well,
    Say, as you sound Death's solemn knell,
"She died, as near as we can tell,
    Of daily doughnut!"

That was a summer of peace and quiet and growth.

Once when my sister and I had been carrying in wood from the shed and carrying water upstairs, and then lifting my wooden chair and table to the apple-tree study across the road, she said, "Kate, you remember what Mr. Micawber said about his periods of 'pausing' before a leap? I'll go and get 'David Copperfield' and read it to you. I can't recall the entire extract, but I believe a vigorous leap on your part will be the result of this perfectly quiet and uneventful summer."

"You are no stranger to the fact, Copperfield," said Mr. Micawber, "that there have been periods of my life when it has been requisite that I should pause, until certain expected events should turn up; when it has been necessary that I should fall back, before making what I trust I shall not be accused of presumption in terming — a spring! The present is one of those momentous stages in the life of man. You find me, fallen back, *for* a spring, and I have every reason to believe that a vigorous leap will shortly be the result."

My sister Nora often proved a prophetic Deborah in our household!

XXV

THE STATE O' MAINE BECKONS

You remember that Lewis Carroll's Red Queen said that it took all the running *she* could do to keep in the same place; if she wanted to get somewhere else, she would have to run at least twice as fast; and this latter achievement was one that I managed so continually in these days that the saying was worn threadbare in my family circle. There was, indeed, one jocular friend who never called me anything but the Red Queen, because we so resembled each other in rapidity of action, accompanied by the never-catching-up quality.

The peaceful summer in Hollis was made adventurous only by the fact that the whilom tenant of the so-called Carll House, fronting on what we in Salmon Falls called the Court End of the main street, had fled in the night without having paid his rent for three months.

The house had been originally the finest in the village, and though rather dilapidated had about it a kind of ancient splendor. It was full of associations for us, too, for, as I have just said, it was there that we had boarded for two summers before my mother's second marriage, and it was quite near the cottage where my childhood was passed.

The moment it was vacated we were possessed with all the demons of covetousness. Night after night, as soon as supper was finished, we sped down the Akers's hill to view the beloved object; to gaze in at all the windows of house, shed, or barn where the blinds were not closed; to sit down on piles of autumn leaves (it was now late September) and imagine the felicity of inhabiting that then rather dolorous house filled with such beautiful possibilities.

Miss Sarah Moulton, my oldest friend in Buxton, just across the bridge, knowing the desire that was fast consuming us like a flame, advised us to rent the house even if it should prove impractical to occupy it the following season. It was owned by five or six heirs of Mrs. Carll, but managed by one of them in the town of Gray, fifty miles away.

"He won't ask much," said Miss Moulton, "for he has to pay more insurance if it isn't occupied, and, anyway, hardly anybody has paid him his rent for some years back."

With trembling hands I wrote Mr. H. in Gray, and received by return mail a most cordial letter, saying that he regarded me as an ideal tenant. (I suppose he had in mind former ones who had left without warning.) He reminded me that the premises were entirely run down, and that the inside of the house would need a considerable expenditure in order to put it into livable condition. He therefore said we should have to make our own repairs, which would add to the value of the property, and named an annual rental he considered fair under the circumstances. I refuse to make the sum public. It had a four in it, and the family, not being quick at figures, immediately conjectured that Mr. H. had left out nearly all the ciphers — so much arithmetical knowledge being in our stock of learning — namely, that the more ciphers you added to a figure the greater the sum.

When Miss Moulton confirmed Mr. H.'s figures as to the number of ciphers, remarking that it was "full enough" to pay for a house completely out of repair, I fell into something that would have been a swoon in a Victorian novel, and on being revived sent a check to Mr. H., and the family spent the night in determining what they would do to the house when they had any money with which to do it.

That, I think, was my first Micawber-like "leap." I had heretofore been a boarder. I was now a house and land leaser, temporary proprietor of ten acres of hayfield, the most beautiful maples and elms in the village, and a more or less defunct apple orchard, seven or eight hundred square feet of leaky roofs on house, shed, and barn, the said barn having sunk two feet off the perpendicular — all acquired at an unrevealed rent, except that it had a four in it.

I was invited to read in Kotzschmar Hall, in Portland, October 19, 1893, for some local charity, and no one probably suspected that the enthusiasm I transmitted to the audience was caused by the fact that I felt myself now a citizen, a householder, and (I feared) a taxpayer of the State of Maine; and that the manuscript stories I was reading had been written under a decrepit, neglected, and alien apple tree which was now my own property, and would be harrowed, ploughed, and dressed within an inch of its life, since its happy future was to pay for its own revival and that of several other enfeebled fruit trees.

Returning to Hollis, I did my first piece of civic work in Maine by reading unpublished stories for the minister's salary fund, in the old Tory Hill Meeting-House at Buxton Lower Corner, the first of many, perhaps thirty, others of the kind.

Mr. Micawber's "leap" now became a matter of daily conversation, for a letter arrived from Mrs. Alice Wellington Rollins, a dear friend of all my New York life, saying that she and her family had removed to Lawrence Park, Bronxville, and that she had found a furnished cottage with reasonable rent near hers, and thought it an admirable place for us to spend the six winter months.

We took it at once, having grown so used to "taking" fences and hurdles of all kinds that our courage resembled lunacy. If a State House and Post-Office had been offered us, I think we might have considered them, though investments were not our "long suit," the collapse of the "land boom" in Santa Barbara having taught us caution at an early age. We never had a debt, under any circumstances; but we were mortgaging the future a trifle in renting a summer and winter residence on literary earnings.

We stayed just long enough in Hollis to nominate Miss Sarah Moulton as our adviser and fiduciary agent, and Mr. John Guilford our chief workman in such preliminary repairs as we thought we could afford during the first season. We spent blissful hours over John's books of wallpaper samples, and were continually harassed by the neighbors who said it wa'n't no use to fix up a house that had a leaky roof!

I became so tired of the allusions to the roof that I told the carpenters to go ahead, and immediately raised my fee for readings, the requests for which had begun to come in rapidly. To my delight, nobody minded the sum, and replied that in any case they were sure to reap a generous surplus for the cause involved. This extra sum was a boon; but I discovered later on that one could read, write, even cipher, and spell, continually, yet what are called in New England "a set of buildings" could never be kept watertight on a hundred-year-old house. The only feasible plan is to have seven sons and to keep them all on the roof.

We departed for Lawrence Park November 1st, and settled ourselves in the comfortable little cottage chosen for us. We spent two or three weeks in moving every article of furniture into a different room or place, upstairs and down, that being our customary habit of happily settling ourselves in any habitation. We are not physically strong, but possessed of extraordinary skill in moving furniture, even to grand pianos and kitchen ranges.

Amanda, our maid, who regarded every change as an evidence of at least harmless (she hoped) insanity, re-marked, from the depths of an armchair where she was resting, "I hope you won't take the grand piano up them rounding stairs when you change it again. I'm good for 'most anything 'on the flat,' but I'm weak in the waistline when it comes to stairs."

Mother attended to the housekeeping, and my sister entered upon what proved to be long months of revision of my lectures to the Kindergarten Training-School in San Francisco, together with chapters of her own, which finally became a work of three volumes — "The Republic of Childhood," i.e., "Froebel's Gifts," "Froebel's Occupations," and "Kindergarten Principles and Practice" (1895-1896). She confessed that she was writing chiefly for the good of humanity, but had an eye on some lovely rag carpets for the halls and stairs of our country residence.

I used Lawrence Park — delightfully situated, with very pleasant society — chiefly as a port of call, for I was there only a few days each week. I submit my itinerary to show that I was not idle and was remembering the leaky roof and the carpenter's bill.

Reading, "Uncut Leaves," New York, November 4, 1893.
"   Pittsburgh, November 7, 1893.
"   Morristown, November 9, 1893.
"   .   Hartford, November 24, 1893.
"   Century Club, Philadelphia, January 12, 1894
"   Albany, January 23, 1894.
Kindergarten Talk, Ministers' Club, Albany, January 24, 1894.
Reading for the Kindergarten at Sherry's, New York, January 29, 1894.

Left for St. Paul, February 2, 1894.
Talk to Kindergartners, Minneapolis, February 5, 1894.
Reading, Minneapolis, February 6, 1894.
Extra Children's Reading, Minneapolis, February 7, 1894.
Overflow Reading, St. Paul, February 8, 1894.
Extra Children's Reading, St. Paul, February 9, 1894.
Talk to St. Paul Kindergartners, February 10, 1894.
Columbus and Youngstown, Ohio, February 14, 1894.
Kindergarten Debate between Mrs. Wetmore and Mrs. Wiggin
    at the house of Mrs. Laurence Hutton, February 19, 1894.
Reading in behalf of Dr. Robert Collyer's Church, New York,
    February 22, 1894.
Reading at Mrs. Hearst's house in Washington, February 26,
    1894, for a Free Kindergarten.
Reading, Brooklyn, March 1, 1894.
Reading, Philadelphia, "The Acorn Club," March 12, 1894.

I also wrote an article on "The Training of Children"
(ten thousand words) for "Scribner's." This article was a
good one, and the reason I know that it was is the fact that
not only was it written *con amore*, but it paid for new
gutters on the house in Hollis, a new drain for the kitchen
sink, the leveling of the front stone steps, and several thousand clapboards.

We dropped work occasionally at Lawrence Park and
had some merry supper-parties on Sunday nights in our
pleasant cottage. They were very informal, and one
person was always chosen to preside at the chafing-dish for
a course or two, while waiters among the distinguished
guests were selected to help our Amanda.

Amanda was self-possessed under ordinary occasions,
but bewildered, dazed, and somewhat given to unseemly
laughter in the presence of genius, and our guests were
"uncommon" gay and witty. I remember one feast at
which there were eggs *à l'artiste*, cooked by Mr. Robert
Reid, the painter, and served by Laurence Hutton; oysters
à la Rufus Choate, broiled by Mr. W. A. Purrington and

passed by my sister; cold fowl and ham, which Amanda served when she could control her feelings; but Clyde Fitch was the waiter who was to follow with the salad, and his flirtatious manner and coruscations of wit were such that he had to bring her from the kitchen in a more or less helpless state every few moments and start her again on her path of duty. No play that he ever wrote was a more brilliant drama than the one he performed that night. Another unforgettable feature of this supper was the magnificent appearance of Robert Reid in cook's costume and his head waiter impersonated by Edward Simmons, the artist, one of the wittiest men I ever knew; a man, too, of incredible velocity and staying-power in speech. (It was Oliver Herford who printed a large sign and hung it on the fire-escape of the St. Botolph Club in Boston: *"Not to be used except in case of Simmons!"*)

Mr. Simmons on the occasion of this supper-party was "intoxicated by the exuberance of his own verbosity," and made a *succès fou* with his audience. He established a simulated connection with an imaginary kitchen, and gave rapid and successive orders regarding food, service, speed, discipline, peculiarities of guests, criticisms of previous courses — all this in French, Spanish, Italian, and German — winding up at last with a lengthy and very heated argument with the imaginary chef, in which he resigned his position and abruptly cut off connection with the speaking-tube, which was a brass hook that he twisted, flung on the floor, and stamped upon in a fury of rage. No food was eaten while this impromptu act was going on, and so much badinage was indulged in during the supper that most of it was left to be eaten next day.

A few of the cover-verses I scribbled for this party are here appended, the rest apparently having perished with scores of others like them.

TO LAURENCE HUTTON

To one who hoards curios rather than pelf,
The gem of the treasure-house being himself.

There once was a nice little Hostess,
　Who hadn't a sign of a Host
To sit at the head of the table
　And saw up the tough little roast.

Each one of her guests was examined
　The instant he came on the scene,
To see if he'd suit the position
　In muscle and dignified mien.

But when they all came to the table,
　The rest were just laid on the shelf:
The place was bestowed upon Hutton,
　For he was a Host in himself.

TO CLYDE FITCH

To one whose rôle in life's to mould, shut in the workshop of his brain,
the puppets that will dance to the world's piping.

How stage a play that will succeed,
　Pray let me give a hint:
I'll show you how to draw the crowd,
　Win plaudits without stint.

Your soubrette must be very pert,
　And very gay and winsome.
Your funny man must grin himself,
　And make the audience grin some.

My feeling is the ingénue
　Should not be over thirty:
She ought to be ingenuous,
　And just a little flirty.

The low comedian, of course,
　Must be a man of wit:
If you don't put it in your play,
　He's bound to furnish it.

The leading man must have good looks;
　The child must be a prig;

The villain must be tall and dark,
Or wear a bright red wig.

Arrange these things, dear dramatist;
Don't have the moral shady;
I'd like to take it on the road
And be your leading lady.

TO EDWARD SIMMONS, ARTIST AND RACONTEUR

There once was a man with a brush;
O'er his pictures the public would gush;
Whate'er he did sign,
They protested divine,
And they bought up his work with a rush.

The ocean wave that laps the shore,
The wheel that turneth o'er and o'er,
The brook that dashes to the sea,
The squirrel leaping in the tree,
The clock that ticks the hours away,
The earth that rolls the livelong day —
All these are ceaseless in their motion,
The wheel, the clock, brook, earth, and ocean;
But in its steady rise and fall
His power of speech surpasses all!

Still, when he thus to ME discourses,
I never *wish* for any pauses!

XXVI

AN OCEAN ROMANCE

THE early summer of 1894 found me on my way to England
again. My dear mother was inclined at first to think that
these annual journeys across the Atlantic were slightly
extravagant, and a pessimistic aunt said at one time:
"Well, let her go, but Kate'll cross that ocean once too
often!" The same aunt wrote, a few years later when I
was living in an apartment eight stories above the street:
"The New York elevators are fire-traps, of course, but her
life is her own. If she dies a natural death, do the elevators
admit the carrying down of coffins at a funeral? Kate
would be sure to have a large funeral!"

My mother realized before long that the ocean voyages
gave me rest after my exhausting winters, and that I
always came home rejuvenated in body and mind, with a
hundred new impressions valuable in a literary as well as
in a financial way.

The fruits of these travels were finally: "A Cathedral
Courtship," "Penelope's Experiences" (England, Scotland, and Ireland; three volumes), "Penelope's Postscripts" (Wales, Switzerland, Italy), "The Diary of a
Goose Girl," and several short stories.

My sister had gone back to San Francisco in the spring
of this year for lectures at the Kindergarten Training-
School and my mother to Maine to begin fitting up, in part,
the newly rented summer home.

I chose the Britannic for this particular voyage (or at
least I thought I did) because of its commander, Captain
Edward Smith, who was already an old friend and placed
me always on his right hand at table. He was a strong,

sane, modest man, of quick intelligence, wide information, and a decided sense of humor; straightforward, loyal, and fitted for all sorts of companionship. When, years later, he met his tragic end on the ill-fated Titanic, a brave and gallant sailor, a true gentleman, and a stanch friend went to his death, and I mourned him greatly.

Tranquilly I walked up the gangway on that sunny May morning in 1894, looking aloft and waving my hand in answer to the skipper's welcome. I had not the smallest idea that before many days I should be making the most Micawber-like leap of my career, for, standing somewhere on one of the decks, was the man whom I was going to marry.

Neither sense of fear nor strange exaltation crossed my mind; indeed, had a clairvoyant on the dock predicted such a change in my intentions concerning the future I should have said, with dignity and full conviction, "Marriage is the last thing I wish; my life is full and my work satisfies me."

I had a brief interview with the Captain before luncheon, at which, of course, he never appeared on the first day of sailing.

"Captain, dear," I said, "I was never so tired in my life and I must rest on this voyage. I don't want to meet any one except those at our end of the table."

"All right," the Captain replied with a quizzical glance. "You'll agree that I never was much of an 'introducer.' — There's an awfully nice chap on my left, who has made twelve or fifteen voyages with me; the Earl and Countess of R. are seated next to you, and across the table Mr. William Shakespeare, the London musician, and his wife."

"That sounds delightful!" I answered. "No one could 'seat' a dinner-party with more discretion."

I went down to luncheon very late and the people at table

had nearly finished the meal. We all made a brief remark or so to one another, with a view to deciding what sort of companionship might be established on a nine days' voyage. I thought both the Earl and Countess R. had most delightful and democratic manners, and the "nice chap" opposite, named on the list as George C. Riggs, New York City, looked sufficiently the part.

"Not exactly in my line," I thought, "nor I in his. The Captain says he is an American, but he looks British; however, I like that. Is he conventional, I wonder, or just correct? And oh! how could Nature waste such a curly crop of hair on a mere man! Still, it is short! Let us be thankful for that! I dare say that we shall get on!" (And we did!)

That superficial impression recorded, I dismissed him, and all the others, from my mind. When I learned at dinner-time that the Captain would not go down, I dined on deck and went early to my cabin.

The next day at breakfast Captain Smith introduced us all and we had a very merry meal. During the morning I walked with my new acquaintance and went to tea in the Captain's room, where he and one or two others were present. On the succeeding day he mentioned that he had heard much of "Timothy's Quest," but confessed that he had never read one of my books. I told him that up to date I had written none that would interest him. "You are too old for some of them and too young for others," I explained, at which he appeared rather chastened, although he recuperated quickly, with the resiliency of a rubber ball. He was (and is) made up of practically uncrushable material, always dashing into the thick of an argument and sturdily maintaining his position — no matter what the obstacle — which may account for various happenings later on.

I found him very much a man's man, keen on out-of-door sports, golfing, fishing, and shooting, as the result of having spent several years of his childhood in Ireland at school, although he was born in America, thank Heaven. This was all new to me, and I delighted in it as something fresh, boyish, and invigorating. He was not in the least "literary," yet he had a tremendous interest in books, and had never read any indifferent stuff. His reading was wider than mine and on different lines, but we supplemented each other in this direction and it made stimulating conversation.

So the days at sea went on, and we were the best of deck and table companions; but there was a gradual change in our new friendship and strange, unexpected revelations began to appear on the horizon. This much may be confided to a well-disposed public, but there are other memories that belong only to the high contracting parties. By the time London was reached, I was considering something to which I was half antagonistic and yielding to a will entirely superior to mine. G. C. R. had a single-track mind and made it up with incredible rapidity, but I was more cautious, though as it turned out never wiser than he.

I had my usual delightful weeks in London, and he, though much in Scotland and Ireland on business, took many journeys to England to convince and re-convince me on certain points, always succeeding on every occasion.

We saw much of Sir Sydney and Lady Waterlow, at whose house in Chesham Place we often met at tea and dinner, as they heartily approved the probable course of events.

We also went to a charming and distinguished party given for me at the Poultney Bigelows' in their beautiful house in Chelsea. Mrs. Frances Hodgson Burnett, Mrs. Louise Chandler Moulton, Mr. Thomas Nelson Page, and

GEORGE C. RIGGS

Miss Genevieve Ward were there to greet me, as well as many other interesting people.

To show the pleasure and honor given me by my host and hostess I may quote from a brief article in London "Truth":

A representative group of American authors were present last night at the house of Mr. and Mrs. Poultney Bigelow, and the Londoners invited to meet them thought the scene most admirably staged. Mrs. Wiggin, who read some chapters from her books with inimitable charm, was the center of attraction of a brilliant crowd numbering every member of the United States Embassy and the officers of the Chicago, who were also great "belles" on this occasion. The Bigelow residence is one of the most attractive houses in London; its drawing-room is always a picturesque setting for the clever and distinguished people who gather there, and no one with an eye for the artistic taste of its arrangements failed to note how the surroundings became the reader.

The groups of well-dressed men and women, scattered irregularly over the large room, with its deep, cushioned window-seats, had their attention concentrated on a raised platform which occupies about a fourth part of the inner wall and is enclosed on two sides with dark carved oak. The author in her pale yellow brocade could scarcely have found a more becoming background as she sat at ease with a tiny table at her side. A screen of dark oak, pierced and carved, intervened between the window and the fireplace, and against this the beautiful white hair of two or three picturesque elderly women showed to much advantage.

Any woman would have looked her best in that alcove of dark carved oak, and I thought the audience, in its uniforms, decorations, and lovely women, the most attractive I had ever seen, as I trembled before it from my point of vantage.

London has been good to me always, and I was very happy, and very much surprised, at my growing circulation in Great Britain and the Colonies; yet I left it that summer more easily than usual because my new-old house in Maine, and my mother, both called me unceasingly, and

I wanted her to know the man whom I had chosen or who had chosen me!

He came for a week-end in a fortnight after my arrival there, and, not being familiar with New England architecture, fell in love with the old house at first sight. My mother approved of him, but she was both shy and reserved, and I think it was not until after we had been married four years that she timidly called him "George." (The use of Christian names among tolerably new friends is always attended with great difficulty in our family, for some mysterious reason.)

G. made several other week-end visits and was of great interest to the little community which had known me in early childhood. It is recorded that two men at work sawing wood in a barn near my house observed us walking down the village street to stand on the bridge and look at the rapids.

"Who is that feller?" asked one workman of the other.

"Why, don't you know who that is — it's Kate's beau. His name is Riggs!"

"Riggs?" repeated the curious one meditatively. "He ain't the Riggs that used to work down in the shoe fact'ry, is he?"

"Not by no manner o' means; he's far diff'rent from that. They had it up to the Mills last week that he was a winder-dresser in New York City and we thought Kate was making a great match. But he took me out fishin' with him, and he told me himself, when I asked out flat what his business was, that he was a manufacturer and importer, and that looks to me a better job than the other one."

"Mebbe!" was the uncertain reply of the inquisitor.

Another evidence of the public interest in my welfare was that a prosperous farmer in a village twelve miles distant drove over to the livery-stable keeper at Bar Mills to

see if he could get some authoritative details regarding the
character and standing of my future spouse.

It was a rather extraordinary quarter in which to seek
information, but good Dan Palmer had been my friend
from childhood, and he certainly did not fail me at this
awkward moment.

"Well," he said, "you couldn't 'a' come to any one who
knows Mr. Riggs better'n I do, for I've druv him to and fro
from Biddeford the last two months. He's got a kind of a
foreign way of talkin', but he's a good upstandin' neighborly feller and I like him first-rate. Land! But he's good
comp'ny comin' up that twelve-mile drive over a muddy
road!"

Nora's return from San Francisco and her joy over the
acquisition of the summer home in Hollis made life happier
than ever. We intended to buy it sooner or later, but there
were grave obstacles in the path. There were five or six
heirs to the property, their residences being well distributed
over the States on the map, and they might not agree on
the price. There was also a romantic and unique lien on
the estate which might be difficult to adjust. Mrs. Thomas
Carll, the owner, had made an unusual will; so complicated
that only an ambitious village Blackstone could have suggested its terms, and so elaborate that it must be dealt with
in a succeeding chapter which will tell of the birth and
growth of my study.

Meantime, swelling with pride and joy at our present
possessions, my sister and I wanted to name the place.
There was much racking of brains, but no decision. At
length we determined to drive to a place where we had
always hitherto found ideas for stories literally hanging
on the bushes. Perhaps, we thought, the name might come
as we talked of our work and ate our sandwiches at noon.

The process of hiring a horse in Hollis or Buxton was almost as difficult at that time as finding a boarding-place. The method was this: to stroll by Mr. D.'s house with the idea that we might find him engaged in sweeping his barn.

"May we hire your horse this afternoon, please, Mr. D.?"

Prolonged sweeping on his part, attended by reflective chewing of a straw. Finally, speech; laconic and not encouraging.

"Where ye goin'?"

"Four miles up the road to the blueberry plains."

More sweeping, and more profound balancing of invisible difficulties involved in the decision; then:

"How many's goin'?"

"Only two, neither of us heavy."

"Waal, I s'pose I can let you have the horse, though I've just washed the 'buggy.'" (The inference being that it is a poor time to let a buggy when it's clean!)

We drove slowly and happily up the dusty road until we reached a favorite clump of trees. Then we alighted, hitched the horse, and sat down in the shade, inhaling the fragrance of pines and sweet fern.

The outcome of our discussion was that the house should be called "Quillcote," the home of two pen-women. We still think it charming as well as self-explanatory, but it has not always proved so. For some years the newspapers have announced in the heat of early July that Mrs. Riggs has gone to "Grillcote," this being the favorite perversion of the typesetters.

We tried to incite an epidemic of naming the few houses in the community. We had no difficulty in coaxing the Widder Akers to call hers "Twin Elms," nor the Widder Dunn hers "The Brick House," as it was the only one on the street.

"Land, Kate!" they said, "we'll call 'em whatever you

an' Nora say, so long as we don't have to get printed writing-paper and visiting-cards."

We had difficulty with the Widder Sweat in her tiny cottage next "Quillcote." We suggested "The Widder's Mite" (she was great at a joke), or, as her deceased husband had been a doctor, "The Pill Box." I think she accepted neither, and, dying at a great age, left her house unnamed, although we wrote her frequent notes, addressing the cottage by dozens of facetious names to incite her to witty retort.

But no one of us ever goes by the place with a thought of any other personality than that of quick-witted, humorous, quaint, spicy "Aunt Susan," who saw more of life than most of us, through her window that overlooked the immediate countryside.

"I must say that your beau has the use of his legs, Kate," she remarked, when George had been setting chairs and tables for supper under the great maple. And again, when a learned professor, an old friend of my sister's, was paying us a week-end visit, she said: "It beats all, that Nora don't take one of those likely 'baches' [bachelors] that come to your house! I thought this one might bring things to a head, but land! he sets and swings in the hammock, and she in the rockin' chair under the trees, an' they do nothin' but laugh back and forth. When a couple laughs all the time, they ain't makin' love!"

Autumn and metropolitan responsibilities came all too soon. We left Hollis for Bronxville, and the owner of "Grey Arches," a furnished house in Lawrence Park, allowed us to occupy it during the absence of the family in Egypt. It was a beautiful house, but the winter was a severe one with much snow and ice, and I met my many engagements with great difficulty, George sometimes dragging me on a sled down the rocky steeps that lay between house and station.

I went to Wellesley College as the guest of Katharine Lee Bates, head of the English department, and had an unforgettable visit, reading to the College in the afternoon, and at five o'clock going to my room to rest before dinner. It may have been an hour later when I heard a faint, faraway sound of fresh young voices. It grew clearer and clearer until it seemed to stop under my window. Running to see from whence it came, I opened my curtains, and there stood the Wellesley Glee Club giving me their College "call," the most poetic and musical one I ever heard.

W - e - l - l - e - s - l - e - y, Welles - ley!

As it rose in exquisite harmony, three times in succession, from middle C major to the E above, it hung on the highest note like the sound of an elfin flute and rings in my ears whenever I choose to call it up. I spoke a few words of gratitude and closed the window lingeringly until the girls sang their way over the snow-covered lawns to their various dormitories.

On the next morning I met about fifty girls in the gymnasium and taught them from the manuscript of my newly composed "Plantation Christmas Carol"; first the words (Mrs. Ruth McEnery Stuart's) and then my own music. The first, third, fifth, and sixth lines of each verse are sung by a solo voice, and all the others by a chorus. In this case, after they had gone through it three times, the effect was so lovely, with the fresh young voices, the sympathy and the charm of learning it in this friendly way, that groups of girls in the halls, or passing by the windows, dropped in to admire and applaud. I afterwards dedicated it to the Wellesley Glee Club, and, after it was published in a little book of my songs, it was much used at Wellesley.[1]

This Wellesley Reading was practically my "swan song," for I never afterward appeared on platforms, save in the more crowded East Side and upper West Side public schools; at annual meetings of the various organizations of which I was a director or member; and at the old country meeting-house at Buxton Lower Corner in Maine, where I read every summer to enable the church to pay the minister's salary and keep the parsonage in repair.

My marriage took place quietly in All Souls' Church on March 30, 1895, a day marvelously like summer, with birds singing in Madison Square and the young leaves as green as if it had been May. A friend of my girlhood, the Reverend Roderick Stebbins, of Milton, Massachusetts, performed the ceremony before our respective family circles and a little group of intimate friends. Among them were, besides the families, Dr. Clarence Campbell as best man, the Reverend Robert Collyer, Mr. and Mrs. Laurence Hutton, Mr. and Miss Howells, Mr. and Mrs. Charles B. Alexander, Mr. H. O. Houghton and his daughter Elizabeth, Mr. and Mrs. G. H. Mifflin, Mary Mapes Dodge, Clyde Fitch, Mr. and Mrs. Richard Watson Gilder, Hamilton Mabie, Mr. and Mrs. George Haven Putnam, Samuel Elliott, Edward G. Kennedy, and a few others whose names evade me at the moment. I can see their kind faces as I went up and came down the aisle, but when I am calling them to mind my pen falters and my eyes grow dim with tears, for twenty-seven of the number who added to our happiness on that day have gone to the other world and left us that much unbefriended.

[1] *Nine Love Songs and a Carol.* K. D. W. 1896.

XXVII

A WEDDING JOURNEY

THE week afterward was one of heavenly weather in Washington, blue skies, delicious air, trees almost in full leaf, dogwood and lilac in blossom, tulips and daffodils pushing their heads out of the earth in all the gardens. Cynics sometimes refer to Washington as a sort of "island" in the vicinity of "loud, longitudinal New York," as Henry James calls it; but to me it is one of the most beautiful and gracious cities in America, with a charm and distinction all its own. At the end of this visit my husband and I returned to inspect a furnished house for our first home in the autumn, and sailed immediately for our wedding journey abroad. Of course, we chose the Britannic as our ship and Captain Smith as our commander, thinking this a simple act of loyalty. Arriving in London, Sir Sydney and Lady Waterlow offered us, in true English fashion, their country place, Trosley Towers, in Kent, for a fortnight, with servants, horses, carriages, and all that hospitality could include or invent, but G.'s business called him to the north, so we made brief visits in Scotland and Ireland and then set our faces toward Venice, the true port of our desire.

Mr. and Mrs. Laurence Hutton, Mr. and Mrs. Charles Dudley Warner, and Mrs. Clement Waters (Clara Erskine Clement) had taken a large villa on the Giudecca, an island only five minutes by gondola from Venice and St. Mark's, and we had been invited before our marriage to join them as coöperative householders. Mrs. Hutton and I managed the housekeeping, but in reality, as we were so ignorant of markets, customs, and manners, we left matters chiefly to the *padrona* and the servants. All that was dull, monotonous, or conventional was banished from this new life in new surroundings, all so strangely beautiful that each day meant a fresh joy.

We read and re-read in these days our letter from Mr. Howells, received from him some days before our marriage, when he had learned we were to spend five or six weeks in Venice. It seems to me now — as I lift the paper, a little faded and brown, from the books which it accompanied — so kind and tender, in a word, so like the man himself, that I would like to preserve it in print.

40 West 59th Street
March 25th, 1895

Dear Mrs. Wiggin:

I am sending you with more love than I can say, or Mr. Riggs would let me, my book about Venice.[1] I would write it all over again to make it worthy of the occasion, if there were time, but you have given us such short notice that I have not been able to do more than interline the old text throughout with the most earnest wishes for your happiness. They will be legible to no one but yourself and Mr. Riggs, for they are in sympathetic ink of a peculiarly confidential tint. It is the most beautiful of all your beautiful gifts, that you make people long to be of your own quality of friendship, and if these wishes of mine have any grace of the sort, it comes from you.

My book is in two volumes, but it is only one Life — like that now beginning for you both. Such a life began for my wife and me in Venice thirty years ago, and it fondly renews itself in our hearts at the thought of your joy.

Yours cordially
W. D. Howells

I will copy from my Italian notebook a few of the occasional records I kept as reminders for home letters. They are but bald, practical details of wonderful days colored by the heavenly loveliness of Italian sunrises and sunsets, the glory of Italian marbles and paintings, and the never-ceasing delight of the gondola's motion through the shim-

[1] *Venetian Life.*

mering waters of the Grand Canal where the eye met nothing but beauty wheresoever it might turn.

We intended to spend Saturday and part of Sunday in Milan, but, by Friday night, I was very travel-tired, and we determined to press on to Venice where we might settle ourselves. We saw Milan Cathedral, therefore, and nothing more, for the city could never be seen properly in less than a fortnight.

The Cathedral is a thousand times more beautiful than it appears in photographs. It looms in the landscape precisely, as Lowell says, like a "stranded glacier" — the two thousand statues on it are each worthy of study, and of the carving I can only follow Lowell again by saying it looks like frozen lace. . . .

It is a six hours' journey from Milan to Venice — the railway carriages were full, even the first class, and we had a rather uncomfortable trip through a most beautiful country.

Every inch of ground is tilled and given up to fruit and vines. An indescribably lovely and quaint effect is given to the orchards by the planting of vines at the foot of the little fruit trees, and festooning them from tree to tree for miles and miles along the roads.

We arrived in a light rain and were met by Mr. Hutton and his two gondoliers — three, in fact, for he had a separate gondola and gondolier for our luggage. His own two men dressed in white and blue linen sailor-suits are handsome and picturesque. As it had not been raining when they left home they had no "felsa" over the gondola and we had to go up the Grand Canal with umbrellas, so I got no idea of the extraordinary beauty of things at first. . . .

Here we are, on the Canale Giudecca — quite in the country, for it is an island, although it does not look like one, as the houses simply appear to rise mysteriously from the water. The ancestors of this family built the villa nine hundred years ago and the present owners are their descendants who have lived here continuously. It is the Casa Frollo and is immense in size. You alight from the gondola and pull a bell-rope, and Fina, a maid, comes out on the balcony and calls down: "Who goes there?" You answer in Italian: "Friend of the house." She pulls up a bobbin and you enter a court, which in its turn opens on a long strip of garden (twenty acres) that runs back to the Adriatic. We raise potatoes, peas, artichokes, asparagus, and grapes. The red wine is made on the place; the raisins, dates, figs, and nuts grow there. They have never taken lodgers before, but they are heavily in debt and may lose their old home in a few months, although seven American tenants will doubtless assist in lifting the burdensome mortgage.

The Huttons heard of this family through Miss Macy, a Boston sculptor, who has lived in the house four years. It is cheap for Venice, two dollars a day apiece, and a gondola hired from the *padrona*, with one man, costs a dollar a day extra. George and I have a most lovely, spacious room — two beautifully carved bedsteads each about two and a half feet wide — mosaic floor, gorgeous old frescoes, shabby mahogany furniture, and two wide windows overlooking all Venice, one of them taking in the beautiful Campanile Tower and Church of Santa Maria della Salute, the other the Doge's Palace. The great drawing-room and dining-room combined is just out of our room, an immense sort of hall with great wings, its stone balcony looking on the Canal, with windows at the other end facing the garden and the Adriatic. The floor is of marble, the walls and furniture are shabby, but in the evening, with the table covered with bronze bowls of pink roses and tall branched candelabra, part of the room in bright moonlight and part in shadow, it is most romantic. . . .

George and I breakfast in our spacious room by the window — a fresh egg apiece with honey, bread, coffee, and most delicious wild Venetian strawberries. Our own gondola will be ready for us to-morrow and then we shall stay out on the canals all day long. . . .

The Huttons took us to the Grand Canal last evening. The scene was magical: innumerable gondolas moving up and down and collecting in scores by the steps of hotels, where the boats of singers were moored. There is one magnificent singer among them, whom Mrs. Jack Gardner of Boston adopted and educated two years ago. Last night he sang "Non è Ver'" and the "Angel's Serenade," both most beautifully.

On the way home we stopped for beer in the Piazza, where there were crowds of people, and when we slipped out into our own quiet canal, Giovanni, Mrs. Hutton's head gondolier, aged seventeen, sang, rowing at the same time. He cannot read or write, but he sings like a lark. Fina, the waiting-maid, is a pretty little flirt, with a rose in her hair and a rose-red flush on her brown cheeks. She has been engaged seven times up to date, and an eighth lover, a brickmaker, is now on the horizon. Three months is the average duration of her affection, then she packs the suitor off with any system of fibs that she can devise.

The mistress of our kitchen is a contralto and sings beautifully. (If she cooked half as well, we should be in clover!) The woman that makes the beds is a fair musician, a mezzo-soprano, but not quite equal to the rest of the servants — the artists, perhaps, I should say! We do not criticize our meals, inasmuch as they are cooked and served by vocalists and are as good as could be expected.

Sunday night Mrs. Hutton gave a dinner to some Americans in Venice. Her gondolier in white gloves helped wait on the table, and the dinner was of Venetian dishes. Fina had a red rose in her hair and coquetted continuously with Giovanni in the intervals of serving. After dinner we climbed the stairs to Miss M.'s studio which occupies all the space under the roof. A great stone platform had a little hearth-fire of twigs in the middle of it and the open windows with broad cushioned seats looked out on the shimmering water with all the light in Venice shining in it and the reflections of a hundred marble palaces on its surface. . . .

George puts on his bathing-suit, runs to the water's edge, and swims under our bedroom windows, or in sight of them, every morning. He enjoys it hugely, although there is always an embarrassing crowd of little street urchins to watch his departure and welcome his approach to the shore. Nobody seems to swim here. I hope they bathe, but my water-pitcher holds less than a quart and my wash-bowl is the size of a soup-plate. . . .

One afternoon this week the Huttons, Mrs. Clement Waters, and the Warners went to the Lido in their gondolas at two o'clock. We followed at three-thirty and found them in one of the little cabins made of rushes on the seashore, where we made tea and sat in the sunshine for an hour and watched the bathers. There is a tram-car running from the point where one lands to the opposite side of the island — about a third of a mile. We seated ourselves in an empty car and had a voluble conversation with a conductor; at least he conversed, and we occupied ourselves in trying to discover the price of the fare. George paid it at length, though he thought it exorbitant, and we started, the only passengers in the tram, which maintained a furious pace. In discussing the matter later we found that we had paid four times the usual rate. Mrs. Waters speaks Italian fluently and, interviewing the conductor, discovered that we had apparently ordered a *special train*, not wishing to wait five minutes for the regular one! George thinks this too ingenious a translation of his Italian and says he shall not talk any more save in English. . . .

Every evening after dinner, about eight-thirty, we order our respective gondolas and float up and down the Grand Canal listening to the music, some of it astonishingly good. The musicians have boats lighted with gay lanterns and they row from hotel to hotel.

There is a certain new and splendid palace that has broad marble steps and an immense veranda or piazza with marble pillars supporting the second story. It makes a most marvelous sounding board for the voice of the celebrated Guglielmo, the popular tenor here for the last four years. The other night he stepped off his boat and disappeared through these marble arches and in a moment the little orchestra and chorus began the "Miserere" from "Trovatore." They sang it wonderfully, and when Manrico's Prison Song floated out from the mysterious darkness of a stone stairway where he was hidden, the effect was simply thrilling. . . .

George and I take Howells's "Venetian Life," have the canopy put on the gondola, and go off and stay from three to six. We alight when we feel like it, and by the aid of a map thread our way through the alleys and over the bridges, meeting our gondolier at some point where George has told him to be. How George manages to find the way is a mystery to me; but he seems to have a map of Venice in his head. . . .

At three to-day we took the gondola in a new direction, past the Arsenal and then through some of the smaller canals and lagoons. At five we alighted in the Piazza. It was a fête day and three gorgeous flags floated from the three towering cedar flagstaffs from which in the old days floated the banners of Cyprus, Candia, and the Morea. There was a brilliant sun, and I cannot describe the front of St. Mark's with its bulbous domes and arches all radiant and sparkling with gold and ruby and blue. It is like an immense jewel-casket, and nobody on earth can put it into words but Ruskin.

We took our cup of tea at Florian's Café just opposite, a café that has never been closed day or night for four hundred years. (They have changed the head waiter several times, however!) The Huttons had friends to dinner, and at nine we all went up the Giudecca to see the Public Gardens illuminated. The lights were thousands in number, in the Italian colors — red, white, and green — and arranged in pendant form from tall poles so that they looked like great trees of light. There was a band and the effect was like fairyland. . . .

We stay an hour in San Marco whenever we can, and we have visited two or three other magnificent churches, Santa Maria della Salute, the Frari, and della Formosa, full of Titians, Tintorettos, Veroneses, Palmo Vecchios, and Gian Bellinis, master of Titian. . . .

Last night we went to the Malibran Theater for the opera "Crispino e la Comare" and a ballet, both rather poor, but we only paid a few pennies a seat and it was a new experience. We reached home at ten o'clock and rose at seven-thirty instead of nine as usual, to go with Miss M. W. to see the Corpus Domini feast at San Marco.

We improved the time to ascend the stone staircases and make a tour of the galleries and arcades of the inside and top of San Marco to see the frescoes, which are all mosaics, made from A.D. 1200 to 1895. . . .

We have just heard of another and the last procession to be seen during our stay. To-morrow is the Day of San Antonio of Padua. Boats have been put sidewise across the Grand Canal and a bridge built upon them. On this the procession will pass from San Marco to Santa Maria della Salute, the votive church built in the sixteenth century after the second plague had ceased — fifty thousand deaths in sixteen months in Venice alone. . . .

We have a kind, faithful gondolier, but we have most unsatisfactory conversations with him. I would give anything to talk freely to these people, for no foreigner ever makes any true headway until he knows the native tongue. The gondoliers do not speak a word of English or French, and very few of the shopkeepers — none of the small ones. We gave our gondoliers — four of them — a lira each for a "standee" ticket to the opera last night, so that they need not wait outside until after midnight. Mrs. H. has two (Giovanni and Alfredo), we one (Angelo), and Mrs. W. one (Bastiano). He has been Wagner's, Liszt's, and Ruskin's also — an extraordinary record. As soon as we leave them to go into a gallery or church, they fall fast asleep. Such beautiful manners they have! "Good morning," "Good evening," "Good repose!" Hats always off in saying the slightest word, and a most graceful arm extended for you to rest upon as you get out and into the gondola. As we went into the theater they bowed to the ground and wished us good amusement and a happy evening. When we offer Angelo beer, he says, in Italian,

"Have I your permission?" Then, "Thanks, Signor, Signora, and your very good health." . . .

A Mrs. Eden of England lives in Venice and has a beautiful house on this island of Giudecca, so we have flowers literally from the garden of Eden. It is a blessed experience altogether, and the pictures we have seen will be a lasting joy. . . .

Thursday night Miss M., Mrs. H., Mrs. W., and I gave a gondoliers' ball here at Casa Frollo. It was a great success. We invited about ten Americans; our gondoliers, their friends and their wives; a few gardeners and others. The hour was nine and they stayed until after midnight. They danced in the court hung with lanterns, and had supper in the great "sala," where we sit and dine. The long table had a strip of orange and white sail-cloth down the center and three huge copper vessels filled with scarlet poppies. We bought plates and mugs at three or four cents apiece of cheap, brightly colored ware, and between the flowers stood two enormous Venetian pitchers holding a gallon each. These contained the common red wine, and each man poured it into his own mug. We had two rolls for each, bologna sausage, cherries, Venetian sweetmeats, and "frittati" — sweet dough, fried, and very good. They sang a great deal at table, played the concertina for their dancing, and were generally jolly. . . .

It is all over, this delicious life on the Giudecca! Every hour has been filled with precious memories. Before we can come again, what may not happen to Venice and to ourselves! To-morrow we shall know for the last time "the quick silent passing" of the only Venetian cab.

" How light we move, how softly! Ah,
Were life but as the gondola! "

TURIN, *June 20th,* 1895

Mr. and Mrs. Hutton rose early to see us off, also Miss M. and the whole family of Casa Frollo, who were most sorry to have us go. As we were among the few persons who did not criticize the management of hotels and cafés and declaim in public and private about the lying and trickery and extortion of the natives, we were naturally great favorites.

We took all our luggage in our own gondola, my small trunk, George's hat-box, immense hold-all, my dressing-bag, a Venetian guitar, bought for Nora, and George's new mandolin. I have not spoken of this addition to our belongings, but a young Italian gentleman, an architect, gave him two lessons and refused to accept any remuneration, saying that it was a pleasure "to forward the interests of an illustrious-and-entirely-in-sympathy-with American." This sort of English is most interesting and gives us a keen desire to hear our own Italian literally translated.

We had a hot but not oppressive journey to Florence, reading, and eating the sparse luncheon put up by Padrona Angela of Casa Frollo. We arrived at Florence at six-thirty, changed our traveling clothes and took *table d'hôte* dinner; then drove in a comfortable old phaeton for an hour and a half to get an idea of the city.

For once we were out early next day and were at the door of the Palatine Gallery (Pitti Palace) at ten when it opened. We could only see it hastily, so we passed by scores of great pictures to see the very greatest, which were even then too many to take in or digest. On finding that a corridor or bridge connected this gallery with the famous Uffizi, we concluded to get a taste of that and leave the rest as needing superhuman strength. Accordingly we entered the corridor, which was about ten feet wide and seemed to be built, not in a straight line, but with turnings and windings. It was lined on both sides with paintings, engravings, old plate, woodcuts, portraits of queens for an eighth of a mile, then kings, then painters, then sculptors, then cardinals, but knowing they were not valuable, save in a historical sense, we did not pause to examine them. When we had walked nearly half a mile (I sitting down on the floor periodically and George holding up a stone lion or griffin for support), we concluded we were incarcerated for life. Gleams from the latticed windows gave us no clue to our position. It was too far to go back, and there seemed no end in sight. I finally sat down on a marble Mother and Child and consulted the Guide-Book. It seems that some old emperor, thinking he would like to have the two greatest things in Florence "under cover," so to speak, calmly ordered the Pitti Palace, his own dwelling, to be joined to the Uffizi Gallery. That it was across the river made no difference to him; so this covered corridor goes over the housetops, along shops, and roofs, around corners, until it comes to the Arno, when it follows the bridge line, winds through another section of Florence, and ends in the Uffizi. I don't suppose any other two human creatures ever before attempted the two in one day.

We rested till four-thirty, then wandered about the shops a

little, when George exhilarated himself by purchasing an antique liqueur bottle and a dozen tiny glasses, for half what the man asked — old silver filigree and glass, exquisitely beautiful. He also sighed for various old blunderbusses and battle-axes and strongbows. Before we've been in these cities an hour, he finds dozens of these things, the delight of his heart. Marriage seems more portentous to me as I reflect that I must see that they are all kept free of dust and rust.

There is the queerest arrangement for a bath in this Turin hotel. The maid takes a huge sheet adorned with many mysterious tapes, and lines the big tub with it as smoothly as possible. Then she turns in the water and you get into the sheet and bathe, the only difficulty being to keep it down, as it has a way of rising in billows and bubbles and throwing you off your balance. I saved myself from drowning several times. . . .

George is much grieved to-day because, having made up his mind to spend his morning in the Armory of the Royal Castle, the most notable collection in Italy, it turns out to be St. Peter's Day and everything is closed. He could not buy anything either, so I am very sympathetic. As we shall dwell in an ordinary New York apartment or house, I cannot imagine how these warlike acquisitions, added to those already in his possession, can ever be exposed to the admiring public. . . .

Three months married to-day! The hours and weeks have gone like lightning, although it seems years since we sailed from New York. How I wish my brain were arranged in tightly walled compartments, and all my memories, carefully catalogued, were written there in indelible ink! Alas, instead of that, my statues totter on their pedestals and my Madonnas and Holy Families lie in confusion, even refusing to stay in the respective galleries where they belong. A neat, orderly mind would take care of all this disorder, "tidy up" the impressions and leave me serene and confident. Yet I have had a new vision of beauty, of genius, of fountains pouring crystal water through gleams of golden sunshine, of a creative energy that is, and ever will be, deathless; of colors that will glow on the canvas forever, of gigantic marbles unstained by time; of towers and turrets like frozen lace — oh! yes, I am a far richer woman than I was three months ago; I shall forget details, but the vision will remain.

XXVIII

DINNERS TO CELEBRITIES

"HOME again from a foreign shore!" We had rented the charming furnished house of a sculptor in the downtown, old-fashioned part of New York, near Washington Square, and there the first two years of our married life were passed.

When one opened the front door one went up a short flight of stairs and, after confronting, during the ascent, a beautiful portrait by Zorn, found one's self in a pretty green-and-white drawing-room, connected by wide doors with the dining-room. On the floor above were a large sunny sitting-room, two bedrooms, a bath, and a sewing-room, and on the top floor more bedrooms small and large. All this was comfortable and homelike, but the real magnet that drew us to the house was the sculptor's studio, reached by a broad passage from the street door. It was an enormous room, two stories high, built out over the land in the rear, for the sculptor modeled large figures and groups. The walls were of mellowed brick; and being a studio it was lighted from the top. There was also a magnificent fireplace into which one could fling logs a yard long. Near by was a curious erection of bricks about five feet square, with accompaniments that made it a sculptor's forge. This seemed a difficult object to combine with other furnishings for a room destined to be devoted to wonderful parties; however, George solved the difficulty by inventing a sizable wrought-iron brazier with a gridiron at the top and coals underneath, and lo! we had a place to broil English chops, lobsters, oysters, and other goodies, so that in time we no longer called the place a studio, but the Michelangelo Grill Room. (The choice of this title was a conscientious effort to placate the sculptor, although he was abroad and had given us *carte blanche* to do anything we liked.)

We bought such pieces of furniture and as many rugs as would be useful in our own home after this delightful dwelling should be released to its owners, and placed them in attractive positions in this colossal space which simply ate up furniture and then cried for more. A huge Steinway grand helped at the farther end, and half a dozen inexpensive tables here and there hid their youth under covers of Venetian brocade. If the room ate up furniture, it swallowed light, and there was no electricity, which would have been an anachronism in any case. George has a passion for collecting articles of beauty rather than of use, and had acquired twelve or fifteen Roman lamps during our stay in Italy. They needed the services of one person to keep them filled with crude oil, the brass polished, and the wicks clean, but when set on stone or brick ledges or plaster brackets, with their two, three, or four little points of light gleaming out from dim corners, they were as lovely as fireflies. Half a dozen huge church candlesticks were added, and sooner or later shaded lamps in the darker zones. The more difficulties the room presented as a general gathering-place, the more we loved it and lavished ourselves on it, until finally we purchased four small gas radiators and concealed them behind screens so that they might supplement the great open fire; otherwise the temperature was close to zero.

The Grill Room was a very expensive but a very precious toy! For our first dinner I bought many plants, and the new butler arranged flowers in all the cut-glass bowls and vases that had been among our wedding gifts. When the feast was over, the last guest gone, and the lights and the fires extinguished, a whirling snowstorm descended, and next morning plants were frozen and all the cut-glass broken. The party was worth it, we declared, for it was a dinner for Sir Henry Irving and Ellen Terry; the other guests being Mark Twain, Clyde Fitch, Mrs. Craigie ("John Oliver Hobbes"), Mr. W. D. Howells, Mr. and Mrs. George W. Smalley, Mr. Carl Schurz, Mr. and Mrs. Laurence Hutton, Richard Harding Davis, and Mr. W. A. Purrington, a lawyer friend, famous for his chafing-dish cookery.

There was a quaint little balcony or gallery across the entrance end of the room, wide enough for an upright piano and high enough for music or theatricals. This was lighted with two tall rose-colored lamps, and there from time to time "The Singing Girls," a quartette of which I was the godmother, gave us old English songs. The great open fire shone on our bewildering array of copper and brass all burnished to the last pitch of brightness, and as I gazed at the spectacle I could have fainted with joy; George was proud, too, but a trifle nervous. He wore a white linen cook's coat and cap and hovered anxiously over the new grill that he had designed with such pride; but the chops were inclined to smoke, and he occasionally muttered words to the effect that meals were better cooked in the kitchen. All went well, however, and never was there a greater outpouring of good talk; and, besides, every one always looked beautiful in that room, which is a great thing to accomplish at a party! The Roman lamps helped, the flickering firelight cast soft shadows, the women's frocks stood out against a perfect background, and, when the dining-table had been bereft of its many leaves and pushed into a corner, and the coffee and cigarettes were passed, a glow of happiness settled upon the friendly company.

Here is the bill-of-fare.

OPENING OF THE MICHELANGELO GRILL ROOM

131 West Eleventh Street, December 1, 1895

This "plat-du-jour" is old and plain;
We feel it, though, no shame,
For every old, old dish to-night
Has got a new, new name.

Soup, Consommé Beatrice

It's warm and it's bubbling,
It's fragrant with spice.
If not nice as She is,
It's awfully nice!

Purrington Oysters, Sauce Mephistopheles

To change a graybeard to a youth
Mephisto mixed a potion.
The Devil in our sauce, forsooth,
May make a graybeard of a youth,
And age us all, both hair and tooth,
According to his notion!
Take heed, ye sinners all, the while
Mephisto stirs his potion!

English Mutton Chops, Henry VIII Style

A good hot stake was much esteemed
By English kings in days of old;
But Henry loved a nice fresh chop
And axed his wives to take it cold.

Cardinal Wolsey Broiled Tomatoes

Grilled Quail au Robert Blanc

Salade Olivia

I'd rather be a singing bird
And tilt on boughs so blithe and merry,
But if I were the eating kind
I'd die to grill for Ellen Terry.
Imagine then the feelings of
A modest quail who lately knew
That he could die for Terry first,
And then could grill for Irving too!

Toasted Biscuits   Camembert   Bar-le-duc Confiture

"Bread and cheese and —" 'lack-a-day! We may not add the "kisses."
Climate, customs, morals here, do not permit such blisses!

FRUIT TARTLETS AND CREAM
Little English tarts
For an English Queen of Hearts

COFFEE AND 'BACCY
What matters it the bill-of-fare,
   If brains be served with every course?
And who e'er flouts a homely dish
   When friendship furnishes the sauce?
To dine on lukewarm broth or chop,
   It doth not vex me in the least;
Nor toughened oyster, rocky tart,
   So wit and genius grace the feast.

My friendship with Sir Henry Irving and Ellen Terry was one of long duration and great tenderness. I met them first at a dinner given for them in New York by Mr. and Mrs. Laurence Hutton in 1894. It had been a brilliant affair, and, having a slight headache, I slipped upstairs to rest in some quiet corner for a bit. Discovering a vacant bedroom, I went into it, and, as I tried to find the sofa in the dim light from the hall, I nearly fell over Miss Terry.

"Come in!" she said. "I was fond of you at first sight! Lock the door and let's talk. I must have ten minutes of darkness; the lights always weary me."

We sat down together and came out of the room friends. I never forget how Beatrice Harraden, the English novelist, described her. Miss Harraden is a simple, sincere, sensible person, and she said to me: "Ellen Terry is bewitching, gifted, enchanting, lovable — but it doesn't end there. For unadulterated *goodness* there is no one to match her!"

Sir Henry during that season was always sending seats to my mother, my sister, and me, and we saw each new performance more than once. I believe he would have been happy if the whole house could have been given away instead of being sold. His fast friend and admirable manager, Mr. Bram Stoker, must often have tried to curb

IRVING AND TERRY

his generosity. I sent Mr. Stoker a book of mine, "Timothy's Quest," that winter, and in thanking me he wrote: "It is a charming story, but I don't mind confessing to you that I like just a little more to happen in a book." A week later he sent me his own novel, "Dracula," which is full of vampires that crawl down outside castle walls, like bats, holding to stones by tiny hooks on ends of wings. They do blood-curdling things, of course, that haunt one's dreams for weeks. I wrote to him:

DEAR BRAM STOKER:
  Your "Dracula" is, indeed, a dramatic story, but I don't mind confessing that I like books in which not quite so much happens!
                                                    K. D. W.

During the winter of '95 and '96 my husband and I saw much of these gifted personages. Sir Henry was the kindest and most considerate of friends, lavish in gifts of flowers and of his own company, even in his busiest days. In our first acquaintance, when, at the request of Mr. Hutton, I had read a little story of my own when he was present, he said to me afterward: "Hutton says you are just beginning your literary career. If it does not result in success, just knock at the Lyceum door when you come to London. I cannot say what I can find for you, but at least it will be something better than bringing on a lamp or announcing a visitor!"

Later, after my marriage, he whispered to me at a dinner: "You were wise! The man you chose is better than anything that could have happened had you knocked at the Lyceum door."

One winter afternoon Sir Henry sent to Evelyn Smalley and me seats for his last performance in Brooklyn. It was a matinée of "Louis XI," and we were to have tea in his dressing-room. A blizzard developed by eleven in the morning; the cold was bitter, and the streets were icy, but nothing could weaken our loyalty, and we made the journey. He had sent me a royal poinsettia plant the day before with at least twenty vivid blooms. I cut off two and pinned them carefully under my fur coat to brighten my dark dress. The theater was packed, but the storm had caused many late arrivals and there was restlessness and coughing in the audience. When we went behind the scenes after the second act for tea, he welcomed us with outstretched hands.

"Brave girls!" he said. "You should not have exposed yourselves to this storm."

"The audience shows that more than a thousand others did!" I answered.

"Yes, but they came to wriggle and cough," he replied, "and you to help me act. The house is cold; I could hear the wind roaring, I felt the audience slipping away from me, I was quite unhappy till I saw your friendly scarlet flowers in the third row; then I warmed myself with their color and acted better!"

I had often been a guest at the famous suppers on the Lyceum stage after a notable first or final performance, but the last time my husband and I saw our friend was on his reappearance in London after a severe illness. All literary, dramatic, and artistic London was in the stalls, and the pit and upper reaches of the house were crowded with those who had loved and honored him for years. His reception was thrilling, but the end of the play furnished the greatest ovation I ever saw given to an actor. Cheers came from throats choked with emotion, tears were in many eyes. The applause gained in volume until it was a deafening roar, and continued till it was evident that Irving was too feeble to do more than acknowledge briefly his appreciation and indebtedness to the audience. His speeches, as all will remember, were brief, gracious, modest, and beautifully phrased. He proclaimed himself frequently as the "grateful servant of the public," and that ardent and loyal public will be his so long as memory lasts.

And while I am discussing dinners I remember two among many others at later dates, both of them, alas! in a new home, minus a grill room. I was, and still am, rather pleased with the *carte-du-jour* of the Kipling dinner.

JUNGLE DINNER

To Mr. and Mrs. Rudyard Kipling

"What food on the way?" said the Jackal.

SMALL BLUE POINTS
"Thou art leader, little brother!"

CONSOMMÉ EN TASSE
"Kaa was licking his chops at the thought of his dinner to come."

CRABS IN THE SHELL
"For my cousin who is a fish-eater, does not always know the good
from the bad."

SWEETBREADS AND MUSHROOMS
"All are very good eating."

SADDLE OF MUTTON
FRENCH PEAS, NEW POTATOES
"I got my girth in that season!"

SQUAB; SALAD OF TOMATOES AND ESCAROLE
"Was no other game afoot?"

CRACKERS AND CHEESE
"A small thing, but acceptable," said the Adjutant Crane.

ICES, SMALL CAKES, FRUIT
"For a crocodile is never quite full."

APOLLINARIS, SHERRY, CHAMPAGNE, WHISKEY, SODA, LIQUEURS
"For though the Jungle People drink seldom, they must drink deep."

COFFEE

"Baloo and Bagheera both echoed: Leave men alone!"

TOBACCO

"What does the lean thing do now?" "He blows smoke out of his mouth,"
said Mowgli.

"All thanks for this good meal," said Tabaqui, licking his lips.

"JUNGLE-FAVOR GO WITH THEE!"
K. D. R. — G. C. R.

There had been plenty of work as well as play in the
beloved downtown house. I had been Vice-President of
the New York Kindergarten Association for several years,
serving successively under the presidency of Mr. Richard
Watson Gilder and Mr. Hamilton Mabie, and the work of
the Association was very arduous at that time. I was also
President of the Wednesday Afternoon Club, an organization of literary women, my duties requiring considerable
study and regular attendance at committee meetings.
The Three Arts Club and work among crippled children
and babies' hospitals claimed much attention, as they
were especially in the line of my interests and experience.
Later, I was on the Art and Literature Committee of the
Colony Club, and for five years one of its Governors and
Chairman of the Library Committee.

Six books had come out since "Timothy's Quest,"
though several, published in 1895 and 1896, had been
written before that date. My "Nine Love Songs and a
Carol" and "Marm Lisa" appeared in 1896. I clearly
recall the desk in my sitting-room and the very hour in
which I read a letter from Mr. Edmund Gosse in regard to
"Marm Lisa." He raised me to the seventh heaven by his
praise of "Mrs. S. Cora Grubb" as a character-study, and
then lowered me to the depths of despair by saying that
"Mistress Mary," my heroine, was little more than a wax

doll with a blue sash! It seems to be my temperament to agree heartily with any piece of honest though ferocious criticism, but to be skeptical about praise, if it is very ardent. "Marm Lisa" has had its admirers, however, in an unexpected direction. The book has for its central character a mentally defective child of fourteen, capable of education, and morally sound to the core. I had certain of these pitiful types in my kindergarten at Silver Street culled from dark alleyways in my visits to the children. I experimented on them one at a time in my own way, and finally succeeded in aiding to found an institution, twenty miles from San Francisco, where they could be properly taught and made self-supporting.

My book reached a distinguished physician in Massachusetts, whose life-work had been given to such cases, and he wrote me as follows:

DEAR MADAM:

I have read with great interest your "Marm Lisa" and marvel that without any specific training you have invented so many ways of reaching and helping such children. My work takes me all over the country to observe institutions and their methods for teaching defectives, and I have seldom visited one where I have not found a copy of "Marm Lisa" as well as many of your other books. It is no mere conventional compliment, dear Madam, when I assure you that wherever I go I find you the favorite author of the feeble-minded.

Sincerely yours

X. Y. Z., M.D.

This is perhaps my favorite letter, and I constantly try to extract some grain of comfort from its honest praise. The only trouble with the good doctor, in fact, is the absence of a sense of humor.

On the day when "Penelope's Experiences in Scotland" appeared in book form, we had a Publication Dinner with "Ian Maclaren" (author of "The Bonnie Briar Bush") as guest of honor, in common with two members of the firm of Houghton, Mifflin & Company, from Boston. The new volume in its dress of Royal Stuart tartan was laid near the cover of every guest, and we had as many dishes notable in Scottish culinary art as our cook could accomplish.

There were brief speeches by Mark Twain, Thomas B. Reed, Hamilton Mabie, and Ian Maclaren, but I cannot help thinking that my husband's verses carried off the palm.

He had remarked while shaving that he should not come to the table if he had to make a speech. I assured him that it was not necessary, but somehow in the succeeding fifteen minutes he had evolved a clever rhyme and pushed it under the plate of a trusty friend who could read it aloud if an emergency arose. It ran thus:

"There was a time when we were boys,
And had our kites and other toys; ·
But every kite then had a tail
To guide it when it went to sail.
The tail was an important part
Of every young kite-maker's art;
But now they're building those box-kites
That have no tails; they're awful sights!
And here's the thought that makes me pale —
Will all kites fly without a tail?
For I, blest mortal, lucky wight,
Have been the tail of my wife's kite!
I've soared in booky atmosphere;
I've met both good and bad and queer: ·
But on the whole it's jolly nice
And 'twould be hard to sacrifice.
But if invention is not stopped
The chances are that I'll be dropped!
I hope I'm tied a 'double tight'
As tail of Kate D. Wiggin's kite."

G. C. R.

XXIX

LONDON AND OXFORD

I HAD been going abroad every spring since 1890, although, after I became possessed of a country house in Maine, I always returned there for July, August, and September. My husband's business interests were largely in Scotland and Ireland, and for a few years in Germany also, so that we always sailed early in April and generally spent three months on the other side of the Atlantic, mostly in Great Britain.

England, Scotland, and Ireland became second homes to me, and until the World War, with all its cruel changes, narrowed my list and prevented my annual visits for a time, I had as many acquaintances and friends there as in America. From the year 1900, when the three volumes of "Penelope's Experiences" had been published, my life every summer was one continuous round of happy and stimulating contacts. I did nothing for myself — the books did everything for me. They brought me unexpected and inspiring friendships with great people, and gave me entrance into hearts and homes, where I could never have hoped to find a lodging. Some of the open doors were in cottages and some were castle gateways, but the warm welcome was always there. One personage gave me letters to another and the second to the third and fourth, so that I was passed on from hearthstone to hearthstone in all three countries where Penelope had been read. If I had told my own experiences instead of inventing those of my three heroines, Penelope, Francesca, and Salemina, the books would have been more interesting, perhaps, certainly more piquant and provocative of discussion, but I should have been discourteous and ungrateful, indeed, had I carried a notebook and set down actual records of places and people and events.

I think I may fairly say I had unequaled opportunities of knowing my backgrounds without special study or business-like collection of facts and material, a task for which I am not fitted, either by temperament or training. My husband's unselfishness and generous devotion to any work I had in hand, his lively interest and pride in any small achievement of mine that he thought worthy and good, was a sustaining force from the beginning. During days or weeks of separation we have always been united in those standards and ideals of living that promote and preserve true companionship. Often, when important business affairs kept him from sharing some unexpected experience that would have been as delightful to him as to me, he always encouraged my acceptance and made the way easy for me. His many foreign relations, both business and social, added to our mutual pleasure in life abroad, and the fact that he was (and is) a good shot, a good angler, and a good golfer often gave me a reflected glory in circles where his talents were more esteemed than mine.

In Scotland, for instance, we not only knew Edinburgh intimately — its plain and its titled people, its schools, its teachers, its literary and professional circles; but during various seasons we were householders in a small way in Upper Largo (Fifeshire), Lochearnhead, in the North, and Inverary, in the West Highlands. There were also regular visits to St. Andrews, North Berwick, and Troon, for my husband's golf, and, although I myself was a hopeless failure at the ancient and honorable game, I was experienced enough to talk about it, and, what is more important, to listen at luncheon to the thrilling accounts of the morning's proceedings.

A LONDON PHOTOGRAPH OF 1896

As to Ireland, I have made long visits in Buncrana, Belfast, Newcastle, Dublin, Killarney, and Valentia Island, taken coaching trips through the length of the West, made a jaunting-car journey to all the Irish literary shrines and birthplaces of her heroes, poets, and authors, and made visits to the Protestant Primate, the "Grand Old Man of the Church of Ireland," successively Bishop of Derry and Archbishop of Armagh, at the Bishop's palace in that northern town.

Two especially brilliant and noteworthy events were my invitation in 1900 to be the guest of Alexandra College, Dublin, during Queen Victoria's visit, and a wonderful week in 1906 at the Vice-Regal Lodge with the Lord Lieutenant and his wife, the Earl and Countess of Aberdeen. These occasions will be described in a succeeding chapter.

Were I a Prime Minister, a Secretary of State, a great general, a lady of fashion, a famous explorer, or any personage whose reminiscences might merit preservation in two fat volumes, there are a hundred and one stories I could tell of my life in the British Isles, as well as in Germany and Italy, stories rather amusing, sometimes pathetic, even dramatic, but I am only a modest, old-fashioned "one-volume autobiographer," whose experiences lie mostly before a war that has submerged all unimportant occurrences and wiped out all minor personalities, leaving them "without form and void." We live in the present and the near future in these agitating years of transition, and my story has a perceptible odor of lavender about it that belongs to other days. For lack of space, therefore, I will lift from my store of memories only a few of those most likely to be interesting.

London would mean merely a mention of dinners and luncheons, from which one must omit all brilliant, serious, memorable, and quotable conversation, and give lists of names that spell awe or delight to all who have broken bread and sipped wine at the same table.

Looking at me as I write I see the faces of Mr. Gladstone; Archbishop Alexander, the Protestant Primate of all Ireland; Professor Samuel Butcher, the Greek scholar; Sir James Barrie; Edmund Gosse; Henry James; Lord Justice Fletcher-Moulton; Sir Johnston Forbes-Robertson; Thomas Hardy; Lord Tweedmouth; Frederic Harrison; Sir Edward (now Viscount) Grey; Lord Rosebery; Lord Haldane; Anthony Hope; Lord Tennyson; Eden Phillpotts; Sir Arthur Quiller-Couch; Richard Whiteing; Henry Labouchère; Rudyard Kipling; H. G. Wells; Maarten Maartens; Lord Reay; Owen Seaman; Sir Henry Lucy; Sir W. S. Gilbert; and Lord Roberts. (I must stop to breathe here, and say that just before luncheon at the American Embassy the great "Bobs" asked me if Gertrude Atherton, author of "The Conqueror," were in the room, as he much desired to sit by her. I knew that I was to have that honor, but I fled to the hostess and had the places changed, so she must report the hero's conversation in *her* autobiography.)

Then follows a list of charming and gifted women: Alice Meynell, Mrs. Humphry Ward, Lucy Kemp-Welch, Mrs. J. R. Green, Lady Bell, Miss Macnaughton, Mrs. W. K. Clifford, Mrs. L. B. Walford, May Sinclair, Countess von Arnim (now Lady Russell, but always "Elizabeth of the German Garden"), Lady St. Helier, and many others not so often met or so well known as these, whose faces and voices come back to me readily and vividly as I write.

There were always many literary dinners in London, those of the Royal Literary Fund, the Women Writers' Society, the Whitefriars Club, the Authors' Society, and others. I was often asked for after-dinner speeches

and responses to toasts, for women are called upon in
London more frequently than in New York. On the occasion of a certain annual dinner of the Authors' Society I
shared the response for "The Guests" with Right Honorable the Lord Collins, Anthony Hope having proposed it.
George Meredith, the President, was absent because of
illness, the great Swinburne had just died, and the sad
end of John Davidson, the poet, had been a matter of
sorrow among authors. Edmund Gosse, LL.D., was in the
chair, and I unconventionally made my speech in rhyme
as follows:

Mr. Chairman, good friends, fellow authors at table,
I fear I shall find myself not very able
To deal with that difficult subject "The Guests";
Still, one cannot evade Dr. Gosse's behests.
If only he'd said: "Talk of 'Palates of Snails,'
'The Uses of Radium,' 'Women in Jails,'
'Revisions of Tariff' or 'Copyright Laws,'
'The Prospects of Holland' or 'Rumors of Wars'" —
You can "read up" such topics in encyclopædias;
You're sure of your facts, if you're frequently tedious!

I myself am a guest from across the blue wave; —
"The land of the free and the home of the brave"
Native singers have styled it, and yet, I suppose,
We cannot monopolize phrases like those.
Notwithstanding your Princes, your Kings, Courts, and
        Thrones —
Institutions our infant Republic bemoans —
Your "freedom," your "bravery," needless to tell,
Appear to be standing the test rather well!

Do you know what I see as I stand here the guest
Of the flower of London, its cleverest, best,
Its dramatists, editors, novelists, sages?
I see *you* as you *are*, then, as heirs of the ages!
Your laurels are green, I see others unfaded,
Tho' centuries cold are the brows they once shaded:
See ghosts of immortals whose eloquent words
Made England a forest of rare singing birds;
Magicians whose tales are still fresh to the ear,
They spoke, they still speak, and the world bends to hear.

I own the same tongue, so I share in the glory
That makes Britain famous in song and in story.
(We imperiled our heritage slightly, you'll say,
When we ventured from out your dominion to stray,
But not one Pilgrim sailed for his bleak Plymouth Rock
Till Shakespeare was born, so we're stock of his stock!)

Later, gods grew more scarce and the half-gods appeared;
'Twas the same on our side: lower altars we reared
When our Emerson, Longfellow, Whittier passed,
With Hawthorne and Holmes, and dear Lowell at last.
Yet though we meet often the Homer who "nods,"
We still pour libations to gods and half-gods —
Those who smile, grave, serene, from the heights of Olympus,
And smaller ones, somewhat addicted to simpers!
We must bow to a genius whenever we see one,
If heroes aren't worshiped there'll soon cease to *be* one!
They used to be big, now the little ones lead:
They can always *write* books if they can't always *read!*
Soon, among the small fry, with their hustlings and jostlings,
Instead of a critic like Gosse we'll find *Gosselings!*

Our pedestals stand rather empty of late,
Each for its Colossus doth patiently wait.
One is just newly filled; golden voice, heart of fire,
What eloquent strains he has swept from his lyre!
The thrushes that sing o'er that freshly made grave
Make music no sweeter than Swinburne once gave
To a world that talks less of a poet's bird-notes
Than armies and navies and feminine votes.
Is it this that puts bitterness into the heart
Of a singer who lives *for*, but not *by* his art?
Poor John Davidson's gone: he was hopeless and sad;
If now he's at peace, we can only be glad
That the "weariest river" when once it flows free
Finds somehow and somewhere its path "to the sea."

Now from sorrow to gratitude; blessings are many,
Tho' up to this moment I've not mentioned any!
There is one splendid voice that is still ringing true,
One that's worthy to rank with the undying few;
Old or young he's as full as a reed is of pith —
Your President, bless his name, George Meredith!
The novelists needn't lose courage and mope,
For while they have Hawkins they always have *Hope;*

Or if they're depressed in a casual way
There's a tonic just out — Wells's "Tono-Bungay" —
And the knowledge that cheers us, encourages, heartens,
That "nothing's the matter" with Herr "Maarten Maartens."
(I give him his pen-name: my Muse never courts
A Dutch rhyme for Herr Van der Poorten und Schwartz!)

These, then, fellow-scribes, are the thoughts of a guest
Who tacitly in her first sentence confessed
She hadn't a notion of speeches at dinners,
For on these occasions the men are chief sinners.
I thank dear Edmund Gosse for the honor conferred
In letting me speak for the guests this brief word;
Lord Collins I thank for dividing the toast,
Especially when in himself he's a host.
And last, friends and authors, I'm glad to be here,
Not alone for the wit and the mirth and good cheer,
But because we are sounding the praises to-night
Of an art in whose service lies keenest delight.
Talk of angels! Poor angels, they play and they sing,
But never a quill do they pluck from a wing!
They have only their harp-strings, no paper, no ink;
I'd rather be author than angel, I think;
I'm nearly submerged in a crowd of my betters,
But proud to be counted a woman of letters!

The friendships made in the British Isles, in all the years
that lie between, have never been completely severed save
by death. In unhappy, perturbed Ireland they still flour-
ish by occasional correspondence, and in Scotland, more
often revisited, the ties that bind us continue to be very
strong. Two intimate Edinburgh friends have visited us
in America, the Reverend Cameron Reid, of Glasgow, who
received signal honors in the war, and Henry Johnstone,
also a valiant worker among the troops in France.

Long ago I adopted this highly gifted person, Henry
Johnstone, without his knowledge or consent, as a sort of
Private Poet Laureate, for he has the charming habit of
writing personal verses to his friends on special occasions,
verses so delightful and so finished in style that they merit
preservation.

Having great difficulty in calling any one, male or female, by his or her Christian name short of a twenty years' acquaintance, and having progressed in friendship far beyond "Mr. Johnstone," I christened him "Olaf," the O.L.A.F. standing for Old, Learned, Anecdotal Friend. In the summer of 1904 I was in London, but unable to visit Edinburgh, whereupon my P.P.L. sent me these lines:

LAMENT

The simmer birds are here again,
O' their sweet notes nae broo hae we,
For while they sing their blythest strain,
We're wae to want Penelope!

The King has come, the King has gaen —
A great and gracious monarch he —
But och! he smiled on us in vain;
We're wae to want Penelope!

The ministers, a godly train
Established and United-Free,
In their Assemblies mak' their maen,
"We're wae to want Penelope!"

And ane and a', that hae been fain
And heartsome in her companie,
We sigh and sab, we greet and graen,
"We're wae to want Penelope!"

OLAF

Another happy affair occurred at a London luncheon. Long years before I had attended a Bowdoin College Commencement in Brunswick, Maine, where Sarah Orne Jewett was the only woman in the Academic procession, and the only woman to whom had been given the honorary degree of Litt.D. by the College up to that time.

I spent a few days with her later in the season at South Berwick, and we had many intimate talks in her lovely old sitting-room at twilight. I recall my telling her that her Bowdoin degree was such a well-deserved tribute to her

BOWDOIN COLLEGE COMMENCEMENT PROCESSION WITH KATE DOUGLAS WIGGIN, LITT.D., IN CENTER

beautiful work; and how I loved to see her so honored among the crowds of men, the one feminine figure in a cap and gown in the long procession.

"I do appreciate it," she said, "and these last two Commencements have been very happy occasions; but, do you know, I should be even happier if only I could have my books translated into foreign languages as yours have been."

This was some years before her death, and there was a much-mourned gap in the Commencement procession until it was filled, most unexpectedly, by me, upon whom her mantle had finally fallen. In 1904 the degree of Litt.D. was given me "*in absentia*," and the cable announcing the news reached me in London on the occasion of the annual luncheon of the Society of American Women. There were many cordial congratulations and much generous applause, the rising of two or three hundred women to give me greeting, with waving of handkerchiefs and merry calls of "Hail! Doctor."

My associations with Bowdoin College have been both intimate and continuous, and I well recall the occasion of my first appearance in cap and gown when our former President, William DeWitt Hyde, prayed, in the old Congregational Church, "for all Bowdoin's sons and for her only daughter." [1] I felt a new sense of pride and responsibility which has never grown less, and now, in 1923, as President of the Society of Bowdoin Women — an organization of the mothers, daughters, wives, and sisters of the Alumni — I have full opportunity to show my devotion to President Kenneth Sills, to the College, and to all it represents.

My good friend and Edinburgh poet did not fail to congratulate me on my new honor.

[1] Two daughters have since been born.

TO THE FAIRE MISTRESS RIGGS

Worthilie Admitted to the Degree of Doctor of Letters, in the
College of Bowdoin, beyond Seas

When of Penelope I hear the Name,
I call to Minde not wise Ulysses' Dame,
But You, that sometimes deigne to sojourn here,
Whom every Muse and every Grace holds deare;
Who smile at Envie, and can bring with Ease
All to confesse Your sovran Skille to please.
For Britaine's Sake then, whose Three Kingdomes show
One Minde in honouring and praising You,
And for my Sake, who ever did prefer
Your Bookes to other Tomes and weightier,
Permit my lines to have a free Accesse,
To kiss Your Hand, most Daintie Doctoresse.

H. J.

Next to London in my affection comes Oxford, where my
sister and I first went to the Clarendon Hotel for Commemoration Week, an especially gay one that season, for
the Duke and Duchess of York [1] were guests of the Dean
of Christ Church, and there was much royal state.

The wonderful old town of colleges and cathedrals is
never so gay as in June days, and, although it was my first
visit, so many friends had heralded my coming that every
hour of our time was filled with engagements. Eminent
dons escorted us to garden-parties and concerts, we dined
with heads of colleges, lunched with their ladies, and
breakfasted with merry undergraduates up flights of
breakneck stairs and down corkscrew passages.

Everybody breakfasts with everybody else in Commemoration Week, and no youth so poor in relatives but
he has his mother, or his grandmother, or his aunt, or his
elder sister with him at this time to chaperon his matutinal
feasts and his afternoon teas.

Oxford appealed so clearly to my literary instinct that
I felt that each new pleasure or event which was offered

[1] The present King and Queen.

to me was of value, and so I passed from boating on the "Char" to the Christ Church ball, from a luncheon at All Souls', graced by the presence of England's future sovereigns, to an open-air performance of "As You Like It" in Worcester Gardens.

I made the acquaintance of the then Master of Balliol, during that first visit (James Leigh Strachan-Davidson), and for three successive seasons I was his guest for Commemoration Week. These days are full of bewildering and thrilling memories, the presence of my brilliant young cousin, Whitney Shepardson, a Rhodes scholar at Balliol, winner of many honors and a favorite of the Master, adding greatly to my pleasure. The Encænia, at which our Mark Twain and Whitelaw Reid, England's Rudyard Kipling and General Booth, of the Salvation Army, and France's Saint-Saëns and Rodin received degrees, called together a specially brilliant assembly of guests. Lord Curzon (a Balliol man) was the Chancellor, and there was a noteworthy luncheon at All Souls' after the presentation of degrees. I was very nervous about Mark Twain, for the "undergrads" in the galleries, who evidently adored him, bawled so incessantly and sometimes with so much humor that I feared Mr. Clemens with his ready wit might talk back. He behaved like an angel, however, and was a miracle of dignity, possibly because his daughter, Clara,[1] had cabled him that morning, "Remember proprieties!"

My sister and I occupied two places in the seats of the mighty at the Sheldonian Theater, and the chief object of our admiration was a foreign personage in glittering dress, his brown skin and dark eyes heightened in effect by a magnificent turban from which hung a sapphire the size of a robin's egg. An Indian potentate, of course, but which one? At the close of the exercises the crowd slowly melted

[1] Mrs. Ossip Gabrilowitch.

away and a smaller stream turned toward All Souls'
quadrangle; still no card had reached me as promised by
the Master, giving me the name of my escort and seat-
mate at the luncheon. Suddenly, as the theater was almost
empty, I saw him hurrying toward me arm in arm with the
picturesque Indian potentate! My heart sank, for in the
excitement of the moment I did not think of him as an
English-speaking person.

He drew nearer and the Master made known to me the
Maharajah of Bikanir. (He did not add G.C.S.I., G.C.I.E.,
A.D.C. to the King-Emperor. Some of his honors were
mercifully withheld till later!) I tremblingly acknowledged
the introduction and accompanied him to the great hall in
All Souls' where the luncheon was to be held. Even by
that time I had discovered he was an Oxford man and
spoke much better English than I; and I later learned that
he ruled over an immense territory, was a Colonel in the
Second Bengal Lancers, and had raised and equipped a
Camel Corps for Imperial defense. He was a very fine
sportsman, devoted to big-game shooting, and a good
polo, racquet, and tennis player.

All these heroic virtues did not come out at luncheon,
but I hereby declare that he was one of the most friendly,
entertaining, sympathetic, delightful companions I ever
sat beside for two hours, and I wrote my mother that he
could appear at a barn dance in Hollis and hypnotize the
whole village.

He asked me as an American and an author to present
him to Mark Twain whose work he knew and admired, and
feeling somewhat like "Alice in Wonderland" I escorted
the magnificent being through the quadrangle to Mark
Twain's side. Mark, "most amiable and charming sir,"
as the Chancellor had called him in Latin, was in great
form, the idol of the crowd; his wonderful white hair

glistening in the sun, and the Oxford gown with its brilliant hood setting off his fine head and face.

"I like the degree well enough," he confided with his usual informality to the Maharajah; "but I'm crazy about the clothes! I wish I could wear 'em all day and all night. Think of the gloomy garb I have to walk the streets in at home, when my whole soul cries out for gold braid, yellow and scarlet sashes, jewels and a turban! If there's a dearth of Maharajahs any time in India, just cable me, sir, and I'll take the next train."

XXX

EDINBURGH AND HOLYROOD PALACE

As for Scotland, I might have been bred on porridge and haggis, scones and shortbread; Scottish ballads might have been the literary inspirations of my childhood; the bagpipe might have been my native musical instrument, so fully, freely, and instantaneously did I fall under the spell of that enchanting country!

Edinburgh has the (reputed) hospitality of a Texas ranch, and, if it gave me a heartier welcome than I merited, I paid it back in ardent affection and loyalty. Charles Reade says the Scotch ice is very cold, but if one thaws it one reaches the Scotch fire, warmer than any sun of Italy or Spain. I never felt the ice, only the cheery, delicious warmth.

I will give extracts from a few letters preserved by my dear mother who was keeping the home-fires burning in our summer place in Maine. She was delighted that her two daughters could be together in Scotland, very busy and active and quite enthralled with the task of getting the house in order, the house where she spent twenty-five happy and useful seasons.

EDINBURGH, 18 ATHOLL CRESCENT
May, 1897

DEAREST MOTHER, guardian of the house and home, preserver of all the village traditions, beloved parent without whose aid we should never have come into this bewilderingly interesting world, we love you and can see you at this moment, desperately sewing on ruffled white muslin curtains, feverishly embroidering centerpieces, and eagerly covering sofa cushions in wool-work, cross-stitch and appliqué, all to welcome home your prodigal daughters now disporting themselves in high society. I am feeling unusually haughty as the Edinburgh Philosophical Institution has invited me to deliver a lecture on American Fiction. As I have declined the honor on the pretext of leaving Scotland earlier than the date fixed, they will never know how badly I should have done it.

George, who returned from a penitential journey to Auchtermuchty, Dunfermline, and Glasgow this morning, says I must write you of my appearance at Holyrood Palace last night, an appearance attended by some unintentional and unconventional features. I have told you in former letters all about the great May Assembly, which fills Edinburgh with ministers and clerical dignitaries from all over Scotland, and among the functions are the dinners and entertainments given by the Lord High Commissioner for the Queen (in this year of grace the Marquis of Tweeddale), who, with the Marchioness, their daughter Lady Clementine Hay, and several ladies-in-waiting, is "in residence" at Holyrood Palace.

Nora declined to be "presented" in last night's grand affair, preferring a Holyrood luncheon and garden-party, instead. (To show you the hospitality of our Edinburgh friends we have received eleven invitations to the palace for Assembly week!)

Lord Kinnear had asked the pleasure of "presenting" me, and I gladly accepted his escort, as he is so well known, so agreeable, and so clever.

We were to leave the house at 8.45. I wore my Dresden China silk with the little bouquets of roses on a white ground, narrow black velvet ribbon on the flounces, and pink and silver embroidery in the low neck. George had provided an enormous shower-bouquet of pink, white, and pale lavender sweet peas interspersed with a delicate, long-stemmed trembling flower that looks like pink star-dust. I was not positively regal, but I could not have looked better with such charms as I possess! I rested after a good tea at five and spent at least ten minutes in continuous curtsying before a long glass, wearing during this unaccustomed exercise my black satin, low-heeled, "reform model," bedroom slippers, as I knew that I might have a long wait in line before my curtsy came.

My toilette was much approved by Nora and various callers assembled in the sitting-room, and just as I was going for my opera cloak Lord Kinnear was announced, ten minutes ahead of time. I disliked to keep him waiting and made haste to don my wrap and depart.

We entered the line of carriages at nine and alighted at the palace door at 9.30. Then came a quarter of an hour in the crowded cloak-room and at least twenty minutes in the crush that moved through the great portrait-gallery toward the narrow door of the throne room.

I could see the Lord High Commissioner and the beautiful Marchioness, who looked like Cleopatra in a vivid scarlet gown with a brilliant display of rubies and diamonds and a lovely little coronet that well became her lustrous dark hair.

Notwithstanding the long wait I felt no fatigue, indeed, indescribably gay and well, for I had many friends in the line, and Lord Kinnear was, of course, directly behind me. I watched the curtsies carefully to see how those "to the manner born" carried themselves, and as I neared the Lord High Commissioner I noted one young lady, virtuous, I am sure, for she was extremely ugly, who allowed a long bony foot and ankle to appear as she swept aside her train.

I glanced down to enjoy the effect of my own white satin shoes with crystal buckles, when lo! I beheld large, black, reformed bedroom slippers on my feet!

No words can describe my confusion! I could easily have fainted, but an instant's thought showed me that I should make a scene at Court, and when borne out by Lord Kinnear my shoes would attract immediate attention, probably fall off and be handed to him by the Purse-Bearer, or a titled Aide-de-Camp. I summoned all my courage and when the awful moment came, made the deepest and most distinguished of curtsies with one end alone in view, that of concealing my feet.

As ill-luck would have it, the Marchioness shook hands and delayed the waiting line by speaking with me as an American stranger, and her daughter, Lady Clementine Hay, remembered me as having given her favorite Children's League of Pity a dozen books for its library. I was obliged to stand, of course, but I accomplished a physical miracle by standing down into myself, decreasing my stature at least two inches.

"You are pale, and I fear very tired," said Lord Kinnear as we wedged our way through the crowd into another room. "Shall I get you an ice? And may I introduce Lord B. who wishes you to dance the opening quadrille with him?"

"I think I won't dance this evening, thank you. I really am tired and must not stay very late," I said.

We walked through the beautiful rooms hung with priceless

tapestries and portraits, meeting many people we knew. There was supper, but I could not eat, hold my shower-bouquet, keep my train from being walked on, and hide my feet — it was too complicated! There was a band playing in the quadrangle, the flowers and palms were superb, the palace was a dream of beauty, for it was mostly lighted by hundreds of candles. It would have been a red-letter evening for me had I not been so enraged at my absent-mindedness. Will you not gather the Hollis neighbors, especially "Aunt" Susan, "Aunt" Hannah, and Jane Akers, and read this letter to them? They will say in chorus: "Land! don't that beat all! Wa'n't Katie careless, and she so used to company, too!"

I must not forget to tell you the most humorous thing that ever happened in our family. Nora and I are invited to luncheons, teas, and dinners, so we have discovered, not because we are beautiful, wise, rich, or gifted, but because we are reputed to sing so delightfully together! I hardly expect you to believe it, for you know our repertory of old plantation melodies, negro spirituals, and Spanish folk-songs. We were never asked, never, indeed, allowed to sing in our native land, at least to "company," yet here we are led to the piano and begged to honor the guests with some of our quaint American songs. We have a little upright piano in our sitting-room and enlarge our collection daily, singing everything from memory, as has always been our habit.

One evening at a dinner at Lord Dunedin's we were asked if American ladies sang! We acknowledged that we could sing old plantation melodies and the like, and went to the piano. We were not self-conscious, for many of our good friends were there. There was Henry Johnstone, known as "Scholar Johnstone" at Oxford — a real lover of boys and a wonderful Master at Edinburgh Academy; a poet, a historian, and the best raconteur in Edinburgh. Rev. Cameron Reid of St. Giles's was there — you will hear much of him from us — and Rev. Hugh Black of Free St. George's, perhaps the most admired, discussed, and loved of all the younger ministers in Scotland. There was Mrs. Sellar, the belle of every dinner, even at seventy years; Miss McLeod, daughter of the famous Dr. Norman McLeod, Queen Victoria's favorite preacher; James Cadenhead and Robin Lorimer, both well-known painters, and several others.

To our surprise they loved and demanded a second hearing of "Nelly was a Lady," "Doan' you cry, ma honey!" "Swing Low,

Sweet Chariot," and "Lubly Melinda" (your favorite)! We thought of you when Mrs. David Masson, wife of the noted professor at Edinburgh University, leaned forward and said: "Do sing it again! Melinda is such a gay little name!"

"I doan' want to stay here no longer!" so full of the indescribable pathos and spiritual yearning of negro music, brought Hugh Black to the piano, with a request for its repetition. "Dem Lubly Little Courtin's by de Door" received special applause, and at the end a grave and distinguished doctor of philosophy asked: "Do I understand that this — this — custom is common in America?" I laughed and answered, "I thought it was practically a universal custom, sir!" . . .

A later letter runs as follows:

INVERARY, ARGYLLSHIRE
May, 1897

DEAREST MOTHER:

Here we are in Inverary, George, Nora, and I. Our dear preacher-friend, Cameron Reid, formerly of St. Giles's Cathedral, Edinburgh, but now established here, met us at Rothesay, where we took the steamer Lord of the Isles for this heavenly spot. (I wish we in America needn't name our small steamers, The Mary Jane Hobbs, or The John C. Higgins!)

The wee village is built on the curve of Loch Fyne, so near that the tide washes almost up to our doorsteps. The hills and mountains across the Loch are beautiful and Inverary Castle at the other end of the village magnificent in itself and superbly situated. At the back of our street is a most wonderful avenue of beeches, part of the Duke of Argyll's estate. It is about a mile and a half long, and the trees are two hundred and fifty years old; we are allowed to cycle in it by the Duke's special permission. Indeed, we are all in clover, for the Duke has given George the fishing of his private preserves, so that his face is radiant with joy and anticipation.

We have taken a little pink-washed cottage and our landlady does the cooking with the help of a scullery maid. It is very near the Manse, which is what we particularly wished, and Cameron has made it so lovely inside, using exquisite taste in the simple furnishings. It is a fine old stone house with two acres of ground, and the Duke put it in perfect order when he offered Cameron the living, restoring the little church at the same time. . . .

Extract from a later letter:

Oh! why did we ever come to Inverary, since we must leave it, and may never see it again? Our visit has been ideal from first to last. Cameron spends every leisure moment with us and Nora and I make parochial calls with him, visiting the cottagers and becoming acquainted with the dear soft-voiced Highland folk. Whenever we cycle in the Castle grounds, we stop and go in, proudly presenting the Duke's permit, although now the servants in residence have learned to know us, and Cameron is generally one of the party. He is a great deal at the Castle, but the Duke and Duchess only spend six months there. The great hall was an armory in olden times, and as a Duke of Argyll always had to fit out his whole clan at an hour's notice you can conceive the splendor of the arms ranged in semi-circles and circles and oblongs on the walls. The hall appears to be three stories in height, and the men could go on the galleries opening into it and seize their weapons as they hung in stacks. Suspended from this gallery on the right are seven battle-flags, torn and blood-stained, and from the opposite side the private banner of each son and daughter of the present house, with arms and insignia, the Marquis of Lorne, Lord Archibald Campbell, and the others.

All Highlanders seem to be educated. Is it not curious, for instance, that Archie, the Duke's head keeper, introduced "Penelope's Experiences in Scotland" at Inverary, put it in the Library, and recommended and lent it here and there?

Yesterday Mrs. Jack Fleming (Rudyard Kipling's sister and author of a couple of charming novels) came to spend the night at the Argyll Arms Hotel. Neil Munro, author of "John Splendid" and a volume of exquisite Highland stories called "The Lost Pibroch," is spending June here, as it is his native place. We all met at the Manse, and it seemed odd to see four authors gathered in one room in that tiny remote village.

The Duke will think twice before he gives George the fishing of his private preserves again, for he made a wonderful record, and if the weather had not been so hot he wouldn't have left a fish in the lochs! There is a keeper for each set of lochs, and George had one of them and a boat when necessary all day and every day he fished. The keepers all said they were sorry His Grace was not at home, as he would have liked to see Mr. Riggs cast a fly. . . .

Wednesday night, the seventh, we dined at the Manse. Nora

and I wore evening dress, just to make it seem a festal occasion, though we had not dressed for dinner before during our three weeks' stay. I send you the dinner menu with the tunes played by the Duke's piper, written on the back. The piper appeared at half-past seven on the lawn in front of the dining-room windows and walked up and down the garden paths playing at intervals all through the meal. I shall never forget the evening. It is not even dusk till 9.45 in the Highlands, though the sun ostensibly goes down at 8.30. The blue loch is just outside the low stone wall that surrounds the Manse garden; the beautiful mountains, all in a kind of rosy haze, encircle the opposite sides of the water; cuckoos were calling and the mavis singing in the wood, and not another sound but the piper!

Sutherland played in this way until dessert and then came into the dining-room and played as he walked around the table. It is at this time that the melancholy pibrochs are played. The pipes, as carried by a Highlander, are most beautiful and graceful things, and the piper himself is a picture in his kilt and bonnet with the tartan streamers floating out from his pipes. The Duke's head piper is the only person out of the family who wears the "silver salmon." This Argyll insignia is so pretty! The Duke's shooting-jacket and some of his others to wear with kilts have, on the shoulder and up and down the front, these clasps, made of two long silver salmon meeting head to head. After Sutherland finished his pibroch, he stood behind my chair, doffed his bonnet, drank his whiskey, and gave a Gaelic toast. He came out of compliment to us, but George gave him a sovereign afterwards. The Inverary visit was a perfect and radiant and unforgettable success for all three of us. It is the most beautiful place on earth and the weather was (mostly) like heaven.

"Farewell to the Highlands, farewell to the North,
The birthplace of valor, the country of worth;
Wherever I wander, wherever I rove,
The hills of the Highlands forever I'll love."

XXXI
EXPERIENCES IN ERIN

I MUST content myself with a bird's-eye view of my many visits to Ireland, choosing only to recall two events of special interest.

Alexandra College in Dublin has each year a Conference Day of the College Guild, to which former graduates come from all parts of the British Empire, and guests of honor from other countries are invited to take part in the programme. In 1900, made notable by the visit to Ireland of Queen Victoria, I was chosen as the delegate from America, and gladly accepted. I wanted to see hundreds of well-educated Irish girls together, and I had met Miss White, the accomplished and scholarly Principal of the College, on a previous visit, and was much interested in Irish educational problems, taking as my subject for the Conference: "The Kindergarten as a Profession for Women."

George put me and my maid off the steamer at Queenstown, and, while he proceeded to Scotland on business, I went to a hydropathic in Blarney to gather strength for Dublin engagements, and to write my address.

April 17th found us established at Boswell's Hotel in Dublin, my good Katie Horan wild with excitement and delight at this propitious return to her native land. "This hotel is full of Royalties and Bishops and Archbishops," she told me. "There's such confusion I can't get a mouthful to eat, but I don't care!"

The Conference was not to be until May 5th, but meantime there was the opening of Alexandra's new buildings by Her Royal Highness the Princess Christian on the afternoon of the 20th, a grand reception of College Societies in the evening, at which I was to read a brief New England story, and on the 21st the grand, the world-famous "Review on the Fifteen Acres," Phœnix Park, by Her Majesty the Queen.

There seemed to be no limit to my good fortune. A friend in London had begged the kind offices of Lady Betty Balfour [1] in my behalf, that I might know each day the particular hour and the gate by which the Queen would leave the Vice-Regal Park for her usual drive. When the telegram arrived from Dublin Castle, Katie and I would mount a side-car and speed to the appointed spot, a great advantage, as any likely point of view was filled by suffocating crowds. We saw Her Majesty many times in this way — oh! so tiny, so weary, yet so royal, so intrepid a Majesty, clad in sober black with just a touch of white or gray, a black lace parasol, and a plain dowdy little bonnet surmounting the head of a real Queen! Katie and I wept together on all these occasions, perhaps from excitement, but I kept thinking to myself: "She is so little, so old and so frail, to make this friendly gesture, after years of absence from this part of her kingdom!" For the same reason, I suppose, I cried at the Review, my companion being "May Laffan," author of "Hogan M.P." and "Flitters, Tatters and the Counsellor," a brilliant Irish novelist always "ag'in' the Government" and Dublin Castle.

Boswell's Hotel was, indeed, full of notables. I had letters to some of them, and at late breakfast or luncheon there might be seen the Right Honorable W. E. H. Lecky, M.P. and historian; Sir John and Lady Constance Leslie; Jane Barlow, the Irish novelist; Lady Gregory, the playwright; Edward Dowden; Alfred Perceval Graves, the Irish poet; the Bishop of Ossory; and, merrier and more

[1] Sister of the Earl of Lytton, wife of Mr. Gerald Balfour, then Chief Secretary for Ireland.

genial than all, an occasional guest in the person of the Very Reverend H. H. Dickinson, Dean of the Chapel Royal, a great Bible scholar and a famous wit. It was he who introduced me when I read at the Alexandra College Reception, chiefly to an audience of titled personages, varied by Chancellors, Vice-Chancellors, Canons, and Deans. Nothing but the feeling of being a plain American under fire ever preserved my life and reason through this ordeal. The only other occasion when I was really frightened was before an audience of a hundred excessively bad boys at a Reform School. They had not begun to reform when I endeavored to amuse them, and they took pains to show me that I was not *persona grata*. My Irish audience was kind and responsive, however, and viewed my reading as a most unique and hitherto unknown form of entertainment.

A few years after the Alexandra College incident, I was asked, because of a friendship begun in Scotland, and carried on in England, to stay a week with Lord and Lady Aberdeen at the Vice-Regal Lodge in Dublin. The house-party was scheduled for the 21st, but there was a specially interesting dinner on the 19th, to which I had been bidden on an enormous card announcing that the State Steward and Chamberlain was directed by Their Excellencies the Lord Lieutenant and the Countess of Aberdeen to ask Mrs. Riggs to dine at the Vice-Regal Lodge on the 19th of May at 8.15 o'clock. (The hour was heavily underscored.)

As my "trousseau" for this week of high and perilous adventure was not entirely ready, I ordered it sent after me and crossed to Dublin via Holyhead on Wednesday the 16th, going to the Royal Hibernian Hotel in Dawson Street, accompanied by my invaluable companion and secretary, Miss Minnie Alford.

The day of the dinner was an example of all that Ireland can accomplish when it wishes to rain. It poured in sheets, not in drops. Questions of huge import arose. Could my newest frock escape rain without the protection of a mackintosh in which to enter and exit from the hired brougham? Would American rubbers be *de rigueur*, or should I take my satin slippers in a bag and wear shoes? In that case how could I get rid of the bag and shoes and rubbers? And so on.

I arrived precisely on time, mounted the steps sheltered by the driver's umbrella, and entered a long wide hallway. One of many footmen approached me and removed my cloak, for there was no dressing-room and no mirror. I thanked Heaven, fasting, that I had left my mackintosh at home and my rubbers in the brougham. With the serenity that marks the caste of Vere de Vere I ascended the crimson-carpeted stairway and was wafted by the hand of one footman after another through many large and beautiful apartments till I heard laughter and conversation, and saw before me eighteen or twenty people in a magnificent drawing-room.

I was announced of course, and, as nobody had ever seen me before, the company concluded that I must be some stray friend of Lady Aberdeen. Lord Anson, one of the young A.D.C.'s, approached and greeted me, showing that I was expected.

At this moment I fell from my high elevation — fell fast, hard, and ingloriously! My eyes searched the various corners of the room, and I murmured timidly, "Lady Aberdeen is not in the room?"

Removing his monocle, Lord Anson remarked instructively (but *not* patronizingly), "Their Excellencies do not come in until all the guests have arrived."

My error could never be retrieved; I was conscious of

LORD ABERDEEN
A photograph inscribed "To the Lady of the Twinkle and the Tear"

that; and approaching the plainest and least regal lady in my vicinity I made a remark of some sort, not a pearl, I fear, nor even a synthetic Roman pearl, but it served. I had chosen wisely. The lady was the delightful and learned tutor of Lady Aberdeen's niece, and informed me at once that she had read all my books to her mother who was blind and that she had looked forward to my visit.

Then Their Excellencies *did* come in, and showed by their affectionate welcome to me that, though I might be ignorant, I was a nice person. I must say in passing that I wish hosts and hostesses in humble society could wait until their guests arrive before coming in to greet them, and how much more do I wish that they could leave the party when they choose, as Viceroys and others of that ilk are permitted by royal etiquette to do.

The week was an altogether dazzling one to me. Every afternoon I accompanied Lady Aberdeen to a hospital, a workhouse, an old lady's home, or a school, for she is an ardent philanthropist. The laying of corner-stones and the opening of bazaars must grow sadly monotonous in time, but it was all new to me, and I loved going "in state" with fine equipages and outriders, holding the inevitable bouquet.

Her Excellency never liked a closed carriage on account of disappointing the people, so that I offered four expensive hats on the sacrificial altar, for it generally rained on these triumphal pilgrimages.

As to the dinners, and the guests, words fail me! Naturally every statesman, great man of affairs, world-traveler, government official of high degree, any personage of note from Canada, Australia, New Zealand, South Africa, India, who came to England, crossed to Ireland to discuss this or that project or topic with the Lord Lieutenant. The procession of learned, interesting, and notable men in every walk of life seemed endless. We sat down to dinner twenty to twenty-four people each night, Lord Aberdeen (the soul of courtesy and kindness) keeping me at his left hand and choosing with great consideration my famous neighbors, telling me their achievements beforehand, thus rendering it easy for me to make acquaintance with them. (I remember at a large dinner, given me once in London by Lord and Lady Aberdeen, he sent me by his secretary a brief written biography of every guest with a diagram of the table and arrangement of the seats. How easy to be at ease under such circumstances!) I ceased at length to feel any terror of Dukes or Duchesses, Earls or Countesses, Masters of Horse, Masters of Buckhounds, Chancellors, Lord Advocates, Q.C.'s or K.C.'s or K.C.B.'s; — they all seemed an integral part of the life I was so miraculously living in their company. Not that I was for a moment unmindful of my opportunity for gathering valuable information of every sort, and of wending my way unobtrusively along roads I had never thought to travel. On the contrary, I was eager to get the different points of view and enlarge my own horizon, and continually I was asking myself: "How did I happen to be here?" I never hungered and thirsted for these opportunities, never plotted nor planned, nor harbored feverish ambitions. The experiences simply came my way and I accepted them gratefully, but, indeed, the chronicles of these later years and the varied records on the milestones of the journey must seem strange to the faithful reader of my first chapters, where the diary of the "truly" little girl depicts her life in a Maine village, where, in the opinion of the worldly-wise, nothing ever happened!

The books did it, as I have said before! The children in them opened certain hearts to me, while "The Cathedral Courtship," "The Goose Girl," and other international stories, with their fresh point of view concerning things immemorially old and stable, coupled with their light-hearted manner and the deep respect that underlay the nonsense, beguiled others and disarmed criticism. One can imagine that people would listen to the tone of a golden trumpet, but why they should pay any attention to the faint music breathed through a reed I can hardly understand.

I never overrated my work myself, and I never shall! I have a sense of literary values, and a camel sees himself truly when he goes under a mountain. I am much in the company of mountains and they do not encourage vanity. Nevertheless, my books have brought me such joy and such richness of compensation that I can only hope that some of it has overflowed the cup and given pleasure elsewhere, for I should always like to be a "sharing" sort of a person if I might, believing with Lowell that the gift without the giver is bare.

XXXII
BOOKS AND THEIR BACKGROUNDS

Books appear on almost every wall in every corner of every house in which we live, but there is one particular bookcase which contains a practically complete file of my own work, and to glance at it casually would seem to give the impression that from my earliest days I had been a drudge, a slave to the pen and inkwell, which is very far from the truth.

On the top shelf stands the uniform ("Quillcote") edition of my books, ten volumes, but many more than ten stories, because the too-brief ones have been bound together, sometimes three under one cover. My old-time friend, Mrs. Frances Hodgson Burnett, wrote, as a labor of love and without my knowledge, a most beautiful tribute to this edition in the way of Introduction.

Mr. John Galsworthy says in a preface to one of the volumes of his latest edition: "*I am convinced that he is in luck to whom the unseen hander-out of bottles offers the pint!*" This unseen benefactor (or enemy, as the case may be) has gone further in my case than Mr. Galsworthy, I think, would have advised — he has sometimes handed me out "splits" — if that word is known elsewhere than in America.

My habit of work has been, generally speaking, to write what was uppermost in my mind and to stop when I had nothing more to say about it. I have done many wrong things in my life, but I have never done a long thing! This may have been discretion, but it is quite likely that it was lack of matter! At all events, very few quart-bottles have ever been handed out to me; but I am hoping that the "unseen hander-out" of Mr. Galsworthy's amusing theory has kept one empty champagne "magnum" left over from pre-Volstead days for this autobiography, since it is easier to remember than to create. Perhaps, even then, the book may not turn out to be a magnum opus! (Forgive the pun, it is not one of my usual sins, and will be the only example between these covers, but, led on by Mr. Galsworthy's figure of speech, Walter Pater himself would have yielded to temptation!)

Proudly erect beside the ten volumes of the Quillcote uniform edition stand the fifteen books edited or written in collaboration with my sister Nora ("The Children's Crimson Classics"); three books on Kindergarten Theory and Practice ("The Republic of Childhood"); "Children's Rights," "The Story Hour," and two beautifully illustrated editions of the "Arabian Nights" and "Scottish Chiefs," with slightly revised or abbreviated texts and new Introductions.

As I gaze upon these various milestones set along the road of a literary life, I wonder which of them all is dearest to me. The inquiry is, happily, almost out of fashion among readers, although it sometimes occurs in unsophisticated circles of society, where an author is still considered a person of unique powers. It was always a foolish question, and an embarrassing one to answer. No one would ever think of asking a mother which one of her children she regarded as most interesting, yet, if she felt any difference and chose to reveal the secret reason of preference, she would seem to be less directly responsible for the beauty, virtues, or faults of her offspring than the author is for the children of her brain.

The author clearly has no one but himself to blame if he has written a poor book — that is, if he has spared no pains and done his conscientious best. As to his favorite, what shall he say if by chance he is confronted with the question?

There is the First Book, never to be forgotten, whether it was the flat failure that, through discouragement, led to greater concentration and effort, or the signal success that laid the foundations of the future.

Then there is the Last Book, very tenderly cherished for the moment, like an unexpected baby arriving after a considerable interval of time.

There is the Book that had the best circulation, a positively shameless and unwieldy popularity; finding itself among the "best-sellers," where the author didn't particularly wish it to be, because of the critics who invariably remark that the Walter Paters, the George Merediths, the Samuel Butlers, and the Matthew Arnolds have to content themselves with a small but select company of readers, while the best-sellers cater to an ignorant, ravening mob.

Then last of all there is the Book for which the author has an indefensible affection. Only eight or ten thousand people ever agree with him and a hundred thousand set their capricious affections elsewhere; but, if you wish to win the undying gratitude of a writer, praise that particular volume!

I have accomplished much less literary than active practical work of various kinds, yet, in temperament, desire, and passionate absorption in the task while it lasts, I feel myself, first of all, an author. From a truly literary point of view a rather negligible one (even wide circulation tells only a half truth), but still an author dyed in the wool. I see, hear, think, like an author. As to quantity of production, my life, circumstances, responsibilities, indifferent health, and several other factors too numerous to mention, have led me to write few books and brief ones. I never seem able to free myself from external activities, and therefore I lack concentration; but I am still an author, diverted for the time being from her true task, this view of things being a common and most agreeable form of vanity. If I haven't anything to write, I am just as anxious to "take my pen in hand" as though I had a message to deliver, a cause to plead, or a problem to unfold. Nothing but writing rests me; only then do I seem completely myself! And then the compensations! They exist, to be sure, in all creative work, but they are so instantaneous, so rich, so personal, so affectionate, so delicious in authorship!

There is another curious thing about an author's books, and that is connected with the places in which he writes them; the mysterious effect they have upon his work; the lively memories they evoke, so that, whenever he opens a certain volume, the scene of its creation, like a picture in a dream, makes a background for the story absolutely inseparable from it.

I have slept or tarried or lived in hundreds of rooms in years of travel abroad and at home, and I cannot recall the features of a single one save those in which I have worked. On the other hand, there is no room in which I have done any writing which ever fades from my memory. It is not only the room itself, but the carpet and every article of furniture, together with the views from the windows, that are stamped upon my brain. I think I can draw every table or desk at which I have ever written a chapter or a book, put it in the exact position it occupied when I was working, and see myself, sometimes in the very dress I wore at the time, bending over the paper.

There is no confusion in my mind as to where any particular book grew into being, although on all other points I have the most treacherous of memories. One might well

suppose that Thomas Carlyle would remember the place
where he wrote an epoch-making work like "The French
Revolution"; but the uncanny fact remains that wherever
the act of creation takes place that spot seems to be stamped
forever on the brain of an author, even if the product is a
very modest one.

I remember a large bedroom in San Francisco — it
overlooked the Golden Gate and the low green slopes of the
Marin shore — where I wrote my first book, "The Birds'
Christmas Carol." It was not to be published, but merely
printed, put between paper covers, and sold for the benefit
of the Silver Street Free Kindergartens where my life-work
lay at the moment. The book was a good friend to me. It
earned the wherewithal to take a group of children out of
the dangers of the squalid streets and transport them
into a place of safety and gladness. Then it took me by
the hand and led me into the crowded world where the
public lives. It brought me friends in strange places, it won
for me the love of mothers and children, that ever blessed
little book of less than a hundred pages.

"The Story of Patsy" was written in that same bedroom
and for the same purpose, though later the two volumes
were to prepare my entrance into the real world of publishers and reviewers, copyrights, and translations.

"Marm Lisa" had the same California background, and
so had "Polly Oliver's Problem," but both of these were
written in New England. How well I recall the farmhouse
in a little Maine village, unpoetically named "Spruce
Swamp," where I wrote "Polly Oliver." The white, green-
blinded cottage lay at the end of a grass-grown lane nearly
an eighth of a mile from the main road, and no lovelier
solitude for work ever existed. The dear people who owned
the house and took me in gave up to me the parlor. Closing my eyes I can still see the gray-painted floor with

flecks of white on it, the drawn-in rugs, the whatnot in the corner, the cedar trees outside, and the enormous bed of lilies-of-the-valley underneath the window. The black haircloth sofa was cool and comfortable enough for a rest when the story "gave out," or when I had to wait for inspiration to begin again.

The first half of "Timothy's Quest" was written at Quillcote (Hollis, Maine), years before it became my property. I left the manuscript behind me in America and went abroad for the first time, not intending to write during a year of travel on the Continent; but a pressing letter from my publishers determined me to take up my story in time for publication that year.

Eventually, after having discarded some of the fairest spots in England, I settled down at Stratford-upon-Avon, in one of the smaller hotels. I did not beguile myself with the belief that the Muse of Shakespeare might still be haunting the river-banks of the lovely country that surrounded Anne Hathaway's cottage, but the Falcon Inn pleased me and I entered my name in the visitor's book. The landlady gave me the public sitting-room for my private use; I bade an affectionate farewell to my friends at the railway station, came back to my writing-table, and took up my pen, only to find that I had forgotten the names of some of my characters and what they had said and done in the eight or nine chapters left with my publishers in America.

I do not know whether people nowadays read Lucretia Hale's book, "The Peterkin Papers," and the delicious chapter in which Solomon John determines to be an author. A certain ingenious lady from Philadelphia is the heroine of the tale, helping the Peterkin family all through their whimsical difficulties, even suggesting to Elizabeth Eliza, who is of a musical turn, that if the sitting-room is

too small for the piano she may easily put her chair outside on the piazza and practice through the window. The
Peterkins build a large and commodious house, furnish it
from turret to foundation stone, and arrange a library for
Solomon John that is calculated to inspire any person of
literary tendencies. The walls are lined with books, the
solid mahogany table has everything that the most indus-
trious scribe could desire, and Solomon John retires into
its solitude and takes his pen solemnly in hand. In a few
moments he opens the door of the apartment and seeks
Elizabeth Eliza in the garden.

"We have taken the trouble for nothing, Elizabeth
Eliza," he says despairingly, yet with a note of amazement
at the fact. "I cannot be an author after all, for I have
nothing to say"; and Solomon John Peterkin vanishes at
once from a list of the world's "best-sellers."

As I seated myself at the window of the Falcon Inn in
Stratford, and looked at the sweetly flowing Avon, I could
only remember Solomon John Peterkin, and, going to the
village post-office, I cabled to my publishers asking them
to send the first chapters of "Timothy's Quest." Pending
their arrival, I wrote another story, and then happily
finished the book so inauspiciously interfered with by
circumstances. The moment I re-read the manuscript,
Stratford and the Muse of Shakespeare disappeared; my
State o' Maine dialect came back to me and I belonged
entirely to the land of my fathers. For a month I forgot
that I was in an English village; the Avon became the
Saco! I discerned only dimly the people and the things
that surrounded me, for I was living in the blissful dream
that we call "writing a book"!

My three volumes, "Penelope's Experiences," in England, Scotland, and Ireland, have often been considered as
filled with true incidents, whereas they are fiction almost

to a page. I chose the three heroines advisedly — Penelope, the artist; Francesca, a charming and rather capricious society girl from the West; and Salemina, a delightful middle-aged spinster from Massachusetts — as giving me an opportunity to write three different love stories, each having its own background.

The English Penelope was written partly at Bramall Hall, Cheshire, and finished at North Malvern, Worcestershire, where I spent six weeks at what is generally known in England as a "village pub." "Mrs. Bobby's cottage," the picturesque and ideal retreat where Penelope is supposed to have written her Experiences, was farther along the village street. Inasmuch as the owner thereof took no boarders or lodgers, I could not settle myself on her most enchanting premises, but had to live at the wayside inn and try to make myself believe that I was dwelling somewhere else.

If I were an artist I could paint the shabby but comfortable English sitting-room, with the matchless views of the Worcestershire Hills from its windows, its open fire, its pictures of Queen Victoria, Prince Albert, the Prince of Wales, and Gladstone adorning its walls.

I remember that on a certain day there was a great deal of agitation and excitement on the part of the landlady and Julius the waiter who served my meals. It was breathed to me that this commotion simply meant that the Weavers' Union of Worcester were going to have "an 'igh tea" on Saturday afternoon; so large an affair that all the downstairs rooms and the garden would be required to entertain the company.

On the eventful Saturday there ensued such a driving downpour of rain as only England can furnish when a festive occasion is in progress. At noon the tables from the garden were taken under cover, while Julius and the landlady sat down to await their fate. At three, four covered barges drew up at the front door, and from my window I watched the company disembark: cold, wet, bedraggled, but strangely hilarious. More pathetic than any other figure among the would-be merry-makers was a woman with a six-months-old baby, who apparently had to bring her child to the party or else stay at home herself.

A quarter of an hour later, when I sat at my desk trying to pay some attention to my work, there was a knock at my door and in walked the woman with the baby, holding it carelessly, upside down, as if all responsibilities of maternity had vanished in the intoxication of anticipated joy. She explained that she did not realize that the sitting-room was private, but, seating herself on my sofa, she asked me if I would mind looking after the baby for "just 'alf an hour, miss, while the dance is going on."

When she further confided to me that she had been married two years and had never had a pleasure excursion of any kind or danced a step, although the "light fantastic" had been her chief joy, I could not possibly deny her plea, and rather timidly assumed the charge of the unknown baby. The mother said, of course, that the infant never did anything but sleep and crow, and that her own participation in the dance would be a brief one; but, as a matter of fact, she must have been the belle of the ball, because two hours passed and she never returned to inquire after the health of her offspring.

Meantime, after a brief interval of comparative quiet interrupted only by wrigglings, contortions, and mysterious signs of unfulfilled desires, the baby began first to whimper and then to cry lustily. I rang the bell repeatedly, but Julius was far too busy to answer, and I faced the prospect of being an unintentional and unwilling mother to a strange child for the rest of my existence. I showed

the baby all my jewelry, for which she evinced a rude
contempt; I gave her small pieces of sugar, which she
ejected immediately. She viewed with derision graphic
sketches which I drew upon paper. I paced the floor with
her, showing her every object of interest that the apartment contained, and could stop her screaming only by
bobbing her laboriously up and down before the picture
of Mr. Gladstone. Apparently her political convictions lay
in the direction of the Liberal Party, and the countenance
of her leader proved a quieting influence.

At five o'clock I succeeded in getting a word with Julius,
but, after a prolonged absence with the weavers, he returned with the news that no lady in the company owned
up to the possession of this or any other baby.

"Try again, Julius!" I said. "Just stand in the middle
of the floor and say that a lady upstairs is caring for a
baby that doesn't belong to her; a heavy Liberal baby
weighing about forty pounds. Say that the lady is about
to become a Conservative and will throw the baby out of
the window if not called for in twenty minutes."

Finally there was a great scraping of chairs, and then
there floated up to my room the sounds of the "Doxology,"
the most curious thing, it seems to me, to insert as a wedge
between a dance and 'igh tea.

Then at last the irresponsible mother appeared and
breathlessly hoped that she had not been too long absent,
but that she had been enjoying herself so much that she
entirely forgot her maternal duties. "I'm sure baby's
been company for you this dreary afternoon, miss," she
ventured, turning the weeping infant upside down, wrong
side out, and giving it a bottle — which succeeded even
better than the picture of Gladstone — and I was too
weary to contradict her; but I never open a certain chapter
in "Penelope's English Experiences" without seeing that

bedraggled tea-party of the Worcester weavers, and the weaver's baby that was the object of my care during the afternoon.

In these backward-looking thoughts I have mentioned six characters: Carol Bird, Patsy, Marm Lisa, Polly Oliver, Timothy, and the Penelope whose "Experiences" in England, Scotland, and Ireland were to furnish me with work so delightful that during several years it seemed play.

Strangely enough, no unkindly criticism ever came from the countries described. Indeed, the London "Spectator" was kind enough to say that the Penelope books had made Mrs. Wiggin one of the most successful of ambassadors between America and Great Britain.

I have been asked daily, if not hourly, for more than a quarter of a century — asked by word of mouth and by letter — if these characters are real and the various experiences are true.

Even my dear old friend, Mr. Howells, assured me that I might tell him forever that I was not Penelope and he could hardly believe it; but he would not say the same of some of my other heroines, who, to him, as a realist, would doubtless seem a trifle "too bright and good for human nature's daily food."

The fact is, it is utterly impossible for me to dissect and pin to the wall any man, woman, or child whom I have ever known. It requires a different kind of art from that which is native to me. Instead of being simpler and easier for me to describe a personage I have seen, or with whom I have come in contact, it is more difficult than to imagine a character from the ground up. If Mr. Howells thought Penelope "real," it is because I might conceivably have comported myself as she did in similar circumstances. The fact is that the experiences in my book are as purely fictitious as the characters. If either of them seem "true" to my readers, it is because they are so simple and so probable.

Of course, had I not been a kindergartner in my youth there never could have been a Patsy or a Marm Lisa; however, these are but composite photographs of the hundreds of physically and mentally pitiful children under my care. As for "incidents" and "experiences," they may be patterned on my own, but they never are my own and never will be.

One thing only I strive to make as true and as real as possible, and that is the background, whatever it may be. As for the speech of my fictitious characters, I never create a character whose mental processes and language I do not feel that I know as well as if they were my own.

The rooms and the houses in Scotland and Ireland where the imaginary Penelope wrote the various chapters of her imaginary "Experiences" are many in number and extraordinarily different in character.

There are but two ways to write books of travel, or dissertations upon strange countries. One is to delve deep into social, political, and racial conditions and find something new and illuminating to give the world. This is the method of the scholar and presumes a talent for national psychology. My sense of humor saved me from any vast ambitions. If anything unique or valuable was to be said about Great Britain — already somewhat familiar to the gentle reader — obviously I was not the person to say it. On the other hand, undeterred by friends who agreed with me that I could add nothing to the sum of human intelligence, and who advised me further not to till old ground lest I be dull and trivial, my pen refused to be quiet, but continually leaped from my desk and begged me to cast a happy, careless, fresh eye on the enchanting scenes amid which I was living.

If a man loves a woman he does not stop to consider how much better her relations and friends know her, nor what has already been said about her; he is never satisfied unless he can pay his own personal tribute. That was precisely my case. Nobody could delight in England, Scotland, and Ireland more than I, and to hold my tongue while I was being consumed by this inner fire of affection and interest was quite impossible. Had I been a better workman the result would have been more worth while, for no one ever had wider or more unique opportunities.

The "Experiences" were written before I had grown from first impressions into the deeper knowledge which is not so apt to spend itself in words; where the scenes have grown unspeakably dear and familiar and the shock of the unexpected has become less provocative. Scotland grew to be home to me, and so did Ireland in its turn, but it was while they were still strange and new to Penelope's eyes that she set down her bird's-eye views and impressions.

Once I selected the island of Iona as a fitting place to set down the "Scottish Experiences." I had seen pictures of Columba's ancient cathedral; but, after taking an expensive but beautiful sea trip to the lonely island, I found but one person who could accommodate an author with meals and lodgings, the price asked being equivalent to twenty dollars a week! It transpired on inquiry that William Black had written "Macleod of Dare" on the island and raised the price of board to authors for all time.

It is extraordinary how one's own stories vanish completely from the memory in course of time, as if one had never had any part in them. During an attack of illness which seizes me at intervals — and which is never wholly unendurable, because it gives me a chance to re-read at least six volumes of Jane Austen — I took up "Penelope's Experiences" and had a most enjoyable day with them!

Not only did I add to my stock of information, for the volumes were full of facts entirely new to me — history, romance, balladry, all delightfully blended with stories — but I smiled continuously at the pleasant humor of the text! Many times during the day I said to myself: "What delightful books!" I remember Mrs. Frances Hodgson Burnett telling me that her sister always knew when she was reading one of her own novels after a long interval, because she never looked so interested under any other circumstances!

This naïve conceit may seem repellent to the gentle reader, but I can only say that apparently it can exist side by side with the most depressing humility — a doubt of one's own powers so extravagant that the author wishes for the moment to think of her works as tied about her worthless neck and drowned with her in the most convenient ocean.

A woman who could not have gleaned something of value from the intimate and varied associations that were my good fortune in Ireland must have been dull, indeed. They ran through several years, though the choicest and most unforgettable were the weeks passed in an inexpensive Angler's Boarding Establishment near Killarney, where most of the Irish Penelope was written.

Few writers, at least in time of peace, can have passed through fiercer fires than these weeks furnished, when I forsook the beaten path of American travelers and good hotels and fled, not without warning from "high society," to places unvisited by the gentry, determined to see a side of Irish life not possible under ordinary circumstances.

There is no need of dwelling on details; it is enough to say that I did see life, and leave it at that! Half my time was spent in sweeping, dusting, house-cleaning, carpentering, plumbing, repairing, bedmaking, and dishwashing, although there were no discounts for service in the weekly bill! The remaining hours were of inestimable value to me, for I felt Irish to the bone while I was writing that book! Not Irish like the "classes," but Irish like the "masses"; not poetic, historic, fashionable, administrative, literary Irish, but the fascinating, "deluthering," hospitable, inconsistent, warm-hearted, head-in-the-clouds daughter of Erin who can discern fairies more clearly than dirt. Faith, now, come to think of it, I was not Irish at all, at all; I was just plain Biddy while I was writing certain chapters of "Penelope's Experiences" in the Green Isle.

My influence on this establishment for the entertainment of anglers was, to my own mind, highly beneficial. I had my own meals served privately, but the anglers had theirs, and more punctually than was the rule of the descendant of the Irish Kings who was disguised as the landlady. This was merely because a lady from New England was modestly acting for the good of the human race in general. One of the maids had assured the Boots under my window one day that Number 5 must sleep with one clock under her pillow for wakin' in the mornin', and another in her stomach to tell her when it was the meal hour, for nothin' else could explain the way the crathur kept account of the time — her that had no need to dip a pen in the inkwell, unless she liked. "It's my belief," she added, "that the woman has a taste for work that is like a man's for strong drink! She cannot abide doing nothing herself, and she'd like to keep the rest of us as busy as she is." She might have added "Bad cess to her," but as I always mingled my admonitions with generous fees, she had no valid reason for disliking me personally.

This ever-so-slight tendency to interfere with the established order of things — which is, I confess, one of my striking characteristics, and which I endeavor to keep in

its proper place, as a virtue, knowing that at any moment
it may become a vice — led me into writing "The Diary of
a Goose Girl." My sister and I both had books to write —
that is, they were really finished, but, as Alexandre Dumas
said of a certain novel, they had only to be "written down."
We were in England and we took daily trips from London
to find the right spot for work. One was full of tourists,
another too near colonies of American friends, one was too
damp, another too windy, one too expensive, another too
cheap.

We saw a great deal of the English countryside on these
various drives to secure apartments. Alighting at a station,
we always secured a competent-looking horse, and an intelligent driver to whom we confided our desires. He in
turn told us the price per hour, and it was extraordinary
the number of miles we could cover without coming across
the sign "Apartments to Let." Our excursions by a certain day in June had involved us in expenditures far beyond any royalties that might chance to accrue from our
literary labors, and it was within an hour of the time of
going back to London when we came suddenly and accidentally on a gate bearing the magic and long-wished-for
placard. We ordered the driver to stop. No sign of human
life appeared, but there was a soft, uninterrupted chorus
of clucks, peeps, crows, gobbles, honks, and hisses which
led us to peer curiously over the gate.

"It won't do, miss; it's a poultry farm," remarked the
driver.

"It looks rather interesting," I ventured.

"It sounds rather noisy, miss, and, if you'll excuse me,
it smells rather smelly."

"That's because the chicken coops are so near the gate;
they ought to have been set behind the house, with all that
beautiful land going to waste, and they're not well kept

either. Oh, look! Way over there under the oak tree in the corner there are dozens and dozens of rabbits — big brown ones!"

"Belgian hares, miss. I don't think you'll fancy them — not that near — shall I drive on, miss?"

The more the driver discouraged us, the more we determined to interview the landlady. She and her husband had just bought the place and their desire for lodgers was very evident. They showed us two large bedrooms, rather bare but clean, and an inoffensive little dining-room the charm of which was somewhat marred by a profusion of family photographs, with many geological and piscatorial souvenirs. I don't know why people who rent apartments are always so faithful to their relations, when they are uniformly so plain, nor why their affections run to shells!

"I don't think you'll find the poultry disagreeable, ladies," said the would-be landlady. "I don't know much about the business, but my daughter Ella has had two months' apprenticeship and we shall rely on her not to allow our boarders to be disturbed. The cocks are a little trying in the morning, but, if you are late risers, Ella can have a few of the loudest crowers killed for roasting and shut the rest in a dark chicken house a little distance in the rear."

This care for our prospective comfort won our hearts, and, promising to come back the next day, we drove to the station, our charioteer being wholly out of sympathy with the undertaking.

The book I intended to write never was touched, for my sister and I applied ourselves heart and soul to the rehabilitation of the poultry farm on scientific principles discovered by us as we went along. We didn't care at all for Ella's methods, which were dull and commonplace, never evoking any interest or surprise in the ducks or geese, or arresting the attention of the Belgian hares for a moment. Ella's father believed in us from the start. "American citizens, even if only females," he remarked, "have a kind of instink for success."

So "The Diary of a Goose Girl" was written! Of course, I invented a different village, landlady, husband, and daughter to suit my literary needs; also a romantic hero. ine with a little story to carry the book along; but the cocks, hens, chickens, and turkeys, the ducks and geese and rabbits and hares, were real! We put the poultry to bed at night and fed them in the morning; we changed the places of all the coops and runs; in every department we introduced educational methods that were at least twenty years ahead of the times. We were revolutionary and audacious, but in some way or other we evaded disaster. We practiced both medicine and surgery without diplomas, but none of our patients died under our hands.

XXXIII

COLLABORATIONS: TRANSLATIONS

THERE have been brief seasons of collaboration in my literary life. The shining example of those twin stars of the English stage — Beaumont and Fletcher — comrades and successors of Shakespeare, may have inspired others in their time. Two hundred years later, Sir Walter Besant and James Rice were fertile and successful co-workers in the realm of fiction, and before and after these there have been numbers of men and women who, for one reason or another, were willing to sacrifice a certain amount of individuality for the pleasure and profit of a companion-mind, dissimilar, yet stimulating and helpful. In our own day there are perhaps no striking instances of collaboration in fiction, but playwrights and builders of musical comedy seem to prefer working as twins, triplets, or even in flocks and herds.

It was inevitable that my author-sister and I, interested in the same subjects and having similar tastes, should occasionally work together, although our attempts have been only in educational fields and in the making of anthologies. The method was simple. The younger sister read, perhaps, uncounted tomes of fairy tales, culled from the literatures of all languages, and decided on the choicest three hundred for the purpose of selecting the best one hundred and fifty. These were the subjects of long discussions and frequently of spirited argument, until we agreed on one hundred, the situation becoming so acute that now and then we were obliged to "trade off" our individual favorites, the elder or the younger partner saying with heat: "I will never give up this one, if you persist in choosing that!"

These volumes of educational essays, and these books of verse, fairy tales, fables, and legends, compiled for young people with such solicitous care, were scarcely looked upon as serious collaboration. The task was something like marriage, that "halveth trouble and joy doth double"; but it doubtless prepared me for working with others.[1]

Seldom have I had more delightful experiences than collaborating some years ago with three talented Scots-women: Mary and Jane Findlater and Charlotte Stuart — the latter having written several historical novels under the pen-name of "Allan Macaulay."

We were together in Torquay, longing for a holiday away from that lovely but somewhat woman-ridden town, with its long succession of manless afternoon teas. Much correspondence brought us no offer of a cottage on Dart-moor, romantically attractive to us as readers of Black-more, Hardy, and Eden Phillpotts, but we finally found some one who would take us in as lodgers and provide our meals, so we departed forthwith in the gayest spirits.

Long before this, at Lochearnhead in the Highlands, we had talked vaguely of writing something together, purely for amusement, but the moment might never have arrived had it not been for a long season of untoward weather.

We halted at the little station of Stoke Babbage at three o'clock on the fine afternoon of a spring day. Life was stirring everywhere. The sallows were pale gold, the amber buds of the oaks had cast their sheaths, and we could see, far in the distance, an impetuous little moorland river dancing and glimmering in the sunshine. Beyond, rose hills and mountains as in a pageant, their summits

[1] *The Children's Crimson Classics.* 8 volumes. Doubleday, Page & Co.

crowned in misty clouds. We took a station fly, and at the top of a gentle slope discovered in the near distance a scattered village; a quiet one, when we reached it, where only the crowing of a cock, the drone of a harmonium, or the voice of a child disturbed the silence. Then came a slope of rocky hillside leading up to Gray Tor, a mountain of granite, then a comfortable-looking inn that we passed with prophetic reluctance, and in a few minutes we drew up at Mrs. Buncombe's cottage.

At four we had tea that neither cheered nor inebriated, followed three hours later by a meal described by Mrs. Buncombe as supper. In the meantime we had sampled the beds, finding them unsuited to sleeping, but otherwise beyond cavil. Each of us unpacked her small bag and hung her wrapper and fresh blouse on her bedroom door, with cynical remarks about the apparent impossibility of finding any sort of simple life in which there was a trace of comfort.

"The simple life," I remarked, "can be lived only in a perfect climate where one can eat out of doors, plucking food from trees and bushes in the immediate vicinity. To make it ideal, all traces of civilization should, of course, be banished, but not before open plumbing has been put in, with set baths and hot and cold water."

After supper we gathered hungrily around a small grate fire and talked hopefully of next day, the rigors of the approaching night being studiously avoided in the conversation. The dining-table, built to accommodate a large family of lodgers, was so enormous that our chairs could barely be squeezed between its commanding bulk and the fire, but we were merry, and young, too, and we determined to make the best of it, drowning by the acclamation of three voices the pusillanimous suggestion of the fourth that we should desert our cottage for the inn. I was not

MARY AND JANE FINDLATER

unhappy, for the Edinburgh poet had sent me some verses at which the others were a little envious.

> In Herrick's Devon to delay,
> In Herrick's month of "smiling May,"
> Is prudent and is pleasant. — Nay,
>
> I too would very gladly be
> In Devon with Penelope
> Would Heaven bestow this boon on me!
>
> But since it will not, let her read
> These rugged lines, in which I plead
> That she will not neglect the need
>
> We feel in Scotland of a chance
> To gaze upon her countenance,
> And from her lips and from her glance
>
> To learn that, quit of languor, she
> Is once again our fresh, our free,
> Our ever young Penelope!
>
> H. J.

Next day dawned cold, gray, misty, drizzly, with a cutting east wind. Before we could cross the threshold, it began to rain. Showers we did not mind, with glints of sun between, but the rains on Dartmoor are anything but gentle. Those that greeted us were fierce, steady, and practically continuous for three days. We had few books, and neither sewing, nor cards for solitaire; so at tea-time of the second day despair had practically overshadowed the party, and we felt that we had perhaps undervalued the manless festivities of Torquay.

Suddenly an idea darted into my mind. I paced the narrow strip of floor between the table and the door, formulating my plans. Then I explained: "We will now collaborate on a story, instantly and as long as may be necessary! It will be only for fun; just a sort of life-saving experiment. Take your pencils and pads; don't argue or rebel; sit up to the table and I'll show you the game. Let us pretend that we are four imaginary persons on Dartmoor, staying, not here (Heaven forbid!), but at that nice inn we should never have passed coming from the station. Each of us must choose a character likely to be useful in a plot, and write in the first person the chapters belonging to her, carrying on the story, of course, that has been outlined by her predecessor. I will be an American girl from the South traveling in England with my widowed mother. If none of you want to be the widowed mother, you can choose something different, and the widowed mother can stay upstairs in her bedroom at the inn and appear only by indirection. My name is — let me see — Virginia Pomeroy. I am the heroine; aged twenty-two and more than common handsome. I am sorry to be greedy, but if I have to begin the book I ought to have some advantage. Now think for five minutes by the Buncombe clock and then tell me whom you have decided to be."

At the appointed time "Allan Macaulay" spoke first.

"Before any one else chooses," she said, "I will be the lover, Sir Archibald Maxwell Mackenzie, of Kindarroch, N.B."

"Oh!" I cried. "I am his for the asking, his name is so delightful!"

"Better wait!" she replied. "I have a perfectly detestable, but good-looking and distinguished, third cousin who will do for the hero without change. I shan't have to invent; I shall only present him photographically."

"Our book will at least be read by your own family!" I said. "Next!"

"I will be Mrs. MacGill," said Mary Findlater. "I am an elderly invalid from Aberdeen, recovering from influenza at the Gray Tor Inn." (And here we all shouted, for it was our affectionate belief that no one could draw a stuffy, snuffy, disagreeable, selfish old woman better than the person who had volunteered to do it.)

"There seems to be little left for me," said Jane Findlater. "I had thought of a second British lover for the American girl, but, after hearing about Mrs. MacGill from Aberdeen, I prefer to be Cecilia Evesham, her downtrodden companion. When I see how the hero turns out, 'Cecilia' may fall in love with him, too, and prove, in a plaintive English middle-class way, a rival of 'Virginia,' who, of course, will be rich as well as beautiful."

The rain continued to fall incessantly, and during two days and evenings we played our little literary game, handing our chapters to one another as fast as we finished them and compelling our successors to take up the thread where we dropped it, not only developing her chosen character, but carrying on the story.

So "The Affair at the Inn" was finished, and, although light as a cream-puff and properly unpretentious, it pleased a greater number of readers than "Robinetta," our second and last attempt at four-sided collaboration.

"Robinetta" was a story of life in a certain little Devonshire village, famous for its plum trees and wonderful jam. It was of much better workmanship and substance, and written this time in the third person, with such good "dovetailing," we thought, that no reader could discover where one writer left off and the next began. I never discovered that anybody cared especially to solve the riddle! Very great personages would have to collaborate on a striking piece of work to make the public eager to disentangle it, crediting each with his particular virtue and discrediting each with his special share of failure.

Collaboration now having been discussed, my memory travels from Mrs. Buncombe's stuffy sitting-room and the wonderful Devonshire moorland, to New England, where I suddenly felt like writing a tale of life among the Shakers. As a child I had been taken to attend the religious services and visit the brethren and sisters in Alfred, Maine; and I had seldom let a year go by without renewing my acquaintance with those still living in the settlement. The number has sadly dwindled now, masculine converts being especially few and far between. What wonder when "open confession," "celibacy," and "holding of goods in common" are the foundation-stones of the Shaker creed as laid down by Mother Ann Lee, founder and patron saint of the sect?

When the book was nearly finished, I wrote to Elder Green and Sister Lucinda, outlining my story, and asking if I might come over and stay a few days in the Women's Community House.

A glad welcome came by return post, and, with my manuscript on the seat beside me, I drove along the sixteen miles of country road between "Quillcote" and the Shaker Village.

The background of "Susanna and Sue" stands out more vividly than that of most of my books, because it is a thing apart, so unique, so hidden away, and of such heavenly tranquillity. Busy, indeed, and thrifty are the Shaker brethren in the fields, with their tilling or sowing or harvesting or gathering the hay into the great barns. No less busy are the sisters at their household tasks, their bottling and preserving and pickling, their wonderful basket-weaving and fancy-work, their gathering and putting-up of garden seeds for the market, and other labors well known throughout New England as good, honest, sound, and profitable.

I ate my plain meals in a little dining-room that shone with cleanliness; then hurried back to my equally spotless bedroom, with its white floor, its iron bedstead, its lavender-scented cotton sheets, its straight-backed, rush-bottomed chairs, and pine tables. It was a beautiful place in which to write, and a more beautiful place in which to be still, and think, surrounded as one was by such unworldly examples of cheerful self-denial, temperance, and devotion to an ideal that required all these qualities in a true Believer. After supper I used to play the cabinet organ and sing Shaker hymns with Elder Green and some of the sisters. I really forgot my own personality and always imagined myself as "Susanna" during my entire visit. On two mornings I read to the children of the Community, many of them orphans, or motherless; some of them waifs and strays cared for and taught with the ardent hope that they might upbuild the Shaker faith. I had told the sisters and Elder Green the plan of my story, but it was with some embarrassment that I read it aloud for their criticism, although I had such respect for the unassuming virtues of their lives that I knew I had treated their creed with deference and understanding. As for the two young lovers in my book, who tried hard to believe in celibacy, but failed, and ran away from the Settlement to be married and live what the Shakers call "life on the plane of Adam" — that tragedy they knew, as well as I, had been of not infrequent occurrence in the otherwise tranquil procession of the years.

The Shakers have an affection for "Susanna and Sue," their "own book," as they call it — written as it was by a dear, though religiously misguided friend, and a copy of it lies on the cabinet organ in the sitting-room, just under a photograph of the author.

On the shelf in my study below "Susanna and Sue" are my English and Colonial Editions, even down to a sixpenny "Rebecca," "Mother Carey," and "Waitstill," and, beside them all, my books written before the World War, and published by Tauchnitz. I often re-read them in this form, so inexpensively and so charmingly done — the neat paper cover, the delightful page and type and convenient size.

Dining one night with Dr. Oliver Wendell Holmes at the house of my publisher, Mr. Henry O. Houghton, in Cambridge, we discussed the Tauchnitz Edition and he told me a delightful story. Baron Tauchnitz had never been in the habit of paying royalties to his English or American authors, but always gave them a certain sum in advance — ordinarily fifteen or twenty pounds. Dr. Holmes said he believed in a royalty basis and refused twenty or thirty pounds for his latest book, "Over the Tea-Cups," then just written. "The Baron came out ahead," he chuckled. "It wasn't a success on the Continent, and how much do you think I received in royalties?"

I was too polite to hazard a guess, but did not have to wait long for a reply, delivered with hearty laughter. "Thirty-two shillings and seven pence — one pound twelve or thereabouts; and I had refused thirty pounds."

Under the Tauchnitz volumes in a bewildering and, to me, inexplicable line, come the translations of my books into foreign tongues, many, marvelously many, and for no special reason that I can divine. They have brought me no riches, but many other compensations, and much excitement, for the titles alone are a source of infinite amusement in Swedish, Norwegian, Danish, Dutch, Russian, Polish, German, French, Bohemian, Roumanian, and Japanese. (The three Kindergarten books have been translated into Japanese and Spanish; also into "Marathi," one of the Indo-Aryan languages.)

I look often at the Polish "Rebecca," courageously published in Warsaw, wondering if, or why, anybody in Poland ever read it!

I am not skilled in many tongues, but I am awe-stricken when I regard some of Rebecca's foreign titles:

> Rebecca von Sonnenbach Hof
> Rebeka ze "Stonecznego Potoku"
> Rebekka fra Solbaekgaarden
> Rebecca van "Zonbeek-Hoeve"

— while "The Rebecca Dictionary and Glossary, Compiled for the Use of Pupils studying English in the German Schools," has been the cause of much innocent mirth in its day. Rebecca's conversation is dotted all over with stars and crosses in the School Edition, and the unhappy little victim of misguided German *Kultur* turns to an accompanying Glossary every time my heroine opens her lips to speak.

Then there is "Timothy's Quest" in Bohemian; and another, done by a professor in a college in Roumania, which interests me greatly, because the translator wrote to me, courteously asking me if I would kindly consent to his "slight abbreviation" of "Aunt Hitty's" monologues, as he feared that they might not be thoroughly understood by Roumanian readers!

As the aforesaid Aunt Hitty is a very gossipy and voluble New England house-to-house dressmaker, I begged him to leave her out as much as possible, and I have never heard that Roumania objected to the excisions.

The Japanese "Birds' Christmas Carol," with a truly Japanese paper cover, provokes more exclamations than any other volume on the shelf. When I showed it, long ago, with some pride to a literary friend (Mr. Laurence Hutton), he turned over the pages, printed, of course, in Japanese characters, upside down and other-end-to, and remarked:

"This is all very well, my dear lady, but can you prove

it? It might be 'Clarissa Harlowe' or Lydia Pinkham's 'Memories,' for all that I can see!"

I was a trifle crushed by this unexpected criticism until, turning every page carefully, I discovered in two places the lines of the well-known hymn —

> "Carol, brothers, carol!
> Carol joyfully,
> Carol the good tidings,
> Carol merrily!"

They had been printed in English in the Japanese text, just as we would naturally quote a verse of German or French poetry in the original language.

I held up the page triumphantly —

"That disposes of Clarissa, also of Lydia," Mr. Hutton said laughingly. "I never doubted you; I was simply jealous!"

Translations, be they never so many, are hardly a real proof of the value of a book. It may be only that news of its popularity in its own land has reached the ears of would-be money-makers and that they straightway attempt to win a new public for it.

That my books have been of some value, however, as a medium of communication between nations, the following letter to the Librarian of Bowdoin College will attest:

FREE PUBLIC LIBRARY COMMISSION
STATE HOUSE, BOSTON, MASS.
June 11th, 1914

Mr. George T. Little
   Librarian, Bowdoin College
     Brunswick, Maine

MY DEAR MR. LITTLE,

I was very much interested in the enclosed article in the *Transcript* last night, and I am writing to ask if you could send me a list of Mrs. Wiggin's works which have been translated into foreign languages, giving me the title, language, and publisher. Her books are just the things we ought to put into the hands

LAURENCE HUTTON
From a Portrait

of the foreigners, as pictures of our life, and I shall be glad to
add them to our lists, if we can secure them.

Very truly yours

J. M. CAMPBELL

Director, Work with Foreigners

On the lowest shelf of the bookcase are seven huge volumes of mine which have been printed in raised type, and
I never look at them without remembering the graduation
exercises of a certain Institution for the Instruction of the
Blind in California. Last on the programme for the day
was the reading, from a book then just printed, by a child
of twelve who had a marvelously sensitive touch. She began to read very fluently, and I recognized some of the
lines from my own "Birds' Christmas Carol," and sat up
in my seat in breathless excitement. The test was only
begun, for a long piece of chiffon was handed her and
placed over the page. She finally read the text slowly, but
correctly, through three thicknesses of chiffon, and, having a seat near the exit, I crept from the room in tears.
No book save the Bible, I thought, was worthy of being
touched by those tender seeing fingers.

Last comes "Rebecca of Sunnybrook Farm," which the
world doubtless supposes to be the darling of my heart. I
am not in the least a psychic person, but Rebecca's origin
was peculiar to herself. I was recovering from a long illness
and very early one morning I lay in a sort of waking dream.
I saw an old-fashioned stage-coach rumbling along a dusty
country road lined with maple and elm trees. A kind,
rosy-faced man held the reins that guided two lean horses
and from the little window of the coach leaned a dark-
haired gypsy of a child. I was instantly attracted by her
long braids floating in the breeze and by the beauty of the
eyes in her mischievous face. She pushed back a funny

little hat with an impatient gesture, straightened it on her head with a thump, and, with some wriggling, managed to secure the attention of the driver by poking him with a tiny frilled parasol. That was all. The picture came, and went, and returned, and finally faded away, but it haunted me, and I could recall every detail of it at will. Too weak to write, I wondered who the child was, and whither she was traveling, and whence she came. I could not content myself until I had created answers to my questions and the final answer was, indeed, the book itself. The child even named herself, for the moment I visualized her mother it seemed to me that a romantic novel-reading woman might have so loved the two heroines of "Ivanhoe" that she called her baby after both of them.

"Rebecca Rowena" came to me precisely in that fashion, by a sort of lightning express. My nurse's name was Randall, and, as she was very much a part of my waking dreams just then, she somehow became further entangled in them.

The book was begun at a Southern health resort, carried on a little during a make-believe convalescence, and finished in a sanatorium where I persuaded the doctors that the work was better out of my system than in it.

No room in the world is more vividly remembered than the quiet one looking on to distant hills and mountains, where Rebecca lived with me for a month or more, mitigating my weariness and sense of separation from active life. I could not put all I seemed to know about her into the first volume, and a year or two later wrote the "New Chronicles of Rebecca," which is not a sequel, but a further "filling in" of incidents from the child's checkered existence at Aunt Miranda Sawyer's brick house in River-boro.

Rebecca somewhat changed the current of my life-stream

by bringing me into a wider fellowship and intimacy with girls of all ages. She unconsciously made me a deal of trouble, for she doubled my correspondence as suddenly and efficiently as she had leaned from the stage-window and poked Uncle Jerry Cobb with the ivory knob of her pink parasol. These letters make one glad as well as weary, for, if one cannot do the great, the memorable things in literature, there is something intoxicating in the sensation that one has chanced to create a child who seems real as well as winsome, one that other children recognize as belonging to their favorite circle.

When I feel a trifle depressed that my audience is chiefly one of girls and women, I re-read an occasional letter from men, who are not copious correspondents! Here is one, strangely enthusiastic from an author of Jack London's type. I quote it verbatim because it is an interesting revelation of the man.

HEADQUARTERS
FIRST JAPANESE ARMY
FENG-WANG-CHU
MANCHURIA
May 25th, 1904

DEAR KATE DOUGLAS WIGGIN:

May I thank you for "Rebecca"? "Penelope's Experiences" whiled away the hours for me the other day, but they appealed to my head, while Rebecca won my heart. Of course, I have laughed, but I have wept as well. She is real; she lives; she has given me many regrets, but I love her. I would have quested the wide world over to make her mine, only I was born too long ago and she was born but yesterday. Why could she not have been my daughter? Can't I adopt her? And, O, how I envy "Mr. Aladdin"! Why couldn't it have been I who bought the three hundred cakes of soap? Why, O, why?

Gratefully yours
JACK LONDON

Letters from all over the world come to any author who has written an appealing book of the human sort. They come from lame, halt, blind, and deaf; from young and old, men, women, and children. They do not mean that you have written a classic; alas, no! But the classicists must long to get them sometimes just as a change from bay leaves and sonnets and laudations of critics! They simply mean that you have spoken, and your unknown public has heard and responded. Nobody can explain why people write to you in droves about one book and only by dozens and fifties about another, but these letters are among the chief compensations of the author. They will never enshrine you in a Hall of Fame; they will only make you warm to the very core of your being.

Years and years ago I said: "To write a book that two successive generations of children might love, read twice, and put under their pillows at night, oh! what joy of joys, greater than showers of gold or wreaths of laurel!" Some people would call that a humble wish, viewed from the standpoint of their own ambitions; others would deem it too great to be realized. Fortunately, I shall never know whether I have even once achieved my goal, for only the passage of years can decide the ultimate fate of a book.

XXXIV

A CHANGE OF SCENE

As I look back upon the many months spent abroad (for I have not mentioned Saxony, Bohemia, the Azores, Naples, Rome, Florence, and the Windward Isles in my travels) and recall the numberless advantages they brought me, I am glad that, after all, my long roots were always strongly entrenched in American soil.

Three or four months of every summer were spent in the Maine village of my childhood, and Quillcote-on-Saco has been for more than twenty years my favorite place of work; for there not only the later New England books have been written, but many others have been revised, polished, finished, and proof-read. Quillcote began by being the most idyllic place for work ever known. There were even summers when I wrote the stories in "The Village Watch-Tower" under my own apple trees, and nobody ever looked at me or spoke to me or wondered what I was doing. I had grown up in the village, and, although my neighbors thought me a pleasant, intelligent child, and a nice woman, they did not consider my talent worth mentioning.

Quillcote was then a restful, serene country home; nowadays it is a beehive where not a single drone has a chance to live — a center of village improvement, a beacon light on the countryside on which somebody has to pile fuel every day. It used to bask tranquilly in the sun, twenty years ago, and books issued regularly through the elm-shaded front door with the dark green blinds. Now the door is frequently blocked with earnest persons from near-by resorts, who want to know about our Vacation School, our

Dorcas Society, our Library, or our Village Improvement Association.

There was a time when we didn't care how bad our roads were and what people said about them, privately or in print; but when motor parties began to break down in front of our house, spend two pleasant conversational hours with us, and say that they hoped it would happen again soon, we determined on better conditions.

Once upon a time the road commissioners chopped down the beautiful leafage along our roadsides for fear of noxious insects; and when they left all their rubbish behind them we thought it a habit ordered by the Government, and that we must endure our troubles in silence. Now we never endure and we are never silent, for our grievances are immediately laid before committees who set about redressing our wrongs; and, while they are busily engaged in the task, the Village Improvement Society clears away and carries out of sight all the disfiguring rubbish in order to satisfy our pride and make our village an object lesson to unconscientious and unambitious parts of the United States.

I do not remember that in the good old days there ever was a committee of any sort in the village, or, if so, that it ever met. There was the Ladies' Aid Society, but it was harmless and never induced nervous prostration. It sewed as much as needful, ate a good deal at special meetings, and was a model of its kind. It is the committees that meet regularly, energetically, and often pass resolutions, make by-laws, and appoint subcommittees, that banish all leisure, and devastate and blight human existence.

Our hamlet has only a few dozen inhabitants, with a few dozen more in the sister hamlet across the river, but it has nowadays a wild mania for getting itself on the map of Maine and keeping up with the procession; while I am more often than not mounted on a figurative white horse

QUILLCOTE, WITHOUT AND WITHIN
The east front and the study

somewhere in the front, secretly regretting the dead past, wearily doing my best for the present, and dreading the future when committees will inevitably meet from nine to twelve, one to four, seven to ten, Sundays included.

Until that day arrives, I have a few hours of seclusion now and then in my study, which sentimental strangers (always young and always feminine) enter timidly, asking: "Is this where you have such beautiful thoughts?"

That being a question that cannot be answered without hysterics, I change the subject by drawing attention to the prospect from the rear windows of the "jog." It is without doubt the most beautiful "jog" in the universe, and was made from the former owner's back entrance and kitchen closet thrown together, after which I added three twenty-seven-inch-square French windows opening into the room. These windows, six feet from the ground, are protected from the noonday sun by groves of golden-glow, and, when they are open, the beautiful green stalks and, later in the season, the buds and glorious blossoms, evoke sighs of rapture from the beholder.

A little farther along is an old-fashioned well, and then a fifty-foot stretch — a perfect forest, indeed — of pink and crimson and white phlox, growing in the shade of Quillcote barn. Then there is a gentle upward sweep of daisy-sprinkled grass or yellow hayfield, ending in a fringe of pines, with a wonderful sunset beyond when the twilight hour comes and the different committee meetings have adjourned.

There are three ordinary windows in the room, two of them looking into the apple orchard, and the third giving a glimpse of village road where the would-be callers stray, arm in arm, and youthful motorists break down on purpose. It is but just to say that, if I had a tire on the point of "going flat," I would never pass Quillcote lawn and elms, the glimpse of the sparkling river, the scarlet and white window-boxes, the stone steps and the hospitably open door, for the sake of breaking down an eighth of a mile ahead on a lonely, stony hill. I certainly would do what many others do — gently turn into the driveway bordered by nasturtiums, let the tire go flat, and wait to see if the inhabitants at all match the house in charm and attractiveness. It is felt to be an impossibility, but worth trying.

The little French windows looking through the golden-glow on to Elysian fields I open only when lost to all sense of self-respect, because the life at that point is so much more interesting than any in my books that it interferes with my concentration. In the first place, I always want to ask Gudrun, who is stringing beans on a bench at the back door, what we are going to have for dinner. Then Lydia appears from the little laundry in the alder bushes and goes to the well for water. Lydia has long blond braids and the whitest neck in the world. Crystal beads like dew stand out on her warm white forehead, her cheeks are pink, and I think how infinitely I should prefer to be as young and beautiful as she, rather than to be writing nice, ordinary little books.

I close the window, giving a vague and uncomprehending look at my manuscript, which is devoted to the girlhood of a heroine named Martha Templeton, and then, going to the dining-room and choosing an overripe banana from the silver fruit basket, retire to the side steps to wait for inspiration. I seem to have had a story about Martha in my mind once upon a time, but it has disappeared.

Presently I throw my banana skin into the deep shade of the lilacs, where my abnormally tidy sister cannot discover it until I have gone to New York in October, and rejoin Martha Templeton in the study. I gaze blankly at the last sentence on the paper until at last the luncheon bell rings and the unfolding of Martha's fortunes must be postponed until the morrow.

Still, there are rainy days and hot days and days when for some benign and insoluble reason committees do not meet, and we write, write, write, blessedly and fluently, without any wish to look out of the window or meddle with the processes of the universe. In such moods the "New Chronicles of Rebecca," "Rose o' the River," "Susanna and Sue," "Waitstill Baxter," "The Old Peabody Pew," "The Romance of a Christmas Card," "Mother Carey's Chickens," and "Ladies-in-Waiting" were born and sent into the world of unknown readers.

"Mother Carey," issued at the same time as Mrs. Burnett's "Secret Garden," elicited from her the following word of praise, which I value very greatly:

Thousands and tens of thousands will flock under the wings of Mother Carey. How sweet, how warm she is! She is not a Yorkshire moor woman, but she and Susan in my "Secret Garden" mean the same thing. I think it beautiful that we were making those two mother-creatures at the same time.

I often wonder, as all writers do, I suppose, how far I have transferred to the printed page the atmosphere of my beloved countryside. As there are colors in nature which no pigments can reproduce, so there are feelings, thoughts, and impressions too delicate to be transcribed by the pen. When I am doubtful of my success as an artist, I always read a certain review of my work written by a critic in the "New York Tribune" of November 21, 1920.

My unknown friend (to whom all my thanks) calls his review "Mrs. Wiggin's Country."

One has to travel but a few miles from the region of Howells's Shakers to find himself in the country Kate Douglas Wiggin has made her own. She is precise enough to tell us it is in York County, Maine, on the banks of the Saco, and she gives us a refrain to Howells's novel in her "Susanna and Sue," the last of the trio of her short stories bound together in "Homespun Tales," the setting of which is laid in another Shaker community.

Those of us who know and love the intervales of the Saco Valley can see them even through the curtain of the walls of this great city, just as Mrs. Wiggin pictures them, with the river flowing "from the White Mountains to the Atlantic in a tempestuous torrent, breaking here and there into glorious falls of amber glimpsed through snowy foam; its rapids dashing through rocky cliffs crowned with pine trees, under which blue harebells and rosy columbines blossom in gay profusion." And we sons and daughters of New England, who love her as a mother, feel within us the æolian melody of the author's lovely words: "The last sound I expect to hear in life will be the faint, far-away murmur of Saco Water."

The opening story of the collection, "Rose o' the River," is rich in the lore and customs of a logging season in Maine, and presents a number of perfectly authentic types, notably garrulous, vainglorious old "Kennebec" Wiley: but it is in "The Old Peabody Pew" that we come face to face and heart to heart with that really untranslatable something that is the New England of clean living, proud enduring, and brave dying. The winds from the pines and the hemlocks are in the pages that interpret the soul of the little church through its parishioners. The scent of apple blossoms and prim gardens, with a blaze from the sunflowers over a fence, is wafted along sentences that seem the whispered echo of voices that issued years ago from the lips of actual men, women, and children.

Have I deserved this beautiful tribute? I scarcely know, but I read it with a certain proud humility on discouraged days in my green-and-brown study.

The walls of this room are covered with a woodland paper and the thin curtains of painted mull carry out the idea of a forest glade. The carpet is moss-green, the woodwork is nut-brown, the capacious desk in the "jog" is English oak, and so is all the simple furniture. The owl on the mantel was shot and mounted by my husband, who presented it with the idea, I suppose, that there ought to

GORGE OF THE SACO RIVER, HOLLIS, MAINE

be wisdom somewhere in the study, even if it were only stuffed and set on the mantelshelf.

Interested visitors always ask if the same husband shot the immense brown bear whose skin forms the hearthrug. I have often heard an affirmative answer given to the question; and the sketch of a thirty-pound salmon hanging on the wall is frequently described by the young lady exhibiting the house as the product of the absent husband's skill, for she is not quite sure of the facts and she has to make her conversation as picturesque as possible.

The story of the study itself is rather interesting in its way, and ought to be told some time, so why not here and now?

Long, long ago, before the house was mine and named "Quillcote," as denoting the home of a pen-woman, it was the property of a certain Mr. and Mrs. Thomas Carll, although it was originally built and lived in nearly a century ago by distant connections of my own family.

A young girl of fifteen, Olive Bradish by name, came to live with the Carlls, and, after the fashion of the time, helped Mrs. Carll with the household duties, becoming part of the family, although never legally adopted. Olive, who in my childhood seemed a very old person to me, is one of my earliest memories, for our own cottage was a little farther up the village street, and Olive was very generous in the bestowal of pieces of thin, hard "muster gingerbread."

The years went on and, though Mrs. Carll and Olive had attained a good age, it was the mistress of the house who died first. I was three thousand miles away at the time, but when I returned I found that Mrs. Carll had made a most kindly and complicated will, aided, I should think, by a lawyer of extraordinary ingenuity. She had built an ell to the house during the later years of her life in order to provide a dwelling for the man who managed her farm. This ell she left to Olive, together with a sitting-room and two small bedrooms (one down and the other up stairs) in the "main part"; entrance and exit over the stairs at all times, share of the woodshed and pump and half an acre of garden spot.

But Olive went to live in another village, and in course of time I rented such scattered portions of the domicile and land as could be identified as not belonging to Olive. All went happily. The outcome of a friendly correspondence enabled me to hire first the sitting-room and then the two tiny bedrooms. I did not really need the ell filled with Olive's belongings, and so I was moderately content, yet always burning with a desire to own the entire premises.

The neighbors, however, were pessimistic. "You'll never get Olive's 'part,'" they said. "She won't sell. She cal'-lates to come back and end her days there. She's awful fond of her home and her independence, Olive is, and she sets great store by her 'part.'"

Time rolled on, and at length I was able to buy from the five heirs [1] — residing in four different States with four different views about the property — nine acres of land and the circumscribed bits of the house not owned by Olive, together with such strips of the stairs as Olive was not legally empowered to tread on, and enough of the shed for my purposes, leaving sufficient space for Olive to store wood and coal in case she so desired. Likewise I was able to buy the pump, though with the express understanding that Olive was to wash her clothes and quench her thirst at the same well if so disposed.

Possession, even of this sort, made me very happy; but one summer I plucked up courage and timidly asked Olive if she would consider selling me her "part." She was not

[1] In 1905.

so perturbed or so violent as I had feared, and intimated that she would consider it, though the tone implied that consideration was about as far as she would go. The reflective process occupied two years, and the neighbors meantime held their breath in suspense.

"Don't set your heart on it, Katy," they said. "Olive hasn't got any place to store her furniture. She's got a bed made up in the upper chamber. She'll never move her cookstove out o' the lower room. She's got a candle an' a candlestick settin' on the window-sill, and paper and kindlin' all ready to light up the kitchen fire in case she should come home sudden; and she's got a bag of beans and a beanpot all ready for her first supper. Of course, the pork and cornmeal isn't there; but, anyway, that wouldn't 'a' kept nineteen years, and I should kind o' think the beans would be a little mite dry."

Well, Olive knew that our family loved every timber in the house and every blade of grass around it. She knew that we belonged to the soil and were even then part and parcel of the village life, so she finally said: "Well, Katy, I guess I'll sell you my 'part,' if you'll store my furniture in your barn chamber. I don't want any one but John Guilford to handle it, and I want to be right there to watch it every minute and lift all the small things myself. I don't know as I could ever come back to live, not with any comfort, you have so much gay company; and, anyway, you'll keep up the premises, and after I'm dead I shan't have to worry about its leaking down chimney in the storms."

I assented to all her wishes, and the move was accomplished. With our own eyes we beheld Olive, straight, tall, and slim, make trip after trip from her "part" to our barn chamber, even to the carrying of a brown glazed pot and a paper bag that was known to hold beans!

Then what joy! A new chimney and open fireplace took the place of the ancient cookstove; the sink was taken away, and the stairs were made to descend discreetly from the upper room into the hall below instead of pitching rudely down into the kitchen. The back entrance hall and closet were thrown together, making an alcove for my desk; two more windows were added; and I, who had been an author for twelve years and written on my lap or a pine table, found myself now in possession of a real study. For the benefit of youthful and penniless scribes I will say that the lap answers all purposes, and that I have often sat at my beautiful desk and thought with deep sympathy of Solomon John Peterkin!

So much for the study; but Olive was neither neglected nor forgotten. When everything was finished, upstairs and down, we had an oblong panel of canvas painted with branches, leaves, and ripe olives, and in the center, painted in old English text, were the words "Olive's Part." It was fitted into its rightful niche over the new fireplace, a little fire was laid on the owl andirons, and Olive, now a very old lady, lighted the first fire on the hearth — somewhat tearfully, perhaps, but with great pride. When, that night, we illuminated all the windows of the ell with kerosene lamps and candles, the neighbors gathered at their doors and exclaimed: "Land! Look at 'Olive's part'! There ain't been a light there for twenty years!"

For some time before her death she was wont to visit the house on all occasions when it was open to the public for Dorcas Bazaars, and the like, and she always sat in the rocking-chair in the study for the sake of hearing people ask: "What is that painting over the fireplace? What is the meaning of 'Olive's Part'?"

We had already added to the comfort and beauty of our house (now more than a hundred years old) while we were still living in it merely as tenants. Now we began discreet and gradual alterations.

An artesian well, promised by the contractors to "strike" water at fifty or fifty-five feet, found it at about one hundred and five, just as we had expected daily to break into the Empire of China.

Then came two modern bathrooms, then a spacious addition to the sitting-room, and little by little the adornment of each room according to a secret plan — that of making it beautiful without too great expenditure of money, since we wished it always to be an "open house" calculated to induce everybody who came to it from ugly surroundings to feel an instant desire to make them lovelier. I believe we succeeded in making it in some mysterious way a lovable house, for all who pass its threshold want to sit down and live there, and it has been for a quarter of a century the delight of our eyes, the dear dwelling of our hearts.

One of our distinctive family enterprises was a Village Circulating Library. There had always been a Magazine Club, but the only way of getting books was to buy them at Portland, the nearest city. I succeeded in buying and renovating, near the bridge which knits together the two halves of Salmon Falls Village, an old, high-shouldered house which for years past had suffered a variety of tenants, the last one of which had let it fall into absolute neglect. It had become an eyesore to all passers-by, and so great a trial to us, its summer neighbors, that I seized an opportunity to buy it with all its imperfections on its head. Many weeks of labor were spent upon it, and, when all was completed and its fresh paint and tiny-paned windows were shining in the sun, we decided to use its largest upper room as a Village Library. We promptly wrote to all our literary friends asking for donations from their works, as well as to all the benevolent-minded publishers we knew.

and with a little help from the family purse the Library is now furnished and equipped with two thousand volumes. It is opened every Saturday afternoon, with a Librarian in charge, and is so liberally patronized by the villagers that five hundred and forty-nine books were taken from its shelves last winter, although only twenty-eight families are on its list.

In due time we and our neighbors on both sides the river aided in building a Community House near the old Tory Hill Meeting-House. Every summer I read there to the whole countryside some of the work I have accomplished during the season, and this gives us more money for good causes.

The fever for village improvement spread in all directions, though we had only limited means, and few men to help us in our varied activities. I used to treat the onward march of culture and prosperity in our midst with humorous allusions to the good old days when we slumbered in contented isolation. Nevertheless, despite the fact that leisure was curtailed, there was a glow and delight in writing that came from closer human intercourse, and the glad feeling that I was a living, breathing factor in the rehabilitation of the humble little corner of Maine where my childhood had been passed.

XXXV

THE BARN THAT CAME TO LIFE

THIS is the story of a Barn that came to life.

A hundred years ago it certainly had no idea of what would happen to it in the passage of time. Barns were struck by lightning now and then, and burned to the ground — hay, grain, live stock, and all; but that horses would give way to motors, cows and pigs grow fewer in number, and men-of-all-work drift away from the village — no barn could have foreseen that, not if it had possessed a prophetic eye in every window. So, faithful and conscientious, it was doing its limited duty in the years just preceding our first tenancy. It had harbored a horse, a cow, and an occasional calf. It was not a large building, but there was plenty of room for a pung, a sleigh, a buggy, a wheelbarrow, and a carpenter's bench; also a cupboard for rakes and hoes and shovels; an upper chamber for a fair quantity of hay; and, just outside, a pigsty, the occupant of which could come inside in cold weather and make himself comfortable on straw. (Which reminds me that a well-known character of long ago in the vicinity — a person not quite up to the mark intellectually — said she never could see why folks kep' on changin' their pigs! "Why kill your pig every fall and buy another in the spring?" she asked; — "why not keep the same old pig?")

For some years after we had bought the big white, elm-shaded house, with its long backward stretch of kitchen, bedroom, shed, and carriage-house, terminating finally in the Barn itself, we made no other use of the latter than as a place of storage. Nevertheless, whenever we went out there for boxes or excelsior or bottles or paper or sacking, we gazed admiringly at the view from the windows, and the ceiling with its hand-hewn timbers all in fine condition, and reflected with a sigh that it was not convenient for us to have either horse or cow — a family of women with the head of the house in New York most of the time, and no earthly use for barn work even when he was present! So, a season or two went by, and not until our tiny village, with its two neighboring hamlets, had become imbued with a desire to shake off its tendency to slumber and work for general improvement did we have a vision of what part the Barn might play in our development.

We thought of it first as an occasional recreation center, a sort of Hall of Happy Hours, something badly needed, as we had no audience room save the old meeting-house on Tory Hill, a mile distant. Accordingly, when the germinal idea burst upon our imaginations, we began work in the early summer of 1905. The stalls were torn out, with respectful memories of the Dobbins and Crumple Horns of the past; a wide opening was cut in the back, where two great doors could swing into our green fields with their fringes of pine woods; and several new windows were made to let in more light. Another ancient barn, "over Deerwander way," and almost a ruin, was bought and demolished, that we might use nothing but old, silver-gray, weathered lumber in our repairs, for that in our own building was beautiful beyond price. A new floor was laid, good for dancing, and stained and polished till it was somewhat worthy of its environment. The fine old doors were furnished with antique latches, fishhook hinges, and "keystones" for the arches, picked up here and there in the neighborhood.

Long, narrow benches like settles were made of heavy, weathered planks and put against the walls; the windows were hung with dull-brown Singapore lattice net tied back

VIEW THROUGH THE BARN-DOOR

with raveled rope; great birch-bark vases were made to rest on brackets of the same wood; the eighty-year-old grain-chest was set in one end for extra seats, and the Barn in its new, though not in its final, form was ready for occupancy.

Our beloved house might have been jealous, for we lived in the Barn while alterations were going on, scarcely daring to go to meals lest a nail be driven in our absence and something missed. Once we even stole out quietly at midnight, and with a half-dozen candles tried to imagine how it would "light up." The house had been the family idol in all the stages of its own transformation, but it paled into insignificance before the fascinations of the Barn. Bicycles, motors, the new artesian well, laundry, ice-house, hot-air engine — all these were sordid improvements, compared with the Barn.

I well remember, one bright, cool, September day when the house was filled with guests after an author's reading in the old church, how we all flocked out and, encircling the carpenter's benches and dragging the workmen themselves into the ring, sang and danced "sixteen hands round" in joy at the near approach of the real opening.

That did not come until November, and a nipping, frosty November it was; but I could not bear to leave the dedication until another spring, and, my mother and sister having made all preparations, I came on from New York for the important ceremonies. I had not seen the village with bare boughs and frozen ground for years, but the smaller dining-room was warm; and how good it was to leave city gayeties and luxuries behind for a little, and revel in fishballs, beans and brown bread, spareribs, corned-beef hash, and pumpkin pie, together with the frozen back and the roasted front induced by open fires!

Quillcote had a kerosene lamp in every one of its sixty-three windows, north, south, and east, on the great night in 1905 when the Barn became a neighborhood center.

One reflector lamp had been affixed to an elm tree at the entrance of the grounds and another on the Barn itself, although a brilliant hunter's moon was doing its best to honor the occasion. There were four musicians from the nearest large town, and a new upright piano stood in one corner of the big room, which was lighted by thirty brown japanned lanterns hung on pegs from ceiling and walls. Oil stoves had been concealed behind small screens to heat the place until dancing itself should do it.

Then, when the eighty guests had assembled, the grand march began, according to village custom. This ordeal, including its two and four and eight abreast, its single file, its original features introduced by the leader, also the Winding and Unwinding of the Snail, requires, to my mind, more courage, initiative, and intellectual ability than any other function in which I have ever been engaged.

All the ladies not fortunate in securing partners — we are a painfully feminine community! — as well as the lame, halt, and non-dancing males of the company, sit on the benches along the wall and gaze at the spectacle either enviously, admiringly or with polite derision. I have had two partners of international celebrity, one of whom confessed that he never before knew the torture of self-consciousness, and the other that his knees shook with fright and knocked together like castanets.

On this occasion I led with the Chief Carpenter. My mother followed with the Chief Painter and Paper-Hanger, my sister with the Chief Plumber, and so on until we formed a double quadrille of honor in the center of the floor, in which were numbered all the neighbors who had helped in restoring or repairing the house and barn — the shinglers and clapboarders, the artesian-well diggers — in fact, all who had done service of any sort in making our buildings beautiful to the eye and tight against wind and weather, for no one outside the village had a hand in it.

Such a neighborhood dance! — With no fine clothes, nor French heels, nor programmes, no fuss or feathers, and with a record of three ladies between seventy and eighty joining in "Hull's Victory," "Lady of the Lake," "Miss Brown's Reel," "The Tempest," or "Boston Fancy," with an occasional polka, redowa, schottische, or mazurka to show off the skill of those who remembered these ancient dances.

As for refreshments, we began as simply as we intended to go on, so that there were only doughnuts and cheese, coffee and red apples in November, and in summer, cake, lemonade, and ice-cream.

During the refreshments at this first dance in the Barn the desire to make a speech proved irresistible. I wanted to say part of what was in my heart to say; for had I not been a child in the village, with a friendship extending to every family represented in the company, a friendship renewed after an absence of many years? If I had voiced all my thoughts, they would have seemed sentimental; indeed, I could not have put into words what the Quillcote household really meant the Barn to be, in time, without defeating our very hopes by making them too obvious.

I said, I remember, among other things, that, as we were mostly a village of workers — farmers, storekeepers, black-smiths, masons, painters, or what not, with an occasional lawyer, doctor, or minister thrown in for good measure — I wanted to remind them that I had earned every penny that had been put into the house, outbuildings, fifteen acres of land, and all the additions and improvements. Not a dollar of inherited money, or that provided by anything but work, had gone into the scheme, and therefore the

Barn stood for equal enjoyment and opportunity. My pen was just as good a tool, but no better, according to my opinion, than shovel or plough, rake or plane, needle or scrubbing-board. There were those present, I said, who could remember the days when horses neighed and cows lowed in the stalls, when pigs grunted and grew succulent spareribs in the sty, and the barn chamber was fragrant with hay. Those were good old days, but times had changed, and we with them. The Barn had always been a place of service; our task now was to give it a new lease of life with fresh opportunities for usefulness.

The little speech of welcome, with a hint of purpose lurking in between the lines, was received with friendly enthusiasm, and the village postmaster quickly mounted a chair and gave a delightful response that set hands to clapping heartily. Then little white quill pens, hung from rosettes of white ribbon, were affixed to coats and dresses as souvenirs of the evening; and to the stentorian call of "Take your pardners for Speed the Plough!" we formed into lines up and down the hall for one of the old-fashioned "contra dances" which we intended to revive and keep alive.

These dances, with their pretty figures and their jolly music, so infectious in rhythm, had been more or less laid aside for several years, but there were still many who had not forgotten them and could initiate newcomers and summer visitors into their mysteries. Very like the English morris dances with their precision of movement combined with frolicsome spirit, they are the best of exercises and wonderful promoters of sociability, since you meet and dance in turn with the whole company, sooner or later. A man may choose his heart's dearest for a partner, but he has only a share of her attention, and no more favors than any other man, save the felicity of going "up and down the center" with her and "swinging" her regularly every two minutes, the swinging being decidedly athletic rather than sentimental. The waist of the fair one is, indeed, encircled, but with a firm grip intended to whirl and spin the lady rapidly round and round on her toes during two measures of the music, there being no time for tenderness.

We had Daisy and Goldenrod and Autumn Leaf dances, even one in costume, as the seasons came and went; and they were graced very often with the presence of Bowdoin College professors and students, with now and then a naval commodore, a governor, a mayor, a New York lawyer, or a financial potentate. These celebrities were uniformly dull below the waist, and were always given over to the tutelage of certain village spinsters or matrons famed for their proficiency.

I shall never forget the exhilaration of one of our guests, an old Edinburgh friend making his first visit to America. He was an Oxford graduate and a clergyman of the Established Church of Scotland, and, with an ambition that wellnigh o'erleaped itself, his partner led him proudly to the head of the long line, a place full of responsibilities and never intended for neophytes, for the "head" begins the dance, guided only by the sometimes incomprehensible commands of the "caller-off." Miss Brown's Reel started at a brisk pace, for we are no laggards in the Quillcote Barn, and the Reverend David Alexander Cameron Reid, distinguished by his clerical garments, started on his lengthy journey with never a pause to regain his breath or reason, till, helpless with mirth, he fell exhausted on a bench, his partner waving a palmleaf fan over his prostrate form, and exclaiming proudly: *"Well! I got him through!"*

He was an athletic person and soon learned the secret of "swinging the lady." As I met him now and then in his first triumphant progress down the line, his face beaming with joy and laughter, he would murmur: "Oh! if my Presbytery could only behold me."

They would have thought him the right man in the right place, I fancy, for he has always been that. He was chaplain to a famous Scottish regiment ("The Black Watch," 42d Highlanders) for three years and so close to the firing line and so valiant in service that later on the King pinned a D.S.O. on his breast.

The Barn was such an immediate and overwhelming success that we needed not only more room for our dances, but greater facilities for other entertainments of a more serious nature. We finally solved the problem by building out a jog, fourteen feet by nine, on the north side, making it look as much as possible like an old-fashioned "tie-up" for cattle. A platform a foot high covered the floor of this new space, and four tiny windows, like those in horse stalls, gave light and air. A door opened from it into a little entry from which the young people could get to the Barn chamber, shed, or kitchen to dress for tableaux, and, by moving the piano from its old position on the floor, we had more ample space for audiences. If only the old building possessed a thinking apparatus, it might have a hundred interesting memories, for no "lightning-change artist" ever had more varied aspects, moods, and experiences.

There were village-improvement concerts, sewing and quilting meetings of the Dorcas Society, apron sales, reading of manuscript stories by their authors; and once a week during July and August the walls echoed to the voices and the marching and dancing feet of the thirty-odd members of the Quillcote Vacation School.

My memory holds most clearly three very different occasions in the passage of the years.

If we had not named the house Quillcote, when we were searching for an appropriate name for the home of two pen-women, of course we should never have thought of having a burnished golden quill for a weather-vane. When the long-awaited box arrived, and the different parts of the vane were taken from their wrappings, first one golden ball, then another and another, then the gilded points of the compass standing out brilliantly against the wrought-iron bars, and last, the shining quill itself — we exclaimed with one breath, "It must have a party!"

There used to be a "Hanging of the Crane," said we; and now that pothooks and trivets and brick ovens have given place to the depressing and unpoetic range, that good old method of housewarming has vanished. Would not the "Setting of the Weather-Vane" be quite as proper and de-lightful a ceremony? We decided that it would be, and accordingly sent to the neighbors who were too far distant for verbal invitation this card:

Setting of the Weather-Vane

on

Quillcote Barn

Independence Day, 1906,

at 3 P.M.

The pleasure of your company is requested.

Dancing in the Barn from 4 to 6 o'clock.

There are no hard-and-fast lines in neighborly gatherings like this. Everybody who has a home, and is interested in other people's ways of housewarming and homekeeping, is heartily welcome. The lawyer's daughter came to lend her charming voice to one of our songs, the doctor's wife to another, and there were present in the company all the professions, together with dozens of farmers and a few of the proverbial New England Jacks-of-all-Trades.

As they all came up the quiet village road, the white dresses of the women and children dappled with shadows from the great trees above, the scene was very quaint and picturesque, and the company was really most imposing when at last it was settled on the rustic chairs and benches drawn up on the lawn in front of the old red Barn.

At this juncture two of the neighbors, who had made all preparations, climbed to the central peak of the Barn, where the new weather-vane lay hidden. It took only a few exciting moments to set it in its socket, the long golden quill, perfectly balanced by its makers, resting between the shining standards pointing North, South, East, and West. Then, when the men had clambered down to the cheers of the children and the applause of the grown-ups, the quartet sang my "Song to the Weather-Vane," set to so simple a tune that the company joined in the chorus after they had once heard it.

THE SONG TO THE WEATHER-VANE

Weather-vane, weather-vane, shining and bright,
Standing so proudly aloft on your height,
Opening gladly your arms to the air,
This is the message we sing to you there:

Turn to the North, turn to the South,
Turn to the East or West,
The wind that blows is the wind of God;
He knoweth which wind is best.

Weather-vane, weather-vane, pointing so true,
Bearing so bravely your quill in the blue,
Snows they will fall and the rains they will beat,
But after the storm sunlight's ever more sweet.

Weather-vane, weather-vane, we shall grow old,
Years will rob you of your glittering gold,
But ageing together we'll vow to the end,
No stress of life's weather our metal shall bend.

Turn to the North, turn to the South, etc.

The emerald green of the lawn, the splendor of the old trees, the daisy-sprinkled hayfields stretching up to the pine woods, the group of interested people, the beauty of the glittering vane, the underlying thought of the occasion drew the bond of neighborhood closer, and when the last couplet was sung:

> The wind that blows is the wind of God;
> He knoweth which wind is best,

there were tears in many eyes. We were uplifted; ready for the larger truths of the Declaration of Independence and the singing of "America" and "The Star-Spangled Banner."

A young lawyer, a capital speaker, was to deliver the patriotic address from a piazza that is within twenty feet of the Barn, and this I prefaced with a little talk about the love of home as preceding, and leading up to, the love of country.

The child loves first his own home acres. As he grows older, his affections cluster about his own hearthstone, and he wants to defend it, keep it safe, honorable, and respected.

Then he awakes to the dignity of village or town life and becomes an embryo citizen. If he bears his part in civic life, he is ready for the vision of what the State and Nation mean to him, as well as the realization of his own duties, responsibilities, and privileges.

"We are assembled, on this Independence Day" (I finished by saying), "to re-dedicate this home to the good of its housemates, the Village, the State, and the Nation in which it must play its loyal, though humble part. 'Except the Lord build the house, they labor in vain who build it.'"

XXXVI

THE BARN'S HOSPITALITIES

The second occasion was Sally's wedding breakfast. She needs no surname here, but if Sally seems too informal and unfinished, let her be written down as Sally Nonesuch, for that she surely was to her friends. Everything of merry wit and bewildering nonsense, of charm and audacity, of natural gifts and royal sharing of them, of butterfly impulses mingled with the industry of a bee, of laughter and love and courage — all this, compacted, was Sally.

Her ancestors came from the village, and she returned to it in summer-time for a sufficient number of years to make the ones that came before and after rather dull and dreary to remember and to contemplate. And then, arriving very early one June morning from New York to take possession of the little cottage next door to Quillcote, she danced into our sitting-room, flung herself on the sofa and exclaimed: "All pay attention! I don't want any breakfast! I'm engaged to be married!" Whereupon she buried her head in a sofa pillow and rocked back and forth in delight at the fullness of her surprise.

Unbounded joy was not our first emotion. Giving something to one man that had heretofore been the delight of a whole village might be just, but it seemed almost quixotic. Sally's harmless summer flirtations had given zest to the community life, and even to the victims themselves. She could have wheedled several estimable young men up the middle aisle to the altar at almost any moment. But she had been apparently holding herself back for some "not impossible He" that existed in her imagination; and when

SILHOUETTE, 1909

he appeared on the horizon, his decision and hers came with lightning rapidity.

Sally agreed rather grudgingly that perhaps she ought not to be married in the Barn, but at least that the wedding breakfast must be there, and so it was.

The wedding was on a heavenly afternoon in September, when, after an early frost, the leaves had turned to scarlet and russet; yet the air was that of summer. It was like all that pertained to Sally — unique.

The old meeting-house on Tory Hill was trimmed with branches and vines and late goldenrod. A leafy screen hid the choir rail and wheezy cabinet organ, which, played by a genius, seemed a noble instrument. The neighbors from two villages had gathered there to await the bride, and nothing was ever prettier than the departure of the little cortège from Quillcote.

There were three or four open motors, the Episcopal clergyman from the city giving distinction to one of them by his white surplice, an article of attire certainly never seen before or since on our village street. Next came a quartet of pretty girls, all smiles and frills and curls and bouquets, with their muslin flounces billowing over the edges of the car. Last, from a third, there floated out a long white trail of happiness, the bridal veil of tulle that seemed to cry joyously: "Come, haste to the wedding!"

Four of the bride's summer friends were the ushers, each in his Sunday suit, whatever it happened to be; for Sally's nuptials, although correct in every detail as to costumes of bride and groom, were highly unconventional in many respects, having a gay, haphazard, careless, human quality not commonly a part of weddings.

Next came the Barn's turn, when it received the bridal party and the twenty or thirty guests invited to the breakfast. Its interior had received one of its manifold transformations at the magic hands of my sister. Birch-bark vases were filled with great branches of autumn boughs and goldenrod, and other fall flowers were at every point of vantage, but the bride's table, at which covers were laid for fourteen, was a dream of color and beauty. Along the whole length ran a beautiful branch from a horn-beam tree, ranging in color from deep glowing garnet and ruby, through brightest scarlet to orange and gold, and gleaming satin ribbons of orange were caught in its leaves making a wonderful color scheme. It was a merry break-fast, interspersed with speeches and songs by Sally's friends; and as it neared the time to say good-bye, the bride herself, her face radiant with smiles and her eyes bright with unshed tears, ran to the upright piano in front of the wide-open doors, and sang to us in the old way — her own way, like no other.

No picture ever made in the Barn ever equaled this. The sun shone full on the singer, giving a dazzling luster to the white satin that fell in thick folds on the dark pol-ished floor. It struck mysterious, iridescent rays from the cloud of tulle that floated from her yellow hair, so that she seemed more spirit than woman. But the sun did some-thing more — something unexpected; something dramatic! It made a broad golden pathway of light across Quillcote's upward slopes directly to the house where Sally's father and grandfather had lived; so that the elms that arched over the door formed a frame for her head. Nobody could have invented or staged that tableau. It simply happened.

"Oh, how beautiful everything is!" Sally cried, as she whirled on the piano stool and came back to her husband's side. "How beautiful it is, and how I should like to be married every day!"

Everybody laughed.

"Land sakes!" whispered an old lady to me; "don't

that girl beat all? She'd say whatever come into her head, even *'twas* at her weddin'. But mebbe she'll tame down some when she's been married a spell."

Well, she never did "tame down," thank Heaven! And she is dead — Sally Nonesuch! At least that is what we say in our clumsy speech when a bright shape has vanished from our sight and a blithe voice no longer charms our ears. She is still radiantly and buoyantly alive to those who knew her best. Yet her ashes are lying in the old Tory Hill churchyard, just a stone's throw from the spot where she was married.

Her voice and her gifts of interpretation were so enchanting, so unique, that people were always crying *Brava!* to her all her life. She passed on, as she had lived, so beautifully and so gallantly, that at the very end we could still whisper with a catch in the throat: *Brava*, Sally!

The Barn had many good concerts, for we had loyal and talented helpers in our enterprise, some of them sufficiently near to be called upon in any emergency, and emergencies fancied or real occurred frequently at Quillcote. Our most faithful "artists" were Sally herself, and Edith Chapman Goold, both sopranos, and Evelyn Dutton Fogg and Edna Webb True, contraltos. Tableaux, community choruses, amateur theatricals, and Mothers' Meetings gave variety to our entertainments, and we set apart a Sunday evening now and then for a simple church service.

We chose a moonlight night for our meetings, when our audiences could be gathered easily from up and down the river and across the hills.

The Barn has a wonderful way of adapting itself; of being all things to all men; of making a background and an atmosphere perfectly in harmony with the occasion, whether it is a reading of Browning's "Saul" or a children's game of "London Bridge." When there is a dance,

it is the merriest place in the world and the floor answers
delightedly to the springing feet; but on a quiet Sunday
evening one might sometimes think there were angels on
the roof. There was such a one when our dear Scottish
parson led the service. While the people were gathering, I
played softly on the piano, old hymn tunes mostly, tunes
of which the words were so familiar that they were remembered silently as they followed one after another —
"Come, ye disconsolate," "Jerusalem, the Golden,"
"Abide with Me," "Oh! for the Wings of a Dove," "Sun
of My Soul," and others.

The neighbors stole into the seats quietly. There were
only a few lanterns lighted. The moon shone through the
wide-open back doors. A bird perched on an apple tree
just outside of one of the little windows in the "tie-up"
where the piano stands. He cocked his head, his bright
eyes glancing from side to side, and when I paused a second
between the tunes he chirruped, as much as to say, "More,
please!" — while one of the children whispered: "He's
come to the meeting, Mother!"

Then the minister prayed, and it was as if he were talking to God, for there was no pulpit and he was standing
among us voicing our secret aspirations. Some one in a far
corner started a verse of "Sweet Hour of Prayer," and
after that a very old lady began, quaveringly, "I'm a
pilgrim and I'm a stranger"; for we often sing without
books, and only the hymns forgotten in the cities.

Then came the sermon, and it was just a Bible story
that almost every one had forgotten, an incident in the life
of Jeremiah during the reign of Zedekiah, King of Judah.
The prophet, the reader will remember, had been let down
with cords into a deep pit or dungeon; "and in the pit was
no water left but deep mire and black ooze, and Jeremiah
sank in the mire."

A certain Ethiopian, servant of the King, said to him: "This is an evil deed and the prophet will die."

Then the King commanded the Ethiopian to take thirty men and drag the prophet from the dungeon. And so he did, but first he went into the King's house and under the treasury found "cast clouts and rotten rags." These he took with him, and when he reached the pit he called to the prophet: "Put now these old clouts and rotten rags under thine arms that the cords may not wound thee." "So they drew up Jeremiah from the deep pit."

It needed few words to draw from the story the lesson of life's little services; of kindliness, sympathy, forethought, that might all be likened to the merciful thought of the Ethiopian.

There was more singing, the moon rose higher; hundreds of stars came out in the blue; insects chirped in the long grasses of the fields; a breath from the pine woods stirred the air. Something was happening to us who listened. It seemed as if we were all sitting with the best foot forward. Could it be that in the unaccustomed, disarming atmosphere of the Barn we were, so to speak, "getting religion"? I shouldn't wonder! At any rate, the bearers of heavy burdens shifted them a little and smiled; shoulders straightened; the wrinkles were smoothed out of tired faces; the discouraged, drooping mouths took an upward curve.

The Barn service was over; and when we, remembering Jeremiah's story, heard the minister say, "God help you to gather up and renew the rags and cast-off garments of your faith and consecrate them to deeds of mercy," we all bowed our heads to the benediction and said Amen! in our hearts.

The light-hearted days before 1914 vanished from the

earth, and in 1917 and 1918 life took on a soberer hue. In all the land no one responded more quickly to the call to arms than the boys of our Maine village. Dancing gave place to marching and drilling, and the Barn went to work with a right good will, just as if it had a soul and realized that it must be a background for something bigger than gayety and good cheer.

There was a flag in the "tie-up" then; and in the window over the entrance door — the window framed in verdant hop vines in summer and with snow wreaths in winter — there was a Red Cross, to show the passer-by that the Barn had entered into a new phase of existence. It had heretofore tried to stand for the highest in community life, for the State cannot be any stronger or wiser or more loyal than the sum of its villages. Now, like the human beings who guide its activities, it strove to widen its horizon, for, behold! the old things had passed away and all things had become new.

XXXVII

A VILLAGE DORCAS SOCIETY

"WELL, I swan!" exclaimed one good old Republican farmer who had come twenty miles by rail because his wife wanted to see our Dorcas Fair. "Well, I swan! You Dorcases beat anything I ever see! There warn't ever but one human creetur in Maine that could draw two thousand folks anywheres, and that was James G. Blaine — and I'm blest if he'd 'a' taken the resk of chargin' 'em ten cents apiece to git in!"

Now, how do we do it? We never arrived at our present height of success all at once, you may be sure. A dozen years ago our Dorcas Society was an ordinary little rustic organization. We are three tiny villages — Salmon Falls, Buxton Lower Corner, Bar Mills — on the brink of the Saco River, in York County, Maine. You would never discover the fact of these villages for yourself, for the geographers — who have no eye for beauty or talent! — persist in keeping us off the map. We are small, to be sure, and, sad to relate, we are not as big as we used to be fifty years ago; but we have no intention of dying out. Like all other Maine villages we are mostly "women-folks," and have to bear some responsibilities that do not properly belong to us.

We began by helping the historic old Orthodox Church on Tory Hill in Buxton. Although we began on the church as the center of the neighborhood's intellectual and social life, as well as its spiritual center, after we had renovated the parsonage within and without, we extended the sphere of our activities to include many departments of village work, such as buying certain educational luxuries for the district schools, giving donations toward various neighborhood improvements and pledging a substantial annual subscription to the minister's salary. All this has meant a considerable expenditure of money, the most of which we earn at the Dorcas Fair given every August for many years at Quillcote, my summer home.

The Dorcas membership — wholly non-sectarian — is almost entirely local, our own family and one or two others being the only distinctly "summer people." We meet at one another's houses, save in July and August, when The Event Toward Which the Whole Creation Moves is near at hand. Then we have such a large attendance and such mountains of work-materials that we are obliged to assemble in the Quillcote Barn. Of course, the meetings are fewer in winter on account of cold weather and bad roads, but the sewing and knitting and crocheting and planning go on, and there is a splendid bulk of "something to sell" when June comes round. The members of my family and those of the few other summer residents do their full share of practical work for the Fair by serving on the various committees, and their names are sometimes among the trustees of the society; but they never accept office, having no faith in "absentee landlords." Those who truly represent the neighborhood are the ones whose interests are linked to it all the year round — those who stand by it when it is buried three feet deep in snow.

Looking back over the years, I know quite well how and why we have grown and waxed strong; we have never had a quarrel or a disagreement in the ranks; there has never been any jealousy or self-aggrandizement; we have simply worked shoulder to shoulder, each doing the thing for which her talent, smaller or larger, fitted her. "Land sakes!" said a neighbor, "I can't sing in the Barn concerts or dance around the Maypole, but I can wash the lemonade glasses, so count on me!"

I have worked with various organizations both here and abroad, and I never saw anything more admirable than the unselfish labor, the energy, pluck, spirit, and skill that were developed in our membership as the work grew and demanded greater effort. We little suspected that we were going to be a "habit," but gradually we noticed that summer visitors at the hotels twenty to thirty miles away stayed in the vicinity till the date was announced, and that hundreds of people planned their vacations so as to "take in" the Dorcas Fair.

Quillcote, as I have explained in an earlier chapter, is neither splendid nor spacious; it is simply a big, white, century-old mansion, well situated for an outdoor festivity. There are magnificent elm trees, wide lawns in front, orchards at the sides, and a beautiful field of eight or nine acres stretching back and up to a fringe of pines. My sister superintends the arrangement of booths and all outside decoration, and makes everything "tone in" with the landscape; so the public is barred out by long garlands of yellow and green looped and rosetted between the elms, while the tall entrance-gates are of goldenrod and hemlock. The booths are all of yellow-and-green striped awning cloth, and the ropes that hold them in place are entwined with goldenrod. Time was when all the articles for sale were displayed within doors, but nowadays the fifteen rooms of the house, and the sheds and the barns, are always so full of visitors during the Fair that the full assortment of our wares cannot be shown properly. Do not suppose that any advantage is taken by the crowd from the fact that the house is open to all — a reception committee doing the honors — for at the end of the day we never find a pin misplaced. There is nothing rare, nothing expensive to be seen, but the rooms furnish rather pleasing object lessons to some of the tired women visitors whose lives have been passed in lonely farmhouses half a mile from the post-office or from any neighbor.

Inexpensive fancy articles are sold in the blue parlor, and jellies, jams, dish-towels and hand-towels, etc., in the dining-room. The study is given up to souvenirs, posters, and photographs, with all sorts of reminders of the literary work of members of the household, and in the old-fashioned rag-carpeted sitting-room are dolls and children's toys. In the orchard we have booths for the sale of ice-cream, aprons of all kinds, and autographed books; also there is one marvelous apple tree hung with hundreds of five-cent and ten-cent packages wrapped with bright-colored tissue paper. These mysterious "fruits" are removed from the tree by the children with the aid of a long, hooked pole.

The Dorcas aprons, we may as well confess, are our pride and joy, although our prices are so reasonable that we really get little for our labor. Everything practical that can be made of gingham is there, and everything dainty that can be fashioned from white or colored nainsook, muslin, lawn, or organdy is in our stock. The good old "apron habit" is not yet entirely out of fashion in Maine. So many housewives do their work without help that kitchen aprons are a necessity, and our pretty saleswomen are not blind to the effect of a coquettish afternoon apron when they try it upon a casual masculine beholder. There never was an article of woman's attire more expressive than the apron, and it is a thousand pities that there is no room for it in city life. James Whitcomb Riley wrote me years ago: "I shall see and know you some time, and oh! what joy if you should turn out to be a little woman with a blue apron, and a dab of flour on your nose!"

The Book Booth needs a little explanation, perhaps even

an apology, as at first sight it does not seem to be intended to foster a love of general literature, it being devoted exclusively to the humble productions of Kate Douglas Wiggin and her sister, Nora Archibald Smith! Not that these authors are the only ones read by the community, but — don't you see? — their books were written at Quillcote, either in the study or in the painted chamber or under the apple trees. Even you would not buy Milton's "Paradise Lost" as a souvenir of a Dorcas Fair! You would purchase an autographed copy of some book written by a Dorcas author, and leave Milton until you went to a bookshop at Christmas-time. The first Book Booth some years ago was a small table with a few books upon it donated to the good cause. Now it is a business, and the Dorcas Society, by buying the books at wholesale — the authors giving their royalties and their inscriptions — earns a delightful sum for the treasury. The autographing is a task that involves much labor, but the result justifies it, and the persons who have no interest in aprons or fancy-work like to have some tangible souvenir of their visit. There is a post-card table under a big Japanese umbrella, and here we sell photographic cards of the river, the falls, the rapids, the meeting-house, the library, and of Quillcote itself.

As to ways of entertainment at the Fairs, we are not without them. Our Barn seats one hundred and twenty-five — on compulsion — and we give continuous ten-cent concerts, admitting each audience through the front door and dismissing them by way of the back door after fifteen or twenty minutes of charming music and brief recitations, furnished sometimes by artists from New York or Boston.

At intervals eight of the junior Dorcas members give morris or Maypole dances on the greensward, fan and parasol reels and old-fashioned "contra dances," wearing picturesque costumes suited to the period, the music being furnished by a band from the nearest large town, which entertains the crowd by playing every quarter of an hour.

The little cottage next to Quillcote on the quiet village street is sometimes pressed into service as a tea-house, and here a committee of six or eight members makes a brave attempt to serve light refreshments to a few of the hundreds who have come to the Fair expecting a local hotel with all modern conveniences. I have called the village street "quiet," but it is anything but that at the height of the fray, between three o'clock and half-past five on a bright summer afternoon.

Four gayly decorated haycarts deposit those visitors who have come by rail and have alighted at the station a mile up the dusty road; automobiles, often several hundred in number, are standing in neat rows on the level grassplots some distance below Quillcote; a large barge freighted with girls from an outdoor school sixteen miles away awakens great excitement, for the occupants are young, ardent, strong of lung, and devoted to their school "yell." As for the horses and nondescript equipages of all sorts, nobody has ever had time to count them, but two men work for hours putting up hitching-rails in the great fields back of the house, placing them near the fringes of shade, so that the horses will be comfortable and the beauty of the landscape preserved. Groups of the oldest inhabitants gather under the trees and look with awe and pride at the wonderful scene brought into being by the ingenuity and energy of their "women-folks." Well, it takes both ingenuity and energy, there is no denying that.

Each season must have its novelties. One year, for instance, we had a four-page newspaper, some folk-dances by a dozen charming girls, and a Registry Booth where persons from twenty-two different States signed their names and paid two cents apiece for the pleasure; we also had a

Dorcas Cook Book neatly printed and prettily bound in Delft-blue boards, with a yellow Colonial back. We try, indeed, to have something new in every department to pique the attention and hold the interest of old friends who make annual pilgrimages to the Fair. So much for "ingenuity."

As for "energy," perhaps you can imagine the labor involved in giving a festival of this kind in a tiny village a mile from a railway, a village where nearly all the women do their own household work; perhaps you can imagine, I say, the brains and pluck and devotion to the good of the community needed to call this great crowd together and win its approval. We have our ideals in this direction, a sort of flexible Dorcas creed built out of our clientage, our experience, and the purposes we have in view: No lotteries nor raffles; no exorbitant prices; no keeping of "the change"; no pursuit of customers; and no solicitations to purchase.

The Dorcas members, who wear washable dresses, long white aprons, and Priscilla mob-caps, do all the selling, always remembering that they are serving country neighbors or city guests who have come a long distance to aid the cause.

Comparatively little money is earned from all this outlay of time and strength; partly because we are too far from the cities to take care of the even larger crowds we might find means to attract, partly because the village is literally too small to hold the Fair, and partly because we cater chiefly to people of modest means. We don't mind very much! We have a thousand good ways for spending money, but, after all, we are glad and grateful to make a holiday for the whole countryside. The old-fashioned "Training Day" and "Muster" are no more, but the Dorcas Society can bring as many people together, in as picturesque a setting, as did any of those ancient festivals.

And how we love to hear our beautiful river praised, our

shade trees extolled, our neat farmhouses approved, and our historic meeting-house admired by those who see our neighborhood for the first time! And then, too, how much we have gained by working together as neighbors for any and every good cause that will make the community a better place for the children to live in, or bring back a single family to an abandoned farm!

Perhaps some of my readers will say that an author who has been writing books for thirty years has a public of her own, and that that public would be likely to be a factor in the success of the Fair because the author would dispense a personal hospitality that would convert an ordinary bazaar into a sort of mammoth garden-party. That has really very little to do with the case. It helps, of course, but every community has its author nowadays, and you have only to annex her or him to possess all our small advantages, with perhaps an absence of our great disadvantage of isolated position. Or it may have a local artist or sculptor or singer — who will be sure to fling himself or herself whole-heartedly into anything that promises to add to local prosperity or good-fellowship.

An author is convenient for signing books and photographs, otherwise she or he does not begin to be as valuable as a millionaire, who will not only open his splendid establishment to the public, but who will also attract other people of wealth to the desired spot. We have a lamentable lack of millionaires. Whatever may be said of them — and I generally find them just as agreeable as paupers — they are certainly at their best on an occasion such as I have described; and the Dorcas Society of Hollis and Buxton would gladly give even a modest Crœsus free admission could they secure his presence at a Fair. We have drawn two thousand people to our Fairs under present conditions — what could we accomplish with a spectacular, generous millionaire!

XXXVIII
ADVENTURES OF A PLAYWRIGHT

I AM accustomed to speak of myself as a late playwright, not because I am extinct, but because such playwriting as I have done came very late in my literary career.

Why it ever came at all, I do not know. My earliest years were spent in a Maine village, and surely nothing was there to stimulate a love of the drama, for life flowed on as quietly as the stretch of river beneath our cottage windows. There were no theaters anywhere in the vicinity, and, if there had been, children would never have been allowed in them until they had attained a ripe and discreet age. I do remember, as long ago as I remember anything, there were white paper "fliers" thrown along our elm-shaded roads, announcing an Indian entertainment in the little hall over our principal country store. The parental judgment was decidedly against my attending this function, but, though I was a docile little person of ten, my imagination was inflamed by the printed promises of Indian dances, pappooses, medicine-men, and war-whoops. I was finally allowed to go under the chaperonage of what was then called the "hired girl."

The "hired girl" regarded the troupe of Indian players with considerable incredulity, even identifying one of them to her own satisfaction as an Irishman that used to work on her father's farm. I felt only a warm enthusiasm for, and simple belief in, the feathers, paint, and bright colors. "I am sure they are really truly Indians, Mary," I whispered. "Nobody else *could* whoop so." A rather realistic imitation of a scalping scene sent Mary and me somewhat prematurely from the entertainment, and, as I clung to her hand going downstairs, I still murmured loyally: "I know they are Indians, Mary! Nobody else *could* scalp so."

Months, and, for aught I know, years passed, and the next thing I recall is a performance of Swiss Bell-Ringers in the brick schoolhouse. This was allowed to be high art, and the entire family attended in a body. According to my recollection it was a truly inspired entertainment, imitated by the neighborhood children for months afterward. It seemed to me then that life could offer no greater joy than to travel from village to village, and schoolhouse to schoolhouse, receiving the plaudits of entranced throngs, often numbering as many as thirty to forty persons!

At the age of twelve I chanced to see "Othello" in the hall of a neighboring manufacturing town. I found it harder now to match my unconscious ideals and developing standards with the impersonations of a barn-storming theatrical company. The all-too-brief, machine-stitched, flannel night-robe worn by the Moor in the strangling scene irritated my dawning sense of beauty, and I wished that Othello had covered his bare feet with bedroom slippers, even though they had not been the fashion in Venice. Desdemona's blond wig was ample in length and thickness, but was so crudely applied that I lost interest in her fate and suffered very little when she was strangled, which shows that an æsthetic tendency plays havoc with ethics.

The Maine village gave place to a home in Southern California, and there, too, there were no dramatics, our out-of-door diversions being much more healthful for growing girls; but, a little later, amateur theatricals loomed up in my life, and the fascination of submerging myself in imaginary characters exercised itself upon me greatly.

By this time I was a full-fledged kindergartner working whole-heartedly among the heterogeneous population in a crowded section of San Francisco. There was drama enough, I can assure you, in my daily contact with a hundred small children and their extraordinarily variegated backgrounds! Our "Circle Plays" became matters of curiosity and interest to many visitors. I had just sufficient skill in singing and accompanying to make the musical side attractive and my study of Froebel gave me due regard for simplicity and directness. Leadership there was, but I tried my youthful best to be a child with the children, forswearing self-consciousness and artifice, and encouraging as much joyous expression of personality as was compatible with perfect coöperation.

From playing with my own hundred children, and later on with many another hundred; from daily telling of stories to this insatiable horde of youngsters; from writing the stories down and selling them in order to open new kindergartens — all this gave me whatever training I had for future literary work. The books, that had been written because they were my only means of contributing to a cause grown inexpressibly dear to me, now found their way to a publisher and there were no more amateur theatricals! Life was real, life was earnest, in another and a new way, but the love of the theater persisted. When the play was bad, I was always "tinkering" it in my mind. If the acting did not convince me, I sometimes imagined myself as doing it better, and, as I was never asked to prove my superior skill, my self-respect never received a shock.

The characters in my books now assumed first place and pushed everything else out of sight and hearing. When they talked together, I always saw them moving, gesticulating, crying, or laughing. It became my habit to read all my dialogue aloud to see if it were as natural, as musical, as simple, as eloquent, as, with my limited powers, I could make it. Many blunders of over-emphasis, clumsiness of speech, repetition of words, sentences foreshortened, or made too long to be clear disappear under this test, when the eye has not detected them. At any rate, if I had not read aloud in the quiet of my own study, I might never have tried to do it for the pleasure of others.

Another element for activity opened after the publication of "Rebecca," for then came swarms of letters from young readers, chiefly in the public schools. Would I come to the weekly Assembly some time to read to the girls? Once the whole English Department of a Girls' High School formed itself into what it called the "Rebecca Composition Club." The Secretary wrote ingenuously that if I could not come and read at Assembly, would I please walk up one aisle and down another so that they could look at me? I concluded that I should run less risk by reading and I faced my first audience of eighteen hundred girls.

In my early visits to schools, I was often regaled with dramatizations of scenes from my stories played by the pupils, and there ensued a positive bombardment in the shape of beseechings to make these scenes for them and make them better. So, in course of time, as the result of these various experiences, "Rebecca of Sunnybrook Farm" came to the real stage, with real actors and a real public.

In "Rebecca," "Mother Carey's Chickens," and "The Birds' Christmas Carol" (dramatic form), I had the aid of a collaborator who not only helped me in planning the scenes and arranging the book-material to be used, but who stood by in the hope of giving me a plot, a suspense, a conflict, a problem, a crisis, or a curtain, leaving all the dialogue to me. Alas, although the characterization and dialogue are as natural to me as breathing, I am absolutely deficient in the other useful adjuncts of the drama. I have sometimes been offered delightful little plots, but I find that they generally "stand out" so obtrusively, even with the most delicate dovetailing, that in despair I have to reject them, though exceedingly anxious to avail myself of their manifest advantages.

No one realizes better than I the dangers that lie in the dramatized book, and I would never have undertaken the task had I not been beguiled, indeed, almost browbeaten into it. When your book lies open in your lap, the people seem rather lifelike, but, when you pry them out from between the covers and attempt to stand them on end in a play, they are sometimes transformed into dummies.

George Moore, in criticizing a certain American novelist, says: "Certain things may have happened before his story opens — burglary, arson, bigamy, forgery, battle, murder, and sudden death; but bang in front of the reader nothing happens!" When I first read that felicitous phrase, written of my betters, my soul shrank to the size of a mustard seed, realizing how true it was of my own work.

The reading and the witnessing of plays has always been my chief recreation. Considering this intimacy with dramatic literature, together with my constant attendance at plays in America, in England, and on the Continent, it is curious that the controlling interest has never had any effect upon my literary work, which is as undramatic as it was in the beginning. Neither is it the fact that I attempt to master these very desirable qualities and fail. I simply never try to alter my natural bent, knowing quite well what is for me, and what, emphatically, is not.

Nevertheless, I have frequently been solicited to write light comedies. Clyde Fitch often asked me to write a play with him, he, of course, to furnish all the movement of the drama, I to contribute the dialogue and the feminine part in the love scenes.

The persons who prefer these requests, must, of course, believe that I have a latent gift, which will develop, if sufficiently urged. I disagree, and continue to adopt the line of least resistance, not because energy and industry are lacking, but because I think that usually one's real gift, if it is real, draws one like ropes of steel!

But when the twenty-seventh person (they were none of them names to conjure with) had asked if he or she might send me the "little play" he or she had made of Rebecca, I began to consider the matter of trying it myself. I felt that I could protect the spirit of my own book, and preserve its simplicity, better than any one else. The result could only be an unpretentious drama, very different from the accepted forms, but it might possibly be an amusing, touching, human sort of thing, pleasing in spite of its slightness.

I suppose because at the age of eighteen I was called "The Mother's Companion" and "The Children's Friend," people will always look for a "purpose" in me. I had a definite desire to write a merry, frolicsome, tender, natural little drama, with ever so many smiles in it; a hearty laugh here and there (not too loud a laugh), a tear now and then, a throb of sympathy. I wanted the fragrance of an innocent childhood and girlhood to steal out over the footlights. I longed to make a verdant little spot in the heat and dust of Forty-Second Street, a New England haying-field in July, and coax all the men and women who had been country boys and girls to come in and rest their tired nerves with a vision of their "little past," lived, perhaps, in some such village as the one to which Rebecca comes, in an old-time stage-coach.

It seemed better to begin with Rebecca. She had made her own following, more or less; at any rate, she "did herself," as the children say, and I had always appeared to my own view as a joyous and somewhat accidental parent. Perhaps (I thought) she will hold some of her friends on the stage as she did in the book. Of course, if she fails I shall have been a very cruel literary mother, dragging my child from the spot where she was beloved, and transplanting her to one where people might shake their heads at her and say: "Why didn't you stay at Sunnybrook Farm where you belonged?"

The play was finished, and, still more remarkable, was accepted for early production. Even more marvelous, the managers who purchased it were those who controlled massive theatrical enterprises. Although they had for years ploughed their managerial path through forests of plots, they welcomed little Rebecca, who brought nothing with her in the way of properties save a nightgown in a brown paper bundle in case she should be asked to stay overnight in any theater. (Later on she took an old-fashioned "hair trunk," because she was invited to remain in Boston for eleven weeks, and needed a change of clothes!)

The whole experience of the work with the stage-director,[1] which preceded rehearsals, and the rehearsals themselves — all this was delightful, illuminating, and chastening, and I issued from the experience wiser as well as humbler. "Authors seem to be absolutely opaque to all dramatic situations!" he would explain; and I would retort; "And stage-managers seem to be blind and deaf to anything that is simple and human and natural!"

This one was wonderful with the children, however, as well as most ingenious in inventing stage business, and in all our differences we each preserved respect and admiration for the other's work. I "wrote in" bits of dialogue, at rehearsal, for delightful persons who had not nearly enough to say for the salaries they received. I took home certain pathetic scenes very dear to me, and brought them back next day wreathed in smiles; as everybody concerned, from the Olympian head himself to the fourth stage assistant, detested tears and approved of laughter, both on moral

[1] Lawrence Marston.

and financial grounds. Why they deplored my gentle April showers of pathos when the rivers of tears that flow in such plays as "Madame X" wash thousands of dollars into the box-office, I shall never understand; but so it was.

Rehearsals brought a new set of friendships. Where can you find a more gallant "working together" than a playwright, even a beginner, finds awaiting him, from the moment the parts fall into the actors' hands?

"Theirs not to reason why"; theirs but to speak or die the lines given them to speak; and how grateful they are for every word with which it is possible for them to secure a smile, a chuckle, a quiver of the lip, a responsive look, or, above all, the coveted applause.

The stage-hands are meantime doing their best that the author's work shall not be judged a failure. They are interested spectators and, I doubt not, pretty good judges of the outcome of affairs.

There was a red-letter day at the Liberty Theater when Rebecca's stage-coach was first rehearsed. With the help of interested friends and much motoring, a wonderful old Concord coach had been discovered in a shed near Prout's Neck, Maine, and Rebecca's managers had persuaded its owner to sell it. He was pleased to have it receive a new distinction, as it had taken many prizes at county fairs and was a sacred object.

The first act of the play was being rehearsed and the coach's moment had arrived. At first you hear the village children crying: "There's the stage!" Then there is the sound of horses' feet, the crack of Uncle Jerry's whip, the rumble of wheels, and in a twinkling the good old State o' Maine stage is at the brick-house gate.

From the window, framed by the fringed taffeta curtains, smiles Rebecca's elf-like face. Afraid that Uncle Jerry had missed the house, she puts her head out of the

EDITH TALIAFERRO

window with an exasperated dab at the hated porcupine quills on her hat, and pokes the driver with her pink parasol.

At that moment I heard a stage carpenter say to his mate the first authentic words of encouragement.

"Horses and kids! It's a combination you can't beat!" was his criticism as to the effect of the scene on an audience.

One stage-coach does not make a play, I think I hear the critics say. An incontrovertible remark, but I experienced some moments of extreme felicity during that winter when these simple happenings in a child's life were received with favor by audiences. To see dozens of young people lunching at one o'clock in great trepidation lest they be late at a matinée; to find them in the theater, gazing, in eager ranks, at the stage; to watch their shining eyes and parted lips when Rebecca steps from the coach — this outweighs many an hour of labor, and makes one marvel one can win such a darling welcome by such simple means.

Children and young people were but a small fraction of the audiences, because there seems an increasing number of men and women who enjoy plays in which the child and the dreams of childhood have a part.

My Rebecca play was accepted in April, 1909, and produced in November of that same year in Springfield, Massachusetts, remaining on tour for several months and opening in New York, October, 1910.

A pleasant feature of its last appearance in Washington was an invitation which my husband and I received from President and Mrs. Taft to dine at the White House and go with them to the theater in their box. The players were tremendously uplifted by the sight of their friend, the author, sitting side by side with the President of the United States, and the management could not conceal its pride at seeing him smile or wipe away an occasional tear.

The second company opened in Richmond, Virginia, October 30, 1911, and the original cast, intact, appeared in London in September, 1912. The play did not reach stock production till the end of its sixth season, and it is still occasionally performed at intervals up to this moment (1923).

On the occasion of its three hundredth night, at the Republic Theater, New York (April 8, 1911), I wrote a little epilogue for Edith Taliaferro, the last lines of which I give below.

> We wonder why you've liked our simple play!
> Did mem'ry conjure up some "long ago" —
> Some bright-hued moment in life's dusty way,
> Some old brick house with hollyhocks a-row?
> Did just a whiff of wholesome country air,
> Blowing o'er clover-fields and wayside flowers,
> Drift to your velvet-covered seats down there,
> And set you dreaming of dear, by-gone hours? —
> Or did the spirit of the eternal child,
> That works such magic in the human heart —
> Did youth, with just its native wood-notes wild,
> Charm and beguile, without a conscious art? —
> We only know we've won your smiles and tears;
> You've made our daily task a pure delight;
> You've changed to hope and joy our earlier fears,
> And so we thank you all! — good-night! good-night!

It might not be amiss to give in the next chapter a letter to my husband describing Rebecca's reception in London, where it ran but six weeks, although better plays written by veteran authors have sometimes been removed in as many days, a poor sort of consolation, however, for lack of distinguished success!

XXXIX

REBECCA GOES TO LONDON

YORK HOTEL
ALBEMARLE STREET, LONDON W.
September 8, 1912

DEAR GEORGE:

It is a week to-morrow since "Rebecca's" first night in London, and yet I have not had a single moment in which to tell you any event of the days before, or of the day itself.

You may wonder what I have been doing during this week, but, for one thing, I had sixty-two telegrams, from Germany, France, Italy, Brittany, Switzerland, Scotland, and all parts of England. These were, of course, not from strangers, but from Geraldine Farrar in Munich, the Robinson-Smiths in Paris, Edward Riggs in Florence, the Findlaters in Devonshire, and so on and so on.

To begin at the beginning, I had asked Mr. Nevill, of Bramall Hall, to come and stay at this hotel on the Monday of the play, and he wrote saying that he wanted a week-end in London and would arrive on Friday.

Cousin Whitney Shepardson arrived from Oxford on Saturday night, and Henry Johnstone, on the way from France to Edinburgh, came on Monday morning. Ellen Terry's telegram from her country place enlivened the day: "I have taken four seats for your first night. Good luck to it! I loved it in New York and feel certain of its instant success in Old Smoky!" Another delightful figure in the house-party, and a most unexpected one, was old Lady Constance Leslie. You will remember her as a friend and contemporary of Thackeray, and, indeed, of all the great people of her day and this. She intended to pass the night and go to the play with Mrs. Jordan Mott, who, however, was weather-bound on a yacht off the coast of Holland. Lady Constance wrote me from Brighton in apparently such a disappointed mood that I telegraphed back asking her if she would not dine and sleep as my guest at this hotel and go to the play with our party. She telegraphed an acceptance and arrived after tea with her maid. She had offered to send the maid to her own empty house in Manchester Square, but, when I bethought myself that my guest was over eighty, and Lord Beresford's cousin or sister (I forget which), I handsomely engaged two bedrooms on the ground floor of the hotel, and told her to let her maid remain with her, for all which she seemed as grateful and pleased as if she were not a great personage.

The house-party sat down to dinner at seven o'clock, and a more delightful old darling than the same Lady Constance could not be found in the world. She and Henry Johnstone kept the table alive with good anecdotes. One of hers was that she met a lady at a bazaar in a dimly lighted room and told her that her face was so familiar she felt she ought to speak to her, although she could not remember her name. The lady laughed and replied, "I am the Queen!" Queen Mary has sent for her twice since this episode, and says it was so delightful to be asked her name, just as if she had one!

It is needless to say that I could eat nothing, and heard the conversation only as if it were being uttered at a long distance. Mary Anderson (Madame de Navarro), and her son had offered to come to the hotel to dine and spend the night if they would be of any comfort to me in the great undertaking, but I asked her to await me in her box at the theater. Think of her beautiful kindness in journeying from Broadway, in Worcestershire, to encourage an American friend!

The house was full. I do not know who comprised the audience, for I recognized only fifteen or twenty out of the twelve hundred. Mr. Nevill, Mr. Johnstone, Whitney, Lady Constance, Ellen and Marion Terry sat together as my guests in the orchestra stalls.

One of the most touching things to me was the presence of my devoted secretary, Miss Minnie Alford, who had gathered her six sisters from Manchester, Brighton, Hove, and Tunbridge Wells, so that seven loyal Englishwomen sat together in the front row of the balcony to witness the first night of my American play.

The performance went without a hitch, and every act was welcomed with real appreciation and enthusiasm. There were many recalls in each act, and so many calls for the author at the end that I stepped behind the scenes from my box, as Mr. Brooks had planned, if necessary, and appeared through the curtains for two recalls, one of them with "Rebecca." I refused to make even the briefest speech, and, when I think of the attitude of many newspapers next day, I can never be sufficiently thankful that I was as modest as any violet could possibly be, although the attitude of the first-night house, its enthusiasm and applause, would have justified anybody in momentary conceit. Edith, as "Rebecca" made a decided personal success — that was evident from the start. "Uncle Jerry" and "Aunt Miranda" did just what we expected them to do, repeated all their American successes, and called forth loud praise on every side. There was not, indeed, a weak spot in the cast.

I had refused two or three invitations to supper, because Mary Anderson had announced her intention of supping with me and drinking my health, so I made all arrangements to come back here to the hotel. I offered nothing in the way of refreshments but champagne, chosen by Mr. Nevill, and various kinds of dainty sandwiches, preceded by cups of hot consommé. There were four small round tables, and the guests were my house-party, also Marion Terry, Mary Anderson and her son, Henry Van Duzer and his niece from New York, Elsie de Wolfe and Gertrude Robinson-Smith, of New York, "Rebecca's" manager, Mr. Joseph Brooks, and Sir Hugh and Lady Bell, who had come five hours by train from their country house for the performance. They stayed only a short half-hour, and, after a few minutes' private talk with my three men guests (who called themselves the "bodyguard"), all went to bed a trifle after midnight.

At this moment all that is pleasurable about the affair ends abruptly. Cousin Whitney gathered all the morning newspapers before nine, and, when we met in my sitting-room for breakfast (Lady Constance being served in her bedroom downstairs), they were as choice a collection of bad reviews as I should suppose ever greeted a playwright's eye. The "Morning Post," which, perhaps, is the most distinguished paper of the lot, gave nothing but unstinted praise, and the "Telegraph," next most important, though mingling praise and blame, gave a wholly delightful and appreciative review to which nobody could object. The others seemed to dislike the play with such violence that I wonder they were able to sit in the theater. The afternoon papers were nearly as unsympathetic as those of the morning, and I was in a fine state of anguish by six o'clock.

Mercifully the house-party had all gone. Lady Constance departed at eleven in the morning, all the gentlemen having fallen head over heels in love with her. She is afraid of taxis and ordered a four-wheeler. Leaning out of the window before she drove off, she said to Mr. Nevill: "I think perhaps Mrs. Riggs would be interested to know how much I wished to do her honor at this time, so I must tell you that, although I am nearly eighty years old, this is the first night that I have ever passed in a London hotel!" (The house where all her married life was spent, and where her children were born, is Stafford House, a magnificent mansion in the fashionable center of London. I have been there many times during its tenancy by her married daughter, but it has now fallen into other hands. Its ceilings are decorated by Angelica Kauffmann, and all the interior decoration is by the Adam brothers.)

Whitney and H. J. left, one for Cornwall and the other for Edinburgh at four, and Mr. Nevill for Bramall at four-thirty, whereupon I sank on the bed in my darkened room, and wondered why I was ever born. I took some comfort in thinking that bringing the play to London was not my suggestion, and that I never urged it for a single moment; also that I thought, from the beginning, criticism might be very severe; but I had not the smallest idea it would be so patronizing in tone. They say that plays by women are seldom reviewed with anything but condescension here, and it is idle to pretend that American plays are sympathetically regarded at the moment. However, I do not believe personally, and never did, in these forms of antagonism. If it had been a better play, it would have overcome the peculiar form of aversion it seemed to evoke from the critics, but it chanced to be the very sort of thing which had positively no charm for them, although it had for nine hundred critics out of a thousand in America. These appear to dislike the rural districts of America and everything pertaining to them, although I've never had anything but praise in England for my books, as you will remember.

At half-past ten the next night, Miss Virginia Brooks (daughter of my manager) called at the hotel and asked me if I would not drive to the Globe Theater where she was going with her father. I stoutly refused at first, feeling that I never wanted to see that spot again, but finally yielded. We entered the place, my tottering feet almost refusing to support me as we opened the glass doors that commanded a view of the audience. I expected to see several people sleeping here and there in the stalls, and an actor or so wandering in a melancholy way across the stage. What was my surprise to find the house seven eighths full and as delighted and responsive an audience as one could desire.

The applause and the recalls for the actors were as warm as on the preceding night, and so it has occurred at every performance this week. The upper circle, dress circle, and pit are always filled; the stalls only one third. This is the case in September in many theaters, because the "stall audience" is out of town, but I think very likely that "Rebecca" will not make a large appeal in London to those persons who pay half a guinea a seat.

A charming telegram from Sir Arthur Pinero arrived this morning and greatly cheered me:

> Thank you for a very happy evening. My wife and I were charmed and moved by your tender play and by the acting of the ladies and gentlemen engaged in it. "Rebecca" and her friends will always hold a place in our memories.
>
> ARTHUR PINERO

I must remember that up to this time Rebecca has been one of the happiest experiences of my life. Never a difference of opinion with the managers, Klaw and Erlanger, and Mr. Joseph Brooks; the closest friendships with the players in both companies, the support of the public in greater measure than any one could possibly have predicted. I should be able to bear a slight disappointment with philosophy.

KATE

The dramatization of my first book, "The Birds' Christmas Carol," [1] has much the same appeal as "Rebecca," and was not made until I had been besieged for years by requests from Jew and Greek, bond and free, for permission to make such a version, the writers frequently accompanying their pleas with manuscripts somewhat more notable for bulk than for value.

The "Ruggleses' Dinner-Party" had long been played by amateurs before my own more finished effort appeared in print, and it was given in Cambridge at one time amid great hilarity by a company of Harvard Professors, nine of whom took the parts of the Ruggles children from Sarah Maud down to Larry, while the famous historian, John Fiske, honored me by impersonating Mrs. Ruggles.

[1] Dramatic version. Houghton Mifflin Company.

It was again given in Cambridge in 1900 by the boys and young men of the Perkins Institution for the Blind, who made their own dramatization, printed it in raised letters, and played it most delightfully.

From that time on my own version has been continuously played in the small and large towns of almost every State in the Union, sometimes entire, and sometimes in selected scenes.

My latest excursion into comparatively untrodden fields — perhaps it has been an *in*cursion — is my dramatizing for country churches my book, "The Old Peabody Pew."

Our Dorcas Society, as the reader knows, beginning as a tiny acorn, had grown into an oak tree of considerable size and beauty. The historic old meeting-house on Tory Hill had been badly in need of repair, and our efforts for several seasons had been devoted to its rehabilitation; new shingles, clapboards, bell-tower, painting within and without, new blinds, furnace, piano, and at last carpets; but at a certain moment the treasury became empty and the repainting of the pews was an impossibility. At a meeting of carpet-sewers in the church, a valiant spirit suggested, as a humble compromise, the scrubbing of the pews. The idea was received with laughter and applause. A meeting was appointed forthwith, and an amendment to include a picnic-luncheon was enthusiastically carried. I never recall a merrier or more exhilarating October morning than the one when the Dorcas members scrubbed the pews of the Tory Hill Meeting-House at Buxton Lower Corner. After the workers had dispersed, I sat in the quiet church, waiting for the old horse and carry-all to take me on its second trip down the hills that led to home. The afternoon sun shone in the open doors drying the sweet, clean, soap-scented pews, and all at once a story took shape in my mind. The Dorcas members made a background, and then the pew in

which I sat filled slowly with personages that fitted themselves into their rightful places, personages that had to do
with a love-story begun long ago, in which the youth and
maiden were separated for a dozen years; a story that had
its happy end, as it had had its beginning, under the shelter
of the old steeple. I closed my eyes and dreamed it out,
even to naming the hero and heroine Justin Peabody and
Nancy Wentworth. They wrote themselves down unbidden, and the story of "The Old Peabody Pew" was almost
finished and dedicated to the Dorcas Society before I left
the church. It was pure fiction, but it gained a wider hearing from being connected with a specific place. Passers-by
(the meeting-house stands on a shady common where seven
roads meet) soon began to demand that the sexton should
show the Peabody Pew, and were disappointed — even
resentful — when told that there really wasn't any!

This popular and growing belief regarding the existence
of a real pew, in which a real family of Peabodys once sat,
shows how easily a myth is made. In vain do I say, and
repeatedly say, that I selected the name of Peabody solely
because it did not occur in the church records; in spite of
these protests summer motoring parties continue to arrive
at the old meeting-house in pilgrim mood and decline to
believe that they have not reached the desired shrine.

Several years ago, when groping for an idea by which to
earn money for our village enterprises, I determined to
make a play of the book, a play that could be done in any
old country meeting-house, without sacrificing the reverence due to a consecrated building or rousing the least
opposition from the most orthodox parishioner. To this
end I abolished all thought of stage, scenery, curtain, or
theatrical lighting. We pushed the pulpit back close to
the wall, and the platform, the right and left "wing pews"
(one of which was supposed to be the Peabody Pew), the

two aisles up and down which the players made their
entrances and exits — these were my substitutes for all
the myriad aids of the theater.

The church bell, rung by the sexton to quiet the audience and herald the opening of the acts, was our only orchestra. Our only music was a hymn of long ago, "By Cool
Siloam's Shady Rill," that chanced to be a vital part of the
original love-story. If we had been a company of geniuses
trained to the height of our powers, we might have tri-
umphed by sheer audacity when thrown thus upon our
own resources, but we were wholly untrained and we had
no audacity.

"Very well," I said, with a sinking heart, as we began
the first rehearsal, "we cannot hope to produce an illusion,
under the circumstances, so we will simply try to present
a piece of life. Remember, now, not a trace of effort, of
artifice, of self-consciousness! There is to be no make-
believe about this performance; it is to be the real thing!"
(I concealed from the cast the fact that the presentation
of "the real thing" has difficulties peculiar to itself!)

Our players belonged to the village, and their work was
the voicing of the community spirit which for twelve or
fifteen years we had been fostering in every possible way.
Their performance was a miracle of simplicity and directness, and the response on the part of audience after audience was overwhelming in its manifest delight and breathless interest.

I should never have attempted an afternoon performance of the play had there not been so great a demand from
the visitors at the various summer resorts — twenty and
even thirty miles distant; for I was certain that the glam-
our of the evening lights had bridged our difficulties, concealed our weaknesses, and helped to give the atmosphere
that had seemed in evidence on all previous occasions. Lo

and behold! the garish light of the summer day, streaming in at ten huge windows, each with its three dozen seven-by-nine panes of glass, had no damaging effect at all.

Lack of scenery, of theatrical make-up, of numberless aids of ordinary stage production — their absence apparently made the heart grow fonder, for the audiences laughed more freely and wept more copiously in the afternoon than in the evening performances. My cast seemed to be an aggregation of stars, but I never claimed, and they certainly never did, that they could have played "Camille" or "Diplomacy." I am also quite sure that the same effect could never be achieved in the vast spaces of a handsomely cushioned city church, with vestibule, organ-loft, baptismal font, altar painting, and stained-glass windows. I wrote the play for old-fashioned country meeting-houses, and that is where it belongs. It was for that reason I tried to keep the humor wholesome, genial, and discreet, letting it circle about church and ministerial activities with only good-natured retorts and pleasantries that left no sting behind them. My Dorcas Society talked no scandal, you may be sure, though it did discuss the foibles of men-folks, "widders" and old maids, deacons, ministers, and ministers' wives.

One of the obvious weaknesses of the play is that, because we were debarred from change of scene and costume, I had to read from the book a carefully arranged prelude to the first act, perhaps five minutes in length, and an interlude of perhaps ten minutes before the second act, to inform the audience concerning the youthful love-story of Justin and Nancy and prepare them for the romantic reunion that was to take place in the church after the supposed lapse of ten years. These readings, brief though they were, ought by rights to have killed any play; but "The Old Peabody Pew" had the resistance of iron or leather. The complete printed version of the play only fails to please when an elocutionist of the aggressive type does the reading and usurps the center of the stage that should belong to the players.

The dramatization of "Mother Carey's Chickens," in which I had the coöperation of Miss Rachel Crothers, was my next effort. It had a wonderfully good cast of my own choosing, headed by Edith Taliaferro, the dainty, exquisite little fairy who played my Rebecca all over the United States and in London. My Mother Carey was a beautiful woman, my Osh Popham a genial and delightful comedian, my Cousin Ann perfection; indeed, each player seemed born for his character. The first performance was given in Poughkeepsie, and it played a whole season in the large cities on tour, before opening for a six weeks' engagement at the Cort Theater, New York, in September, 1917.

After touring again for a season, it appeared in stock here and there, for several years, but its career was continually hampered by bad financial management and ill-advised bookings. The critics were uniformly kind, calling it a "Peg o' My Heart," a "Rebecca multiplied by four," and other pleasant names. I loved it myself and all the dear people in it, and semi-occasionally paid their salaries when nobody else would or could.

Adventures in play-making, that is what "Rebecca of Sunnybrook Farm," "The Birds' Christmas Carol," "Mother Carey's Chickens," and "The Old Peabody Pew" have been; just innocent escapades, indulged in to vary any monotony that might creep into a literary life. There was the intoxication of a new interest, a fresh method of work, of putting things into unaccustomed forms, a renewal of mental energy, an indescribable joy in a novel task. An author is never able to watch people laughing, crying, or sleeping over his book; he never sees them enchanted or bored with it before his very eyes; he never knows whether he has pleased the public, or how greatly, save through the reviews, the publishers' semi-annual statements, and the number of letters he receives. With a play, on the other hand, he is able to realize the results of his efforts from minute to minute. He may sit in the shadow of a box and watch the faces of his unconscious critics — pleased, friendly, delighted, absorbed. He may even stand in the foyer, and if his play is a success he knows every few moments what scene is being enacted, and how it is being received. He can hear the laughter, gentle or uproarious, the impetuous applause following an exit, the sudden eruption of handkerchiefs, as if influenza had overtaken the audience. He knows when the laughs and the tears come, and what lines and situations provoke them. Oh! what rapture, when all is well with the play, the players, and the management, which it might as well be confessed happens very seldom for any length of time. Nevertheless, the fascination persists in foul as well as in fair weather.

The adventures, even of a modest playwright, are markedly different from those of an author.

For instance, when His Excellency Earl Grey was Governor-General of Canada, he conceived the idea of encouraging an interest in music and the drama throughout the Dominion by bringing together amateur dramatic societies from the principal cities of British North America. An important part of the plan was to provide an opportunity for the members of various clubs to make one another's acquaintance and to acquire a feeling of affection and loyalty for the Federal City of Ottawa.

Accordingly ten dramatic and musical organizations presented themselves to compete for Earl Grey's trophy, a large bronze group of figures representing Comedy and

Tragedy, which, by the way, after the competitions were over, was awarded to the Winnipeg Club.

The performances were given in the principal theater of the city on every evening of the week of January 29, 1907, and I had been chosen, most unexpectedly, by His Excellency as one of the judges in the competition, the far more discriminating ones being Langdon Mitchell, the dramatist, of Philadelphia, and George W. Chadwick, of Boston, the musician and composer.

We were all guests of Government House for the week, and every description of delightful entertainment suitable for a Canadian winter was given us. A replica of Earl Grey's trophy, presented by His Excellency, now adorns a shelf in my study and serves to remind me of a delightful and unique experience.

An author may forget a book the week after it is published, but a play once produced can never be out of mind for a day until it has finished its prosperous journey, or been peacefully interred in the theatrical storehouse. A book is a solid, corporeal fact, but a play is a quicksilver sort of thing that indulges in sudden unexpected, mysterious, unaccountable changes. It seems to present one aspect in Buffalo, and another in Boston. They may love it in Pittsburgh, and loathe it in Peoria; the critics praise it in Syracuse, and revile it in Schenectady. It seems better than it really is when the players are well, happy, and delighted with their several parts, and worse than it really is when they are not. It is better on Fridays than on Mondays; on Saturday matinées than on Wednesdays; and although it may have faults it is always a perfectly delightful play when the "Standing Room Only" sign decorates the outside of the theater, giving a style and distinction to the sidewalk that no other placard in the world possesses. And this, mind you, is really not so much because the box-office is prosperous as because it means eager, sympathetic, responsive audiences, who almost make and unmake plays at will. Audiences themselves really do need a little educating, I must confess. They sometimes laugh too boisterously, and laugh in the wrong places: they weep at bathos more readily than at pathos; but we must remember that they would not have a chance to weep at bathos if we did not give it to them.

When people are bored with simple, straightforward material, it is because the true simplicity, which is the highest art, has not been achieved; because we have not the genius to be human and universal and thus appeal to the common mind and heart. Audiences are not stone-blind. It is merely that we who write for them have not seen the vision clearly enough ourselves to make them see it in turn. They are not deaf. It is simply that our particular message has not been framed so that it will reach their ears.

There is one quality possessed by every writer who has the world with him: it is the infectious spirit of enthusiasm. Would that we all had it! There are some who possess the magic touch; who have the same effect as a beautiful morning that never reaches noon. Under their spell one's mind is braced, one's spirit re-created; one is ready for any adventure, even if it only be the doing of the next distasteful task light-heartedly. Heaven send us more such writers!

XL

"ENTERTAINING STRANGERS"

THE season from October to April always brings a succession of distinguished and interesting playwrights, musicians, novelists, essayists, and poets to New York. They come to see America; but of course they must know beforehand that they are likely to get only a glimpse of so vast a country. Few of them can spare the time, it appears, to travel from the rock-bound coast of Maine through the Middle States, the Middle-Western, and from thence to California, that garden spot of America on the Pacific Coast. They go to cosmopolitan New York, as Americans go to London, to take what is offered in the way of different climate, customs, food, and pleasures, and they expect, no doubt, or should expect, a variety of disappointments and disillusions. The writers among them commonly visit the large private schools for girls and boys, and the colleges and universities where they are invited to lecture or read their poems, and thus become somewhat acquainted with our young people and our educational systems. All this is, I hope, of some use to them, and I am sure it is salutary for us, whether we are praised or censured in the volumes that naturally result from a series of new experiences in a hitherto unknown country.

There were many delightful seasons when we were "not forgetful to entertain strangers," from 1909, when my Rebecca play gave me such continuous and unspeakable pleasure, up to the winter of 1914. New York hospitality is always generous, and especially so, if talent or genius is to be seen, heard, or known. This eagerness of hospitality is often misunderstood, especially when the nerves and digestion of the grateful recipient happen to break down under the strain. It comes largely from a keen desire on the part of the public to meet and know a person who has enriched by his art, in one way or another, hundreds of lives. They have read his books, seen his pictures, heard him sing or play; they may never wander with him on his native heath, or dine with him at his own table; now is the opportunity to penetrate into something beyond the novel, the poem, or the painting, to get a closer touch, and to show by their presence in his audiences their respect, admiration, and enthusiasm.

Nobody supposes that thousands of dwellers in Michigan or Minnesota went to hear John Masefield and John Drinkwater read their own poems because it involved any social aggrandizement, nor because they were empty-minded and craved pleasure. They knew the author in his books, and they longed to get still nearer to him.

I had met many distinguished persons in London in earlier years, but I was now only too glad to meet others, to renew my old acquaintances, and return some of the favors bestowed upon me in England.

During our various winters as householders in New York, we have been privileged to entertain, at one time or another, Rudyard Kipling, Mrs. Craigie (John Oliver Hobbes), Mrs. L. B. Walford, Mrs. W. K. Clifford, and Lady Gregory; in a later group, Mrs. Humphry Ward and her sister Ethel Arnold, Mary and Jane Findlater, Ian Maclaren, May Sinclair, Sir Herbert Beerbohm Tree, Sir John Hare, Sir Johnston and Lady Forbes-Robertson, Lord and Lady Aberdeen, Geraldine Farrar, and, still later, John Masefield, Lord Dunsany, Alfred Noyes, John Drinkwater, Hugh Walpole, and scores of others.

I remember especially Miss Ellen Terry's return to New

York, this time only for talks on Shakespeare's Women and for illustrative recitations.

How regal and how beautiful she looked in her white draperies, worn as no other woman ever wore them. I recall in this connection driving home in a hansom from an Irving-Terry performance in London with Sir Frederick Leighton, who had designed the costumes of the principal characters in the play. He sighed, as he leaned back in his corner, and said: "After planning things for Ellen Terry, I cannot bear fiddling with lesser women's clothes. They simply put them on, but she *wears* them. Great Heaven! how she wears them!"

I saw very much of her during the winter of 1910–11, attending her talks in New York, and often going out of town with her on an engagement near by. She had many kinds of gay, irresponsible ways that made her presence ever more and more endearing. She had a notion, for instance, of bringing two or three roses when she came to call, always in a small vase with a little water.

Entering my apartment unexpectedly with her floral tribute, she once said: "Penelope, you have lived in this place ten years, and yet they do not appear to know you. I have asked four times of the doormen and lift-boys, and they have never so much as heard of Penelope. They denied that such a woman had ever lived here. 'Take me up in the lift,' I said, scornfully, 'and I think I shall know her door!' I did; and as I passed into the apartment, I looked back with disdain, while they remarked, rudely: 'You didn't mention Mrs. Riggs. We *do* know her.'"

On another occasion she took me to the theater, as she often did when she was not on the bill, as on the nights when Sir Henry played "Louis XI," or "The Bells." She always sat in the front row, by the way, a place which I should never occupy from choice.

"Why do you always like to be so near, Miss Terry?" I asked one evening. "What becomes of your illusions when you sit in these seats?"

"Ah, Penelope," she answered, "I never have any trouble about keeping my illusions. I always take 'em along with me!"

And so she did and still does until the present moment!

Her difficulty in remembering the lines of her part was always a trial to her. She used to hide various cues and speeches, so she said, in the workbaskets, flower vases, stuffed chairs, or under the sofa-pillows; but a new anxiety arose from the necessity of remembering where she had placed them. Names of characters easily escaped her, also.

"When I call the hero 'Mr. Thingumajig,' in 'Captain Brassbound's Conversion,' it doesn't make much difference," she said; "it may even pass for a pleasantry; but when we revived 'The Merry Wives of Windsor' with such success, and I could never remember the names of the other two wives, being obliged repeatedly to accost them as 'Mrs. What-do-you-call-'em?' the effect was anything but Shakespearean and I was thoroughly ashamed."

I remember that I once asked Mrs. Kendal, who played one of the "merry wives" in the great revival, why the company didn't give Miss Terry her cues.

"Oh! it would have been quite confusing," she answered. "Miss Terry knew that the prompter, at least, would rescue her in course of time. She very seldom makes disastrous lapses, and the audience always adores her — whether she forgets for a moment, or remembers. Ellen Terrys are not subject to common laws."

At the end of Miss Terry's lecture-season in America, she was tendered a dinner by five or six hundred of her admirers. (No building in New York would have held all who loved her!)

I was one of those privileged to respond to a toast at this dinner; and I repeat it here, not for its own significance, but as a tribute to an artist of unparalleled charm:

"We are saying good-bye to that elixir of sunbeams labeled by her parents, Ellen Terry. She is going home to England. Her heart may be beating with anticipation, but her American friends will miss her sadly. I confess that a country having ninety-five millions of people and no Ellen Terry in it seems a foolish sort of a place, a little dull and not quite well furnished. Going home! Do you remember that scene in 'The Vicar of Wakefield' where Olivia, after her lover leaves her, is waiting alone in the coffee-room of the old inn? Do you remember the oak bench against the wall and the map of England hanging over it? Then you will recall the beautiful moment when this Olivia (was there ever another?) used to float across the width of the room, alight on the bench, and point with a happy finger to that sheltered, that forgiving, that protecting spot on the map which stood for home. No one who saw it could ever forget it. Was it a wave of the sea, a bird on a bough, a butterfly on a bending lily-stalk? Did muscles that move the ordinary being carry her through space? Such loveliness does not stop at the eye; its eloquence ravishes the senses and touches the heart like some perfect line of Keats or Shelley.

" 'She walks in beauty like the night' might have been said of every one of the matchless women in Ellen Terry's portrait gallery. We too seldom say it nowadays, alas! for the raiment prescribed in modern drama altogether forbids 'walking in beauty.' The 'poetry of motion' is fast becoming hobbled prose!

"Mrs. Patrick Campbell said of her performance in 'Imogen': 'When she entered, I felt she had come from the moon. No one has ever had her magical step — that extraordinary happy haste that makes you feel she must presently arrive at the gates of Paradise.' "

As an impersonator of Shakespeare's women, if Miss Terry was not that immovable post, perfection, she was "a dancing sprig of the tree growing beside it." She was a reed through which all things blew into music. I have never made up my mind which was the more potent quality in her Juliet, her Viola, her Beatrice, or her Portia: was it art, or was it *heart?* Mere intellect, histrionic ambition, fine technique, could never have produced these women: they could only have been conceived in love.

She always made me think of Wordsworth's Nightingale. There are plenty of actresses to essay the Stockdove in the poem, but few "earth-born, Heaven-fallen stars" to play the Nightingale, that "creature of a fiery heart" who

> "Sang as if the god of wine
> Had helped him to a Valentine."

Miss Terry's art was never dazzling, like the diamond. It was a lovable, luminous, iridescent thing, compounded of sunshine and dew, for there was an invisible fountain playing in her heart that kept everything about her cool and sweet and fresh. There was nothing cut and dried, nothing academic about it: it seemed all radiant spontaneity. It had in it the essence of the bubble and the rainbow, and of all things filmy and fair.

In this wise I set down my little tribute of love and fealty this afternoon, and when I saw the words written in black and white I was suddenly overcome with a sense of their banality and futility. Into this mood came the suggestion of a poet-friend — not at all like healing balm — rather like the prick of a spur; and here it is, in rhyme most informal, made on his model:

> One morning when snow had been falling all night,
> Walking out after breakfast I saw an odd sight —
> A grave-looking man somewhat strangely equipped
> With a pot of white paint and a brush, which he dipped
> In the paint very often, and swept to and fro,
> In the hope, he assured me, of whitening the snow.

> A day or two after I met on the strand
> A lady who carried a bag in her hand;
> A bag full of salt which, she told me, she shook
> From the tails of the birds that her gardener took:
> "And I need every grain I can get," added she,
> "For the purpose of properly salting the sea."

One Midsummer Day when the sun in the skies
Was shining superbly and blinding men's eyes,
I found a small boy with twelve tapers a-row
And twelve polished mirrors poised neatly below,
Who asked my approval for what he had done
With the praiseworthy object of brightening the sun.

So, by devious ways I arrive at my goal,
For these tasks so superfluous, seen on my stroll, —
This of whitening the snow, this of salting the sea,
This of brightening the sun when 'twas bright as could be,
This plating fine gold, or this reddening the cherry, —
Are precisely like trying to praise Ellen Terry!

The winters that I have chronicled in this chapter were
not all play by any means, though few manuscripts ever
issued from our New York dwellings; but somehow, in off-
seasons, came "The Story of Waitstill Baxter" (1913),
"Penelope's Postscripts" (1915), "The Romance of a
Christmas Card" (1916), "Ladies-in-Waiting" (1919; a
collection of tales hitherto unpublished in book form), and
several short stories in magazines.

My interest in Free Kindergartens, Babies' Hospitals,
Crippled Children, Improved Tenements, and so on, continued unabated; but I longed for something especially my
own to add to my work for these causes, and my body of
girl-readers found it for me. One day came an eager request
from the English Department of a Girls' High School for
me to come and read some of my own stories at the morning
assembly in the great auditorium. Eleven o'clock was the
hour appointed, and thirty minutes the time allotted to
me, though, as it happened, I was urged to go on and read
for twice that time.

Every girl in the school naturally went home and reported that an author had been reading extracts from her
own books to the school, and every principal who heard it
immediately wrote and asked if I would not come to his or

her girls or boys. I read most frequently at High Schools, and I freely confess that it is with great trepidation that I approach boys. Truth to say, I have only a few selections fitted to amuse and edify them; so girls from twelve to sixteen form the major portion of my audiences. The girls invariably complain when two or three hundred youths are thrust into our assembly by some English master, because they say that I pay so much more attention to the boys than to them. It is quite true, although I did not imagine it was obvious; but I am secretly terrified by youthful persons of the male sex — afraid of not pleasing them, knowing that a great inventor, explorer, or aviator could give them the needful things. I try to select something of mine most humorous, most universal, most human, however, and endeavor by my manner to show them my spirit of comradeship.

In this way an entirely new calling has been opened in my life, one that has a hundred voices and appeals in a hundred different ways. There seems to be no other free-will offering, for me, at least, that is so useful and so much appreciated. Many authors are so prolific that they have no leisure to devote to such tasks; many of them have not sufficient voice; others, writers of books much greater than any I have achieved, have no place in the school libraries, where all of mine are read to tatters; others have had no experience with young people, and thus do not find the audience ready and waiting to welcome them. So, once every two or three weeks, from October to May, I read for half an hour, sometimes to an audience of twelve hundred, sometimes to two thousand, and I find these occasions heart-warming and exhilarating beyond words. They are fruitful, too, so the teachers assure me, for when I read my own experience, "A Child's Journey with Dickens," the pupils take "David Copperfield," "Great Expectations," or "Pickwick Papers" from the library for the first time, and there is a run on the ever-beloved writer.

It is true also that the readings of an author from his own books give these children and young people a more vital touch with literature in general. I can hardly explain why it is, but it infuses a new ambition into the writing of themes and gives a fresh impetus to reading in general. It would need the word of some spectator on these occasions to describe the warmth, affection, and heartiness of applause that greet my coming. It would seem egotistical if I should write of even a fraction of the scenes of delight that have been my happy portion these last few years. There have been triumphal arches, flower-decked rooms, K.D.W. Clubs, with special banners, badges, and decorations, five or six hundred boys at railway stations to meet me, school bands playing marches composed for the occasion by the Musical Director; cheers for the school, cheers for the day, and cheers for K.D.W. — all the school windows open and crowded with heads of boys and girls shouting "Welcome."

A flower-trimmed motor car meets the train, or my taxi, if it is a town school, and great personages in the way of Class Presidents hang to the vehicle in all sorts of perilous positions, I, between laughter and tears, trying to keep the frolic within some sort of proportion; the effect to the ignorant bystander being that it is General Joffre, or Clemenceau, who is being welcomed to a grateful country.

I think the fact that I have been a teacher in past years, though only of four-year-olds, gives me a ready friendship with all teachers; and at all school assemblies the Faculty, twelve or thirty strong, sits on the platform behind me. I shall never forget, nor cease to be grateful for the opportunity of meeting these armies of young readers and teachers,

WELCOMES AT PUBLIC SCHOOLS

thousands upon thousands in number. I have never had anything but beautiful and heart-warming welcomes at the seventy-five schools where I have been a visitor; and had I space I would print the name of each, that its Principal and students might know that what I said to them in gratitude at the time we met is just as fresh in my memory now as then, for I see, looking backward, each individual group, and recall the events of the morning.

Even if the publishers have to put in an extra leaf, however, I must record my twenty years' friendship with the Maxwell Training School for Teachers, in Brooklyn, where Miss Emma Johnston, one of the noblest women and most influential teachers in America, directs an enormous body of students, to whom for some reason I seem to belong, as a sort of school Godmother. Next in affection comes the Wadleigh High School in New York where I am the official Valentine and read every year in February; and very close to this come the Washington Irving and Julia Richman High Schools.

Newtown High School at Elmshurst, Long Island, is perhaps the most remarkable among my scenes of activity. I shall recall to the end of my days the receptions of such unparalleled triumphs there as were probably never showered on any other head, deserving or undeserving, for they are poetic and musical and artistic and dramatic (as well as energetic) at Newtown, and when they invite anybody to come and do something for them, they go into retirement themselves, like Cicero in his tent at Tusculum, and invent the programme for the day. The results may not be quoted here; but their beauty and originality are beyond belief.

So I here write down my devotion to all the thousands of young people whom I have met in this delightful way, and pay especial homage to the spirit of the schools I have chanced to know best. There are hundreds of others on my waiting list, and every one of them will, I am sure, give me a beautiful and helpful experience when I am privileged to visit them.

XLI

THE HEART OF THE HOME

AMONG our many happy winters, there was one beyond measure sorrowful, for in February, 1921, we lost our dearly beloved mother. She had passed her ninety-first birthday, so we ought perhaps to have been content with so long a possession of her love; but she was of all friends the dearest, the closest, and most loyal, the object of our hourly thought and care, the focus of our little family life; so that when she went, a great deal of what we were, or had been, seemed at first to go with her. She had leaned on us in everything, why then should we suddenly have felt that we had nothing ourselves on which to lean? Never, in all the vicissitudes of life had she once failed us. In seasons of prosperity she bore herself with modest pride, but in adversity she had been full of courage.

She had extraordinary personality; I think I never knew a woman in the least like her. She was rather below medium size, while her charming figure, her exquisite coloring, her regular features, and wealth of wavy brown hair made her very good to look upon. She loved pretty clothes up to the very last, though she rigidly objected to anything "too young" or "too conspicuous." I remember during her very last summer she said to me: "Kate, my clothes are so *dull* this season! I should think I might have had just a sparkle of jet on my black ones and some fringe or lace on my gray."

She was a very whirlwind of activity until a serious lameness in her later years confined her many hours a day to a wheel chair. But even then she was never idle; mending, sewing, doing all sorts of embroidery on linen, and wool-work on canvas, knitting, crocheting, basket-making, and delighting in any new sort of employment that could be brought her from the art shops. She took some pride in my sister's neat plain sewing, but sorrowed over the fact that she had brought forth in me such a failure in handiwork.

During the War I sat by her side knitting mufflers, asking her continually to count my stitches or turn a corner for me.

At such moments she sometimes said: "It seems as if no person of your intelligence could really be so stupid and clumsy, Kate!" At which remark we all laughed, I most heartily of all.

My afghans for War Babies were subjected to the same criticism. She hoped they would reach only the lower classes of infants, they were so rough, uneven, and ill-made. "The Red Cross will never accept them, and at any rate be sure and don't put your name on them," she said.

She was very reserved, and though eagerly interested in life and in people, and pouring out love and interest in our work, she was always chary of compliments. After her death my sister and I read with tears an old letter sent to us by a friend, one that she had written during a visit away from home.

"A. and G." (ran a postscript) "think their oldest son a musical prodigy and their two daughters of eighteen and twenty, brilliant beyond compare. I say nothing, but I only wish the poor things could see my boy and my two girls!"

She was an omnivorous reader of the best current magazines and books of all sorts. Just why she always read carefully and in its entirety the column of deaths in the Boston newspapers she could never quite explain. I was fond of quoting to her the saying of an elderly country neighbor who declared that she had given up taking a local

MRS. BRADBURY
Mother of the Author

newspaper, "The Biddeford Journal," because it had so few deaths in it!

She was upright and downright in her speech and truthful to a really painful degree, for she didn't like a word added to a good story. If she happened to be the subject of it herself, she would say, "I allow that there was something ludicrous about the incident, but when Kate gets through with it, though everybody will laugh, they'll never know what really happened!"

Oh! what a miracle of neatness and tidiness and order she was; and how she instilled into us from childhood her instinct for good housekeeping! And what a capital cook she was of New England dishes! I can see her even at eighty-eight, trundled into our great country kitchen to make the filling for her own currant pie, a marvelous piece of culinary art that brought her unfailing applause. When the table was spread for a picnic, rows of seven or eight persons would shout in chorus: "We want to sit near Mrs. Bradbury's currant pie!" and mother would beam with delight.

After she reached the age of eighty we made great celebrations of her birthday (February 6th). A matinée was always her choice for the afternoon, usually one where her favorites were acting, notably Mrs. Fiske or Margaret Anglin, with whom we had a personal acquaintance. I am almost certain that the afternoon of her eighty-ninth birthday was passed at a play and at any rate those of the years from eighty to eighty-eight were generally so spent. Oftentimes the star told some of the company that a lady in her eighties had chosen their play for her birthday treat and that they would see her in an aisle seat with a cane by her side.

I used to whisper, "Keep your cane well in evidence, mother, and look as old as you can, for I am afraid they will take me for you!" After having her cloak arranged she would put on her glasses and open the programme; then with a deep breath of satisfaction she would say: "It is in four acts; I am so glad; there will be more of it!"

She was a good audience to play to, to sing to, to read to, because she was extraordinarily full of appreciation and an eager and responsive listener, while she had a remarkable gift of reading aloud most beautifully, though to no one but her children.

What wonder that such an individual little personage should be missed from the circle she had so enlivened?

There is a bay window in the living-room at Quillcote. In one corner was the high rocker into which my mother stepped from her wheel chair. Behind her was her standing workbasket and on top another shallow one with spools of cotton, her gold thimble in its case, and her scissors. In the center within her reach was the revolving Queen Anne table, both of its deep sides laden with different kinds of fancy work. There were five windows in the bay and a view of our beautiful elms and maples as well as a glimpse of the quiet village street. There my mother often sat from morning till night and her actual presence seems so engraved upon the spot that it never fades for an instant. When we come into the room nowadays it is not easy to sit in Mother's Corner; we miss the bright head, the white lawn apron, and the busy hands twinkling over her work. Her own particular chair is never offered to any one, though an old friend often occupies it unconsciously. No place in all the house, nor in the barn where she passed many happy hours, nor in all the green fields that surround it, not one of them holds the picture of our mother like the corner by the window in the living-room. That was always the heart of the home; it still is, and always will be.

The winters of 1920 and 1921 were spent by my sister and mother at a delightful family hotel in Portland, Maine, as mother's increased lameness had made the journey to New York impossible. I was with her a large part of both summers, but a severe illness kept me from making a visit in the early days of January, 1921, though my sister's letters had given me cause for anxiety. On February 7th, I was allowed to go to her, though the temperature was ten degrees below zero and the snowdrifts seven feet high. The hotel was flooded with sun, however, and mother's sitting-room looked like a conservatory, as the day before had been her birthday. The hour that the sleeping-train arrived from New York was half-past six in the morning and I reached the hotel before seven, but mother was dressed and had asked that I look at the breakfast table before she came out. A beautifully embroidered center-piece lay upon it, of pink wild roses and their leaves, and an elaborate scalloped edge, which she had finished and pressed the night before. I could barely glance at it for fear of breaking down, and then she appeared through her bedroom door in her wheel chair, looking as she always did, like an exquisite piece of fragile china. She was all smiles, but the tears came soon and I was glad, for then mine seemed more natural. She seemed so little, so little, and so white, and I felt that she had been waiting for me so that she could have her two daughters together. Never in my life did I feel such a sudden swift heart-pang, such a certain knowledge of what was to come.

We spent a few quiet, dear-to-be-remembered days together. They were happy ones because the shadow was never in her heart, but in ours, and she still worked for a half-hour at a time on a center-piece of pansies for a friend.

She leaned over my shoulder when I was playing Patience and helped me with the moves; scolded Nora for the tight stitches in her knitting, and laughed, oh! so many times, when we were indulging in reminiscences over hard times in California. I recall with unspeakable gratitude and joy the laughter in that tired face, for it was the last time we saw it there.

There was another nurse now, but the end came very quietly in a few days and there was no consciousness on her part that it was so near. Indeed, she was so weary and her nights had long been so restless that sleep would have been a blessed thing in her imagination. There were no precious last words to be recalled later, no looking into eyes that saw, and in seeing, could show love, no remembrance of all the days gone by, nor sadness in parting — just sleep — and then the gentle passing from one life to another.

It was Sunday and a heavy snowstorm raged outside, keeping the streets quiet. There was no hurry or bustle. All the needful things were done under the superintendence of my mother's old friend and sometime nurse, Mrs. Lord, and my secretary, Miss Alford, both, in truth, members of the family. When all was ready my sister and I were called to the sitting-room, even then filled with flowers, and left there together, but these are not moments to describe. . . .

At length we noted her fragile hand with its worn wedding ring, the hand that we had never before seen still. A thought came to us both at the same time, and Nora brought the little pansy center-piece she had worked on only two days before. We folded it and put it beside her, with the threaded needle and the violet silk just as it had been left ready for the next stitch. Then we laid her tiniest workbasket near her, with its dainty reels of silk and cotton and its gold thimble at the top and we felt that she was ready for her journey.

My dear brother was no longer living, having died two years before in California, so the only lack in our little family circle now was that of my husband, who was on a visit to the Bahama Islands. In the twenty-seven years of our marriage my mother and he had been the best of friends with never a word of difference between them. It seemed peculiarly hard, therefore, that no steamer sailed from Nassau that would reach us for a fortnight or more, so she must miss her son-in-law's last tribute.

We took her to lie in the old churchyard on Tory Hill, Buxton, Maine, where she had attended every summer service for many years. Our place had long been chosen, and a young pine tree on the edge of the lot was growing large enough to shade us all in good time.

Kind hands had helped the officials to make ready the resting-place through snow and frozen ground, but our trusty country doctor had inspired the task and helped in it.

The old church was nearly filled with friends, although horses could not long be kept out in such weather, and it was a sight to strike the heart to see the old people bending against the wind and walking through the snow in the piercing cold, that they might do my mother reverence.

The simple service in which we were upheld and comforted by our old friend, Rev. Roderick Stebbins, was soon over, and among the beautiful remembrances were the garlands of evergreen with which the windows had been trimmed by the ladies of the Dorcas Society and the wealth of wreaths and flowers sent by old friends from Maine to California.

It seemed in no sense a funeral, but a good-bye to a friend; and the one thing that brought tears to those who saw it was that little symbol of her active life under her hand, the bit of unfinished embroidery with the threaded needle ready for the next stitch. If they had stopped to think, they might have considered it unconventional, perhaps even unorthodox, but it moved them deeply.

Then a dozen or two who could brave the weather

walked through shoveled paths and walls of snow to the place of rest. The day was very cold, the sun bright, and the new snow was whiter than down, and every crystal in its frozen surface dazzled the eye and made it beautiful beyond words. Hillocks, mountains, and dales shone white and the branches of the trees were hung with glittering garlands.

The fear that I had thought to feel never came. There was nothing chilling about the scene; it was celestial!

The grave was lined with green hemlock branches and it seemed peaceful and wonderful for the beloved one to go softly down into the green, to have the flowery garlands thick above her, and then billows of pure white snow to cover her safely, just as they were keeping warm in the earth all the beautiful things that would bud and flower and bear fruit later on.

The page was turned; the new life was begun, shorn of a passionate interest; but it must be lived bravely and lived all the better because what had been, now was to be no more. But I cannot think as I write this tribute how there can be any women who do not care for motherhood, or how they can belittle the privilege of proving a benediction to their children all their days, and when the end comes, of leaving them, not with a leaden sorrow, but with a golden memory.

XLII

" THE SONG IS NEVER ENDED! "

OF late years scarcely a week has passed without the publication of several autobiographies, some of which have been compiled for the soundest of reasons, and others, perhaps, for motives less honorable to the persons involved.

Many have been written by great soldiers and sailors whose briefest word concerning their victories in the field, or on the seas, has brought thousands of readers under their spell. There have been also statesmen and politicians who could await no longer the right moment to reveal the secrets that would either vindicate their policies, if vindication were needed, or place at once the public seal of approval on their final achievements.

Then a bewildering company of artists has given us enchanting stories concerning their careers as actors, painters, sculptors, and musicians; and travelers in unknown countries have led us to see life in some of its stranger phases.

The octogenarians and nonagenarians in other days used to keep autobiography pretty well in their own hands, for it was not then thought either dignified or discreet to write one's life before eighty or, better still, eighty-five years had been passed. To undertake such a thing would have been considered in the past a sure sign of such hoary old age as to indicate a speedy senility which would interfere with all future books from the same pens.

However, "other times, other manners," for here is that rascally young novelist, Hugh Walpole, writing memories of his infancy, boyhood, and downy young manhood, because, perhaps, he is afraid of forgetting some of the delightful details of that period and its many interesting associations, although I can assure him, from my point of vantage, that he never will do so.

And what shall we say of that horde of uncatalogued autobiographers that has arisen in our time and of which unfortunately this very page includes another? You may any day see in the newspapers that a man who holds a swimming or a boxing record, or a woman who weighs five hundred pounds and travels with a circus, will either of them gladly write down their memories if they can find a publisher.

I asked a literary friend the other evening the plain question, "Just why is it that all these autobiographies are written?" and he replied, with Satanic satisfaction: "Because all you quill-drivers like to talk about yourselves! You can never get in so many words on that special subject in any other way. You'd have to die before a biographer did it, and then you'd miss the fun, if the public liked his book about you."

I was annoyed with his sordid views and delighted to hear very soon from an intimate friend that the gentleman in question had his own autobiography written in most finished style up to the very hour he had made the uncivil remark to me. He is only forty, but he has no idea of allowing a falling roof or a shipwreck to take him away from a world unprepared to endure his loss and unconsoled by a record of his achievements.

It is well enough to treat this subject lightly, but at this moment (I quote from memory) some lines by James Branch Cabell come into my mind: "We are not quite content to be put by, finished with forever. . . . Not only does the shallow-pated artist appeal for remembrance, . . . business men enter demurrers in the public libraries. There is no modest tombstone but insanely appeals to posterity to keep in mind the owner's name and date of birth and death, *for we will to continue here in the world well known to us, if only as syllables; we would not be forgotten utterly.*"

I wonder if that is any answer to such autobiographies as mine, having no appeal to the great public, but inciting a sympathetic interest in a body of friends by no means small — friends known and unknown, with whom somehow one has come into contact in a thousand ways, even setting aside the direct one of author and reader.

I was pondering these matters when I recalled a remark of Mrs. Sellar, my dear and witty old friend of Edinburgh. (Thank Heaven, she wrote *her* memoirs in good time!) "The only way, my dear, that old age can be faced without dismay, is to love knitting, enjoy cards, and be able to repeat the Psalms from memory."

At one blow I felt myself defenseless. A poor and reluctant knitter I have always been; a card-player of such dense and impenetrable ignorance that one solitary game of Patience has been my only resource; and finally, though fairly familiar with the Psalms, the committing to memory of the whole one hundred and fifty was so obviously impossible a feat to me that I perceived Mrs. Sellar could never serve as my model of old-ladyhood.

My mind must have been working somewhat in this fashion when my autobiography began to loom in the dim distance. The idea took no positive hold at the time, perhaps because I made an unfortunate visit to the New York Public Library one day and became depressed by the number of books already written and the excessive facilities for their preservation. Rooms and rooms, alcoves and alcoves, shelves and shelves, filled with books! I regretted my own innocent works, and realized gladly that they were few in number and small in size. I, at least, had not taken up much room on shelves that should stand empty, awaiting a volume from an immortal pen.

Coming home I passed the house of a friend, a great bibliophile, and found him standing on his front steps, looking at a van of packing-cases.

"I have just rid myself of fifteen hundred books," he said; "packed 'em off to my country-house library."

He showed no emotion, and I thought he looked younger than usual, as if he might just have come from a Turkish bath. My heart sank, for he had been a critic for twenty years and had never printed a word between covers.

"You will miss your books," I said, feebly.

"Nonsense!" he replied, cheerfully. "This is my second mental house-cleaning. Twenty years ago I weeded out fifteen hundred others, the accumulation of my salad-days."

The autobiography vanished into thin air at that moment, but later it again and again took bodily form. It received a little extra discouragement, however, when I sat beside a Minister of Education one night at a London dinner.

He told me, whimsically, that the shelf-room demanded by the complete works of Hannah More kept him from buying other books; but he could not make up his mind to sell them, since it would be equivalent to circulating them. He felt, it seems, that the enervating fog of their impeccable dullness ought not to be allowed to creep into other libraries, and he buried the twenty-four morocco-bound volumes in his garden, amid the cheers of his family.

I took this to heart, as showing that the true bookman is a man of comparatively few books; but still I wanted to write an autobiography, even if it should prove as dull as the works of Hannah More.

The idea first began to haunt me in permanent shape,

day and night, under the inspiration of a nursery rhyme which seemed to me to epitomize a life journey:

> "How many miles to Babylon?
> Threescore miles and ten.
> Can I get there by candlelight?
> Yes, and back again."

If Babylon in this case were a kind of symbol of all one longed to hear and learn and experience, then I thought I had at least been within the city walls. I had begun to inquire the way and seek the road I should follow, early enough in life to be sure of arriving in daylight, that I might see clearly the towers and spires, the tall pillars, and the glittering domes of my imagination; and at noonday I had had time to sit in the sunshine, drink in the fragrance of roses and lilies, dream dreams, and see visions.

The road thither and the road home again had been full of unexpected beauty, rich with innumerable experiences, and, above all, with those opportunities for helping strangers who were, as I was, making the pilgrimage, an endless procession of Youth.

I have made the journey, and here I am back again, well within the threescore-years-and-ten allotted to travelers, and still it is hardly candlelight. Even before sunset I can walk through the garden of memory, plucking here a pansy, here a sprig of rosemary, there a branch of lavender; by the brook a cluster of forget-me-nots, over the arbor a bunch of roses for the days of youth, and later on I can bind the posy together with the long grasses that grow by the pool of meditation.

And, after all, it is not alone the marvelous deeds, the great moments, the magnificent achievements, that make the record of a life worth setting down, though I will allow they always make more fascinating reading.

To believe that the sometimes trivial details of one's

own months and years are worth preservation would indeed be unutterable vanity; but, on the other hand, we have in a book of memories the means of transmitting the theory of life and truth which we bear within ourselves, humble though it may be. And so, when the literary impulse sweeps aside everything else, with great as with little artists alike, we write, not always, indeed, a life that like a rich tapestry reveals a rich personality behind it, but a simpler, soberer, merrier, more unpretentious sort of thing, perhaps, that is "us," "ourselves," and somewhere in the world there are readers waiting for it. It is wonderful, it is all but incredible, but it is true; and when the people find it for whom it was unconsciously written, they often see in it something far, far better than the author ever put there. It is something that the reader's heart creates for himself, he reads between the lines; and there are moments, across seas and mountains and continents, when a miracle happens and he who writes touches hands with him who reads.

It is only this fact, verified a thousand times, that makes me bold enough to remember what Palacio Valdés says: "If it has happened that thy books have made a slight imprint on the souls of thy readers, that imprint, no matter how slight it may be, will never be erased."

In childhood, whenever I read Hans Christian Andersen's fairy-tales — which was all too seldom, for we had but one copy of the book — I always turned first to the story of the Flax; and as my sister and I grew older and were incessantly telling or reading stories to children, it exerted a great fascination, indeed a great influence, over me. It seemed a little piece of religion, and in some way a philosophy of life.

Do you remember how the Flax said to itself one fine summer morning? — "I am strong and tall. I am in full bloom; and every day something delightful happens to me. Oh! this is a beautiful world!"

A Hedge-Stake, near by, you know, overheard the Flax and grumbled: "It takes those who have knots in their stems to know the world!" — and he creaked out a mournful song:

> "Snip, snap, snurre,
> Basse lurre:
> The song is ended!"

"Oh, no!" cried the Flax; "the song is not ended, it is hardly begun. Every day the sunshine gladdens, or the rain refreshes me. I know that I am growing. I know that I am in full blossom. I am the happiest of all creatures."

I used to feel even then that the Hedge-Stake was wrong in his philosophy of existence; but very soon in the story the Flax, now full-grown, was pulled up by the roots, laid in water till it was almost drowned, and set by the fire until it was almost roasted.

"One must not complain," said the Flax. "If I've suffered something, I'm being made into something." And when it was put upon the wheel and spun into thread, and the thread woven into a web, still it sang its song of content as the wheel whirred and the shuttle shot to and fro. (I think two little girls, sitting by an open fire, with a few tears falling on the page of the beloved book, learned something just then — not through the head, but the heart!)

Then the Flax was spread upon the grass as a long piece of white linen, the finest in the parish, and there were many changes after that — snipping and cutting and making into garments — and the Flax said: "See how little the Hedge-Stake knew when he told me the song was ended; look what I have become! This was my destiny. Now I shall be of some use in the world. I am the happiest of all creatures."

At last the garments were worn quite to rags; and then they were cut into smaller bits and softened and boiled till they became white paper.

"What a glorious surprise!" cried the Flax. "Now perhaps a poet may come and write his thoughts upon me. See how I am led on from glory to glory — I who was only a little blue flower growing in the fields. Ah! the poor Hedge-Stake, how little he knew about life!"

And truly a poet did come and write beautiful thoughts on the shining white leaves, and they were sent to the printers and made into books.

"This is best of all!" said the Flax. "Now I shall sit at home, like an honored grandfather, and my books will travel over all lands. How happy I am! Each time I think the song is ended, it begins again in a more beautiful way!"

But now the paper was thrust into a barrel and sold to a grocer for wrapping his butter and sugar.

"I had not thought of this!" said the Flax (though the two little girls had, and a hundred readings could not prevent momentary tears). "But, after all, it is better, for I have been so hurried from one stage of my life to another that I have never had time to think! After work, it is well to rest. Now I can reflect on my real condition."

But it did not happen as the Flax had thought, for the grocer's children were fond of burning paper on the hearth. They liked the flash of the flames up the chimney, the gray ashes below and the red sparks careering here and there, and they often danced and sang when the fire was flashing its brightest; so they pulled all the paper from the barrel one day and set it afire.

Whis-sh! went the blaze up the chimney. It soared higher than the Flax had ever lifted its blue flowers, and glistened as the white linen had never glistened.

"Now I'm mounting straight up to the sun!" cried

a voice far above the chimney, and, more delicate than the flames, invisible to human eyes, a myriad tiny beings floated in the air above, many, many more than there had been blossoms on the Flax.

Down below, the children sang the rhyme of the Hedge-Stake over the dead ashes:

> "Snip, snap, snurre,
> Basse lurre:
> The song is ended!"

But the little invisible beings in the air above them sang together, as clearly as if there had been a thousand voices in unison: "The song is never ended; the most beautiful is yet to come; we know it, and therefore we are the happiest of all!"

I am at one with the little invisible beings in the air — they who had begun as blue Flax flowers. The song is more joyous in youth, fuller and stronger in middle age; it quavers a little as the years go on and on: but the song itself is never ended.

THE END

APPENDIX

TRANSLATIONS OF THE BOOKS OF KATE DOUGLAS WIGGIN

THE BIRDS' CHRISTMAS CAROL

FRENCH: L'Oiselet de Noël. Traduit par Auguste Monod. Paris, 1895.

SWEDISH: Lilla Julrosen: Tvenne Berättelser af K. D. Wiggin. Ofvers. från engelskan af Hedvig Indebetou. Albert Bonniers Förlag, Stockholm, 1894.

GERMAN: Die Geschichte von Vogels Weihnachts-Röschen. Von K. D. Wiggin. Aus dem Englischen von M. von K. Verlag von Peter Hobbing in Darmstadt.

JAPANESE: [See cut]. Tokyo, 1895.

GERMAN: Die Geschichte von Vogels Weihnachts-Röschen (Birds' Christmas Carol). Hobbing & Büchle, Stuttgart, 1900.

GERMAN: The Birds' Christmas Carol in English with German Glossary and Dictionary for use in German Schools. Edited by Elizabeth Merhaut. 1906.

SWISS: Hosianna (Birds' Christmas Carol). Translated by Louise Leneste. Carl Hirsch, Konstanz.

TIMOTHY'S QUEST

SWEDISH: Två Små Hemlösa, Berättelse af Kate Douglas Wiggin. Ofvers. från Timothy's Quest, det 30. tusent, af Hedvig Indebetou. Andra Upplagan. Albert Bonniers Förlag, Stockholm, 1893.

DANISH: Tim og Gay, To Forældreløse oversat af P. Jerndorff-Jessen. N. M. Kjaers Forlag (Døcker & Kjaer). København. Fr. G. Knudtzons Bogtrykkeri, 1894.

BOHEMIAN: Za Maminkou. Anglicky Napsala K. D. Wigginová. Přeložila G. B. Cěchová, v Praze, 1912. Nákladem Spolku Komenského-Tiskem Edvarda Leschingra.

GERMAN: Flossy's Geheimnitz. Dresden, 1899.

GERMAN: Wie Timotheus sucht und findet. Berlin, 1900.

GERMAN: Zwei Kinder suchen sich ein Heim. Hobbing & Büchle, Stuttgart, 1900.

REBECCA OF SUNNYBROOK FARM

GERMAN: Rebekka vom Sonnenbachhof. 2 Bände. Autorisierte Übersetzung aus dem Englischen von Natalie Rümelin. Verlag von J. Engelhorn, Stuttgart, 1907.
GERMAN: Rebekka vom Sonnenbachhof. Autorisierte Übersetzung aus dem Englischen von Natalie Rümelin. Verlag von J. Engelhorn, Stuttgart, 1905. (1 vol.)
POLISH: Rebeka ze "Słonecznego Potoku." Powieść przez Kate Douglas Wiggin z upoważnieniem autorki tłómaczyła z angielskiego Teresa Lubińska. Druk Piotra Laskauera, Nowy-Świat 41, Warszawa, 1912.
DANISH-NORWEGIAN: Rebekka fra Solbækgaarden. Autoriseret Dansk-Norsk Udgave ved L. Stange. Omslag af Alfred Schmidt. E. Jespersens Forlag, Kjøbenhavn. Cammermeyers Boghandel, Kristiania.
DUTCH: Rebecca van "Zonbeek-Hoeve." Uit het Engelsch door Mevrouw Beelaerts Van Blokland. Hollandia-Drukkerij, Baarn, 1905.
GERMAN: Rebecca in English with German Glossary for use in German Schools. Arranged by Elizabeth Merhaut. Published by G. Freytag, Leipzig, and F. Tempsky, Vienna, 1906.
GERMAN: Rebecca Dictionary. For use in German Schools. Compiled by Elizabeth Merhaut and published by G. Freytag, Leipzig, 1906.

A CATHEDRAL COURTSHIP

FRENCH: Une Cour à travers les Cathédrales. Published by Attinger Frères, Neuchâtel, 1899.

PRINCIPLES AND PRACTICE OF THE KINDERGARTEN

SPANISH: Principio y Práctica del Kindergarten. By Estefania Castañeda. City of Mexico, 1907. This educational work is also translated into Marathi, one of the Indo-Aryan languages.

THE STORY OF PATSY

GERMAN: "Die Geschichte von Jochen." Hobbing & Büchle, Stuttgart, 1900.

TITLE OF THE JAPANESE TRANSLATION OF
"THE BIRDS' CHRISTMAS CAROL"

APPENDIX

POLLY OLIVER'S PROBLEM

SWEDISH: Polly's Planer. Albert Bonniers Förlag, Stockholm, 1894.

TAUCHNITZ EDITION. BERNARD TAUCHNITZ, LEIPZIG

Timothy's Quest, 1893. Penelope's Irish Experiences, 1901. Rebecca of Sunnybrook Farm, 1904. The Affair at the Inn, 1905. Rose o' the River, 1906. New Chronicles of Rebecca, 1907. The Old Peabody Pew, 1910. Susanna and Sue, 1910. Robinetta, 1911. Mother Carey's Chickens, 1912.

BOOKS IN RAISED TYPE FOR THE BLIND

The Birds' Christmas Carol — The Story of Patsy — Timothy's Quest — Rebecca of Sunnybrook Farm — Mother Carey's Chickens.

INDEX

H. M. & Co., 179; written in San Francisco, 325; 231.
The Story Hour, in collaboration, 178 n., 323.
Susanna and Sue, and the Shakers, 346, 347, 359, 360.
Timothy's Quest, where written, 182, 327, 328; its success in Great Britain, 182; translated into Bohemian, 349; 231, 265, 289.
"Tom o' the Blueberry Plains," 251.
"The Training of Children," 259.
"A Village Stradivarius," 252.
The Village Watch-Tower, 251, 252.
The Story of Waitstill Baxter, Mrs. Burnett quoted on, 359; 347, 422.

Wiggin, Samuel Bradley, marries *W.*, 163; his death, 164, 165.
Wilkins, Mary E., 214.
Willard, E. S., 235.
Wilmington, Del., 222.
Winnemucca, Sarah, 158.
Winnipeg Club, 414.
Winter, William, 214.
Women's Unitarian League, readings at, 218.
Wordsworth, William, "Ode on Intimations of Immortality," 126; 99, 151, 221, 421.

York, Duchess of (now Queen Mary), 304, 305.
York, Duke of (George V), 304, 305.